Employee Engagement in Theory and Practice

In recent years there has been a weight of evidence suggesting that engagement has a significantly positive impact on productivity, performance and organizational advocacy, as well as individual well-being, and a significantly negative impact on intent to quit and absenteeism from the work place.

This comprehensive new book is unique as it brings together, for the first time, psychological and critical human resource management perspectives on engagement as well as their practical application. *Employee Engagement in Theory and Practice* will familiarize readers with the concepts and core themes that have been explored in research and their application in a business context via a set of carefully chosen and highly relevant original case studies, some of which are co-authored by invited practitioners.

Written in an accessible manner, this book will be essential reading for scholars in the field, students studying at both undergraduate and postgraduate levels, as well as practitioners interested in finding out more about the theoretical underpinnings of engagement alongside its practical application.

Catherine Truss is Head of the People, Management and Organization Group at Kent Business School, University of Kent, UK.

Rick Delbridge is University Dean of Research, Innovation and Enterprise and Professor of Organizational Analysis in Cardiff Business School at Cardiff University, UK.

Kerstin Alfes is Assistant Professor in the Department of Human Resource Studies, Tilburg University, The Netherlands.

Amanda Shantz is Assistant Professor in the School of Human Resource Management at York University, Canada.

Emma Soane is Lecturer in the Department of Management at the London School of Economics and Political Science, UK.

Employee Engagement in Theory and Practice

**Edited by Catherine Truss,
Rick Delbridge, Kerstin Alfes,
Amanda Shantz and Emma Soane**

Routledge
Taylor & Francis Group

LONDON AND NEW YORK

First published 2014
by Routledge
2 Park Square, Milton Park, Abingdon, Oxon OX14 4RN

and by Routledge
711 Third Avenue, New York, NY 10017

Routledge is an imprint of the Taylor & Francis Group, an informa business

British Library Cataloguing in Publication Data
A catalogue record for this book is available from the British Library

Library of Congress Cataloging-in-Publication Data
Employee engagement in theory and practice / edited by
Catherine Truss, Rick Delbridge, Kerstin Alfes, Amanda Shantz, and
Emma Soane.
pages cm
Includes bibliographical references and index.
1. Employee motivation. 2. Employees–Attitudes. I. Truss, Catherine.
II. Delbridge, Rick. III. Alfes, Kerstin. IV. Shantz, Amanda. V. Soane, Emma.
HF5549.5.M63E475 2013
658.3'14–dc23
2013016186

ISBN: 978-0-415-65741-9 (hbk)
ISBN: 978-0-415-65742-6 (pbk)
ISBN: 978-0-203-07696-5 (ebk)

Typeset in Times New Roman
by Keystroke, Station Road, Codsall, Wolverhampton

Dedications

Katie
To my late parents, Rodney and Gwenda Truss

Kerstin
To my parents, Rita and Manfred Alfes

Rick
For Rachel

Amanda
To my loving parents

Emma
To all the employees who have participated in our research

Contents

Figures and tables

Figures

Tables

Contributors

Kerstin Alfes is Assistant Professor at the Department of Human Resource Studies, Tilburg University, The Netherlands. Her research interests are human resource management, employee engagement, volunteering, and change management. She has a PhD from the University of Berne.

Arnold B. Bakker is Professor of Work & Organizational Psychology at Erasmus University Rotterdam, The Netherlands, and Adjunct Professor at Lingnan University, Hong Kong. He is past president of the European Association of Work and Organizational Psychology. He is interested in positive organizational behaviour.

Jenny Bergeron is the Director of Educational Research and Assessment at Harvard University, a role she previously held at Stanford University. She received her doctorate in psychometrics from the University of Florida. Her current work focuses on student engagement and learning.

Kristi M. Bockorny is an instructor at Northern State University, Aberdeen, South Dakota. She holds a B.S. in Finance and Business Education and a Masters in Management. She is currently pursuing a PhD in Human Capital Management at Bellevue University.

Liz Bramley is Head of Employee Engagement & Diversity at The Co-operative Group and is responsible for leading the management and development of structured, strategic engagement and inclusion programmes that are supporting successful change and improvement across 6,000 trading locations.

Brooke Buckman is a doctoral student in Organizational Behavior at Arizona State University. Her current research focuses on better understanding the intricacies of employee engagement at both the individual and team levels of analysis.

Christopher Chan is an Associate Professor, School of Human Resource Management, York University and an Honorary Research Fellow, Faculty of Business, Australian Catholic University. Chris's research interests are cross-cultural management and religious ethics.

Eean R. Crawford is an Assistant Professor of Management and Organizations at the University of Iowa. He received his doctorate in management from the University of Florida. He conducts research on employee engagement, team effectiveness, networks, and personality.

Gillian D'Analeze is a Senior People Policy Specialist for Marks and Spencer plc. In addition, Gillian was actively involved with the Engage for Success Taskforce as the Nailing the Evidence Sub Group Co-ordinator and 'The Evidence' co-author.

Rick Delbridge is University Dean of Research, Innovation and Enterprise and Professor of Organizational Analysis in Cardiff Business School at Cardiff University. His research interests include the nature of work and employment relations in contemporary capitalism. He is Associate Editor of the *Academy of Management Review* and an Academician of the Academy of Social Sciences.

Elaine Farndale is Assistant Professor, Labor Studies and Employment Relations, at the Pennsylvania State University (USA), and is affiliated with the Human Resource Studies Department at Tilburg University (Netherlands). Her widely published research encompasses the broad field of international human resource management.

Luke Fletcher is completing a PhD at Kent Business School, University of Kent on employee engagement within medium-sized organizations in the UK. He has been involved with projects, both in practice and in academia, that examine employee engagement measurement and strategy.

Kathleen Gosser is the Director, HR at KFC/YUM! Brands leading the KFC University, and an Adjunct Professor at the University of Louisville and Spalding University. She is the former president of the Louisville Chapter of Women MBA International and serves on the University of Louisville Business School Advisory Board.

David E. Guest is Professor of Organizational Psychology and Human Resource Management in the Department of Management at King's College, London, where he has worked since 2000. He has written and researched extensively in the areas of human resource management, employment relations, the psychological contract, and careers. His research interests are in HRM and performance, employment contracts, the psychological contract and workers' well-being, and careers theory.

Emily D. Heaphy is Assistant Professor of Organizational Behavior at Boston University. Her research focuses on positive work relationships and the differences they make at work, and how individuals influence organization change.

Joyce Henderson is Principal Insight Consultant in the Organization Design and Development team in the Department for Work and Pensions.

Veronica Hope Hailey is Professor of Management Studies and Dean of the School of Management at the University of Bath. Her research interests focus on the changing nature of the employment relationship, particularly looking at the concepts of trust and engagement, and she also examines strategic change and corporate renewal.

William A. Kahn is Professor of Organizational Behavior at Boston University. His current research focuses on the social, cultural, and structural dimensions of caring for organizational members exposed to painful stress and trauma.

Tom Keenoy, Honorary Professor, Cardiff Business School, has research interests in organizational discourse analysis, the social construction of HRM, and sensemaking in academic work. He has no hobbies but reads much of the night and would like to go south in the winter.

Clare Kelliher is Professor of Work and Organization at Cranfield School of Management, Cranfield University, UK. Her principal research interests are in the organization of work and the management of the employment relationship, and she has published widely in this field.

John Purcell's expertise is in the areas of strategy and HRM. He worked in the universities of Manchester, Oxford, and Bath before rejoining the real world at Acas while being a research professor at Warwick. He is now proving that professors don't retire, they just lose their faculties.

Bruce Louis Rich is an Associate Professor of Management at California State University San Marcos. He received his doctorate in organizational behaviour and human resource management from the University of Florida. His research on employee engagement has received honours for scholarly achievement from the Society for Industrial and Organizational Psychology.

Dilys Robinson is a Principal Research Fellow at the Institute for Employment Studies (IES). Since 2002, she has led IES's research into employee engagement (definition, measurement, and drivers) and more recently into engaging managerial behaviours.

Tonette S. Rocco is Professor and programme leader of adult education and human resource development at Florida International University, a Houle Scholar, a Kauffman Entrepreneurship Professor, and a former board member of the American Society for Training and Development, Certification Institute Board of Directors.

Sebastiaan (Ian) Rothmann (PhD) is a Professor in Industrial/Organizational Psychology at the North-West University (Vanderbijlpark). He is author/co-author of 151 articles in peer-reviewed journals. His research focuses on the flourishing of people in work and organizational contexts.

Jordan Schoenberg is a student at the London School of Economics, pursuing a Master's degree in business management. Jordan is currently researching the impact of financial regulation on the occurrence of incomplete markets for his Master's dissertation.

Wilmar B. Schaufeli is full Professor of Work and Organizational Psychology at Utrecht University, The Netherlands, and Visiting Professor at Loughborough Business School, UK and Jaume I Universitat, Castellon, Spain. He is a Fellow of the European Academy of Occupational Health Psychology, a licensed occupational health psychologist, and works part-time as an organizational consultant.

Amanda Shantz is an Assistant Professor in the School of Human Resource Management, York University, Canada. Amanda's research interests are employee engagement, motivation, and skill development.

Brad Shuck is an Assistant Professor of Organizational Leadership and Learning at the University of Louisville. Shuck was the 2010–11 Malcolm Knowles Dissertation of the Year Runner-Up and recipient of the 2011 Advances in Developing Human Resources Issue of the Year Award for the special issue on employee engagement. Shuck's research is focused on the use of employee engagement and positive psychology in HRD.

Emma Soane is a lecturer in the Department of Management at the London School of Economics and Political Science. She received her doctorate from the Institute of Work Psychology at the University of Sheffield. Her research focuses on personality, leadership, decision making, and engagement.

Paul Sparrow is the Director of the Centre for Performance-led HR and Professor of International Human Resource Management at Lancaster University Management School. His research interests include cross-cultural and international HRM, HR strategy, performance-led HR, and the employment relationship.

Maria Tims is Assistant Professor of Work & Organizational Psychology at Erasmus University Rotterdam, The Netherlands. She is interested in proactive work behaviours, job crafting, and employee well-being. She has published in the *Journal of Vocational Behavior* and *The Leadership Quarterly*.

Gary Tomlinson is Head of HR for Kia Motors UK and Ireland. He is a Fellow of the CIPD and has an MA in HR specializing in his subject of passion and employee engagement.

Catherine Truss is Professor of Human Resource Management and Head of the People, Management and Organization Group, Kent Business School, University of Kent. She has a PhD from London Business School and her research interests are in engagement, strategic human resource management, and individual experiences of work.

Selma Suna Yeltekin Leloglu received her MSc in Organizational Behaviour from the London School of Economics with distinction for her dissertation on victimization in the workplace. She received her BA (Hons) in Economics from Sabanci University, Turkey with merit scholarship.

Carolyn M. Youssef-Morgan is the Redding Chair of Business at Bellevue University, Nebraska, USA, co-author of *Psychological Capital* (Oxford, 2007) with Fred Luthans and Bruce Avolio, and a leading researcher, author, speaker, and consultant on positivity in the workplace.

Acknowledgements

The editors would like to express their thanks and appreciation to the Economic and Social Research Council for their grant supporting the seminar series, 'Employee Engagement, Organizational Performance and Individual Wellbeing: Exploring the Evidence, Developing the Theory' (RES-451-26-0807), which provided the inspiration for this book. We would also like to thank all the speakers, contributors, and delegates involved with the seminar series for their enthusiasm and insights into the topic of engagement.

Thanks are also due to the Chartered Institute of Personnel and Development for a series of research grants awarded to four members of this book's editorial team to support research into employee engagement from 2006 onwards, and also of course to the members of the Employee Engagement Consortium 2007–2012, from whom we learned so much.

Rick Delbridge would also like to acknowledge the support of the ESRC through its grant to the ESRC Centre on Skills, Knowledge and Organizational Performance (SKOPE), RES-557-28-5003.

Introduction

Catherine Truss, Rick Delbridge, Kerstin Alfes,
Amanda Shantz and Emma Soane

The notion that individuals can be 'personally engaged' in their work, investing positive emotional and cognitive energy into their role performance, was first proposed by William Kahn in 1990 in his seminal paper in the *Academy of Management Journal.* Since then, there has been a steadily growing stream of research, notably within the psychology field, that has sought to further explore the meaning and significance of engagement (Wollard and Shuck, 2011). Perhaps the reason that engagement has garnered so much attention lies in its dual promise of enhancing both individual well-being and organizational performance (Bakker and Schaufeli, 2008; Christian et al., 2011; Harter, Schmidt and Hayes, 2002), sidestepping the traditional trade-offs and tensions that exist between employers and employees that have for so long been the subject of debate within the human resource management (HRM) and industrial relations domains.

The potential for employee engagement to raise levels of corporate performance and profitability has been noted by government and policymakers as well, and has led in the UK, for instance, to the highly influential work of Engage for Success (www.engageforsuccess. org). Engage for Success, led by David MacLeod and Nita Clarke, is a voluntary movement involving public, private and third sector employers, alongside representatives from government, trades unions and professional bodies, as well as consultants and academics. The espoused aim of the movement is to provide employers with free tools, techniques and guidance on how to raise the engagement levels of workers, based on the premise that a highly engaged workforce will perform better than one that is disengaged, as well as enjoying higher levels of personal well-being, thus ultimately helping bolster the UK economy (MacLeod and Clarke, 2009; Rayton et al., 2012). There have been few, if any, precedents in the UK or other countries, of similar informal coalitions forming to promote a particular approach to managing people.

The concept of engagement has therefore caught the imagination of both academics and practitioners, yet, despite the volume of material that has been written, the concept remains more contested than perhaps much of the practitioner literature would suggest (Soane et al., 2012). In consequence, Christian et al. (2011: 89–90) conclude: 'engagement research has been plagued by inconsistent construct definitions and operationalizations'. Debate continues within the academic community concerning the meaning of engagement, its antecedents and consequences, and its theoretical underpinnings, and there is an emerging disconnect between the way 'engagement' is regarded within the academic world, where it is broadly viewed as a psychological state, as compared with the practitioner sphere, where engagement is conceptualized as a workforce strategy.

Although scholars in the psychology field have been researching engagement for the past 20 years or so, it is only very recently that HRM scholars have turned their attention to the topic, and studies examining the HRM implications of engagement are just starting to emerge (Alfes et al., 2013a, 2013b; Brunetto et al., 2012; Shuck et al., 2011; Truss et al., 2013). Moreover, analyses of engagement from a labour process, critical management studies and collectivist standpoint are also now being developed (Jenkins and Delbridge, 2013; Arrowsmith and Parker, 2013). These studies challenge the unitary assumptions underpinning much of the extant research on engagement, and locate engagement within the broader setting of ongoing debates within the HRM and organizational studies literature concerning structure, agency and the employment relationship (Truss et al., 2013).

It is within the context of this burgeoning interest in engagement on the part of the HRM community that we have produced this edited collection of articles written by leading scholars in the field. The inspiration behind the book has been the seminar series led by the editorial team: 'Employee Engagement, Organisational Performance and Individual Wellbeing: Exploring the Evidence, Developing the Theory' funded in the UK by the Economic and Social Research Council (RES-451-26-0807), which ran between 2010 and 2012 (http://www.kent.ac.uk/kbs/ecg/news-events/esrc-general.html).

This series of five seminars featured presentations by several of the authors who have contributed to this book, and attracted large audiences of academics, consultants, policymakers and practitioners. Through the lively debates that took place during the series, we became aware that these various groups are largely talking past one another, lacking a shared vocabulary and understanding of engagement. This has been exacerbated by the fact that, until very recently, engagement has not featured in university or business school generalist or specialist programmes at any level, and so many practitioners are unfamiliar with its academic foundations. Scholars therefore debate the meaning and status of engagement without reference, in many cases, to the needs and concerns of practitioners, and practitioners often do not have access to the thinking and insights that are being developed in the academic world.

There seemed to be a need to bring this multiplicity of perspectives together in one place, allowing diverse voices to be heard, and permitting the reader to form a rounded view of how engagement sits, not only within its foundation discipline of psychology, but also of how it is being shaped and conceptualized within the HRM arena, as well as its enactment in daily practice within organizational settings.

In this book, we do not seek to impose any one definition of engagement or any one perspective on the engagement construct, but rather we have deliberately sought out authors with varied and, at times, challenging views. The book includes chapters written from a range of perspectives; some are theoretical or conceptual contributions that outline the authors' views on particular aspects of engagement, whilst some report on empirical studies that the authors have undertaken. Reflecting the plurality of possible interpretations of engagement, some authors refer to 'work engagement', others to 'personal engagement', 'employee engagement' or 'organizational engagement'. In addition, we have included chapters that explore engagement in practice. Throughout, we have aimed to adopt an international and inclusive perspective, and a style that is accessible to all readers with an interest in the field.

The aim of this book, then, is to bring together for the first time a set of contributions from world-leading authorities that shed light on the multiple facets of engagement relevant within the HRM context. We hope that readers will gain an understanding of the roots of engagement within the psychology discipline, and insight into some of the controversies around the various meanings and applications of 'engagement'. Our intention is to contribute to nascent discussions within HRM and critical management studies about engagement, and to provoke debate about the range of possible future directions for engagement research, thinking and practice.

In Part 1, 'The psychology of engagement', there are four chapters that address the foundation of engagement within the psychology field, particularly within the positive psychology movement, examining the way that engagement has been defined and conceptualized, and exploring organizational contextual features that have been found to affect engagement levels. In Part 2, 'Employee engagement: the HRM implications', we turn to the question of how engagement fits within the context of debates and discussions within the HRM field with six chapters that explore the relevance of engagement within different domains of the HRM arena, from strategic HRM through HRD, job design, leadership and international dimensions.

Part 3, 'Employee engagement: critical perspectives', comprises three more critical chapters on engagement. Here, the authors raise some important fundamental questions about the nature and meaning of engagement, its status as a distinctive construct and its unitary foundations. Finally, in Part 4, 'Employee engagement in practice', we include three chapters on engagement in practice, and the authors here explore how engagement has been measured within the academic and practitioner communities, and the ways in which countries around the world have embraced engagement, together with a series of extended engagement case studies.

The psychology of engagement

Employee engagement is a problematic construct. Even the term itself is subject to a number of variations, including 'work engagement', 'personal engagement', 'job engagement', 'staff engagement', 'employee engagement' and just simply 'engagement', each lending itself to a range of different definitions. MacLeod and Clarke (2009) found as many as 50 different versions of engagement, and suggested that there may well be more.

Kahn's original (1990) research suggested that engagement is the personal expression of self-in-role; someone is engaged with their work when they are able to express their authentic self and are willing to invest their personal energies into their job. Since then, engagement has been defined as the antithesis to burnout (Maslach and Leiter, 1997), as well as a distinctive positive psychological state in its own right, comprising a range of affective, cognitive and, sometimes, behavioural facets, depending on the precise definition adopted (Schaufeli et al., 2002; Soane et al., 2012).

In Chapter 1, Wilmar Schaufeli outlines the complex and contradictory history of the development of engagement as a construct in its own right, and provides an overview of research that has explored whether, and how, engagement differs from related constructs such as job satisfaction and commitment. He concludes that there is now sufficient evidence to suggest that engagement 'reflects a genuine and unique psychological state'. Schaufeli and his team developed the Utrecht Work Engagement Scale (UWES), which measures vigour, dedication and absorption as the three constituent facets of engagement, and is the most extensively used academic measure of engagement.

In his chapter, Schaufeli situates the UWES within the context of other contributions to the field, and shows how not only the UWES, but also other measures, capture what is unique about engagement and provide the basis for demonstrating the link between engagement and an important range of outcomes including health and well-being, organizational citizenship behaviour, turnover intent, absence and in-role performance. This topic is picked up again in Chapter 15, where Luke Fletcher and Dilys Robinson discuss a range of different measures that have been developed by both academics and practitioners to evaluate levels of engagement.

Another contribution of Chapter 1 is a discussion of relevant theoretical frameworks. In appreciating what is unique and distinctive about engagement, it is important to understand on what basis claims about the link between engagement, its antecedents and its consequences, are made. Schaufeli concludes that the job demands–resources model (JD–R), which suggests that individuals' job and personal resources combine to energize employees and foster high levels of engagement, has received the strongest empirical support to date.

The chapter concludes with the important point that by defining engagement narrowly as a psychological state, aspects of behavioural engagement that are most important to organizations tend to become lost, whilst a broader, more behaviourally based definition, would lead to the loss of specificity that would blur the boundary between engagement and similar constructs.

In Chapter 2, Carolyn M. Youssef-Morgan and Kristi M. Bockorny situate the concept of engagement within the wider positive psychology movement. Historically, workplace psychology has been based on a 'deficit' approach, whereby the focus is on identifying problems and challenges and then working out appropriate solutions. In contrast, an 'abundance' approach is based on identifying positive, peak experiences and identifying their enablers and drivers (Linley et al., 2010). Alongside this, the emphasis has shifted in the past 20 or so years to positive psychology and organizational studies, and engagement's status as an active, motivational state clearly fits within this overarching paradigm (Stairs and Galpin, 2010).

Youssef-Morgan and Bockorny show how current thinking on engagement draws on a rich seam of historical research on positive aspects of organizing work, including motivation and job satisfaction theory, and outline the limitations of negatively-based research and organizational practice. They show how engagement can be linked with a wide range of positive features of organizing work including positive organizational behaviour, positive organizational scholarship, appreciative enquiry and notions of individual hope and resilience. The practical implications of their ideas are brought to life through a case study of the North Lawndale Employment Network, based in a deprived area of Chicago, which shows how the principles of positive psychology can be used to address some of the most pressing social issues of today.

Eean R. Crawford, Bruce Louis Rich, Brooke Buckman and Jenny Bergeron turn their attention in Chapter 3 to the factors that have been found to drive up levels of engagement. In particular, they build on the work of Kahn (1990) to suggest that the experienced psychological conditions of meaningfulness, safety and availability lie at the heart of engagement models, and discuss research findings on organizational factors that affect each of these. In exposing the critical role played by job design in influencing engagement levels, they anticipate the themes pursued by Maria Tims and Arnold B. Bakker in Chapter 7. In addition to job design, Crawford and colleagues explain how the organizational context, in particular in areas such as leadership, social support, workplace climate and justice perceptions are relevant for engagement. Pursuing the notion introduced earlier by Schaufeli, they also reveal how excess job demands such as role overload or work-role conflict can deplete individuals' resources and decrease engagement levels.

One of the most pressing questions asked by practitioners concerns the relative importance of the wide range of factors that have been identified as engagement drivers. In a world of diminishing resources, which areas warrant most investment? Crawford and colleagues provide some insight into this, although the answer may not be what most practitioners would wish. Overall, their conclusion is that most research to date suggests that antecedent factors have unique effects on engagement levels, in other words, potential antecedent factors such as appropriate job design, value congruence and transformational leadership, in those studies that have considered combinations of these, each appear to be relevant for engagement. In a case study of Shands Healthcare, a hospital in Florida, Crawford and colleagues show how managers have used the findings of staff engagement surveys to develop holistic engagement strategies.

The final chapter of this section of the book, written by William A. Kahn and Emily D. Heaphy, focuses on the relational contexts of engagement. William Kahn's own lasting influence in defining the field can be seen throughout the book as each chapter acknowledges his legacy as 'founding father' of the concept of engagement. In this chapter, Kahn and Heaphy turn their attention to the role of work relationships in enhancing or depleting levels of engagement, an aspect that has hitherto received less attention than areas such as job design or leadership. In doing so, they reclaim engagement as originally conceived as 'personal engagement' in contrast to 'work engagement', whereby employees fully express themselves in physical, cognitive and emotional terms during the performance of their work (Kahn, 1990). Kahn and Heaphy revisit the relational aspects of the original psychological conditions for engagement identified earlier by Kahn – meaningfulness, safety and availability – thus complementing Crawford and colleagues' discussion of job design in relation to these three states in Chapter 3.

Relational aspects of work such as a sense of belonging, high-quality connections, meaningful contact with beneficiaries, together with the importance of 'holding environments' where workers feel supported, enabled and affirmed through their work relationships, can all assist in creating a setting conducive to personal engagement. The authors also highlight the importance of positive and energizing group dynamics for high levels of engagement and, conversely, show the depleting effects of psychologically unsafe environments. In a case study focusing on a hospital pharmacy technician, Kahn and Heaphy show how positive work relations that foster meaningfulness, safety and availability can turn around an individual's sense of engagement at work.

Employee engagement: the HRM implications

Having set the scene in Part 1 with an overview of the foundations of engagement, in Part 2 we turn our attention to the HRM implications of engagement with six chapters focusing on different aspects of HRM.

In Chapter 5, Paul Sparrow addresses the question of how human resource strategy is linked with engagement in practice, and particularly focuses on the underpinning assumptions about engagement and its link with performance within the context of two overarching strategic imperatives: innovation and 'lean' management. Sparrow argues that the focus should be on the engagement strategy as the unit of analysis, rather than individual levels of engagement, and highlights the challenges involved in developing and embedding an 'engagement narrative' within the organization, and with understanding the link between engagement on the one hand, and performance outcomes on the other.

In the chapter, Sparrow identifies three streams of thinking that underpin engagement narratives: a focus on process improvement, a focus on engagement as the direct link between individual attitudes and performance and a focus on engagement as alignment of corporate and individual objectives. He shows how a more nuanced understanding of performance at various levels, alongside the deconstruction of engagement strategies linked with overarching strategic imperatives, will be required as approaches to engagement in practice mature.

Brad Shuck and Tonette S. Rocco in Chapter 6 examine the implications of engagement within the context of human resource development (HRD). HRD is concerned with the development of both human and social capital within the organization, and there has been increasing focus in recent years on the relevance of engagement in enhancing individual performance and the individual experience of work, a movement that has been spearheaded by the authors. In particular, they highlight the emerging definition of engagement within the HRD field as being the cognitive, emotional and behavioural energy an employee directs towards positive organizational outcomes. This definition has clear commonalities with the work of the Utrecht group and others. The authors highlight the role that HRD can play not only in raising levels of engagement, but also in reducing levels of disengagement.

From a practical perspective, the authors indicate some of the ways in which the HRD function can enhance engagement through organizational development, workplace learning and career development initiatives.

The link between employee engagement and job design is the focus of Chapter 7, written by Maria Tims and Arnold B. Bakker. The authors explore the history of job design theory from its roots in scientific management and socio-technical systems theory. More recently, a steady stream of research has examined whether job design can specifically affect levels of engagement. For example, some studies have shown that levels of job resources such as coaching, social support and feedback can affect individuals' engagement. Social exchange theory and basic need fulfilment theory can at least partially account for the linkage. Tims and Bakker outline the practical implications of their review for HR managers, and suggest that employers need to be especially mindful of ensuring employees have sufficient resources to fulfil their role requirements.

In Chapter 8, Emma Soane addresses the link between leadership and engagement. A considerable amount of research effort over the years within the engagement domain has focused on the role that leaders can play in enhancing engagement levels. Notably, Soane highlights the importance of transformational leadership, which has several dimensions: idealized influence, inspirational motivation, intellectual stimulation and individualized consideration. Through interview data drawn from a manufacturing organization, and set within a context of social exchange theory, Soane brings the model to life, showing how leaders within the company enacted these roles in practice. There are links between the relational context for engagement highlighted in this chapter, and the broader relational engagement contexts referred to by Kahn and Heaphy in Chapter 6. In anticipation of the discussion in Chapter 15, Soane demonstrates the valuable role that measuring engaging leadership styles can play in identifying problematic areas and concludes with the point that leaders 'have a duty to create optimal working environments'.

In the context of increasing multiculturalism and diversity, in Chapter 9 Ian Rothmann argues that more consideration is needed of engagement's cultural and psychological roots. He notes that much of the research on engagement to date has taken place within the USA and Europe, and its applicability and relevance have yet to be explored in detail in other contexts. Further, he raises concerns about the validity and reliability of attitude surveys across cultural boundaries, and about whether theoretical frameworks often used within the engagement field, such as self-determination theory and job demands–resources theory, can meaningfully be generalized around the world.

Clare Kelliher, Veronica Hope Hailey and Elaine Farndale build on the themes raised in Chapter 9 and focus in Chapter 10 on the question of engagement in the context of multi-national corporations (MNCs). This is an important area, since many models and frameworks tend to assume that engagement will be similar across national settings, whereas both common sense and evidence from related areas would strongly suggest that this will not be the case. Kelliher and colleagues draw on qualitative data from three MNCs operating in the UK, the Netherlands and India and, in contrast to some of the other chapters, they use Saks' (2006) distinction between 'job' and 'organizational' engagement to frame their analysis. Further, they situate their argument within an institutional context, thus extending the range of factors that are relevant for engagement beyond the boundaries of the organization. They note the challenges that may be faced by Western MNCs in choosing to locate in India, given cultural, structural and societal dissimilarities with Western contexts, as well as the potential differences between the UK, a liberal market economy, and the Netherlands, a co-ordinated market economy.

Their study shows that both corporate HR teams and local managers stressed the importance of engagement with the job, and with the organization itself, but that there were differences in terms of the antecedents of engagement across the various settings. For example, job and personal resources acted as stronger drivers of engagement with the employer in more individualistic settings, whereas meaningfulness was derived from the closer links that existed between the employer and the community in India than in Europe. The authors highlight the point that although engagement may have some commonalities across diverse settings, the variables influencing engagement vary, and that economic, social and cultural factors play an important role.

Overall, this section of the book represents a first effort at bringing together expert opinion on how the debates in engagement that have been taking place in the psychology field are relevant within the context of human resource management.

Employee engagement: critical perspectives

In this third part of the book, we turn our attention to more critical views of the engagement construct in three chapters that examine engagement through divergent perspectives. Such critiques of the topic are to be encouraged, since it is only through subjecting engagement to critical and analytical scrutiny through a range of lenses that the field can progress.

In Chapter 11, Tom Keenoy draws on critical management theory, actor-network theory and discourse analysis to critique the notion of engagement as it has been developed and operationalized by policymakers, consultants and practitioners. He particularly highlights the problems that arise when engagement is not adequately defined, since it can become a catch-all with no explanatory power. Similarly, he raises the concern that the engagement agenda risks being hijacked by consultants and others aware of the potentially lucrative nature of the engagement 'industry'. As he notes, many of the so-called drivers of engagement cited in recent years frequently amount to no more than the kind of advice given to managers 50 or more years ago.

Perhaps more trenchant still is his critique of the managerialist agenda underpinning engagement within both the academic and the practitioner spheres, and he argues that much of the writing on engagement downplays or ignores both its political and economic context and its potential 'dark side'.

David E. Guest, in Chapter 12, questions whether engagement is simply a transitory and fashionable fad enjoying its 'day in the sun'. Distinguishing between 'academic' and 'consultancy' type approaches to engagement, Guest shows how the academic literature on engagement has now accumulated a sufficient body of evidence to suggest that it does indeed represent something conceptually and statistically 'different' from what has gone before. However, he expresses more significant reservations about the 'consultancy' perspective on engagement, and notes that the measures developed so far are problematic, concluding that the longevity of the consultancy version of engagement is difficult to assess. Alongside this, he also notes the ethical issues raised when employees are expected to participate in cost-saving exercises that may ultimately affect jobs, and in expecting employees to contribute more, for no greater personal reward.

Chapter 13 picks up this point again and addresses the link between employee voice and engagement. Here, John Purcell notes his concern that the engagement agenda relegates employees to a passive role as engagement initiatives are perceived to be driven by the organization and done 'to' rather than 'with' employees. He further points out the hierarchical inequalities within formal voice mechanisms that often remain unacknowledged within the engagement literature.

Purcell suggests that some engagement writings seem to imply that employees should have super-human levels of energy and performance that may be unrealistic; by definition, he argues, if engagement is associated with exceptional attitudes and behaviours, it must be a 'minority activity'. Developing the point raised in Chapter 10, Purcell considers the question of what it is that we are asking employees to be engaged with, and proposes that the notion of 'organizational engagement' is perhaps more valuable than job engagement, since this acknowledges the firm as a social entity. He discusses the role of trust in relation to engagement and asks what has happened to engagement during the recession, citing evidence from some studies that engagement initiatives had in some cases been withdrawn due the prevailing economic climate. Another important issue raised in the chapter is that of collective versus individual voice, and the significance of informational justice.

Employee engagement in practice

In Part 4, we move on to consider employee engagement in practice in three chapters addressing international agendas, the measurement of engagement and, finally, a series of in-depth case studies.

In Chapter 14, Amanda Shantz, Jordan Schoenberg and Christopher Chan explore the interesting question of the extent of uptake of the engagement agenda by professional associations around the world, such as the UK's Chartered Institute of Personnel and Development and the People Management Association of the Philippines. Through a detailed analysis of the websites of 120 such associations, Shantz and colleagues show that there are significant variations in the way in which engagement is adopted and promoted by these groups. In particular, they found that reference to engagement appeared more frequently in Western professional associations than those in other parts of the world, lending further support to the points expanded in Chapters 9 and 10 concerning the cross-cultural dimensions of engagement.

In an analysis aimed at helping practitioners understand some of the complexities and challenges of evaluating engagement levels, Luke Fletcher and Dilys Robinson examine in some detail in Chapter 15 the principal ways in which engagement has been measured and operationalized within the academic and practitioner literatures. As perhaps might be expected given that engagement is a relatively new area of interest, a number of divergent views can be found. Starting with an overview of the status of engagement as a construct, and focusing on measures of engagement as a psychological state, Fletcher and Robinson review the well-established UWES, alongside measures developed by May et al. (2004), Rich et al. (2010) and Soane et al. (2012), comparing them in terms of their individual facets. This analysis reveals areas of commonality and difference across the measures, raising questions about the overarching conceptualization of the engagement construct, as well as its individual components. They argue that whilst an emotional and a cognitive dimension are evident in most measures, there is less agreement about the third dimension which has variously been conceived as energy and effort, persistence and intensity and social connectedness.

Within the domain of engagement as an attitude towards the organization overall, the authors review measures developed by the Institute for Employment Studies (IES), Gallup, UK National Health Service (NHS) and Civil Service, before considering generalized issues of statistical validity and reliability and the interpretation of results, together with a critique of the significance of benchmarking. Case studies from the NHS and Mace illustrate how organizations have utilized engagement surveys in practice. They conclude by urging some caution in the adoption of any one particular method of measuring engagement, and in interpreting and using the results.

Whilst academics may debate the meaning of engagement and its locus within the extant literature, those working for organizations who are charged with developing and implementing engagement strategies must make the best of the information they have available. In Chapter 16, Kerstin Alfes and Suna Yeltekin introduce four case studies written by engagement practitioners from diverse organizational settings: UK Department for Work and Pensions, Marks and Spencer, the Co-operative Group Pharmacy and Kia Motors. The cases show how each organization measured engagement and implemented an organization-wide strategy aimed at fostering high levels of engagement. Taken as a whole, these case studies reveal the complex and multi-faceted initiatives undertaken, and the ongoing challenges faced by the organizations, particularly in the prevailing economic climate. The variety of engagement measures used in each of the organizations highlights the point made in Chapter 15 that benchmarking and comparing engagement across settings may be misleading.

Conclusions

The chapters in this book represent a first endeavour to build a bridge between psychological, HRM and critical perspectives on engagement, as well as to consider the practical implications of emerging engagement theories. As is normally the case with the development of new constructs, opinions are diverse, and there are more questions than there are answers. As we can see from Chapters 1 and 12 of this book, there is emerging consensus that engagement is a psychological state experienced by employees in relation to their work that is sufficiently distinct from other, similar constructs to be regarded as worthy of investigation in its own right. The ethnographic work of William Kahn as founder of the field and the contribution of the Utrecht group in operationalizing the engagement construct, have been especially salient in establishing the field. The chapters in Part 1 of this book provide an excellent summary and overview of the progress made on engagement to date within the psychology discipline.

However, even within the psychology field, views diverge about the best ways to conceptualize and measure the construct. There is further debate around the drivers of engagement, and research studies that can identify which, of the wide range of potential antecedents matter the most, is still to be conducted.

The HRM discipline has been relatively late in appreciating the emerging importance of engagement, and so the majority of research and insights we have on the topic are located within the psychology literature, and have been conducted within a positivistic paradigm using quantitative methods. This approach is reflected within the usage of engagement by the practitioner community, which is normally based on a model of staff engagement surveys aimed at identifying levels of engagement across organizational units, followed by a range of inteiventions designed to raise engagement levels, as is reflected in the case studies in Chapter 16. The potential problems that may be caused through the adoption of scales and measures that lack the appropriate validity and reliability are discussed in Chapters 9 and 15.

Further, as suggested by the authors contributing to Parts 2 and 3 of this book, there are some significant questions that still need to be addressed in terms of how engagement as conceived within the psychology field can be the subject of research and enquiry within the HRM domain. Recent studies are starting to adopt more qualitative, ethnographic and case-study based methodologies using multiple informants (e.g. Chapters 8 and 10 in this volume and papers published in a special issue of the *International Journal of Human Resource Management*), should begin to yield more nuanced insights into the context of engagement (Truss et al., 2013). Equally, there has been a rising level of interest in the cross-national dimensions of engagement (e.g. Chapters 9 and 10) that start to address some of the culturally bound underpinnings evident within some of the engagement literature to date. Diverse approaches are emerging, such as that proposed in Chapter 10, that question whether the focus of engagement, rather than being on the job itself, would perhaps be better conceived as relating to the organization as a whole.

Contributors to Part 3 of this volume raise further, important questions about the ontological and epistemological status of the engagement construct, and its relationship with similar notions within the HRM domain, such as high commitment work practices. As the authors note, engagement as currently constructed is part of a managerialist agenda, and founded on a unitary view of organizations that paradoxically risks relegating the employee to a passive role if the complex political and cultural realities of organizational life are not taken into consideration.

Taken together, the cumulative evidence presented by contributors to this volume suggests that engagement is more than a passing fad and has entered the lexicon as a significant factor in the management of people. Understanding more about what engagement is, how its presence or absence can be evaluated, the factors that influence it and its potential outcomes, alongside an awareness of engagement's micro- and macro-level cultural context, will be essential to the growth and development of the field. The contributors to this book make a significant contribution to these debates, and to raising awareness of the rich potential of the engagement subject area for practitioners and academics alike.

References

Alfes, K., Shantz, A., Truss, C. and Soane, E. (2013a) 'The Link between Perceived HRM Practices, Engagement and Employee Behaviour: A Moderated Mediation Model', *International Journal of Human Resource Management*, 24, 2: 33051.

——, Truss, C., Soane, E., Rees, C. and Gatenby, M. (2013b – in press) 'Linking Perceived Supervisor Support, Perceived HRM Practices and Individual Performance: The Mediating Role of Employee Engagement', *Human Resource Management.*

Arrowsmith, J., and Parker, J. (2013) 'Delivering Employee Engagement: A Neo-Pluralist Departure for HRM?', *International Journal of Human Resource Management*, 24, 14: 2692–712.

Bakker, A. and Schaufeli, W. (2008) 'Positive Organizational Behaviour: Engaged Employees in Flourishing Organizations', *Journal of Organizational Behavior*, 29: 147–54.

Brunetto, Y., Teo, S., Shacklock, K. and Farr-Wharton, K. (2012) 'Emotional Intelligence, Job Satisfaction, Well-Being and Engagement: Explaining Organisational Commitment and Turnover Intentions in Policing', *Human Resource Management Journal*, 22, 4: 428–41.

Christian, M., Garza, A. and Slaughter, J. (2011) 'Work Engagement: A Quantitative Review and Test of its Relations with Task and Contextual Performance', *Personnel Psychology*, 64: 89–136.

Harter, J. K., Schmidt, F. L., and Hayes, T. L. (2002), 'Business-Unit-Level Relationship between Employee Satisfaction, Employee Engagement, and Business Outcomes: A Meta-Analysis', *Journal of Applied Psychology*, 87: 268–79.

Jenkins, S. and Delbridge, R. (2013) 'Context Matters: Examining 'Soft' and 'Hard' Approches to Employee Engagement in Two Workplaces', *International Journal of Human Resource Management*, 24, 14: 2670–91.

Kahn, W. (1990) 'Psychological Conditions of Personal Engagement and Disengagement at Work', *Academy of Management Journal*, 33, 4: 692–724.

Linley, A., Harrington, S. and Garcea, N. (2010) 'Finding the Positive in the World of Work'. In P. Linley, S. Harrington and N. Garcea (eds) *Oxford Handbook of Positive Psychology and Work*. Oxford: Oxford University Press.

Macleod, D. and Clarke. N. (2009). *Engaging for success: Enhancing performance through employee engagement*. London, UK: Department of Business, Innovation and Skills.

Maslach, C. and Leiter, M. (1997) *The Truth about Burnout*. San Francisco: Jossey Bass.

May, D. R., Gilson, L. and Harter, L. M. (2004) 'The Psychological Conditions of Meaningfulness, Safety and Availability and the Engagement of the Human Spirit at Work', *Journal of Occupational and Organizational Psychology*, 77: 11–37.

Rayton, B., Dodge, T. and d'Analeze, G. (2012) *The Evidence. Employee Engagement Task Force 'Nailing the Evidence' Work Group*. Engage for Success.

Rich, B. L., Lepine, J. A., and Crawford, E. R. (2010) 'Job Engagement: Antecedents and Effects on Job Performance', *Academy of Management Journal*, 53: 617–35.

Saks, A. (2006) 'Antecedents and Consequences of Employee Engagement', *Journal of Managerial Psychology*, 21: 600–19.

Schaufeli, W. B., Salanova, M., Gonzalez-Roma, V., and Bakker, A. B. (2002), 'The Measurement of Engagement and Burnout: A Two Sample Confirmatory Factor Analytic Approach', *Journal of Happiness Studies*, 3: 71–92.

Shuck, B., Reio, T. and Rocco, T. (2011) 'Employee Engagement: An Antecedent and Outcome Approach to Model Development', *Human Resource Development International*, 14: 427–45.

Soane, E., Truss, C., Alfes, K., Shantz, A., Rees, C. and Gatenby, M. (2012) 'Development and Validation of a New Measure of Employee Engagement: The ISA Engagement Scale', *Human Resource Development International*, 15, 5: 529–47.

Stairs, M. and Galpin, M. (2011) 'Positive Engagement: From Employee Engagement to Workplace Happiness'. In P. Linley, S. Harrington and N. Garcea (eds) *Oxford Handbook of Positive Psychology and Work*. Oxford: Oxford University Press.

Truss, C., Mankin, D. and Kelliher, C. (2012) *Strategic Human Resource Management*. Oxford: Oxford University Press.

——, Alfes, K., Delbridge, R., Shantz, A. and Soane, E. (2013) 'Employee Engagement, Organisational Performance and Individual Wellbeing: Developing the Theory, Exploring the Evidence', editorial introduction to special issue, *International Journal of Human Resource Management*, 24, 14: 2657–69.

Wollard, K. and Shuck, B. (2011) 'Antecedents to Employee Engagement: A Structured Review of the Literature', *Advances in Developing Human Resources*, 13, 4: 429–46.

Part 1
The psychology of engagement

1   What is engagement?

Wilmar B. Schaufeli

Introduction

Everyday connotations of engagement refer to involvement, commitment, passion, enthusiasm, absorption, focused effort, zeal, dedication, and energy. In a similar vein, the Merriam-Webster dictionary describes the state of being engaged as 'emotional involvement or commitment' and as 'being in gear'. This chapter focuses on engagement at work, a desirable condition for employees as well as for the organization they work for. Although typically, 'employee engagement' and 'work engagement' are used interchangeably, this chapter prefers the latter because it is more specific. Work engagement refers to the relationship of the employee with his or her *work*, whereas employee engagement may also include the relationship with the *organization*. As we will see below, by including the relationship with the organization, the distinction between engagement and traditional concepts such as organizational commitment and extra-role behavior becomes blurred.

Although the meaning of engagement at work may seem clear at first glance, a closer look into the literature reveals the indistinctness of the concept. As with many other psychological terms, work engagement is easy to recognize in practice yet difficult to define. In large part, as Macey and Schneider (2008: 3) argued, the confusion about the meaning of engagement 'can be attributed to the "bottom-up" manner in which the engagement notion has quickly evolved within the practitioner community'. However, this bottom-up method that flourishes in business is not only at odds with the top-down academic approach that requires a clear and unambiguous definition of the term, but it also hampers the understanding of work engagement for practical purposes. A Babylonian confusion of tongues precludes a proper assessment, as well as interventions to increase work engagement. Therefore the first chapter of this volume tries to answer the crucial question: 'What is engagement?'

The structure of the chapter is as follows. First, a brief history is presented of the emergence of engagement in business and in academia (section 1), which is followed by a discussion of various definitions that are used in business and in science (section 2). Next it is argued that engagement is a unique construct that can be differentiated, for instance from job-related attitudes such as job satisfaction and organizational commitment, and from work addiction and personality dispositions (section 3). The most important theoretical frameworks are discussed that are used to explain engagement (section 4) and the organizational outcomes of engagement are elucidated (section 5). The chapter closes with some general conclusions and an outlook on the future of this intriguing psychological state (section 6).

The emergence of engagement in business and academia: a brief history

It is not entirely clear when the term 'engagement' was first used in relation to work, but generally the Gallup Organization is credited for coining the term somewhere in the 1990s.

Table 1.1 Changes in the world of work

Traditional	Modern
Stable organizational environment	Continuous change
Uniformity	Diversity
Life-time employment	Precarious employment
Individual work	Teamwork
Horizontal structure	Vertical structure
External control and supervision	Self-control and self-management
Dependence on the organization	Own responsibility and accountability
Detailed job description	Job crafting
Fixed schedules and patterns	Boundarylessness (time and place)
Physical demands	Mental and emotional demands
Experience	Continuous learning
Working hard	Working smart

In their best-selling book *First, break all the rules*, Buckingham and Coffman (1999) summarized survey results that Gallup had obtained since 1988 on 'strong work places' of over 100,000 employees. Employees' perceptions of such workplaces were assessed with a 'measuring stick' consisting of 12 questions. Later this tool became known as the Q^{12}, Gallup's engagement questionnaire (see below). The term engagement is only occasionally used in the book by Buckingham and Coffman (1999) that was basically about leadership, as is reflected by its subtitle *What the world's greatest managers do differently*.

Around the turn of the century, other major consulting firms followed suit. Obviously, the time was ripe and engagement was 'in the air'. But why was that so? Why did companies suddenly become interested in work engagement after the turn of the century? Although it is difficult to come up with an unambiguous answer, it can be speculated that a set of changes that were – and still are – taking place in the world of work constitute the background for the emergence of engagement in business. Table 1.1 summarizes the major changes that are related to the ongoing transition from traditional to modern organizations.

Taken together, these changes boil down to what can be called a 'psychologization' of the workplace. That is, most of the current changes that are listed in Table 1.1 require a substantial psychological adaptation and involvement from the part of employees. In other words, more than ever employees need *psychological* capabilities in order to thrive and to make organizations survive. For instance, organizational change requires adaptation, diversity requires perspective taking, teamwork requires assertiveness, working in vertical networks requires communication skills, job crafting requires personal initiative, boundarylessness requires self-control, and mental and emotional demands require resilience.

The bottom line is that more than in the past the employee's psychological capabilities, including their motivation, is taxed. Instead of merely their bodies, employees in modern organizations bring their entire person to the workplace. Or as David Ulrich has put it in its best-selling book *Human resource champions*:

> Employee contribution becomes a critical business issue because in trying to produce more output with less employee input, companies have no choice but to try to engage not only the body, but also the mind and the soul of every employee.
>
> (1997: 125)

Ulrich makes two points here. First, the organization's human capital becomes increasingly important because more has to be done with fewer people. So, people matter more than they

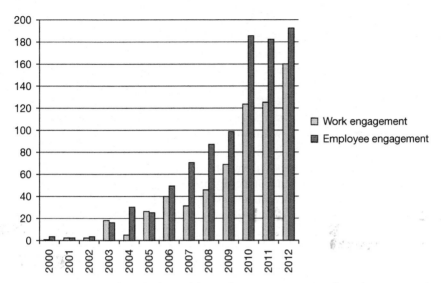

Figure 1.1 Number of publications with 'employee engagement' and 'work engagement'
in the title 2000–11

Source: Google Scholar (January 2013)

did in the past. Second, modern organizations need employees who are able and willing to
invest in their jobs psychologically. And this is exactly what work engagement is all about.
No wonder that companies became interested in engagement at a time of profound changes
in the world of work.

The emergence of engagement in academia is quite well documented, as is shown in Figure
1.1 that summarizes the number of publications on engagement through the years.

Between 2000 and 2010 there was a sharp, yearly increase in the number of publications
and, to date (January 2013), around 1,600 papers have been published with 'work engagement' or 'employee engagement' in the title. In fact, the first scholarly article on engagement
at work was published by William Kahn as early as 1990 in the *Academy of Management
Journal*, but it took another decade before the topic was picked up by others in academia.
Why was that so? Of course, this has to do with the changes in the world of work that were
discussed above and which took place gradually from the late 1990's onwards. But there is
more. At the turn of the century the so-called positive psychology movement emerged. Or
rather the science of positive psychology was proclaimed by a group of scholars working
with Martin Seligman, at that time the President of the American Psychological Association.

Broadly speaking, as discussed in Chapter 2, positive psychology refers to the scientific
study of optimal human functioning that aims to discover and promote the factors that allow
individuals, organizations, and communities to thrive. Clearly, work engagement fits into this
novel approach that has gained significant momentum in the past decade. So, the positive
psychology movement created the fertile soil that made engagement research blossom in
academia.

In conclusion, the emergence of engagement at the beginning of the 21st century has to do
with two converging developments: (1) the growing importance of human capital and
psychological involvement of employees in business, and (2) the increased scientific interest
in positive psychological states.

Definitions of engagement in business and in academia

Engagement has been criticized for being no more than old wine in new bottles (Jeung, 2011). Consultancy firms have conceptualized engagement by combining and relabeling existing notions, such as commitment, satisfaction, involvement, motivation, and extra-role performance. For instance, according to *Mercer*, 'Employee engagement – also called "commitment" or "motivation" – refers to a psychological state where employees feel a vested interest in the company's success and perform to a high standard that may exceed the stated requirements of the job' (www.mercerHR.com). Another firm, *Hewitt*, states that:

> Engaged employees consistently demonstrate three general behaviors. They: (1) Say – consistently speak positively about the organization to co-workers, potential employees, and customers; (2) Stay – have an intense desire to be a member of the organization despite opportunities to work elsewhere; (3) Strive – exert extra time, effort, and initiative to contribute to business success.
>
> (www.hewittassociates.com)

Finally, for *Towers Perrin* engagement reflects employees' 'personal satisfaction and a sense of inspiration and affirmation they get from work and being a part of the organization' (www.towersperrin.com).

Taken together, these three examples suggest that in business, engagement is defined as a blend of three existing concepts (1) job satisfaction; (2) commitment to the organization; and (3) extra-role behavior, i.e. discretionary effort to go beyond the job description. Additionally, the approaches of consultancy firms are proprietary and thus not subject to external peer review, which is problematic as far as transparency is concerned. For instance, questionnaire items and technical details of measurement tools are not publicly available. This is discussed further in Chapter 15.

Recently, Shuck (2011) searched all relevant HRM, psychology, and management databases and systematically reviewed academic definitions of engagement. Based on 213 eligible publications he identified four approaches to defining engagement:

The Needs-Satisfying approach. Kahn (1990) defined personal engagement as the 'harnessing of organization members' selves to their work roles: in engagement, people employ and express themselves physically, cognitively, emotionally, and mentally during role performances' (p. 694). He conceptualized engagement as the employment and expression of one's preferred self in task behaviors. Although important for the theoretical thinking about engagement, the Needs-Satisfying approach has only occasionally been used in empirical research (e.g. May, Gilson and Harter, 2004).

The Burnout-Antithesis approach. Rooted in occupational health psychology, this approach views work engagement as the positive antithesis of burnout. As a matter of fact, two schools of thought exist on this issue. According to Maslach and Leiter (1997) engagement and burnout are the positive and negative endpoints of a *single continuum*. More specifically, engagement is characterized by energy, involvement and efficacy, which are considered the direct opposites of the three burnout dimensions exhaustion, cynicism and lack of accomplishment, respectively. By implication that means that persons who are high on engagement are inevitably low on burnout, and vice versa. The second, alternative view considers work engagement as a *distinct concept* that is negatively related to burnout. Work engagement, in this view, is defined as a concept in its own right: 'a positive, fulfilling, work related state of mind that is characterized by vigor, dedication, and absorption'

(Schaufeli, Salanova, González-Romá, and Bakker, 2002: 74), whereby vigor refers to high levels of energy and mental resilience while working, the willingness to invest effort in one's work, and persistence even in the face of difficulties; dedication refers to being strongly involved in one's work, and experiencing a sense of significance, enthusiasm, inspiration, pride, and challenge; and absorption refers to being fully concentrated and happily engrossed in one's work, whereby time passes quickly and one has difficulties with detaching oneself from work. To date, most academic research on engagement uses the Utrecht Work Engagement Scale (UWES), a brief, valid and reliable questionnaire that is based on the definition of work engagement as a combination of vigor, dedication, and absorption (Schaufeli, 2012).

The Satisfaction-Engagement approach. According to the Gallup Organization: 'The term employee engagement refers to an individual's involvement and satisfaction with as well as enthusiasm for work' (Harter, Schmidt and Hayes, 2002: 269). Thus, like the definitions of other consultancy firms, Gallup's engagement concept seems to overlap with well-known traditional constructs such as job involvement and job satisfaction. This is illustrated by the fact that, after controlling for measurement error, Gallup's Q^{12} correlates almost perfectly ($r = .91$) with a single item that taps job satisfaction, meaning that both are virtually identical. The authors acknowledge this overlap by stating that the Q^{12} assesses 'antecedents to positive affective constructs such as job satisfaction' (Harter et al., 2002: 209). Hence, rather than the *experience* of engagement in terms of involvement, satisfaction and enthusiasm, the Q^{12} measures the *antecedents* of engagement in terms of perceived job resources. The reason for that is that the Q^{12} has been explicitly designed from an 'actionability standpoint' and not from a scholarly perspective (Buckingham and Coffman, 1999). In other words, the Q^{12} was first and foremost designed as tool for management to improve jobs so that employees would be more satisfied. Nevertheless, the Satisfaction-Engagement approach has had a significant impact in academia as well, because Gallup's research has established meaningful links between employee engagement and business unit outcomes, such as customer satisfaction, profit, productivity, and turnover (Harter et al., 2002).

The Multidimensional approach. Saks (2006) defined employee engagement as 'a distinct and unique construct consisting of cognitive, emotional, and behavioral components that are associated with individual role performance' (p. 602). This definition is quite similar to that of Kahn (1990) because it also focuses on role performance at work. The innovative aspect is that Saks (2006) distinguishes between 'job engagement' (performing the work role) and 'organizational engagement' (performing the role as a member of the organization). Although both are moderately related ($r = .62$), they seem to have different antecedents and consequences. Despite its intuitive appeal, the multidimensional approach (i.e. the distinction between job and organizational engagement) has hardly been taken up by the research community.

Taken together, these four approaches each stress a different aspect of engagement: (1) its relation with role performance; (2) its positive nature in terms of employee well-being as opposed to burnout; (3) its relation with resourceful jobs; and (4) its relation with the job as well as with the organization.

Probably the most important issue in defining engagement is 'where to draw the line'. Or put differently, what elements to include and what elements to exclude from the definition of engagement. In their seminal overview Macey and Schneider (2008) proposed an exhaustive synthesis of *all* elements that have been employed to define engagement. Their conceptual framework for understanding employee engagement includes: (1) trait engagement (e.g. conscientiousness, trait positive affect, proactive personality); (2) state engagement (e.g. satisfaction, involvement, empowerment); and (3) behavioral engagement (e.g. extra-role

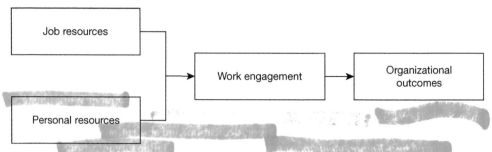

Figure 1.2 The experience of work engagement and its antecedents and outcomes

behavior, proactivity, role expansion). Consequently, as Saks (2008) has noted in his critique, for Macey and Schneider, 'engagement' serves as an umbrella term for whatever one wants it to be. In contrast, Schaufeli and Bakker (2010) proposed a more restrictive model that considers work engagement as an experienced psychological state which mediates the impact of job resources and personal resources on organizational outcomes (see Figure 1.2).

Hence, unlike Macey and Schneider (2008), who present an all-inclusive taxonomy that covers the entire range of concepts which have – in one way or another – been associated with engagement, Figure 1.2 distinguishes the *experience* of work engagement from its perceived *antecedents* and *consequences*. That means that neither resourceful jobs (as in the Satisfaction-Engagement approach) nor employees' performance behavior (as in the business approach) are conceived as constituting elements of work engagement.

Of course, these antecedents and consequences could (and should) be included in research and practice, but they are considered to be distinct concepts. For instance, a job can be resourceful but an employee might not feel engaged because of family problems. Alternatively, an employee might feel engaged but not show initiative (i.e. extra-role behavior) because of constraints at work. As these two examples illustrate, the experience of work engagement is neither inherently linked to challenging work nor to performance and should therefore be treated as a separate entity. Using a meta-analysis that included over two hundred articles Christian, Garza and Slaughter (2011) successfully tested a similar model, as is depicted in Figure 1.2. They included autonomy, task variety, task significance and feedback as job resources and conscientiousness and positive affect as personal resources. In addition, transformational leadership was included that had a direct impact on in-role and extra-role performance as well as an indirect effect through work engagement. So it seems that the model (Figure 1.2) is supported by empirical research.

Moreover, the definitions of engagement as a psychological state by Kahn (1990) and Schaufeli et al. (2002) fit with Figure 1.2. Both academic conceptualizations agree that engagement entails a physical-energetic (vigor), an emotional (dedication), and a cognitive (absorption) component. The similarity between both definitions is further illustrated by their operationalizations. Based on the work of Kahn (1990), May, Gilson and Harter (2004) developed an engagement inventory that consists of three dimensions: cognitive, emotional and physical engagement. The items that are included in this inventory show a striking resemblance with those included in the absorption, dedication, and vigor scales of the UWES (Schaufeli et al., 2002), respectively.

It appeared particularly that the cognitive engagement and absorption scales are strongly related, whereas the physical engagement and the vigor scales are only weakly related, with the emotional engagement and dedication scales somewhere in between

Table 1.2 The correspondence of two engagement questionnaires (example items)

May, Gilson, and Harter (2004)	Schaufeli et al. (2002)
Physical engagement: 'I exert a lot of energy performing my job'	Vigor: 'At my job, I feel that I'm bursting with energy'
Emotional engagement: 'I really put my heart into this job'	Dedication: 'I am enthusiastic about my job'
Cognitive engagement: 'Performing my job is so absorbing that I forget about everything else'	Absorption: 'When I am working, I forget anything else around me'

(Viljevac, Cooper-Thomas and Saks, 2012). Recently, and also building on the work of Kahn (1990) the *Intellectual, Social, Affective (ISA) Engagement Scale* was introduced (Soane, Truss, Alfes et al., 2013). It includes three facets of engagement: (1) intellectual (i.e, 'the extent to which one is intellectually absorbed in work'); (2) social (i.e. 'the extent to which one is socially connected with the working environment and shares common values with colleagues'); and (3) affective (i.e. 'the extent to which one experiences a state of positive affect relating to one's work role'). The first and the third facet of engagement are similar to absorption and vigor, respectively whereas the second facet had not been considered before.

Engagement as a unique construct

The emergence of engagement has been plagued by disagreements about its nature. Most notable is the claim that it is merely old wine in new bottles, as suggested elsewhere in this volume. It follows that it is crucially important to show its conceptual distinctiveness vis-à-vis particular job related attitudes, job behaviors, and behavioral intentions, as well as certain aspects of employee health and well-being, and personality.

Job-related attitudes

From the outset, the concept of engagement has been criticized for its overlap with other, pre-existing notions, such as job satisfaction and organizational commitment. This is not very surprising because, as we have seen in the previous section, particularly in business contexts the distinction between engagement and existing concepts is blurred. For example based on a meta-analysis, Newman, Joseph and Hulin (2010) showed that engagement is closely related – or perhaps even a constituting element – of what they dubbed 'the A (attitude)-factor', a combination of job satisfaction, job involvement, and affective organizational commitment.

Despite their claim, in fact, correlations of these three attitudes with engagement were modest and ranged from .39 to .54, which corresponds with an overlap of 15–29 per cent. Surely, such levels of association do not indicate that engagement is identical with the other three concepts involved. And what is more, engagement shows different patterns of correlations with other variables as compared with satisfaction, involvement and commitment. For instance, Christian et al. (2011), also using a meta-analysis, showed that engagement predicted in-role as well as extra-role performance, *after controlling for job satisfaction, job involvement, and organizational commitment*. This means that the explanatory power of engagement goes beyond that of the three attitudes. This is in line with the study of Rich, Lepine and Crawford (2010) among firefighters that showed that the independent contribution of engagement to in-role and extra-role performance outweighed that of job involvement, job satisfaction and intrinsic motivation. Most likely the reason why engagement is more strongly related to performance than the other job-related attitudes is that it reflects an energetic drive, rather than a feeling of satiation, which is typical for job satisfaction (see Figure 1.3).

So, in conclusion, although engagement is positively related to work-related attitudes such a job satisfaction, job involvement, and organizational commitment, it nevertheless seems to be a distinct concept that is more strongly related to job performance.

Job behavior and behavioral intentions

It appears that engagement is only moderately and negatively related to turnover intention, as is attested by the meta-analysis of Halbesleben (2010). In a study using four independent samples Schaufeli and Bakker (2004) showed that work engagement mediated the relationship between job resources and turnover intention; the more resourceful the job, the higher the levels of engagement, and the lower the level of intention to quit. In a similar vein, Schaufeli and Salanova (2008) showed in a Spanish and Dutch sample that job resources are related to proactive behavior via work engagement. This means that the more resourceful the job, the higher the levels of engagement, and the more personal initiative is shown by employees. This result was replicated in a longitudinal study among Finnish dentists, which showed in addition that personal initiative leads to more innovative behavior at team level (Hakanen, Perhoniemi and Topinen-Tanner, 2008a).

Taken together, these results – which fit with the model depicted in Figure 1.2 – testify that engagement is related to, but can be discriminated from, behavioral intentions and actual behavior that reflects an employee's commitment to the organization and its goals.

Health and well-being

As discussed above, it is claimed that work engagement is incompatible with burnout and is, in fact, to be seen as its positive anti-thesis. Despite the intuitive appeal of this claim, correlations between the three dimensions of burnout and engagement are much less than −1.00 and range between −.15 and −.65 (Halbesleben, 2010; Cole, Walter, Bedeian and O'Boyle, 2012). Typically, correlations with engagement are highest for inefficacy, ranging between −.41 and −.65. This has to do with an artifact, namely that inefficacy is measured with *positively* framed items that are subsequently reversed in order to assess *in*efficacy (Schaufeli and Salanova, 2007). Using data from 50 samples, Cole et al. (2012) refute the claim that work engagement – as assessed with the UWES – is a distinct concept that can be discriminated from burnout – as assessed with the Maslach Burnout Inventory (MBI; Maslach, Leiter and Jackson, 1996). They conclude that Kahn's (1990) description of engagement may offer a better basis to reconceptualize engagement in a way that does not overlap with burnout.

In contrast, numerous studies have documented that, indeed, although being moderately to strongly negatively related, engagement and burnout should be considered distinct concepts. This applies to detailed psychometric studies that assess the relationships between the UWES and the MBI and that show that rather than loading on one overall, indiscriminate, general well-being factor, both instruments assess separate constructs (for an overview see Schaufeli, 2012). And perhaps even more importantly, a host of studies using the job demands–resources model (JD–R), which is discussed below, show that work engagement and burnout have different antecedents (for an overview see Schaufeli and Taris, in press). In conclusion, the discussion about the distinctiveness of burnout and engagement is not yet finished.

There exists an alternative, under-researched state of mind that may act as the counterpart of work engagement as well: boredom at work. Boredom is defined as a psychological state of low arousal and dissatisfaction that is due to an under-stimulating work environment. Like burnout, feeling bored refers to a displeasurable-deactivating affect, whereas feeling engaged refers to a pleasurable-activating affect. As expected, Reijseger, Schaufeli, Peeters et al. (in press), found that boredom is negatively related with engagement ($r = -.46$) and positively related with burnout ($r = .40$). Moreover, their study showed that compared to work engagement boredom is inversely related to job demands, job resources, job satisfaction, organizational commitment, and turnover intention. Future research should further elucidate how far boredom at work is indeed the negative counterpart of work engagement.

Not surprisingly, for engaged employees work is fun, which is precisely the reason why they work so hard, as was shown in a qualitative interview study (Schaufeli, LeBlanc, Peeters et al., 2001). However, the reverse is *not* true; not all employees who work hard are engaged. Although there are various reasons to work hard, such as financial needs, promotion prospects, or perhaps a poor marriage, some do so because they are driven by an obsession to work. These so-called workaholics are not *pulled* towards their work because they like it, but they are *pushed* by a strong inner drive they cannot resist. Following this lead, Schaufeli, Taris and Bakker (2006) define workaholism as the compulsive tendency to work excessively. A series of studies have shown that:

(1) Work engagement – as assessed by the UWES – and workaholism – as assessed by the Dutch Workaholism Scale (DUWAS) – can be measured independently from each other (e.g. Taris, Schaufeli and Shimazu, 2010; Schaufeli, Taris and Van Rhenen, 2008), although some overlap exists as far as absorption is concerned, meaning that both engaged, as well as work addicted employees, have difficulties in detaching from work.

(2) Work engagement is 'good' and workaholism is 'bad'. That is, engagement and workaholism are inversely related with engaged workers scoring favorably and workaholics scoring unfavorably on performance (Taris et al., 2010), distress, psychosomatic complaints and self-rated health (Schaufeli, Taris and Van Rhenen, 2008), quality of sleep (Kubota, Shimazu, Kawakami et al., 2011), and life satisfaction (Shimazu, Schaufeli, Kubota and Kawakami, 2012). More specifically, it seems that the obsessive aspect of workaholism is its most toxic component.

(3) The underlying work motivation of engaged and addicted employees differs fundamentally. Engaged workers are primarily intrinsically motivated, they work for the fun of it, whereas workaholics are primary driven by external standards of self-worth and social approval that they have internalized (Van Beek, Hu, Schaufeli et al., 2012). They work because their self-esteem depends on it and because they do not want to fail in the eyes of others.

In conclusion, it seems that engagement and burnout are two distinct and opposite concepts. Although recent evidence casts some doubts on that claim, at least when engagement and burnout are assessed with the UWES and the MBI, respectively. In addition the evidence that 'good' (engagement) and 'bad' (workaholism) forms of working hard can be distinguished seems rather convincing. And finally the inverse relationship of engagement with boredom is not yet well-established and needs further investigation.

By way of summary, Figure 1.3 depicts a taxonomy of work-related well-being. Various types of well-being, including burnout, boredom, satisfaction and engagement can be

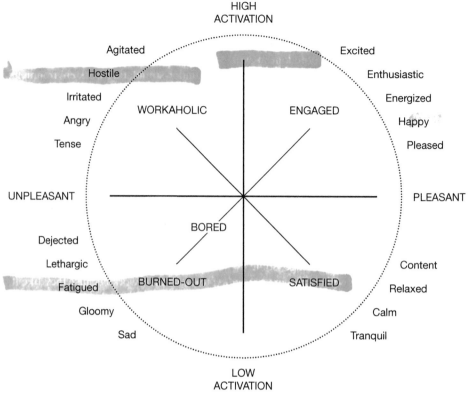

HIGH
ACTIVATION

Agitated   Excited

Hostile   Enthusiastic

Irritated   Energized
            WORKAHOLIC   ENGAGED
Angry   Happy

Tense   Pleased

UNPLEASANT   PLEASANT

                          BORED
Dejected

Lethargic   Content

Fatigued   BURNED-OUT   SATISFIED   Relaxed

Gloomy   Calm

Sad   Tranquil

LOW
ACTIVATION

Figure 1.3 A taxonomy of work-related well-being
Source: Adapted from Russell, 1980

mapped using the circumplex model of emotions (Russell, 1980). This model assumes that all human emotions may be plotted on the surface of a circle that is defined by two orthogonal dimensions that run from pleasure to displeasure and from activation to deactivation. For instance, employees who experience mainly negative emotions may suffer from burnout, boredom or workaholism, whereas employees who experience mainly positive emotions may feel satisfied or engaged. In addition, employees may either feel activated, as in workaholism and engagement, or deactivated as in burnout, boredom and satisfaction.

Personality

As indicated above, engagement has also been associated with personality traits, most notably with conscientiousness (Macey and Schneider, 2008). However, studies that might answer the question whether or not engagement is more than just a personality trait are scarce. Langelaan, Bakker, Van Doornen and Schaufeli (2006) used a two-dimensional model that included neuroticism (i.e. the disposition to experience distressing emotions such as fear, depression, and frustration) and extraversion (i.e. the disposition towards cheerfulness, sociability, and high activity) and found that engagement was negatively related to the former and positively related to the latter. Correlations ranged from −.33 to .50, which means that the overlap with both personality traits is small (11–25 per cent).

A more comprehensive study by Kim, Shin and Swanger (2009) included the so-called Big Five personality traits and found that only conscientiousness was significantly related to engagement($r = .37$ or 15 per cent overlap), whereas neuroticism and extraversion were not. After controlling for job related factors, conscientiousness was still (positively) associated with engagement, but was now supplemented with neuroticism that was (negatively) associated with it.

So, it seems that engagement is a psychological state rather than a dispositional trait. Limited evidence is found for a weak to moderately strong relationship with conscientiousness and, to a lesser degree, with neuroticism and extraversion.

Summary

The conceptual distinctiveness of engagement vis-à-vis other relevant concepts remains an issue. As would be expected, engagement is related significantly and in meaningful ways to job related attitudes, behavior and intentions on the job, employee health and well-being, and personality traits. But the question is: are these relationships that strong, and does engagement overlap to such an extent with other concepts that they are virtually identical? Based on the empirical evidence presented above the answer to this question is 'no', at least for the time being. In addition, it seems that compared to similar, alternative concepts engagement is related in a rather unique way to job demands, job resources and performance. So, taken together, it appears that engagement reflects a genuine and unique psychological state that employees might experience at work.

Theoretical frameworks

A unique theoretical framework for work engagement does not exist. Instead, a number of theoretical perspectives have been proposed that each emphasize a different aspect, but that cannot be integrated into one overarching conceptual model. Below, four approaches are discussed.

The needs-satisfying approach

This approach was introduced earlier in the section on the definition of engagement. Kahn (1990) assumes that employees become engaged when three psychological conditions or needs are met: meaningfulness (i.e. the feeling of receiving return on investments of one's self in role performance), psychological safety (i.e. feeling able to show and employ one's self without fear of negative consequences), and availability (i.e. the belief of having the physical and mental resources to engage the self at work). Meaningfulness is influenced by the nature of the job; that is, its task characteristics and role characteristics. Psychological safety is mainly influenced by the social environment, that is, by interpersonal relationships, group dynamics, management style, and social norms. Finally, availability depends on the personal resources that people can bring to their role performance, such as physical energy.

Kahn's model was derived from a qualitative interview and observational study among counselors from a summer camp for adolescents and architects, and it was first tested by May et al. (2004) in a field study, using questionnaires of employees from an insurance firm. Indeed, as predicted, particularly meaningfulness and to a lesser degree also safety and availability, were positively associated with engagement. They also found in agreement with Kahn's theorizing that job enrichment and role fit were positively related to meaningfulness, whereas rewarding co-worker and supportive supervisor relations were positively related to safety, and personal resources were positively related to availability. So basically, the needs-satisfying approach assumes that when the job is challenging and meaningful, the social environment at work is safe, and personal resources are available, the needs for meaningfulness, safety and availability are satisfied and thus engagement is likely to occur.

The job demands–resources model

A host of studies on work engagement have used the job demands–resources (JD–R) model as an explanatory framework (see Bakker and Demerouti, 2008, and Schaufeli and Taris, in press, for a review). Particularly scholars who believe that engagement is the antithesis of burnout use the JD–R model because it conceptualizes burnout and engagement as two separate constructs that are integrated in an overarching conceptual model.

Essentially, the JD–R model assumes that work engagement results from the inherently motivating nature of resources, whereby two types of resources are distinguished; (1) job resources, which are defined as those aspects of the job that are functional in achieving work goals, reduce job demands, or stimulate personal growth and development (e.g. performance feedback, job control, and social support from colleagues); (2) personal resources, which are defined as aspects of the self that are associated with resiliency and that refer to the ability to control and impact one's environment successfully (e.g. self-efficacy, optimism and emotional stability).

According to the JD–R model, resources energize employees, encourage their persistence, and make them focus on their efforts. Or put differently, resources foster engagement in terms of vigor (energy), dedication (persistence) and absorption (focus). Furthermore, the JD–R model assumes that, in its turn, engagement produces positive outcomes such as job performance. So taken together, the JD–R model posits that work engagement mediates the relationship between job and personal resources on the one hand and positive outcomes on the other hand. This is called the *motivational process*, which is represented by the upper part of Figure 1.4.

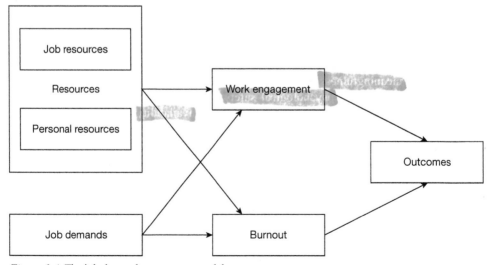

Figure 1.4 The job demands–resources model

Note: See text for the nature of the relationships

But also another – negative – process operates, the so-called *health impairment process*, which is represented in the lower part of Figure 1.4. This process is sparked by job demands, which are defined as those aspects of the job that require sustained physical or mental effort (e.g. work overload, time pressure, role conflict, and red tape). When job demands are high, additional effort must be exerted to achieve the work goals and to prevent decreasing performance. This compensatory effort obviously comes with physical and psychological costs, such as fatigue and irritability. When recovery is inadequate or insufficient, employees may gradually exhaust their energy backup and might eventually burn out. In its turn, burnout may lead to negative outcomes such as depression, cardiovascular disease, or psychosomatic complaints (Melamed, Shirom, Toker, Berliner and Shapira, 2006).

As can be seen from Figure 1.4, cross-links also exist between the motivational and the health-impairment processes. More specifically, poor resources may foster burnout, whereas job demands might increase work engagement. However, the latter is only true for the so-called challenge demands that have the potential to promote mastery, personal growth, and future gains (e.g. time pressure, high workload and high job responsibility). In contrast, hindrances that have the potential to thwart personal growth, learning and goal attainment (e.g. role conflict, red tape, and hassles) do not have an impact on work engagement. Using a meta-analysis based on 64 independent samples, Crawford, LePine and Rich (2010) found that demands were positively related to burnout, but that the relations between demands and engagement varied with the nature of the demand: hindrances related *negatively* and challenges related *positively* to engagement.

Meanwhile, abundant empirical evidence exists for the main assumption of the JD–R model; the presence of a motivational and a health impairment process. For instance, Schaufeli and Taris (in press) reviewed the results of 16 cross-sectional studies from seven countries and concluded that in *all cases* mediating effects of engagement and burnout were found, albeit that in four cases partial instead of full mediation was observed. That means that in addition to an indirect effect of demands and resources via engagement and burnout, also a direct effect on outcomes occurred. Finally, in 13 cases, significant crosslinks were found, particularly between poor job resources and burnout. However, no causal inferences can be made from cross-sectional studies so that it cannot be ruled out that, for instance, high levels of engagement lead to more favorable perceptions of resources (reversed causation).

So what about longitudinal evidence about the direction of causation? A three-year follow-up study among Finnish dentists (Hakanen, Schaufeli and Ahola, 2008b) supported both the motivational process and the health impairment process. It appeared that job resources influenced future work engagement, which, in its turn, predicted organizational commitment, whereas job demands predicted burnout over time, which, in its turn, predicted future depression. No reversed causation was observed – that is, neither burnout nor engagement predicted job demands or job resources. In a similar study among Dutch managers, increases in job demands and decreases in job resources predicted burnout across a one-year period, whereas increases in resources predicted work engagement (Schaufeli, Bakker and Van Rhenen, 2009). Moreover, burnout predicted future absence duration (an indicator of health impairment), whereas work engagement predicted future absence frequency (an indicator of employee motivation).

Another one year follow-up study among Australian university staff showed that job resources predicted psychological strain (negatively) and organizational commitment (positively), but failed to confirm the effect of job demands on strain (Boyd, Bakker, Pignata et al., 2011). Again, no reversed causal effects were detected. In a final longitudinal study spanning 18 months, Xanthopoulou, Bakker, Demerouti and Schaufeli (2009) found that personal resources (i.e. self-efficacy, optimism, and organization-based self-esteem) predicted later work engagement next to job resources (i.e. control, supervisory coaching, feedback, and opportunities for development).

In conclusion, job demands and resources have an impact over time on burnout and work engagement in ways as predicted by the JD–R model. That means that indications were found for the mediating role of work engagement and burnout in the motivational and health impairment processes, respectively.

Mounting empirical evidence suggests the dynamic nature of the motivational process of the JD–R model as far as job performance is concerned. That is, a feedback loop seems to exist that runs back from performance and engagement to job and personal resources (see Salanova, Schaufeli, Xanthopoulou and Bakker, 2010, for a review). This feedback loop is consistent with the notion of resource accumulation after successful performance. For instance, when an engaged employee accomplishes his or her work task successfully, this not only increases his or her level of self-efficacy (a belief that acts as a personal resource), but also leads to positive feedback from one's supervisor (a job resource). In a somewhat similar vein, in their three-wave study Weigl, Horning, Parker et al. (2010) found evidence for the existence of a gain spiral between work engagement and both job resources (i.e. job control and social support) and personal resources (i.e. active coping). Hence, it seems that increases in work engagement lead to increases in resources, and vice versa.

The affective shift model

It has been observed that work engagement waxes and wanes as a person moves through the working day, shifting from one task to another and being exposed to various kinds of events during the day (Sonnentag, Dormann and Demerouti, 2010). The affective shift model seeks to explain this dynamic nature of work engagement (Bledlow, Schmitt, Frese and Kühnel, 2011). This model is based on the assumption that both positive and negative affect have important functions for work engagement. The model proposes that a core mechanism underlying the emergence of high work engagement is a *shift* from negative to positive affect. Negative affect has motivating potential, meaning that it signals that things are not going well and that action should be taken. Subsequent effort then releases this motivating potential of negative affect and a shift towards a positive affective state occurs. Work engagement is most likely to result when this up-regulation of positive affect is accompanied by a simultaneous down-regulation of negative affect. So it is the dynamic interplay of positive and negative affect at work that produces work engagement.

Bledlow et al. (2011) followed a group of 55 German ICT professionals for two weeks and demonstrated that – as predicted by their affective shift model – moving from a situation in which negative events occur and negative mood is present to a situation in which high-positive mood is experienced, was associated with high work engagement. Although so far only one study has tested the affective shift model, the results are encouraging for explaining the dynamic nature of work engagement.

Social exchange theory

In essence, as shown elsewhere in this volume, social exchange theory argues that relationships at work evolve over time into trusting, loyal, and mutual commitments as long as all parties involved abide by reciprocity or repayment rules. For example, when employees receive particular resources from their organization (e.g. a decent salary, recognition, opportunities of development) they feel obliged to respond in kind and 'repay' the organization. Following this lead, Saks (2006) argues that one way for individuals to repay their organization is through engagement. In other words, employees will engage themselves to varying degrees and in response to the resources they receive from their organization. In terms of Kahn's (1990) definition of engagement, employees feel obliged to bring themselves more deeply into their role performances as repayment for the resources they receive from their organization. Alternatively, when the organization fails to provide these resources, individuals are more likely to withdraw and disengage themselves from their roles, which eventually might result in burnout (Schaufeli, 2006).

As noted before, using his multi-dimensional approach, Saks (2006) distinguishes between job engagement and organizational engagement. Not surprisingly, the relationships between *organizational* engagement on the one hand and perceived rewards and recognitions, perceived organizational and supervisor support, and procedural and distributive justice, on the other hand, are stronger than those with *job* engagement. Overall, however, these relationships are relatively weak, so that the current empirical support for the social exchange theory of work engagement is limited.

Recently, using a social exchange perspective Alfes, Shantz, Truss and Soane (2013) showed that the relationships between engagement and citizenship behavior as well as that between engagement and turnover intention was moderated by perceived organizational support and by the relationship with the supervisor. More specifically, when engaged employees felt supported by their organization and when they had a good relation with their supervisor, they exhibited more citizenship behavior and less intention to quit.

Summary

Although various theoretical approaches have been proposed to explain the underlying psychological mechanisms that are involved in work engagement, so far the job demands–resources model has received most empirical support.

Organizational outcomes of engagement

This section focuses exclusively on the organizational outcomes of work engagement; its relevance for individual health and well-being, although documented frequently (e.g. Hakanen and Schaufeli, 2012), is not discussed here. Basically, three kinds of approaches exist to examine the organizational outcomes of engagement. First, engagement levels of individual employees can be related to individual outcomes that are relevant to organizations (e.g. job performance, sickness absence). In a similar vein, average engagement levels of work teams can be related to, for instance, team performance or team absence rates. Second, average engagement levels of business units or entire organizations can be linked with business level outcomes, such as profit and productivity. Although the practical relevance of such 'linkage studies' seems obvious, the validity of averaging individual engagement scores across heterogeneous groups of hundreds or perhaps even thousands employees, is not entirely beyond question. Finally, case studies might illustrate the relationships between employee engagement levels and particular organizational outcomes. Since chapter 16 of this book is devoted to such case studies, these will not be included here. Roughly speaking, the first and the second approach correspond with the way engagement is studied in academia and business, respectively.

Attitudes and behaviors of employees and teams

Earlier, I argued that engagement is a unique construct that can be distinguished from other organizational attitudes and behaviors such as in-role and extra-role performance, organizational commitment, intention to leave, personal initiative, innovativeness, and proactivity. According to the models depicted in Figures 1.2 and 1.4, rather than constituting elements of engagement, these attitudes and behaviors should be considered *outcomes* of work engagement. A recent study among UK employees showed that – in accordance with Figures 1.2 and 1.4 – engagement mediates the relationship between job resources (i.e. task variety, autonomy, feedback, task identity and task significance) and outcomes such as organizational citizenship behavior (OCB), counterproductive work behavior (CWB), and task performance as assessed by the supervisor (Shantz, Alfes, Truss and Soane, 2013). In addition, various longitudinal studies show that high levels of engagement lead over time to more organizational commitment (Hakanen et al., 2008b, Boyd et al., 2011), more personal initiative and more innovative behavior at team level (Hakanen et al., 2008a), less frequent company registered sickness absence (Schaufeli et al., 2009), and better role performance (Xanthopoulou, Heuven, Demerouti, Bakker and Schaufeli, 2008; Bakker and Bal, 2010).

Among students, high levels of engagement at the beginning of the term are associated with a higher grade point average (GPA) at the end of the term (Salanova, Schaufeli, Martínez and Bresó, 2009). In addition, engaged medical residents committed fewer errors than their less engaged peers (Prins, Van der Heijden, Hoekstra-Weebers et al., 2009), engaged nurses are less often involved in needle accidents than their less engaged colleagues (Mark, Hughes, Belyra, et al., 2007), engaged chemical process workers are more committed to safety behaviors than less engaged workers (Hansez and Chmiel, 2010), supervisor performance ratings are higher for engaged workers than for non-engaged workers (Halbesleben and Wheeler, 2008), and engaged employees exhibited more organizational citizenship behaviors and less counterproductive work behaviors than their less engaged colleagues (Sulea, Virga, Maricutoiu et al., 2012). In short, there is ample evidence that engagement is related to positive organizational attitudes and behaviors.

At the team level, it has been documented that levels of engagement of frontline staff in hotels and restaurants are positively associated with customer rated quality of service (Salanova, Agut and Peiró, 2005).The more engaged the staff, the higher the service quality is rated. Moreover, a diary study among staff at a fast food company found that on days when employees were more engaged the financial turnover of the restaurant was higher (Xanthopoulou, Bakker, Demerouti and Schaufeli, 2009). Thus, the more engaged the employees of a particular work shift were, the more food was sold.

Taken together, these academic studies make a strong case that, indeed, work engagement leads to positive outcomes for the organization, both at individual level and at team level.

Business success

Many consultancy firms have claimed that a positive association exists between the average level of employee engagement of an organization and its business success. Recently, Attridge (2009) reviewed the research papers of consultancy firms that have not been published in peer reviewed journals (so-called grey literature) and concluded that 'engagement seems to be good for business' (p. 394). A review of the Conference Board (2006) goes into more detail and, for instance, describes a study that showed that roughly the sales of departments with more engaged employees were twice as high as those with less engaged employees. Another study revealed that that companies with high levels of engagement saw an overall 3.74 per cent increase in operating margin and a 2.06 per cent net profit increase over a one-year period, while companies with low engagement saw a 2 per cent and 1.38 per cent drop in these respective categories.

Perhaps the most convincing evidence for the link between engagement and business success comes from a series of studies that have been conducted by the Gallup Organization. A summarizing meta-analysis that included almost 8,000 business-units of 36 companies (Harter et al., 2002) revealed that levels of engagement are positively related to indicators of business-unit performance, such as customer satisfaction and loyalty, profitability, productivity, turnover, and safety. More detailed analyses revealed that compared to the bottom 25 per cent least engaged business units, the top 25 per cent most engaged units had 2 per cent to 4 per cent higher customer satisfaction, 1 per cent to 4 per cent higher profitability, and 13 per cent to 36 per cent less turnover. Finally, businesses in the top quartile on engagement had, on average $80,000 to $120,000 higher monthly revenues or sales.

In another Gallup study including over 955,000 respondents in the US and 23 other nations, work engagement accounted for 78 per cent of the variance in profitability across 17,339 business units (Harter, Schmidt, Killian and Agrawal, 2009). Those business units with higher levels of work engagement had a 94 per cent higher success rate in their own organization and a 145 per cent higher success rate across organizations.

Despite these impressive results, some caution is warranted. As noted before, most studies of consultancy firms lack scientific rigor and transparency and usually their operationalization of engagement is questionable because it overlaps with traditional concepts such as extra-role performance and organizational commitment, which, in fact, can also be considered outcomes of engagement. For instance, the linkage study undertaken by Gallup uses the Q^{12}, which instead of the experience of engagement assessed its antecedents in terms of perceived job resources. So in fact, the results of the meta-analyses of Harter et al. (2002) indicate that resourceful jobs are positively associated with business success.

In sum: circumstantial evidence exists that suggests that work engagement might be related to business success. However strictly, scientifically speaking, the empirical test of this claim still requires further investigation.

General conclusion and outlook

This chapter sought to answer the question 'What is engagement?' The answer is equivocal. Or perhaps it is more correct to state that the answer depends on one's perspective. Taking a purely scientific perspective, work engagement can be defined as a unique positive, fulfilling, work related state of mind that is characterized by vigor, dedication, and absorption; that can be measured using a valid and reliable self-report questionnaire (the UWES); and that can be explained by the job demands–resources model. However, at the same time – although supported by abundant international empirical research – this perspective on engagement is rather narrow because it does not include its consequential behavior. This is particularly important for business and consultancy, which is the very reason that in these contexts engagement is defined in broader terms and includes employee *behaviors* that are in line with organizational goals. The reasoning here is that employees might feel 'engaged' in their work, but may nevertheless not contribute to organizational success because their 'engagement' is not properly focused. Unfortunately, by defining engagement more broadly, its uniqueness is lost because the distinction with other concepts such as extra-role performance and organizational commitment gets blurred.

So, it seems that we are stuck in a dilemma: either engagement is defined narrowly as an *experience* (i.e. purely psychological state) in which case its practical relevance is reduced, or it is defined in broader terms including its *behavioral expression*, in which case the concept gets fuzzy. A pragmatic solution could be to consider engagement as a psychological state *in conjunction* with its behavioral expression. That way the uniqueness of the concept is preserved and its practicability is guaranteed.

For the scientific community that would imply that future research should focus on the ways in which the experience of work engagement is translated into employee behaviors that are in line with team- and organizational goals. For instance, research on the engagement–performance and on the engagement–productivity nexus. For business and consultancy that would imply that state-of-the art measures to assess engagement as a psychological state should be employed in projects that aim to improve employee performance and productivity. When both parties agree on these implications, a joint collaborative effort can be made for a genuine, evidence based approach to improve employee well-being and increase business success in which engagement plays a key role.

References

K. Alfes, A. Shantz, C. Truss and C. Soane, 'The link between perceived human resources management practices, engagement and employee behavior: A moderated mediation model', *International Journal of Human Resource Management*, 24, 2013, 330–51.

A. B. Bakker and P. M. Bal, 'Weekly work engagement and performance: A study among starting teachers', *Journal of Occupational and Organizational Psychology*, 83, 2010, 189–206.

A. B. Bakker and E. Demerouti, 'Towards a model of work engagement', *Career Development International*, 13, 2008, 209–23.

R. Bledlow, A. Schmitt, M. Frese and J. Kühnel, 'The affective shift model of work engagement', *Journal of Applied Psychology,* 96, 2011, 1246–57.

C. M. Boyd, A. B. Bakker, S. Pignata, A. H. Winefield, N. Gillespie and C. Stough, 'A longitudinal test of the job demands–resources model among Australian university academics', *Applied Psychology: An International Review*, 60, 2011, 112–40.

M. Buckingham and C. Coffman, *First, break all the rules*, New York: Simon Schuster, 1999.

M. S. Cole, F. Walter, A. G. Bedeian and E. H. O'Boyle, 'Job burnout and employee engagement: A meta-analytic examination of construct proliferation', *Journal of Management*, 38, 2012, 1550–81.

Conference Board (2006), *Employee engagement: A review of current research and its implications.* Retrieved on from http://www.conference-board.org/employeeengagement.htm.

E. R. Crawford, J. A. LePine and B. L. Rich, 'Linking job demands and resources to employee engagement and burnout: A theoretical extension and meta-analytic test', *Journal of Applied Psychology*, 95, 2010, 834–48.

M. S. Christian, A. S. Garza and J. E. Slaughter, 'Work engagement: A qualitative review and test of its relations with task and contextual performance', *Personnel Psychology*, 64, 2011, 89–136.

J. J. Hakanen, R. Perhoniemi and S. Toppinen-Tanner, 'Positive gain spirals at work: From job resources to work engagement, personal initiative and work-unit innovativeness', *Journal of Vocational Behavior*, 73, 2008a, 78–91.

J. J., Hakanen and W. B. Schaufeli, 'Do burnout and work engagement predict depressive symptoms and life satisfaction? A three-wave seven-year prospective study', *Journal of Affective Disorders*, 141, 2012, 415–24.

J. J. Hakanen, W. B. Schaufeli and K. Ahola, 'The job demands–resources model: A three-year cross-lagged study of burnout, depression, commitment, and work engagement', *Work and Stress*, 22, 2008b, 224–41.

J. R. B. Halbesleben, 'A meta-analysis of work engagement: Relationships with burnout, demands, resources, and consequences'. In: A. B. Bakker and M. P. Leiter (eds), *Work engagement: A handbook of essential theory and research*, New York: Psychology Press, 2010, 102–17.

J. R. B. Halbesleben and A. R. Wheeler, 'The relative role of engagement and embeddedness in prediction job performance and turnover intention', *Work and Stress*, 22, 2008, 242–56.

I. Hansez and N. Chmiel, 'Safety behavior: Job demands, job resources, and perceived management commitment to safety', *Journal of Occupational Health Psychology*, 15, 2010, 267–78.

J. K. Harter, F. L. Schmidt and T. L. Hayes, 'Business-unit-level relationship between employee satisfaction, employee engagement, and business outcomes: A meta-analysis', *Journal of Applied Psychology*, 87, 2002, 268–79.

J. K. Harter, F. L. Schmidt, E. A. Killan and S. Agrawal, *Q12 meta-analysis: The relationship between engagement at work and organizational outcomes*. White Paper Gallup Organization, 2009. Retrieved from http://www.gallup.com/consulting/126806/q12-meta-analysis.aspx on 10 June 2010.

C-W. Jeung, 'The concept of employee engagement: A comprehensive review from a positive organizational behavior perspective', *Performance Improvement Quarterly*, 24, 2011, 49–69.

W. A. Kahn, 'Psychological conditions of personal engagement and disengagement at work', *Academy of Management Journal*, 33, 1990, 692–724.

H. J. Kim, K. H. Shin and N. Swanger, 'Burnout and engagement: A comparative analysis using the Big Five personality dimensions', *International Journal of Hospitality Management*, 28, 2009, 96–104.

K. Kubota, A. Shimazu, N. Kawakami, M. Takahashi, A. Nakata and W. B. Schaufeli, 'Association between workaholism and sleeping problems among hospital nurses', *Industrial Health*, 48, 2011, 864–71.

S. Langelaan, A. B. Bakker, L. J. P. van Doornen and W. B. Schaufeli, 'Burnout and work engagement: Do individual differences make a difference?', *Personality and Individual Differences*, 40, 2006, 521–32.

W. H. Macey and B. Schneider, 'The meaning of employee engagement', *Industrial and Organizational Psychology: Perspectives on Science and Practice*, 1, 2008, 3–30.

B. Mark, L. Hughes, M. Belyra, Y. Chang, D. Hofmann, C. Jones and C. Cacon, 'Does safety climate moderate the influence of staffing adequacy and work conditions on nurse injuries?', *Journal of Safety Research*, 38, 2007, 431–46.

C. Maslach, and M. P. Leiter, *The truth about burnout*, San Francisco, CA: Jossey-Bass, 1997.

C. Maslach, S. E. Jackson and M. P. Leiter, *The Maslach Burnout Inventory* (3rd edn), Palo Alto, CA: Consulting Psychologists Press, 1996.

D. R. May, R. L. Gilson and L. M. Harter, 'The psychological conditions of meaningfulness, safety and availability and the engagement of the human spirit at work', *Journal of Occupational and Organizational Psychology*, 77, 2004, 11–37.

A. Melamed, A. Shirom, S. Toker, S. Berliner and I. Shapira, 'Burnout and risk of cardiovascular disease: Evidence, possible causal paths, and promising research directions', *Psychological Bulletin*, 132, 2006, 327–53.

D. A. Newman, D. L. Joseph and C. L. Hulin, 'Job attitudes and employee engagement: Considering the attitude 'A-factor'', In S. L. Albrecht, *Handbook of employee engagement: Perspectives, issues, research and practice*, Northampton, MA: Edward Elgar, 2010, 43–62.

J. Prins, F. van der Heijden, J. Weebers, A. B. Bakker, H. van de Wiel, B. Jacobs and S. Gazendam-Donofrio, 'Burnout, engagement and resident physicians' self-reported errors', *Psychology, Health and Medicine*, 14, 2009, 654–66.

B. L. Rich, J. A. Lepine and E. R. Crawford, 'Job engagement: Antecedents and effects on job performance', *Academy of Management Journal*, 53, 2010, 617–35.

J. A. Russell, 'A circumplex model of affect', *Journal of Personality and Social Psychology*, 39, 1980, 1161–78.

A. M. Saks, 'Antecedents and consequences of employee engagement', *Journal of Managerial Psychology*, 21, 2006, 600–19.

A. M. Saks, 'The meaning and bleeding of employee engagement: How muddy is the water?', *Industrial and Organizational Psychology*, 1, 2008, 40–3.

M. Salanova, S. Agut and J. M. Peiró, 'Linking organizational resources and work engagement to employee performance and customer loyalty: The mediation of service climate', *Journal of Applied Psychology*, 90, 2005, 1217–27.

M. Salanova, W. B. Schaufeli, I. Martínez and E. Bresó, 'How obstacles and facilitators predict academia performance: the mediating role of study burnout and engagement', *Anxiety, Stress and Coping*, 26, 2009, 1–18.

M. Salanova, W. B. Schaufeli, D. Xanthopoulou and A. B. Bakker, 'Gain spirals of resources and work engagement'. In A. B. Bakker and M. P. Leiter (eds), *Work engagement: A handbook of essential theory and research*, New York: Psychology Press, 2010, 118–31.

W. B. Schaufeli, 'The balance of give and take: Toward a social exchange model of burnout', *International Review of Social Psychology*, 19, 2006, 87–131.

W. B. Schaufeli, 'The measurement of work engagement'. In R. R. Sinclair, M. Wang and L. E. Tetrick (eds), *Research methods in occupational health psychology: Measurement, design, and data analysis*, New York: Routledge, 2012, 138–53.

W. B. Schaufeli and A. B. Bakker, 'Job demands, job resources and their relationship with burnout and engagement: A multi-sample study', *Journal of Organizational Behavior*, 25, 2004, 293–315.

W. B. Schaufeli and A. B. Bakker, 'The conceptualization and measurement of work engagement'. In A. B. Bakker and M. P. Leiter (eds), *Work engagement: A handbook of essential theory and research*, New York: Psychology Press, 2010, 10–24.

W. B. Schaufeli, A. B. Bakker and W. van Rhenen, 'How changes in job demands and resources predict burnout, work engagement, and sickness absenteeism', *Journal of Organizational Behavior*, 30, 2009, 893–917.

W. B. Schaufeli and M. Salanova, 'Enhancing work engagement through the management of human resources'. In K. Näswall, M. Sverke and J. Hellgren (eds), *The individual in the changing working life*, Cambridge: Cambridge University Press, 2008, 380–404.

W. B. Schaufeli, M. Salanova, V. Gonzalez-Roma and A. B. Bakker, 'The measurement of engagement and burnout and: A confirmative analytic approach', *Journal of Happiness Studies*, 3, 2002, 71–92.

W. B. Schaufeli and T. W. Taris, 'A critical review of the Job Demands–Resources Model: Implications for improving work and health'. In G. Bauer and O. Hämmig (eds), *Bridging occupational, organizational and public health*. Amsterdam: Springer, in press.

W. B. Schaufeli, T. W. Taris and A. B. Bakker, 'It takes two to tango. Workaholism is working excessively and working compulsively'. In R. J. Burke and C. L. Cooper (eds), *The long work hours culture. Causes, consequences and choices*, Bingley UK: Emerald, 2008, 203–26.

W. B. Schaufeli, T. W. Taris, P. Le Blanc, M. Peeters, A. B. Bakker and J. de Jonge, 'Maakt arbeid gezond? Op zoek naar de bevlogen werknemer' [Does work make you healthy? In search of the engaged worker], *De Psycholoog*, 36, 2001, 422–8.

W. B. Schaufeli, T. W. Taris and W. Van Rhenen, 'Workaholism, burnout and engagement: Three of a kind or three different kinds of employee well-being', *Applied Psychology: An International Review*, 57, 2008, 173–203.

A. Shantz, K. Alfes, C. Truss and E. Soane, 'The role of employee engagement in the relationship between job design and task performance, citizenship and deviant behaviors', *International Journal of Human Resource Management*, 24, 2013, 2608–27.

A. Shimazu, W. B. Schaufeli, K. Kubota and N. Kawakami, 'Do workaholism and work engagement predict employee well-being and performance in opposite directions?', *Industrial Health*, 50, 2012, 316–21.

E. Soane, C. Truss, K. Alfes, A. Shantz, C. Rees and M. Gatenby, 'Development and application of a new measure of employee engagement: Ihe ISA Engagement Scale', *Human Resource Development International*, 15, 2013, 529–47.

S. Sonnentag, C. Dormann and E. Demerouti, 'Not all days are created equal: The concept of state work engagement'. In A. B. Bakker and M. P. Leiter (eds), *Work engagement: Recent developments in theory and research*, New York: Psychology Press, 2010, 25–38.

C. Sulea, D.Virga, L. P. Maricutoiu, W. B. Schaufeli, C. Zaborila and F. A. Sava, 'Work engagement as mediator between job characteristics and positive and negative extra-role behaviors', *Career Development International*, 17, 2012, 188–207.

T. W. Taris, W. B. Schaufeli and A. Shimazu, 'The push and pull of work: About the difference between workaholism and work engagement'. In A. B. Bakker and M. P. Leiter (eds), *Work engagement: A handbook of essential theory and research*, New York: Psychology Press, 2010, 39–53.

D. Ulrich, *Human resource champions*, Boston, MA: Harvard Business School Press, 1997.

I. van Beek, Q. Hu, W. B. Schaufeli, T. W. Taris and B. H. Schreurs, 'For fun, love or money. What drives workaholic, engaged and burned-out employees at work?', *Applied Psychology: An International Review*, 61, 2012, 30–55.

A. Viljevac, H-D. Cooper-Thomas and A. Saks, 'An investigation into the validity of two measured of work engagement', *International Journal of Human Resources Management*, 23, 2012, 3692–709.

M. Weigel, S. Horning, S. T. Parker, R. Petru, J. Galser and P. Angener, 'Work engagement accumulation of task, social, personal resources: A three-wave structural equation model', *Journal of Vocational Behavior*, 77, 2010, 140–53.

D. Xanthopoulou, E. Heuven, E. Demerouti, A. B. Bakker and W. B. Schaufeli, 'Working in the sky: A diary study on work engagement among flight attendants', *Journal of Occupational Health Psychology*, 13, 2008, 345–56.

D. Xanthopoulou, A. B. Bakker, E. Demerouti and W. B. Schaufeli, 'Work engagement and financial returns: A diary study on the role of job and personal resources', *Journal of Organizational and Occupational Psychology*, 82, 2009,183–200.

2 Engagement in the context of positive psychology

Carolyn M. Youssef-Morgan and Kristi M. Bockorny

In his inaugural speech as President of the American Psychological Association, Martin Seligman lamented the strong negative bias in psychological research and practice. Before World War II, the field of psychology was believed to have three goals: healing mental illness, helping healthy people become happier and more productive, and actualizing human potential. However, when the war ended, it left many people psychologically scarred and in great need of psychological treatment. Resources and energy followed suit, leading to an out-of-proportion emphasis on containing the damage and fixing weaknesses within a 'disease model'. Human strengths, and even the proactive prevention of mental illness, were for the most part ignored and went underfunded (Seligman and Csikszentmihalyi, 2000).

While research in business psychology may not be as negative, the organizational literature on negatively oriented topics such as poor performance, stress and burnout, work–life conflict, unethical practices and counterproductive work behaviors tends to prevail. This led Luthans (2002b) to call for a shift toward 'positive organizational behavior', which he defined as 'the study and application of positivity oriented human resource strengths and psychological capacities that can be measured, developed, and effectively managed for performance improvement in today's workplace' (p. 59).

The problem is that negatively oriented research and practice is limited in its ability to yield a better understanding of strengths, optimal functioning and actualizing human potential, because positivity and negativity usually represent distinct continuums, rather than opposite ends of the same continuum. For example, freedom from mental illness is not equivalent to flourishing and a fulfilled life, and an 'adequate' job that pays the bills cannot begin to compare with a 'great' job that engages employees physically, mentally, emotionally, socially and even spiritually. This notion has been supported in relation to numerous psychological and organizational constructs (e.g. see Cacioppo and Berntson, 1994; Chang, Maydeu-Olivares and D'Zurilla, 1997; Dunlop and Lee, 2004; Pittinsky, Rosenthal and Montoya, 2011; Sackett, Berry, Wiemann and Laczo, 2006; Taylor, 1991). Thus, positivity needs to be studied, applied and pursued in its own right, rather than extrapolated from negatively oriented practices and findings.

This notion is particularly relevant for engagement, because research supports the view that engagement is a distinct positive concept, not just a polar opposite of its negative counterparts such as burnout. It has different patterns of causes and consequences, which warrants its management in the workplace through different intervention strategies (Schaufeli and Bakker, 2004). If that is the case, then we argue that engagement should be understood and promoted within a positive paradigm, rather than just as an extension of important but negatively oriented models such as those designed for treating depression, coping with stress, reducing work–family conflict, dealing with workplace bullying or toxic managers, and the list goes on. Positive psychology, positive organizational scholarship and positive organizational behavior are examples of positive paradigms that can be applied and leveraged to foster work engagement.

In today's workforce, employees may vary widely in their levels of engagement. Some may hold a job to which they are dedicated, while others just go through the motions. The question of how organizations can help their employees become more engaged at work has become particularly pertinent for many organizations over the past decade due to numerous changes in the nature of work. For example, today's technology and constant connectivity have created new expectations for employees to be available 24/7, which requires additional engagement to face these increasing demands beyond just 'being there' (Rathbard and Patil, 2012). William A. Kahn's early conceptualization of engagement as 'the harnessing of organization members' selves to their work roles' (Kahn, 1990: 694) is consistent with these increasing demands and expectation of being constantly 'on', physically, cognitively and emotionally, in relation to one's work role, rather than just 'being there'.

Similarly, more recent conceptualizations of engagement also view it as a positive state characterized by vigor, dedication and absorption (Schaufeli, Salanova, Gonzalez-Roma and Bakker, 2002). Vigor is described as high levels of energy and effort in one's job, as well has having resiliency and persistence when faced with challenges. Dedication is described as having pride and a strong connection to one's work. Lastly, absorption is the 'pleasant state of total immersion in one's work, which is characterized by time passing quickly and being unable to detach oneself from the job' (Maslach, Schaufeli and Leiter, 2001: 417).

Employers are also increasingly interested in creating an environment that can facilitate employee engagement due to the recognized impact of engagement on productivity and financial outcomes (see Harter, Schmidt and Hayes, 2002 for a meta-analysis, and Cascio and Boudreau, 2011 for a comprehensive review). For example, according to Stairs and Galpin (2010), high levels of engagement have been shown to relate to:

- lower absenteeism and higher employee retention;
- increased employee effort and productivity;
- improved quality and reduced error rates;
- increased sales;
- higher profitability, earning per share and shareholder returns;
- enhanced customer satisfaction and loyalty;
- faster business growth; and
- higher likelihood of business success.

Drawing from positive psychology (Seligman and Csikszentmihalyi, 2000), this chapter offers a unique perspective on engagement in which positivity can help enhance employee engagement and facilitate its desirable outcomes at the individual, group and organizational levels. Positivity can be defined as an emphasis on elevating processes and outcomes, intentional behaviors that depart from the norm of a reference group in honorable ways, exceptional outcomes that dramatically exceed common or expected performance and an affirmative bias toward strengths, capabilities and possibilities, rather than weaknesses, problems or threats (Cameron, 2008). In other words, positivity is going above and beyond by intentionally using strengths to achieve unparalleled results. Positive psychology's focus is to draw attention to the positive aspects of flourishing individuals, groups and organizations. This is different from the deficit model because positive psychology focuses on strengths and positive characteristics rather than weaknesses.

The chapter starts with a brief overview of the more traditional roots of positivity in psychology and management. More contemporary positivity movements, such as positive psychology, positive organizational scholarship, positive organizational behavior and psychological capital, are then discussed in more detail. Linkages between positivity and engagement are proposed and evaluated, and practical implications are discussed.

Traditional roots of positivity in psychology and management

Positivity is not new to psychology or management. Traditional theories and practices in both areas have recognized the importance of positivity. However, the positive psychology movement has triggered increased interest among HR professionals and an exponential growth in scholarly activity to understand and leverage the untapped potential of positivity, as well as a paradigm shift in how positivity should be studied and applied. To better understand the current status of positivity and what is has to offer in terms of increased engagement and productivity, it would be helpful to overview the traditional roots and foundations for its conceptual development and practical applications.

Motivation

Traditional motivation theories have recognized many of the positive concepts that are receiving increased attention today. For example, Maslow's hierarchy (Maslow, 1954) identified five levels of needs. Physiological and safety needs are more basic in nature, while belonging, esteem and especially self-actualization are more aligned with the constructs now increasingly discussed in the context of positivity. More process-oriented motivation theories also place a special emphasis on positivity, especially its cognitive and evaluative dimensions. For example, Vroom's expectancy theory (1964) posits that motivation results from the interactive linkages between perceived effort, performance and the achievement of desired rewards. For example, an employee who perceives a high probability that his or her effort can lead to higher performance (expectancy), and that his or her performance can lead to rewards (instrumentality) that are valuable to him or her (valence), will be more motivated to invest more effort in his or her job. Similarly, goal setting research, which emerged in the 1960s but continues to be highly regarded and foundational for positive theories and practices, shows strong support for the notion that employees are more motivated by difficult and challenging goals than easier ones (Locke and Latham, 2002).

Interestingly, even as early as Maslow's writing, there was a recognition that positive and negative concepts are qualitatively different, rather than opposite ends of the same continuum. For example, Maslow (1968) argues that while physiological safety, belongingness and even esteem needs yield 'deficiency motives', self-actualization is an entirely different type of motivation, namely a 'growth motivation'. This higher level of motivation, or as Maslow refers to it, 'metamotivation', is unique in that unlike deficiencies, it has no satiation point and thus can be a sustainable source of drive. In Maslow's words, for self-actualizing individuals, 'even the casual workaday, moment-to-moment business of living can be thrilling, exciting, and ecstatic', (Maslow, 1954: 215), a notion that is surprisingly consistent with the much more contemporary definitions of engagement throughout this book.

Job satisfaction

The examination of job satisfaction started in the late 1950s when Herzberg explored factors that can make employees happier, and found that job satisfaction and job dissatisfaction are determined by different sets of factors (Herzberg, Mausner and Snyderman, 1993). Job satisfaction is determined by 'motivators' such as job *content*, recognition, achievement, responsibilities and advancement and opportunities. On the other hand, dissatisfaction is caused by 'hygiene factors' such as salary, working conditions and other dimensions of the job *context*. Similar to the notion of 'deficiency motivation', hygiene factors are effective to the extent that their absence can lead to dissatisfaction, but only the more positively oriented motivators are related to job satisfaction.

It is important to note that job satisfaction has been found to be one of the strongest predictors of job performance. There is also significant debate regarding the direction of causality from job satisfaction to job performance. Despite conventional wisdom and the common belief that 'a happy worker is a productive worker', there is also evidence that high performance precedes and predicts subsequent job satisfaction. The relationship between job satisfaction and job performance may also include mediators and moderators. For example, mediators that affect the satisfaction leads to performance model could be intentions and positive mood; whereas mediators that can affect performance to satisfaction are success and achievement (Judge, Thoresen, Bono and Patton, 2001). Particularly relevant to this chapter, critics have debated the value that engagement adds over more traditional job attitudes such as job satisfaction. For example, in their seminal engagement study, Harter and colleagues (2002) defined engagement as 'the individual's involvement and satisfaction with as well as enthusiasm for work' (p. 269). They referred to The Gallup Work Place Audit, which is one of the most recognized measures of engagement, as a measure of 'satisfaction-engagement'. This debate has promoted additional research in order to fine-tune and distinguish the conceptual framework and measurement of engagement (see Chapter 15, this volume).

Job design

While Herzberg has been recognized as 'the father of job enrichment', it was not until the 1970s that additional interest was generated in understanding the specific dimensions of a job that can make it more motivating and satisfying. Most recognized in this area is Hackman and Oldham's (1976) job characteristics model, in which five job dimensions (variety, identity, significance, autonomy and feedback) yield three distinct positive states (perceived meaningfulness, responsibility and knowledge of results), which, moderated through each employee's growth need strength, determines the motivational potential of a job (see Chapter 7, this volume).

Hackman and Oldham's model has shaped many subsequent work practices in HR because of its practical applicability. Particularly relevant to this chapter is its integration of the explicit job dimensions with more covert cognitive processes, yielding meaningful work experience and positive evaluations of one's job. Decades later, these positive outcomes would become foundational to the research and practice of positivity and engagement.

Positive reinforcement

One of the most prominent 'positive' intersections between human resource management and psychology has been the application of reinforcement and behavioral modification theories to the workplace. Numerous studies have demonstrated that contingent positive reinforcement can promote positive behavior at work in similar ways to B. F. Skinner and John Watson's experiments. Specifically, when rewards such as money, positive feedback and recognition are administered contingently upon the desired behaviors, employees learn to habitually behave in the desired ways, yielding higher performance outcomes in their roles.

These impressive and highly relevant findings have been shown to generalize across jobs, industries and even cultures (Stajkovic and Luthans, 1997, 2003), which has triggered a lot of interest among HR professionals seeking better ways to design more effective compensation and benefits packages. Importantly, positive reinforcement has been shown to be more effective than punishment in generating and sustaining the desired work behaviors.

Although effective, behavioral theories have been critiqued for dehumanizing and manipulating workers for employers' gains. This has promoted a more balanced approach to the interactions between cognitive, social and behavioral dimensions of motivation (Bandura, 2001; Kreitner and Luthans, 1984), which has become foundational to positive psychology and its applications in the workplace. More specifically, positive organizational research emphasizes the cognitive, affective, conative, social, behavioral and even spiritual dimensions of positivity. Furthermore, behavioral modification has been recently viewed as simplistic and limited in its applicability primarily to piece-work, but of limited use for today's knowledge workers. As suggested earlier, these knowledge workers need to be more engaged in designing and 'crafting' their roles (Berg, Wrzesniewski and Dutton, 2010) in order to be productive.

Positive and negative affect

Watson, Clark and Tellegen (1988) characterize high positive affect as 'high energy, full concentration, and pleasurable engagement' (p. 1063), and low positive affect with more passive conditions such as sadness and lethargy. On the other hand, negative affect can be represented by more prominent uncomfortable emotions, such as anger and anxiety. This conceptualization, as well as extensive empirical evidence, clearly highlights the qualitative distinctions between positive and negative affect. Positive and negative affect also yield different outcomes. For example, positive affect is more closely associated with positivity, energy, pleasure and engagement, negative affect is more related to unsuccessful coping processes and stress (Watson et al., 1988).

Particularly relevant for positivity and engagement is an important distinction between traits and states. Similar to many personality traits, positive and negative affect have been shown to be relatively stable and trait-like. This limits their use in the workplace to employee selection and placement in order to create an adequate fit between the employee and the demands of the position, a notion that has subsequently become critical in fostering work engagement. On the other hand, the positive concepts recently emphasized in positive research and practice can be represented on a continuum. This continuum ranges from (a) positive traits (genetically determined or 'hard-wired' characteristics), (b) trait-like factors such as positive and negative affect, to (c) malleable state-like resources that are open to development (e.g. the core construct of psychological capital, comprised of hope, efficacy, resiliency and optimism, discussed later), to (d) 'pure' states, such as momentary moods, temporary pleasures and fleeting emotions. Positive traits are constant and are often seen as a baseline or foundation to help develop the malleable states (Luthans and Youssef, 2007).

Based on the timeframe for fluctuations in engagement established in empirical research findings (e.g. Bakker and Bal, 2010; Xanthopoulou, Bakker, Demerouti and Schaufeli, 2009b), engagement seems to most closely resemble the state end of the trait–state continuum, making its development most suited to relatively short interventions. Positive emotional states have also been shown to have a stronger and more direct influence on work attitudes and behavior than their trait counterparts such as positive affect (George, 1991; Ilies, Scott and Judge, 2006). Since engagement tends to also be a state that varies in the short term, it follows that positive emotional states would be more related to engagement than personality traits and trait-like characteristics such as positive and negative affect.

Transformational leadership

Transformational leadership theory generated a great deal of interest in the 1990s, particularly following dissatisfaction with its predecessor, charismatic leadership theory, due to the potential for charismatic leaders to abuse their power and take advantage of their followers for personal gains. Transformational leaders possess the 'gift' of charisma (Conger and Kanungo, 1992), through which they challenge the status quo, rally followers around their vision and take personal risks to achieve success. Their followers view them as heroes, which enhances their credibility and effectiveness (Conger and Kanungo, 1988). However, this should not be confused with charismatic heroism. In addition to charisma, transformational leaders lead through (a) *inspirational motivation*, which is the ability to inspire followers to achieve more than they thought was possible by setting high standards of excellence; (b) *idealized influence*, where they exhibit high standards of moral and ethical conduct that promote followers' respect, trust, willingness to transcend self-interest, and a collective sense of mission; (c) *individual consideration* that provides followers with a supportive environment and attends to their individual needs; and most importantly (d) *intellectual stimulation*, which promotes followers' independent thinking and encourages them to question the status quo (Bass and Riggio, 2006). These additional characteristics can have a more positive and proactively 'transforming' impact on followers than charisma alone.

Importantly, transformational leadership is also distinguished from transactional leadership, in which leaders establish and communicate goals and performance standards, then consistently and objectively reward their followers in exchange for their efforts and performance in achieving these goals and standards. While transactional leadership can be effective and perceived as 'fair' by many employees, transformational leadership differs fundamentally from transactional leadership. Transformational leaders are concerned with helping followers in achieving their full potential, which goes beyond just meeting short-term goals. Although not mutually exclusive, research shows that transformational leadership is significantly more effective than transactional leadership and yields a unique set of positive work outcomes (Avolio, 2011, also see Chapter 8, this volume).

Transformational leaders encourage a range of behaviors in their subordinates. They show concern, encourage thinking, motivate and become role models for their followers. They show interest in their subordinates by assigning tasks based on each individual's strengths and encouraging self-development. They also encourage thinking by allowing followers to re-evaluate problems. These leaders are also open to listening to followers' ideas. They present optimistic visions that can motivate and engage the employees.

Recent positive movements

Three streams of research are recognized in the positivity literature: positive psychology, positive organizational scholarship, and positive organizational behavior. In this section, we discuss these three streams in more detail and build out their conceptual linkages with engagement.

Positive psychology and engagement

The preface to positive psychology is a need to focus on human strengths and their potential to yield flourishing, fulfilled lives (Keyes and Haidt, 2003). The goal of positive psychology is not to do away with negative (or neutral) concepts and practices, but to capitalize on the untapped potential of positive ones. This is also in line with what Luthans and Avolio (2009) refer to as an 'inquiry' approach, in which the value added of positivity is explored alongside the more established, traditional research and practices. The 'inquiry' approach is contrasted with the 'advocacy' approach, in which one set of theories and practices is favored over another, which often leads to defensiveness and focusing on 'deficiency-reduction'. Three specific models from positive psychology are particularly relevant for the linkages between engagement and positivity we seek to establish in this chapter.

The broaden-and-build model of positive emotions

According to Fredrickson (2009), positive and negative emotions are distinguished in terms of the unique cognitive, affective and behavioral mechanisms they trigger. Positive emotions tend to broaden one's thought–action repertoires, leading to a wider, more creative set of solutions. They also tend to build and replenish personal and social resources. Negative emotions tend to do the opposite. They tend to trigger fight-or-flight responses, promote a narrower set of tried-and-true solutions, and deplete previously built resources.

Engagement is both cognitive and affective in nature. Thus, it is more likely for engagement to develop when employees are experiencing positive, rather than negative emotions. This is because positive emotions create the cognitive space, emotional safety, mental energy and resources necessary for employees to experience the vigor, dedication and absorption dimensions of engagement (Schaufeli et al., 2002). Negative emotions such as exhaustion, cynicism, indifference or inefficacy are likely to be associated with employee burnout, rather than engagement (Maslach et al., 2001).

Many managers and employees mistakenly believe that emotions have no place at work and should be relegated to the personal or social realms. However, growing research attests to the opposite. For example, in a meta-analysis of hundreds of cross-sectional, longitudinal and experimental studies, Lyubomirsky and colleagues (2005) examined the relationship between happiness and success in numerous life domains, including work, relationships, health and others. Their findings strongly suggest that happiness and success are not only correlated, but that happiness leads to success, rather than the other way around. Even more specifically, Fredrickson (2009) demonstrated that positivity thresholds need to be met in order for individuals and relationships to thrive. These thresholds occur at a ratio of about three positive encounters for each negative encounter in general work settings. This ratio is much higher in other contexts. For example, it is five-to-one in marriages, and six-to-one in complex decision making situations (e.g. senior leadership). Engaging managers and employees through triggering high levels of positive emotions that help them cross those thresholds and thrive at work can truly pay off.

Experiencing flow

According to Csikszentmihalyi, a state of flow is experienced when individuals are fully absorbed in their work, lose track of time, and find it difficult to step away from an activity. It can be compared to a 'euphoric zone' during which time is perceived to pass very quickly. Flow occurs when an individual's perceived abilities align with the demands and challenges presented by the activity. As a result, the individual enters a state of low self-consciousness, high concentration and a strong sense of agency and control. Flow is also characterized by an ability to automatically perform a task, well-defined goals, timely feedback and an autotelic experience (perceiving the task to be intrinsically motivating and diminished need for extrinsic rewards – Csikszentmihalyi, 1990, 1997). In other words, employees who are in a state of flow often find the process of performing an activity more enjoyable than achieving the end goal. This perception corresponds with Kahn's definition of engagement at the beginning of this chapter.

The notion that flow requires alignment between the demands of an activity and perceived abilities is also consistent with the job demands–resources model (Bakker and Demerouti, 2007), which has been extensively applied to work engagement. In this model, high job demands and low job resources predict stress and burnout, while high job resources predict engagement, both directly and through buffering the cognitive, emotional and social impact of job demands. Thus, although excessive or unnecessary job demands should be managed in order to mitigate negative outcomes, job resources are much more critical for engagement. These job resources include social support, autonomy, opportunities to learn and feedback (Schaufeli, Bakker and Van Rhenen, 2009).

Consistent in the conceptualizations of both flow and engagement is that low demands or unchallenging tasks do not yield flow or engagement. They yield boredom. Instead, a balance between demands and resources or abilities is the key to the absorption experiences that characterize flow and engagement. This implies that easy jobs are not engaging. Rather, challenging jobs, along with adequate resources to meet job demands, can trigger flow and increase engagement.

Importantly, and consistent with the 'perceived abilities' dimension of flow, recent research suggests that the effect of job resources on engagement is mediated through personal resources such as self-efficacy and optimism (Xanthopoulou, Bakker, Demerouti and Schaufeli, 2009a, 2009b). Thus, flow may be an intermediate state that can help explain the relationship between job resources and engagement. For example, adequate job resources can help employees develop personal resources, which can enhance their perception that their abilities match the demands and challenges of their jobs. This in turn can lead to more frequent experiences of flow, ultimately promoting engagement. As discussed later in this chapter, positive organizational behavior, and particularly the construct of psychological capital, explores in-depth various positive personal resources that can promote flow and lead to higher engagement.

Character strengths and virtues

The third and final positive psychology model linking positivity to engagement is character strengths and virtues. According to Peterson and Seligman (2004), there are 6 core virtues with 24 strengths assigned to these core virtues. The core virtues include courage, justice, humanity, temperance, transcendence and wisdom. The psychological strengths assigned to each core virtue represent its 'psychological ingredients' or manifestations. Character strengths and virtues are trait-like, meaning they are stable over time.

In terms of relevance to engagement, some of the character strengths conceptualized by Peterson and Seligman (2004) may be foundational to engagement. Examples of these strengths include love of learning, persistence (which includes perseverance and industriousness), vitality (which includes zest, enthusiasm, vigor and energy) and self-regulation. Indeed, studies support individual differences as antecedents for engagement (e.g. Langelaan, Bakker, van Doornen and Schaufeli, 2006). On the practice side, the Gallup Organization emphasizes the critical role of trait-based talents and strengths in enhancing engagement through proper selection and placement (Coffman and Gonzelez-Molina, 2002). In other words, while engagement may be a state, various positive personality traits and trait-like characteristics, extensively studied in positive psychology, may represent important baselines, thresholds or boundary conditions for the development and management of engagement in the workplace.

Positive organizational scholarship and engagement

Positive organizational scholarship is defined as a 'movement in organizational science that focuses on the dynamics leading to exceptional individual and organizational performance such as developing human strength, producing resilience and restoration, and fostering vitality' (Cameron and Caza, 2004: 731). While positive organizational scholars study a variety of positively oriented topics, their focus tends to be on collective positivity, manifested and promoted within group or organizational phenomena. Of course individual positivity and performance are also considered important. However, positive organizational scholars view group and organizational constructs as much more than the sum of the parts of their individual level constituents. For example, a group of resilient individuals does not necessarily yield organizational resiliency. Similarly, compassionate organizations are more than a group of compassionate employees. In this chapter, three positive constructs from positive organizational scholarship were selected for their potential linkages with engagement. These constructs are: organizational virtuousness, positive deviance and appreciative inquiry.

Organizational virtuousness

Virtuousness refers to 'the best of the human condition or the highest aspirations human beings hold for themselves' (Cameron and Winn, 2012: 231). It is manifested in terms of: (a) positive human impact; (b) inherent moral goodness as a terminal value, rather than means to an end; and (c) unconditional societal betterment that transcends both self-interest and norms of reciprocity (Bright, Cameron and Caza, 2006). While virtuousness tends to be equated with virtues, the latter tend to be individual attributes. On the other hand, virtuousness is an aggregation of human virtues representing moral excellence, inherent goodness and humanity at its best, which can be manifested at the individual or collective level (Cameron and Winn, 2012).

Virtuousness and ethics are not equivalent, nor are they varying levels of the same construct. Similar to earlier discussions of positive and negative constructs being qualitatively different, ethics tend to be deficit-oriented toward avoiding wrongdoing such as harming others, violating the law or otherwise causing damage. However, absence of unethical behavior does not necessarily lead to virtuousness, because virtuousness entails a strong desire to work for the betterment of oneself and others. Virtuousness is also critical in situations where ethical codes fail to provide adequate guidelines. In these situations, organizational virtuousness can transcend situational boundaries to guide moral judgments and the exercise of virtuous behavior (Bright et al., 2006).

In the organizational context, virtuousness has been shown to have an amplifying effect, and a buffering effect. Similar to Fredrickson's broaden-and-build model of positive emotions, discussed earlier, collective virtuousness is expansive, contagious and is manifested in upward spirals. Observing and experiencing virtuousness in an organizational setting promotes positive dynamics that promote even more virtuousness. Organizations can also enable the virtuous activities of their members through various processes or cultural attributes that promote, support or perpetuate these activities. For example, when the spontaneity of seeking positive human impact, inherent moral goodness and unconditional societal betterment becomes part of an organization's culture, it can become self-perpetuating and self-sustaining. Organizational members may also collectively exercise virtuousness in ways that are beyond what any one individual can achieve when acting alone (Cameron, Bright and Caza, 2004). Thus, organizational virtuousness goes beyond the sum of an organization's members' individual levels of virtuousness. Furthermore, organizational virtuousness has been shown to also buffer the blow of negative organizational shocks such as downsizing (Bright et al., 2006).

Organizational virtuousness could promote engagement through several mechanisms. First, organizational virtuousness can be considered a job resource. As discussed earlier, job resources can have a positive impact on engagement. Second, organizational virtuousness can buffer the effects of everyday job demands, as well as the social pressures and psychological burdens of compromising one's moral standards, which can be distracting and a hindrance against experiencing the vigor, dedication and absorption dimensions of engagement. In other words, virtuousness in an organizational setting can produce the balance between job demands and collectively shared job resources that can promote engagement. Third, the inherent attractiveness of virtuousness and positivity in general to all living organisms, also referred to as 'eudaemonic tendency' (Cameron, 2008), can promote the vigor, dedication and absorption dimensions of engagement, especially when work activities are perceived to be sought or promoted for their inherent moral goodness, positive human impact and societal betterment, rather than just for financial gains.

Positive deviance

Positive deviance can be defined as honorable actions and uncommon yet socially desirable behavior that significantly differs from behavioral norms and expectations. Often, deviance is seen in a negative light. However, when an action represents a positive exception to the rule, it is considered positively deviant. In order for a situation to be deemed deviant, two characteristics must be present. First, the action or event should be intentional, not accidental. Second, the action must deviate from the norm by a noticeable margin. Thus, it should be 'radical' and 'norm-defying' enough to be noticeable to those who witness the deviance. Positive deviance tends to be intrinsically motivated, elicited by a desire to help others, and manifested by individuals who are high on self-determination, autonomy, agency, efficacy and courage (Lavine, 2012; Spreitzer and Sonenshein, 2003, 2004). Positive deviance represents the deliberate intention to create a positive outcome by using an unchartered path.

Positive deviance can be instrumental to engagement in several ways. First, the necessary resourcefulness of positively deviant employee in pursuit of a path less travelled (or not traveled at all) may imply that they balance a higher level of personal and job resources with a higher threshold for job demands, leading to exceptional levels of engagement. Second, positively deviant individuals tend to be genuinely motivated to help others, which can promote higher engagement levels in the recipients of their help. Third, similar to organizational virtuousness, the attitudes and behaviors of positively deviant individuals can be collectively contagious and yield self-sustaining upward spirals through promoting positive changes in organizational culture and processes. These organizational changes can in turn further support and perpetuate positive deviance.

Appreciative inquiry

Appreciative inquiry (AI) is a strength-based philosophy that has changed the way of thinking for many organizations (Cooperrider and Godwin, 2012). It calls for fundamental positive changes within organizations, focusing on what is positive, rather than what is viewed as negative or problematic. The AI paradigm involves a collaborative process that engages all employees by taking the organization through a four-cycle process; discovery, dream, design and destiny. In 'discovery', participants are asked to explain the strengths of the organization. In 'dream', they envision where the organization should be. In 'design', they propose action plans to accomplish the dreams. Finally, in 'destiny', the design is put in motion to achieve the desired positive change (Cooperrider and Whitney, 2005). In other words, AI is a continuous process of asking the right questions to promote change that unceasingly revolves around the strengths of the organization.

AI can promote engagement in several ways. First, the high levels of participation required in AI can lead to high-quality relationships, interactions and trust amongst stakeholders, which can promote engagement (Coffman and Gonzalez-Molina, 2002). Second, AI can also lead to engagement through absorption and intrinsic motivation as the participants are challenged by the roles they are responsible for performing (Csikszentmihalyi, 1997). Moreover, since the participating managers and employees have a vested interest in the change, this can promote their dedication to the change and the harnessing of themselves to their roles in the process, which as discussed earlier are critical components of engagement. Indeed, in AI, change agents do not specifically tell the participants what to do and how to do it. Instead, they facilitate a process of collaboration and self-change. Finally, similar to organizational virtuousness and positive deviance, as participants take the initiative to change, they become role models to others, leading to a spiral effect throughout the organization (Quinn and Wellman, 2012).

Positive organizational behavior (POB) and engagement

As defined earlier, positive organizational behavior (POB) applies positive psychology in organizational settings. The following section will examine what is distinctive to POB, the four psychological resources that fit the POB inclusion criteria, and psychological capital (PsyCap) as an integrated, higher order resource.

Unique to POB is that in order for a psychological capacity or resource to be incorporated in POB, it has to meet the following scientific criteria (Luthans, 2002a, 2002b):

1   Theory and research foundation: This criterion differentiates POB from the majority of the popular positive literature that many practicing managers may be familiar with, but which unfortunately does not have this theory and research backup. Such unsubstantiated positivity often leads to management fads and can waste substantial resources in pursuit of 'the next big thing'.
2   Valid measurement: All of the POB concepts are measurable using valid and reliable instruments. This is often the case in positive psychology, but not necessarily across all positive organizational scholarship constructs, many of which are assessed more qualitatively. Moreover, the quality measurement criterion is seriously lacking in practice, leading to many soft measures that do not predict very well what they are expected to predict.
3   State-like and hence open to development and change: This criterion differentiates POB from many positive psychology concepts such as character strengths and virtues which, as discussed earlier, tend to represent stable traits or trait-like characteristics. POB emphasizes psychological resources that can be developed through relatively short interventions (e.g. a training workshop), which are typical in the workplace.

4   Positive impact: POB concepts must show an impact on important work-related outcomes such as job performance, work attitudes and behaviors, recognized in the vast organizational literature for their significant relationships with the organizational bottom line. This quantifiable impact is not emphasized in positive psychology or positive organizational scholarship.

5   Individual level of analysis: As discussed next, psychological concepts of interest in POB all take place within the individual. As mentioned earlier, positive organizational scholarship emphasizes the group and organizational levels of analysis.

Numerous positive constructs have been tested and evaluated, but four specific positive psychological resources have been found to best fit the above criteria: Hope, efficacy, resilience and optimism (summarized using the acronym: HERO).

Hope and engagement

Hope is 'a positive motivational state that is based on an interactively derived sense of successful (1) agency (goal-directed energy) and (2) pathways (planning to meet goals)' (Snyder, Irving and Anderson, 1991: 287). In order to achieve hope, an individual must have the agency or determination to reach a goal, as well as the pathway to achieve the goal. Without both components of hope, hope is lost and motivation to pursue one's goals is compromised. Often, hope gets confused with 'wishful thinking', which is more of an 'emotional high' than a cognitive, motivational state.

Sweetman and Luthans (2010) argue that hope may actually be a requirement for work engagement. Hope can be tied to vigor and dedication, factors of engagement through its agentic determination to achieving one's goals. When a hopeful employee is working towards a goal, he/she will harness more energy and cognitive resources to the work involved in goal pursuit.

Efficacy and engagement

Self-efficacy is 'an individual's convictions (or confidence) about his or her abilities to mobilize the motivation, cognitive resources, and courses of action needed to successfully execute a specific task within a given context' (Stajkovic & Luthans, 1998: 66). Important to the conceptualization of self-efficacy is that individuals' perceptions of their own abilities are what truly affect their confidence levels, which in turn affect the difficulty level of goals they choose to pursue, the amount of effort and perseverance they invest, and ultimately their performance (Bandura, 1997). Individuals who demonstrate a high level of self-efficacy look for a challenge, set goals for themselves and work hard to accomplish them, are exceedingly motivated, and do not give up when faced with difficulties.

It can be argued that efficacy can promote engagement, for several reasons. First, when employees perceive their personal abilities and resources to match the challenges posed by the tasks involved, this can lead to higher levels of engagement. Second, efficacy can promote the critical engagement dimensions of vigor, dedication and absorption as the efficacious individual energetically and persistently pursues challenging goals. Third, efficacy is recognized as developing over time through four distinct mechanisms: task mastery, vicarious learning (learning from relevant role models), social persuasion and encouragement, and physiological and psychological arousal (Bandura, 1997). A sense of mastery can make the job more enjoyable to engage in. The interpersonal dimensions of vicarious learning and social persuasion can increase dedication to the role, team and organization. The physiological and psychological arousal mechanisms can promote vigor and energy, making available more physical, cognitive and affective resources for active involvement. Together, these mechanisms can promote higher engagement in efficacious managers and employees.

Resilience and engagement

Resilience is 'the positive psychological capacity to rebound, to "bounce back" from adversity, uncertainty, conflict, failure or even positive change, progress and increased responsibility' (Luthans, 2002a: 702). Resilience is also the ability to look at the future, full of uncertainty, and continue moving forward (Sweetman and Luthans, 2010). Masten (2001) explains two criteria that must be present for an individual to be considered resilient. First, an individual must experience some type of threat. If an individual has never experienced a threat or roadblock, it would be hard to determine how this individual would handle this type of situation. Second, the way in which an individual handles the threat or roadblock has to be deemed positive. For the individual to simply cope is not being resilient. Overcoming and growing through the event characterizes resilient individuals.

Resilience can be a valuable personal resource that can help employees maintain engagement in the face of obstacles and setbacks through facilitating the necessary balance with job demands. It can also promote engagement through increasing vigor and dedication. As setbacks are experienced, resilient employees harness their persistence to regain their confidence and try again (Sweetman and Luthans, 2010). They endure and remain engaged even in work environments where their less resilient counterparts may experience burnout and are ready to give up (Bakker, Demerouti and Euwema, 2005).

Optimism and engagement

Optimism is a combination of a general positive outlook and a positive explanatory style of events. An optimistic individual attributes successes to internal strengths, as well as permanent and pervasive causes. The optimist also attributes failures to external circumstances that are only temporary in nature. As a result, optimists recognize that they are in control of their lives and take credit for the good fortune they have created (Seligman, 1998). They believe that positive things will come to them and that they can carry this good fortune into the future and control their own destiny (Carver, Scheier, Miller and Fulford, 2009). It is due to this positive outlook that an optimist can have psychological availability. Optimism can also increase the vigor component of engagement by decreasing the amount of thwarting negative spirals of self-blame and cynicism in the workplace.

Psychological capital (PsyCap) and engagement

Psychological capital (PsyCap) is

> an individual's positive psychological state of development that is characterized by (1) having confidence (self-efficacy) to take on and put in the necessary effort to succeed at challenging tasks; (2) making a positive attribution (optimism) about succeeding now and in the future; (3) persevering toward goals and, when necessary, redirecting paths to goals (hope) in order to succeed; and (4) when beset by problems and adversity, sustaining and bouncing back and even beyond (resiliency) to attain success.
>
> (Luthans, Youssef and Avolio, 2007)

PsyCap is a higher-order composite of the four positive psychological resources discussed earlier: hope, efficacy, resilience and optimism. The underlying mechanism linking PsyCap's constituent resources is a positive cognitive, agentic, developmental capacity that promotes 'positive appraisal of circumstances and probability for success based on motivated effort and perseverance' (Luthans, Avolio, Avey and Norman, 2007: 550). PsyCap, as well as each of its constituent resources, has been shown to be measurable, open to development and management in the workplace, and able to yield a wide range of tangible performance outcomes (Avey, Reichard, Luthans and Mhatre, 2011).

As discussed earlier, recent research suggests that the effect of job resources on engagement is mediated through personal resources such as self-efficacy and optimism (Xanthopoulou et al., 2009a, 2009b). Thus, PsyCap may be a more immediate resource set that can help explain the relationship between job resources and engagement. For example, adequate job resources can help employees develop PsyCap, which can enhance their perception that their abilities match the demands and challenges of their jobs, leading to higher engagement. Furthermore, PsyCap's underlying positive cognitive, agentic, developmental mechanism, positive appraisals of circumstances and positive expectancies for success based on motivated effort and perseverance (Luthans, Avey et al., 2007) can help employees not only overcome negativity, cynicism and burnout, but also enjoy an upward spiral of vigor, energy, motivation, dedication and determination in relation to the ever-increasing demands, challenges and uncertainties of the current work environment.

Practical implications

Positivity can affect every domain in one's life, including the workplace (Luthans, Youssef, Sweetman and Harms, 2013; Lyubomirsky et al., 2005). In organizations, managers are beginning to realize the importance of and interplay between positive employees and a positive work environment for organizational success and competitiveness (Avey, Wernsing and Luthans, 2008; Bakker and Schaufeli, 2008; Luthans, Norman, Avolio and Avey, 2008). This chapter proposes that positivity can help promote engagement through a number of positive mechanisms. Thus, positive managers, employees and organizations are necessary for promoting work engagement. In order to promote positivity and engagement in the workplace, positivity should be effectively selected, developed and managed.

Selecting for positivity

When it comes to positivity, the distinction between traits and states is of utmost importance (Luthans and Youssef, 2007). Traits are stable over time, and cannot be developed. Examples of positive personality traits are abundant in the mainstream literature, including the Big Five (Barrick and Mount, 1991) and core self-evaluations (Judge and Bono, 2001). Positive psychology expands the realm of stable traits by emphasizing character strengths and virtues (Peterson and Seligman, 2004). Both mainstream and emerging positive personality traits have been shown to relate to engagement (Coffman and Gonzalez-Molina, 2002; Langelaan et al., 2006). Positive traits also establish a baseline on which more malleable states and state-like characteristics are built (Luthans and Youssef, 2007). Thus, selecting for positivity is a priority for an engaged workforce.

Selecting for positivity is not an easy process. It must be evidence-based both in order to select the right talent and to avoid subjective or discriminatory biases. For example, valid and reliable instruments, now available in the literature and with a track record of success in the workplace, should be used to measure positivity. There can also be a downside to excessive positivity, such as overconfidence (Vancouver, Thompson, Tischner and Putka, 2002; Vancouver, Thompson and Williams, 2001), unrealistic optimism (Peterson, 2000) and false hope (Luthans and Youssef, 2007). Moreover, some jobs require a healthy dose of negativity. Examples include accounting, safety engineering and quality control (Seligman, 1998). However, even in these cases, realistic positivity should be encouraged to create engagement amongst the employees.

Developing positivity

Selection based on stable personality traits may be necessary but not sufficient for engagement. Both positivity and engagement are malleable, to some extent, and thus open to development. Several concepts and mechanisms from positive psychology and positive organizational behavior can help promote positive states, which in turn can promote engagement. One area is to promote positive emotions in the workplace. Positive emotions broaden employees' thought–action repertoires and help build their physical, social and psychological resources, which promotes creativity, innovation and out-of-the-box thinking. Another area is increasing flow experiences by aligning employees' roles and job responsibilities with their qualifications and ensuring they have the proper resources to complete their tasks (Schaufeli and Bakker, 2004).

Another way to increase positivity is to develop employees' psychological capital (PsyCap) through enriching hope, self-efficacy, resiliency and optimism. Luthans, Youssef and Avolio (2007) discuss numerous successful ways to develop PsyCap. For example, hope can be developed through (a) setting appropriate goals that are specific, measurable and challenging; (b) using a stepping method which breaks down large goals into smaller, manageable ones; (c) involving employees in goal-setting decisions when possible; (d) using a reward system that reinforces desirable employee behaviors; and (e) encouraging contingency planning.

As discussed earlier, efficacy can be developed through providing employees with the time, resources and opportunities to experience (a) success and mastery; (b) vicarious learning through observing and learning from seasoned co-workers performing the job; (c) positive feedback and support from managers and coworkers; and (d) physical fitness, positive social interactions, psychological well-being.

Masten, Reed, Cutuli and Herbers (2002) also describe three strategies to develop resilience. Applied by Luthans, Youssef and Avolio (2007), these strategies include: (a) risk-focused strategies, where unnecessary risks (e.g. safety hazards) or stresses (e.g. work–life conflict) are eliminated; (b) asset-focused strategies, where employees are provided with resources that help with success; and (c) process-focused strategies, which teach employees how to cope with, overcome, learn from and grow through risks and setbacks by best utilizing the personal and organizational resources available to them.

Finally, successful development of optimism entails teaching cognitive strategies for re-evaluating successes and failure along the lines of: (a) leniency for the past (giving oneself the benefit of the doubt when something may not have gone as expected); (b) appreciation for the present (e.g. the positive assets the employees bring into the organization and what is going right in the organizational context); and (c) opportunity-seeking for the future based on a positive future outlook, which can lead to a positive approach to goal-setting, an increase in persistence, flexibility in goal attainment, creativity, better outcomes and subjective well-being (Schneider, 2001).

Managing positivity through creating a positive organizational environment

Selecting positive employees and developing positivity in employees are important. However, they do not automatically yield a positive, engaging work environment. Organizational positivity goes beyond the sum of its individual members, to also include the elevating mechanisms, dynamic processes, upward spirals, contagion effects and synergistic collective outcomes that no one individual member of the organization can possibly accomplish alone. Organizations can enable this collective positivity through creating the structural and cultural attributes that promote, support or perpetuate positive deviance and organizational virtuousness. Appealing to humans' eudaemonic tendencies (attraction to what is positive) can yield a more engaged, committed workforce and increase the attractiveness of the organization, both to its current workforce (resulting in higher retention) and in the labor market. Adopting appreciative inquiry as a way of thinking and a process for change can also promote positivity and engagement.

Case study*

North Lawndale, Chicago is a poor community with a population of about 40,000. Unemployment rates are high, and so are criminal activity, drug addiction, homelessness and dysfunctional family dynamics, to name a few of the prevalent problems. Communities like North Lawndale are in desperate need of positivity. Financial resources are nice to have, but are not always available or effective in turning lives and communities around. Many times positive change needs to happen from within. The success story and track record of the North Lawndale Employment Network (NLEN) provide evidence for the critical role of positivity and engagement.

Led by private initiatives, planning and funding, NLEN was established in 1999 to break the cycle of hopelessness and despair. The network achieves its goals through three programs:

- *U-Turn Permitted:* This program equips formerly incarcerated individuals with employment skills. However, it is not just a job placement service or technical skills training. Unique to this program is the engagement of the whole person, including attitudes, habits, thoughts and behavioral patterns. It seeks to develop its participants' self-efficacy through teaching important life and employment skills; building hope through goal-setting, instilling determination and pathways thinking; boosting optimism through creating trusting and helping relationships; and promote resilience through resources and support. Negative behaviors and self-destructive thoughts are replaced with positive alternatives that can broaden the participants' thought–action repertoires and help build their psychological, social and even physical resources.

  Importantly, the program is very selective, and participants are selected for attitudes, not skills. They have to be self-motivated to succeed and have a strong desire to change, or they do not get accepted. The program equips them with a wide range of tools and resources to turn their own lives around, including surrounding them with examples

---

* Based on Thompson, K. R., Benedetto, R. L., Walter, T. J. and Meyer, M. (2013) *It's My Company Too!* Austin, TX, Greenleaf, Chapter 5; Thompson, K. R., Luthans, F., Youssef, C. M., Walter, T. J. and Benedetto, R. L. 'Implications of positive psychological capital in innovative, best practice organizations: A symposium', presented at National Academy of Management, Boston, MA, August 2012; and North Lawndale Employment Network website: http://www.nlen.org.

and role models of positive deviance by counselors who truly invest in them individually and help counter the prevalence of negative deviance in their past experiences. However, it is ultimately up to them to make the right choices and meet the demands of this challenging program, and then, beyond the program, on the job and in life.

- *Sweet Beginnings:* This program provides some of the U-Turn Permitted graduates and others with twelve weeks of transitional employment in the production and marketing of honey and honey-based skincare products. Participants practice first-hand newly learned positive thoughts and behaviors such as teamwork, punctuality and conflict resolution. Again, the positions are competitive, the work is hard, and although the pay may not be substantial, the efficacy that the trainees build is invaluable in equipping them for more permanent employment. Eighty percent of those who work for Sweet Beginnings are able to locate employment within three months, and while the national recidivism rate is around sixty percent, it is under four percent among former Sweet Beginnings employees.

- *The NLEN Resource Center:* This center provides employment-focused resources to the members of the community, including workshops on topics such as resume development and interviewing skills, as well as essential job search tools such as free Wi-Fi, phone, fax, photocopiers and community voicemail. Workforce development coaches offer guidance in numerous ways, from securing rides and suitable clothing for job interviews, to career advancement guidance. This equipping and support can provide hope and optimism, build efficacy, and sustain resilience in those who may be ready to give up.

Setbacks such as those faced by members of the North Lawndale community can make people feel that their lives are out of control, they risk losing hope, and get sucked into a downward spiral of self-destruction. Efforts to increase work engagement can be fruitless when negativity prevails. On the other hand, when positivity is instilled, its broadening and building effects can yield engagement at the personal, social, professional and community level, because while work engagement is desirable, a positively engaged life is certainly more fulfilling.

References

Avey, J. B., Reichard, R., Luthans, F. and Mhatre, K. H. (2011) 'Meta-analysis of the impact of positive psychological capital on employee attitudes, behaviors, and performance', *Human Resource Development Quarterly*, 22: 127–52.
——, Wernsing, T. S. and Luthans, F. (2008) 'Can positive employees help positive organizational change? Impact of psychological capital and emotions on relevant attitudes and behaviors', *Journal of Applied Behavioral Science*, 44: 48–70.
Avolio, B. J. (2011) *Full-Range Leadership Development*, 2nd edn, Thousand Oaks, CA: Sage.
Bakker, A. B. and Bal, P. M. (2010) 'Weekly work engagement and performance: A study among starting teachers', *Journal of Occupational and Organizational Psychology*, 83: 189–206.
——, and Demerouti, E. (2007) 'The Job Demands–Resources model: State of the art', *Journal of Managerial Psychology*, 22: 309–28
——, Demerouti, E. and Euwema, M. C. (2005) 'Job resources buffer the impact of job demands on burnout', *Journal of Occupational Health Psychology*, 10: 170–80.
—— and Schaufeli, W. B. (2008) 'Positive organizational behavior: Engaged employees in flourishing organizations', *Journal of Organizational Behavior*, 29: 147–54.
Bandura, A. (1997) *Self-Efficacy: The Exercise of Control*, New York: Freeman.
—— (2001) 'Social cognitive theory: An agentic perspective', *Annual Review of Psychology*, 52: 1–26.

Barrick, M. R. and Mount, M. K. (1991) 'The big five personality dimensions and job performance: A meta-analysis', *Personnel Psychology*, 44: 1–26.

Bass, B. M. and Riggio, R. E. (2006) *Transformational Leadership*, 2nd edn, Mahwah, NJ: Lawrence Erlbaum Associates.

Berg, J. M., Wrzesniewski, A. and Dutton, J. E. (2010) 'Perceiving and responding to challenges in job crafting at different ranks: When proactivity requires adaptivity', *Journal of Organizational Behavior*, 31: 158–86.

Bright, D., Cameron, K. and Caza, A. (2006) 'The amplifying and buffering effects of virtuousness in downsized organizations.', *Journal of Business Ethics*, 64: 249–69.

Cacioppo, J. T. and Berntson, G. G. (1994) 'Relationship between attitudes and evaluative space: A critical review, with emphasis on the separability of positive and negative substrates', *Psychological Bulletin*, 115: 401–23.

Cameron, K. S. (2008) 'Paradox in Positive Organizational Change', *Journal of Applied Behavioral Science*, 44(1): 7–24.

——, Bright, D. and Caza, A. (2004) 'Exploring the relationships between organizational virtuousness and performance', *American Behavioral Scientist*, 47: 766–90.

—— and Caza, A. (2004) 'Contributions to the discipline of positive organizational scholarship', *American Behavioral Scientist*, 47: 731–9.

—— and Winn, B. (2012) 'Virtuousness in organizations', in K. Cameron and G. Spreitzer (eds) *The Oxford Handbook of Positive Organizational Scholarship*, New York: Oxford University Press, pp. 231–43.

Carver, C. S., Scheier, M. S., Miller, C. J. and Fulford, D. (2009) 'Optimism', in C.R. Snyder and S. J. Lopez (eds), *Handbook of Positive Psychology*, 2nd edn, Oxford: Oxford University Press, pp. 313–21.

Cascio, W. F. and Boudreau, J. W. (2011) *Investing in People: Financial Impact of Human Resource Initiatives (second ed.),* Upper Saddle River, NJ: FT Press.

Chang, E. C., Maydeu-Olivares, A. and D'Zurilla, T. J. (1997) 'Optimism and pessimism as partially independent constructs: Relations to positive and negative affectivity and psychological well-being', *Personality and Individual Differences*, 23: 433–40.

Coffman, C. and Gonzalez-Molina, G. (2002) *Follow This Path*, New York: Gallup.

Conger, J. A. and Kanungo, R. N. (1988) *Charismatic Leadership. The Elusive Factor in Organizational Effectiveness*, San Francisco, CA: Jossey-Bass.

—— and Kanungo, R. N. (1992) 'Perceived behavioural attributes of charismatic leadership', *Canadian Journal of Behavioural Science*, 24(1): 86–102.

Cooperrider, D. L. and Godwin, L. N. (2012) 'Positive organization development', in K. S. Cameron and G. M. Spreitzer (eds) *The Oxford Handbook of Positive Organizational Scholarship*, New York: Oxford University Press, pp. 737–50.

—— and Whitney, D. (2005) *Appreciative Inquiry: A Positive Revolution in Change*, San Francisco, CA: Berrett-Koehler.

Csikszentmihalyi, M. (1990) *Flow: The Psychology of Optimal Experience*, New York: Harper.

—— (1997) *Creativity: Flow and the Psychology of Discovery and Invention*, New York: Harper.

Dunlop, P. D. and Lee, K. (2004) 'Workplace deviance, organizational citizenship behavior, and business unit performance: the bad apples do spoil the whole barrel', *Journal of Organizational Behavior*, 25: 67–80.

Fredrickson, B. L. (2009) *Positivity*, New York: Crown.

George, J. M. (1991) 'State or trait: Effects of positive mood on prosocial behaviors at work', *Journal of Applied Psychology*, 76: 299–307.

Hackman, J. R. and Oldham, G. R. (1976) 'Motivation through the design of work: Test of a theory', *Organizational Behavior and Human Performance*, 16: 250–79.

Harter, J. K., Schmidt, F. L. and Hayes, T. L. (2002) 'Business-unit-level relationship between employee satisfaction, employee engagement, and business outcomes: a meta-analysis,' *Journal of Applied Psychology*, 87: 268–79.

Herzberg, F., Mausner, B. and Snyderman, B. (1993) *The Motivation to Work*, New Brunswick, NJ: Transaction Publishers.

Ilies, R., Scott, B. A. and Judge, T. A. (2012) 'The interactive effects of personal traits and experienced states on intraindividual patterns of citizenship behavior', *Academy of Management*, 49: 561–75.

Judge, T. A. and Bono, J. E. (2001) 'Relationship of core self-evaluations traits – self-esteem, generalized self-efficacy, locus of control, and emotional stability – with job satisfaction and job performance: A meta-analysis', *Journal of Applied Psychology*, 86: 80–92.

——, Thoresen, C. J., Bono, J. E. and Patton, G. K. (2001) 'The job satisfaction–job performance relationship: A qualitative and quantitative review', *Psychological Bulletin*, 127: 376–407.

Kahn, W. A. (1990) 'Psychological conditions of personal engagement and disengagement at work', *Academy of Management Journal*, 33: 692–724.

Keyes, C. L. M. and Haidt, J. (eds) (2003) *Positive Psychology and the Life Well Lived*, Washington, DC: American Psychological Association.

Kreitner, R. and Luthans, F. (1984) 'A social learning approach to management: Radical behaviorists "Mellowing out"', *Organizational Dynamics*, 13(2): 47–65.

Langelaan, S., Bakker, A. B., Van Doornen, L. J. P. and Schaufeli, W. B. (2006) 'Burnout and work engagement: Do individual differences make a difference?' *Personality and Individual Differences*, 40: 521–32

Lavine, M. (2012) 'Positive deviance: A metaphor and method for learning from the uncommon', in K. S. Cameron and G. M. Spreitzer (eds) *The Oxford Handbook of Positive Organizational Scholarship*, New York: Oxford University Press, pp. 1014–26.

Locke, E. A. and Latham, G. P. (2002) 'Building a practically useful theory of goal setting and task motivation: A 35-year odyssey', *American Psychologist*, 57: 705–17.

Luthans, F. (2002a) 'The need for and meaning of positive organizational behavior', *Journal of Organizational Behavior*, 23: 695–706.

—— (2002b) 'Positive organizational behavior: Developing and managing psychological strengths', *Academy of Management Executive*, 16(1): 57–75.

—— and Avolio, B. J. (2009) 'The "point" of positive organizational behavior', *Journal of Organizational Behavior*, 30: 291–307.

——, Avolio, B. J., Avey, J. B. and Norman, S. M. (2007) 'Positive psychological capital: Measurement and relationship with performance and satisfaction', *Personnel Psychology*, 60: 541–72.

——, Norman, S. M., Avolio, B. J. and Avey, J. B. (2008) 'The mediating role of psychological capital in the supportive organizational climate–employee performance relationship', *Journal of Organizational Behavior*, 29: 219–38.

—— and Youssef, C. M. (2007) 'Emerging positive organizational behavior', *Journal of Management*, 33: 321–49.

——, Youssef, C. M. and Avolio, B. J. (2007) *Psychological Capital: Developing the Human Competitive Edge*, Oxford: Oxford University Press.

——, Youssef, C. M., Sweetman, D. and Harms, P. (2013) 'Meeting the leadership challenge of employee well-being through relationship PsyCap and health PsyCap', *Journal of Leadership and Organizational Studies*, 20: 114–29.

Lyubomirsky, S., King, L. and Diener, E. (2005) 'The benefits of frequent positive affect: Does happiness lead to success?' *Psychological Bulletin*, 131: 803–55.

Maslach, C., Schaufeli, W. B. and Leiter, M. P. (2001) 'Job burnout', *Annual Review of Psychology*, 52: 397–422.

Maslow, A. (1954) *Motivation and Personality*, New York: Harper.

—— (1968) *Toward a Psychology of Being*, New York: Wiley.

Masten, A. S., Cutuli, J. J., Herbers, J. E. and Reed, M. J. (2009) 'Resilience in development', in C. R. Snyder and S. Lopez (eds) *Handbook of Positive Psychology*, 2nd edn, Oxford: Oxford University Press, pp. 117–31.

Peterson, C. (2000) 'The future of optimism,' *American Psychologist*, 55: 44–55.

—— and Seligman, M. E. P. (2004) *Character Strengths and Virtues: A Handbook and Classification*, New York: Oxford University Press.

Pittinsky, T. L., Rosenthal, S. and Montoya, R. M. (2011) 'Liking is not the opposite of disliking: The functional separability of positive and negative attitudes toward minority groups', *Cultural Diversity and Ethnic Minority Psychology*, 17: 134–43.

Quinn, R. E. and Wellman, N. (2012) 'Seeing and acting differently', in K. S. Cameron and G. M. Spreitzer (eds) *The Oxford Handbook of Positive Organizational Scholarship*, New York: Oxford University Press, pp. 751–62.

Rathbard, N. P. and Patil, S. V. (2012) 'Being there: Work engagement and positive organizational scholarship', in K. S. Cameron and G. M. Spreitzer (eds) *The Oxford Handbook of Positive Organizational Scholarship*, New York: Oxford University Press, pp. 56–69.

Sackett, P. R., Berry, C. M., Wiemann, S. A. and Laczo, R. M. (2006) 'Citizenship and counterproductive behavior: Clarifying relations between the two domains', *Human Performance*, 19: 441–64.

Schaufeli, W. B. and Bakker, A. B. (2004) 'Job demands, job resources, and their relationship with burnout and engagement: A multi-sample study', *Journal of Organizational Behavior*, 25: 293–315.

——, Bakker, A. B. and Van Rhenen, W. (2009) 'How changes in job demands and resources predict burnout, work engagement, and sickness absenteeism', *Journal of Organizational Behavior*, 30: 893–917.

——, Salanova, M., Gonzalez-Roma, V. and Bakker, A. B. (2002) 'The measurement of engagement and burnout: A confirmative analytic approach', *Journal of Happiness Studies*, 3: 71–92.

Schneider, S. (2001) 'In search of realistic optimism: Meaning, knowledge, and warm fuzziness', *American Psychologist*, 56: 250–63.

Seligman, M. (1998) *Learned Optimism*, New York: Pocket Books.

—— and Csikszentmihalyi, M. (2000) 'Positive psychology', *American Psychologist*, 55: 5–14.

Snyder, C. R., Irving, L. and Anderson, J. (1991) 'Hope and health: Measuring the will and the ways', in C. R. Snyder and D. R. Forsyth (eds) *Handbook of Social and Clinical Psychology*, Elmsford, NY: Pergamon, pp. 285–305.

Spreitzer, G. M. and Sonenshein, S. (2003) 'Positive deviance and extraordinary organizing', in K. Cameron, J. Dutton, and R. Quinn (eds) *Positive Organizational Scholarship*, San Francisco: Berrett-Koehler, pp. 207–24.

—— and Sonenshein, S. (2004) 'Toward the construct definition of positive deviance' *The American Behavioral Scientist*, 47: 828–47.

Stairs, M. and Galpin, M. (2010) 'Positive engagement: From employee engagement to workplace happiness', in P. A. Linley, S. Harrington and N. Garcea (eds) *Oxford Handbook of Positive Psychology and Work*, New York: Oxford University Press, pp. 155–72.

Stajkovic, A. D. and Luthans, F. (1997), 'A meta-analysis of the effects of organizational behavior modification on task performance: 1975–95', *Academy of Management Journal*, 40: 1122–49.

—— and Luthans, F. (1998) 'Social cognitive theory and self-efficacy: Going beyond traditional motivational and behavioral approaches', *Organizational Dynamics*, 26(4): 62–74.

—— and Luthans, F. (2003) 'Behavioral management and task performance in organizations: Conceptual background, meta-analysis, and test of alternative models', *Personnel Psychology*, 56: 155–94.

Sweetman, D. and Luthans, F. (2010) 'The power of positive psychology: Psychological capital and work engagement', in A. B. Bakker and M. Leiter, (eds) *Work Engagement: A Handbook of Essential Theory and Research*, East Sussex: Psychology Press, pp. 54–68.

Taylor, S. E. (1991) 'Asymmetrical effects of positive and negative events: The mobilization-minimization hypothesis', *Psychological Bulletin*, 110: 67–85.

Vancouver, J., Thompson, C., Tischner, E. and Putka, D. (2002) 'Two studies examining the negative effect of self-efficacy on performance', *Journal of Applied Psychology*, 87: 506–16.

——, Thompson, C. and Williams, A. (2001) 'The changing signs in the relationship between self-efficacy, personal goals, and performance', *Journal of Applied Psychology*, 86: 605–20.

Vroom, V. (1964) *Work and Motivation*, New York: Wiley.

Watson, D., Clark, L. A. and Tellegen, A. (1988), 'Development and validation of brief measures of positive and negative affect: The PANAS scales', *Journal of Personality and Social Psychology*, 54: 1063–70.

Xanthopoulou, D., Bakker, A. B., Demerouti, E. and Schaufeli, W. B. (2009a), 'Reciprocal relationships between job resources, personal resources, and work engagement', *Journal of Vocational Behavior*, 74: 235–44.

——, Bakker, A. B., Demerouti, E. and Schaufeli, W. B. (2009b), 'Work engagement and financial returns: A diary study on the role of job and personal resources', *Journal of Occupational and Organizational Psychology*, 82: 183–200.

3 The antecedents and drivers of employee engagement

*Eean R. Crawford, Bruce Louis Rich,
Brooke Buckman and Jenny Bergeron*

Introduction

Over two decades have passed since William Kahn formally defined employee engagement as 'the harnessing of organization members' selves to their work roles; in engagement, people employ and express themselves physically, cognitively, and emotionally during role performances' (Kahn, 1990: 694). Since that time we have witnessed an explosion of scholarly and practitioner interest in engagement – particularly in the last ten years. Engagement has recently been the focus of several narrative reviews (Bakker and Demerouti, 2008; Bakker, Schaufeli, Leiter, and Taris, 2008; Britt, Dickinson, Greene-Shortridge, and McKibben, 2007; Macey and Schneider, 2008; Schaufeli and Salanova, 2007), two books in addition to this current volume (Bakker and Leiter, 2010; Macey, Schneider, Barbera, and Young, 2009), three meta-analyses (Christian, Garza, and Slaughter, 2011; Cole, Walter, Bedeian, and O'Boyle, 2012; Crawford, LePine, and Rich, 2010), and special issues of *Industrial and Organizational Psychology* (2008, March), *Work and Stress* (2008, July–September), and the *European Journal of Work and Organizational Psychology* (2011, January).

By our count, well over 250 articles have been published on engagement since 2000, with over 80 per cent of these published since 2006. Much of the appeal of employee engagement derives from research asserting its competitive advantages for organizations in terms of superior employee performance and bottom line results (Harter, Schmidt, and Hayes, 2002; Schneider, Macey, Barbera, and Martin, 2009; Vance, 2006). The Society for Human Resource Management (SHRM) has consistently listed employee engagement as one of the most important topic areas in employee relations over the last several years (Cohen, 2007: 1016).

Because of its potential for superior business results, researchers and practitioners naturally wonder what key drivers can be leveraged to bring about increases in employee engagement. This has led to research exploring factors such as job design, leadership, perceived organizational and supervisor support, and human resource management practices. As research on engagement has developed, the list of its studied antecedents has grown increasingly large and varied. The purpose of our chapter is to summarize and make sense of this research. In the spirit of Lewin's (1945: 129) statement that 'nothing is as practical as a good theory', we return to Kahn's foundational theory on the psychological conditions of engagement to explain how antecedent factors are linked to engagement through psychological conditions of meaningfulness, safety, and availability. Although scholars do not always explicitly use this framework to conceptually ground models of engagement, the majority of the antecedent constructs studied reflect, to a great extent, these three psychological conditions. Thus it becomes a parsimonious means for comprehending this growing literature. The unifying theme underlying this research is that individuals' perceptions of organizational, job, and personal characteristics affect the experience of psychological conditions, which in turn shape individuals' agentic decisions to engage more completely in their work roles.

Our chapter is organized as follows. First we briefly review Kahn's (1990) theory of personal engagement. We then more thoroughly explore the psychological conditions of meaningfulness, safety, and availability, and summarize research on antecedent factors that drive engagement through these respective psychological mechanisms. This is followed by a discussion of available research on the inter-relationships of these antecedent factors and psychological mechanisms. We conclude with a case study of one organization that has successfully leveraged the psychological conditions to drive up levels of employee engagement within its workforce. Our hope is that readers from both theoretical and applied settings leave this chapter with a greater understanding not only of what factors enhance engagement, but why it is that they do so.

Primary psychological drivers of engagement

In a qualitative, theory-generating study drawing on the work of psychologists (Freud, 1922), sociologists (Goffman, 1961a, 1961b; Merton, 1957), and group theorists (Bion, 1961; Slater, 1966; Smith and Berg, 1987), Kahn (1990) argued that people have dimensions of themselves that, given appropriate conditions, they prefer to employ and express in the course of the roles they perform, even as they maintain boundaries between who they are and the roles they occupy. To employ dimensions of the self is to drive personal energy into physical, cognitive, and emotional labors. To express dimensions of the self is to display real identity, thoughts, and feelings. Those who drive personal energy into role behaviors become physically involved in tasks, cognitively vigilant, and empathetically connected to others in the service of the work they are doing. Those who display the self in the role show what they think and feel, their creativity, their beliefs and values, and their personal connections to others.

Similar to job characteristics theory (Hackman and Oldham, 1980), Kahn observed that people's experiences of themselves and their work contexts influence momentary psychological conditions that drive their willingness to personally engage in work roles. Organization members seemed to unconsciously ask themselves three questions and then personally engage depending on the answers: '(1) How *meaningful* is it for me to bring myself into this performance? (2) How *safe* is it to do so? and (3) How *available* am I to do so?' (Kahn, 1990: 703). These three conditions also accurately reflect the basic logic of contracts. Generally, people agree to contracts when they believe they possess the resources necessary to meet their obligations, when the contract contains clear and desired benefits, and finally, when the contract also offers protective guarantees (Kahn, 1990).

Individuals vary their willingness to invest themselves according to the benefits, or the meaningfulness, and the guarantees, or the safety, they perceive in situations; as well as according to the resources they perceive themselves to have, or their own availability. The combination of these three conditions – meaningfulness, safety, and availability – creates a state of psychological presence (Kahn, 1992) from which organization members are able to employ and express themselves more completely physically, cognitively, and emotionally in their work role performances. To summarize, Kahn's engagement represents the employment and expression of personal physical, cognitive, and emotional energy in one's work role. This personal investment ebbs and flows according to the psychological presence created by individuals' perceptions of meaning, safety, and availability. These perceptions are initially influenced by characteristics of work contexts, interpersonal and intergroup relations, and characteristics of the employees themselves, which we discuss next.

Psychological meaningfulness antecedents

The experience of psychological meaningfulness involves a sense of return on investment of the self in work role performances (Kahn, 1990: 703–4). Individuals who experience meaningfulness feel worthwhile, useful, and valuable – as though they have made a difference and have not been taken for granted, while lack of meaningfulness is connected to individuals' feeling that little is expected of them or that there is little to receive from giving themselves to work role performances. According to Kahn (1990, 1992), the key factors promoting meaningfulness include tasks that are challenging, clearly delineated, varied, and somewhat autonomous; roles that carry identities congruent with how individuals like to see themselves and that confer a sense of status or influence; and rewarding interactions involving appreciation, feedback, and respect that allow individuals to feel valuable and cared for.

Constructs we have found to theoretically fit Kahn's description of psychological meaningfulness and its task and role influences include job challenge, autonomy, variety, feedback, role fit, opportunities for development, and rewards and recognition. These factors are associated with increased engagement because they offer opportunities and incentives for individuals to express more of their preferred selves in work role performances (Kahn, 1992). To the extent that individuals perceive these work elements to offer clear and desired benefits for their personal investments, they ought to exhibit an increased willingness to more fully engage in their work roles.

Job challenge   Job challenge refers to having a high workload, broad job scope, and/or high job responsibility (Cavanaugh, Boswell, Roehling, and Boudreau, 2000). Job challenge is motivating because it creates potential for accomplishment, mastery, and personal growth (Lazarus and Folkman, 1984). This potential triggers positive emotions and an active, problem-focused coping style (e.g. increasing effort) to deal with the challenges (LePine, Podsakoff, and LePine, 2005). Job challenge promotes meaning through individuals' feelings that much is expected of them (Kahn, 1990). Raised expectations have been consistently shown to increase effort, persistence, and performance among individuals and groups (Eden, 1990; Locke and Latham, 1990). Consistent with this, researchers have found engagement to be positively related to cognitive work demands (Bakker, Demerouti, and Schaufeli, 2005; Lorente, Salanova, Martínez, and Schaufeli, 2008), work responsibility (Rothbard, 2001), and a high workload (Bakker, Demerouti, and Schaufeli, 2003; Britt, Castro, and Adler, 2005; Hallberg, Johansson, and Schaufeli, 2007; Xanthopoulou, Bakker, Demerouti, and Schaufeli, 2007). The Crawford et al. (2010) meta-analysis found that both job responsibility (.15) and workload (.13) have significant positive relationships with engagement. The Christian et al. (2011) meta-analysis found that both job complexity – the extent to which a job is multifaceted and difficult to perform – (.24) and problem solving – the extent to which a job requires innovative solutions or new ideas – (.28) have significant positive relationships with engagement. Thus, across different types of job challenges, employees appear to respond to increased expectations with greater engagement.

Autonomy   Autonomy refers to the freedom, independence, and discretion allowed to employees in scheduling their work and determining the procedures for carrying it out (Hackman and Oldham, 1975). It has been the most frequently studied engagement antecedent. Autonomy increases the meaning of work because it provides a sense of ownership and control over work outcomes (Hackman and Oldham, 1980; Kahn, 1990). This is consistent with the notion from self-determination theory (Ryan and Deci, 2000) that the satisfaction of a universal basic human need for autonomy motivates individuals to be proactive and engaged. Extensive empirical findings support these premises as the Crawford et al. (2010) meta-analytic estimate based on 32 studies and a combined sample of over 18,000 individuals put the relationship between autonomy and engagement at .37. An updated estimate from Christian et al. (2011) based on 43 studies and a combined sample of over 24,000 individuals put the relationship at .39. Thus, it is well established that one of the key ways engagement can be enhanced is through increased employee autonomy.

Variety   Jobs with greater variety allow individuals to perform many different activities, or they require the use of many different skills and talents of the employee while carrying out the work (Hackman and Oldham, 1975). Variety promotes meaningfulness because it allows individuals to feel more useful as they draw on a wider range of their personal knowledge, skills, and abilities to complete their tasks (Kahn, 1990). Although it has been less extensively studied in relation to engagement, evidence suggests that it is one of the strongest predictors of engagement. Variety in skill use had strong positive relationships with engagement in two independent samples of Finnish dentists (Hakanen, Bakker, and Demerouti, 2005), a large randomly selected sample of the Dutch workforce (Beckers et al., 2004), large samples of technology workers in Spain and telecom mangers in the Netherlands (Salanova and Schaufeli, 2008), and a diverse sample of employees working in 17 different organizations in Belgium (Van den Broeck, Vansteenkiste, De Witte, and Lens, 2008). Both the Crawford et al. (2010) and Christian et al. (2011) meta-analytic estimates of .53 suggest that job variety has a strong positive relationship with engagement. In sum, mounting evidence indicates that increasing job variety is one of the most powerful ways to leverage greater engagement in organizations.

Feedback   Feedback refers to employees obtaining direct and clear information about the effectiveness of their performance (Hackman and Oldham, 1975). This information results from carrying out the work activities required by the job itself such as when a customer service representative notes how many customer complaints they successfully resolved during a specific time period. It is supplemented by information from supervisors and coworkers such as when supervisors provide regular performance reviews or informal coaching sessions. Feedback promotes employees' psychological meaningfulness because it allows them to evaluate their growth and progress towards achieving goals, as well as helping them feel known, valued, and appreciated in rewarding relationships (Kahn, 1990). Feedback has exhibited significant positive relationships with engagement in samples of information technology workers (Hallberg and Schaufeli, 2006), customer service representatives (Bakker et al., 2003), teachers (Bakker, Hakanen, Demerouti, and Xanthopoulou, 2007; Hakanen, Bakker, and Schaufeli, 2006), dentists (Gorter, te Brake, Hoogstraten, and Eijkman, 2008; Hakanen, Perhoniemi, and Toppinen-Tanner, 2008; Hakanen, Schaufeli, and Ahola, 2008), military personnel (Britt, 1999, 2003), as well as diverse samples of employees from various nations across both private and public sectors (Llorens, Bakker, Schaufeli, and Salanova, 2006; Salanova and Schaufeli, 2008; Schaufeli and Bakker, 2004; Van den Broeck et al., 2008). Crawford et al. (2010) estimated the relationship between feedback and engagement to be .35 in a combined sample of 19 studies and over 12,000 individuals. Christian et al. (2011) estimated the same relationship to be .33 in a combined sample of 10 studies and over 7,000 individuals. Thus, feedback, either from the job itself or from supervisors and coworkers, provides meaningful information that enhances engagement.

Fit   Fit refers to compatibility between an individual and a work environment (e.g. the job, organization, workgroup, supervisor) that occurs when their characteristics are well matched (Kristof-Brown, Zimmerman, and Johnson, 2005). Kahn (1990) referred to employees' fit with the work roles they assumed, such that the roles offered identities, status, and influence consistent with employees' preferred self-images. Role fit offers greater meaning to individuals as it allows them to behave in a manner consistent with how they see or want to see themselves. Roles that offer status and influence allow individuals to feel important and needed, as though they have the power to shape their work environment as opposed to only responding to it (Kahn, 1990). May, Gilson, and Harter (2004) found that work role fit was positively related to engagement and that this relationship was mediated by greater perceived work meaningfulness. Having pride in one's profession was a significant predictor of engagement for a large sample of dentists (Hakanen, Perhoniemi, et al., 2008). In Britt's (1999, 2003) work, consistency between individuals' identities and the behavior prescribed by their job roles was positively associated with their engagement. Rich, LePine, and Crawford (2010) found that greater congruence between the values espoused by individual firefighters and those called for by their departments predicted increased engagement, which was in turn related to higher performance as evaluated by their supervisors. The meta-analytic estimate of the relationship between work role fit and engagement based on six studies and a combined sample of over 4,500 individuals provided by Crawford et al. (2010) is .52. Though fewer studies have been conducted on this relationship, the existing evidence points to work role fit as a strong driver of engagement.

Opportunities for development   Opportunities for development (also referred to as training and development) are planned efforts to facilitate employee acquisition of knowledge, skills, and abilities that improve employees' ability to meet job requirements and customer and client demands (Noe, Hollenbeck, Gerhart, and Wright, 2010). These opportunities make work meaningful because they provide pathways for employee growth and fulfillment, prepare employees for greater job challenge, and expose employees to alternative roles that have potentially greater fit with their preferred self-images (Bakker, van Emmerik, and Euwema, 2006; Kahn, 1990). Opportunities for development were strongly positively associated with engagement in a large sample of Royal Dutch constabulary officers (Bakker et al., 2006). Training proved to be a key organizational resource that was positively associated with employee engagement across 114 hotel and restaurant units (Salanova, Agut, and Peiró, 2005). In a weekly diary study of educators, teachers that perceived they had regular opportunities for development reported enhanced levels of engagement (Bakker and Bal, 2010). Opportunities for development have also been positively associated with engagement in samples of managers (Rothmann and Joubert, 2007), physicians (Hornung, Rousseau, Glaser, Angerer, and Weigl, 2010), public sector workers (Williams, Wissing, Rothmann, and Temane, 2009), soldiers (Chambel and Oliveira-Cruz, 2010), and employees from a diverse array of organizations in Spain and Mexico (Lisbona, Morales, and Palací, 2009). Crawford et al. (2010) estimated the relationship between opportunities for development and engagement to be .47 based on a combined sample of nearly 5,000 employees across six studies. These findings support the idea that providing employees with dedicated training and development is a key way to enhance their engagement.

Rewards and recognition   Rewards and recognition refer to the formal pay and benefits received as compensation associated with a job, as well as the informal praise and appreciation given by supervisors, coworkers, and customers approving of one's work. Rewards and recognition should promote meaningfulness because they represent both direct and indirect returns on the personal investment of time and energy in one's work role (Kahn, 1990). However, in terms of empirical relationships with engagement, results are more mixed. For example, (Bakker et al., 2006) found that financial rewards were actually negatively related to perceptions of engagement, although satisfaction with fringe benefits was positively related to engagement. In contrast, Jackson, Rothmann, and Van de Vijver (2006) found that financial rewards were positively related to reported levels of engagement for a large sample of educators in South Africa. Similarly, Saks (2006) found that rewards and recognition as combined perceptions of pay, promotions, praise from supervisors, and public recognition were positively related to engagement. Bakker et al. (2007) found that informal appreciation from coworkers was significantly positively related to engagement in sample of teachers in Finland. Material benefits comprising financial rewards and public prestige of the profession were positively related to engagement for dentists (Gorter et al., 2008). Crawford et al. (2010) estimated the relationship between rewards and recognition and engagement to be .21. However, the credibility interval for this relationship included zero. In other words, among the population of correlations between rewards and engagement, while it is most likely that researchers observe significant positive relationships, it is also possible for researchers to observe significant negative relationships. This notion is consistent with research suggesting that extrinsic rewards may be damaging to intrinsic motivation (Ryan and Deci, 2000). While it appears that in most cases rewards and recognition are beneficial for engagement, further research examining the conditions under which they are detrimental would be informative.

Summary   The first key driver of engagement is employees' experienced psychological meaningfulness, or the sense of receiving a return on investment of the self in work role performances. Among the antecedent factors conceptually linked to meaningfulness, extensive research confirms that a simple way for employees to experience this return on personal investment is to be given more autonomy. In addition, ensuring greater employee fit with work roles and providing greater variety in the activities and skills comprising those roles are also powerful ways for employees to feel a return on their personal investment. Increasing job challenges and receiving greater feedback also help encourage employees to invest themselves more deeply into their work roles. Interestingly, among these factors, formal pay is not necessarily a strong contributor to employees' willingness to invest their energy into work role performances. This is consistent with research showing that satisfaction with pay is one of the weakest correlates of overall job satisfaction, while satisfaction with the work itself is one of the strongest (Ironson, Brannick, Smith, Gibson, and Paul, 1989; Russell et al., 2004). What is striking among these results is the reality that many job design changes that would increase employee engagement, such as giving employees greater autonomy, increasing variety, or providing more regular feedback, are quite simple and could be made at relatively little or no cost. This should be encouraging to managers and practitioners having to operate in today's business environment of tight competition and resource constraints.

Psychological safety antecedents

The experience of psychological safety refers to a sense of being able to invest oneself in work role performances without fear of negative consequences to self-image, status, or career (Kahn, 1990, p. 708). Individuals feel safe when work situations are trustworthy, secure, predictable, and clear in terms of behavioral consequences, while they feel unsafe in situations that are inconsistent, unpredictable, or threatening such that it is deemed too risky to invest themselves in work role performances. Kahn found that the key factors promoting psychological safety include interpersonal relationships that offer support, trust, openness, and flexibility; leadership styles and processes that show support, resiliency, consistency, and trust; group and intergroup dynamics that minimize divisions in the distribution of authority and power among subgroups; and organizational climates and norms that facilitate clear and shared expectations of member behaviors. Constructs we have found that theoretically correspond to Kahn's conceptualization of psychological safety and its social system influences include social support, transformational leadership, leader-member exchange, workplace climate, organizational justice, and job security. These factors are associated with increased engagement because they contribute to more supportive, predictable, and non-threatening situations in which individuals perceive they can try and perhaps fail without fearing negative consequences (Kahn, 1990). To the extent that individuals perceive these elements of their work social systems as providing protective guarantees for their self-investments, they should become more willing to take the risks involved in more completely engaging in their work roles.

Social support   Social support refers to employees' perceptions concerning the degree to which the organization values their contributions and cares about their well-being (Eisenberger, Huntington, Hutchison, and Sowa, 1986). These perceptions develop through interactions with the organization, supervisors, and coworkers. Support perceptions foster increased safety because it gives employees the flexibility to take risks and perhaps fail without fearing negative consequences (Kahn, 1990). It also fosters in employees a felt obligation to care about the organization's welfare and help the organization reach its objectives (Rhoades, Eisenberger, and Armeli, 2001). Social support from supervisors and coworkers has been positively linked to engagement in dozens of studies. In fact, after autonomy, social support has been the next most frequently studied engagement antecedent. For example, across four independent samples, Schaufeli and Bakker (2004) found that social support was consistently positively related to engagement. Saks (2006) also found that social support was a strong predictor of engagement in a sample of employees working in a variety of organizations. In a study of neonatal intensive care units, Nembhard and Edmondson (2006) found that units whose supervisors actively invited and appreciated employees' contributions reported increased levels of employee engagement. The meta-analytic estimates of the relationship between social support and engagement provided by Crawford et al. (2010) of .33 (33 studies; combined sample of over 17,000 individuals) and Christian et al. (2011) of .32 (38 studies; combined sample of over 18,000 individuals) provide definitive empirical evidence that social support is indeed a key factor associated with enhanced levels of employee engagement.

Transformational leadership   Transformational leaders motivate followers to transcend immediate self-interests to work for goals that benefit the group, organization, or country (Bass, 1997). They motivate followers to achieve more than what was originally expected as followers strive for higher order outcomes (Burns, 1978). Though Kahn (1990) did not explicitly consider transformational leadership, he theorized that supportive, resilient, and clarifying leadership promotes psychological safety because it enhances supportiveness and openness to new ideas. Through the use of inspirational motivation and intellectual stimulation, transformational leaders encourage followers to re-examine assumptions, look at problems in new ways, and think innovatively to challenge traditional ways of doing things (Sosik, 2006; Zhu, Avolio, and Walumbwa, 2009). Through individualized consideration, transformational leaders look for the unique potential in each follower and spend time listening and teaching to encourage the follower to reach that potential (Sosik, 2006). Through idealized influence, transformational leaders model high levels of moral and ethical standards showing that what is right and good to do is important (Bass, 1997; Sosik, 2006). These factors combine to heighten psychological safety as employees are encouraged to try new things and think differently rather than fearing that they may be punished or reprimanded for doing so.

The relatively few empirical examinations of the relationship between transformational leadership and engagement support this theorizing. Zhu et al. (2009) found that senior managers' perceptions of top executives' transformational leadership had a strong positive relationship with their own reported levels of engagement as measured by the Gallup Workplace Audit (GWA; Harter et al., 2002). Transformational leadership exhibited a strong positive relationship with reported levels of engagement for telecommunications employees in China (Aryee, Walumbwa, Zhou, and Hartnell, 2012). Babcock-Roberson and Strickland (2010) reported a strong positive relationship between the idealized influence component of transformational leadership and engagement. Moss and colleagues have also reported positive relationships between various dimensions of transformational leadership and engagement (Moss, 2009; Whitford and Moss, 2009). Most recently, employees' day-to-day perceptions of transformational leadership were positively associated with their daily reported levels of engagement (Tims, Bakker, and Xanthopoulou, 2011). Christian et al. (2011) estimated the relationship of transformational leadership to be .27 based on four studies and a combined sample of 777 individuals. This initial research shows promise for the notion that transformational leaders have leverage in influencing levels of employee engagement. However, more research on the extent and ways in which this occurs is warranted. Leadership is discussed further in Chapter 8 of this volume.

Leader–member exchange   Leader–member exchange (LMX) refers to the differentiated quality of relationships between leaders and their followers based on the effort, resources, and support exchanged between the two parties (Graen and Uhl-Bien, 1995; Nahrgang, Morgeson, and Ilies, 2009). High-quality LMX relationships are characterized by high degrees of interaction, trust, and support; low-quality LMX relationships are characterized by low degrees of interaction, trust, and support (Dienesch and Liden, 1986). High-quality LMX promotes psychological safety precisely because it embodies the supportive, connected, and trusting relationships individuals need to bring their full selves into role performances without fear of negative consequences (Kahn, 1990). Similar to transformational leadership, studies of LMX and engagement have been few in number but supportive of a positive relationship. Xanthopoulou and colleagues found positive relationships between LMX and engagement in samples of electronics and fast food company workers (Xanthopoulou et al., 2007; Xanthopoulou, Bakker, Demerouti, and Schaufeli, 2009b). Bakker and colleagues found similar positive relationships for teachers and call center employees (Bakker and Bal, 2010; Bakker et al., 2003). LMX has also been positively associated with engagement in samples of physicians (Hornung et al., 2010) and Chinese telecommunication company employees (Aryee et al., 2012). Christian et al. (2011) estimated the relationship between LMX and engagement to be .31 based on four studies with a combined sample of nearly 4,700 employees. Clearly more work needs to be done exploring the relationship between LMX and engagement, but existing results confirm that as a leader and follower develop a high-quality relationship of mutual trust and support, followers are more likely to exhibit increased engagement.

Workplace climate   Workplace climate broadly refers to employees' perceptions of their work environment comprised of social, organizational, and situational elements

(Glick, 1985). Frequently its dimensions reference a particular criterion of interest such as climates for safety, service, achievement, quality, and innovation (Schneider and Reichers, 1983). Workplace climates enhance psychological safety because they make clear the organizational norms and expectations for desired employee behavior (Kahn, 1990). This makes situations more predictable and consistent, as climates help people understand the boundaries and consequences for what behavior is allowed and disallowed (Kahn, 1990). Salanova et al. (2005) found that service climates were positively linked to engagement levels in hotel and restaurant business units. Climates of support and encouragement exhibited positive associations with engagement in samples of teachers (Bakker et al., 2007), dentists (Gorter et al., 2008), fast-food workers (Xanthopoulou et al., 2009b), and employed breast cancer survivors (Hakanen and Lindbohm, 2008). Hakanen and colleagues' research with samples of dentists (Hakanen et al., 2005; Hakanen, Perhoniemi, et al., 2008) and teachers (Hakanen et al., 2006) illustrate that engagement is also positively associated with climates for innovation. Crawford et al. (2010) offered a meta-analytic estimate of the relationship between workplace climates and engagement of .28 based on 13 studies and a combined sample of over 10,000 individuals. This evidence reveals that organizations can enhance employee engagement by developing healthy organizational climates.

Organizational justice   Organizational justice refers to perceptions about the fairness of outcome distributions and allocations, fairness of the procedures used to determine the outcome distributions or allocations, fairness of treatment people receive when procedures are implemented, and fairness of the explanations people receive about why procedures were used in a certain way or outcomes where distributed as they were (Colquitt, Conlon, Wesson, Porter, and Ng, 2001). Justice perceptions enhance psychological safety by increasing equity and minimizing concerns over the distribution of power, resources, and authority (Kahn, 1990). Surprisingly, very few studies have examined justice perceptions and engagement, though the few that have find support for this line of thinking. Saks (2006) found that both distributive and procedural justice perceptions were positively linked to engagement. Inoue et al. (2010) found that procedural and interactional justice perceptions were positively associated with engagement. Finally, Siltaloppi, Kinnunen, and Feldt (2009) found that interactional justice perceptions were positively associated with engagement. Clearly more research is needed in this area. However, initial results indicate that increasing organizational justice can enhance employee engagement.

Job security   Job security refers to the relative certainty employees have that they will be able to remain in their positions or with their organizations for the foreseeable future (Sverke, Hellgren, and Naswall, 2002). Job security fosters psychological safety because it forms a foundation underlying perceptions that work situations are predictable and non-threatening (Kahn, 1990). Empirical investigations have usually incorporated job security by studying the relations of its inverse – job insecurity – with engagement. For example, Mauno and colleagues found that job insecurity was negatively related to reported levels of engagement in two separate samples of health care personnel (Mauno, Kinnunen, Mäkikangas, and Nätti, 2005; Mauno, Kinnunen, and Ruokolainen, 2007). Vander Elst, Baillien, De Cuyper, and De Witte (2010) found that job insecurity was negatively related to engagement in a diverse sample drawn from 20 organizations representing service, industrial, and public sectors. Rothmann and Joubert (2007) found that job security (measured positively) exhibited a positive relationship with engagement for mining managers. Once again, although this factor has been the subject of limited research, taken together these results suggest that employees' expectations regarding their security in their jobs and organizations is a source of predictability that can enhance their levels of engagement.

Summary   The second key driver of engagement, psychological safety or the sense of being able to invest oneself without fear of negative consequences, expands the considerations of factors beyond the specific job itself to the organizational system in which the employee works. Among these factors, the most extensive research confirms that employees experience this safety when they are embedded in systems of strong support. As for the other factors, only limited research has been conducted, but results thus far indicate that employees' leaders have significant influence either through their transformational behaviors or their personal relationships they form with employees. Also, organization-wide perceptions of a healthy and fair climate ensure employees feel safer to engage themselves. Finally, efforts to ensure some degree of job security in this fast-paced and dynamically changing business environment can enhance psychological safety, and in turn, engagement as well.

From a research perspective, clearly more work can be done examining psychological safety conditions and their organizational system components. For example, while research has examined how the quality of the LMX relationship affects employees' engagement, less explored is how being involved in high- or low-quality LMX relationships affects the supervisor's engagement. Further, how might a supervisor's engagement or the collective engagement of the supervisor's unit be affected if there is a high degree of LMX differentiation – that is, that the supervisor has high variability in the quality of relationships from very high quality to very low quality within the same unit? Does having a select group of 'favorites' affect the supervisor and unit engagement relative to having more uniformly spread high-quality relationships? Additional research into these questions would be welcome.

From a practical perspective, although organizational development efforts to bring about system-wide changes may be daunting, a starting point might be to focus on the organization's agents – its leaders and supervisors – as individuals often view actions by agents of the organization as indications of the organization's intent rather than solely as actions of a particular individual (Levinson, 1965; Rhoades et al., 2001). Organizations may find that simple efforts to increase the incidence of transformational leadership behavior among leaders and supervisors may bring about many of the positive system changes that enhance employee engagement. For example, results from a field experiment of bank branch managers showed that randomly selected managers who participated in transformational leadership training exhibited significantly higher levels of transformational leadership behavior relative to those who received no training. Additionally, subordinates of those leaders exhibited increased commitment and higher performance as a result (Barling, Weber, and Kelloway, 1996). This suggests that transformational leadership can be learned, and that efforts to train transformational leaders can result in increased subordinate engagement and performance as well.

Psychological availability antecedents

The experience of psychological availability refers to individuals' sensing that they are ready to personally engage at a particular moment (Kahn, 1990, p. 714). Individuals who are available feel they are capable and prepared to invest their physical cognitive, and emotional resources into role performances, while individuals who are unavailable either lack these energies or are distracted or preoccupied from investing them in work role performances.

Kahn observed that the key factors influencing psychological availability include workplace distractions and issues in people's outside lives that have the potential to take them psychologically away from their role performances; existing levels of physical, emotional, and cognitive energies remaining for investment into role performances; and individuals' levels of self-confidence and personal security in their own abilities to invest themselves fully into work role performances. Constructs we have found that theoretically correspond to psychological availability and these personal influences include role overload, work-role conflict, family–work conflict, resource inadequacies, time urgency, off-work recovery, individual dispositions, and personal resources. On the one hand, elements representing distractions and negative self-perceptions are associated with decreased engagement because they tend to preoccupy and consume people's resources, leaving them with little space, energy, or desire to employ themselves otherwise in moments of task performance (Kahn, 1990). On the other hand, elements representing distraction reduction and positive self-perceptions are associated with increased engagement because they allow individuals to feel free and capable of driving their personal energy into role performances. When individuals believe, based on their self-assessments and individual distractions, that they possess the personal energies necessary to fulfill the obligations of their work roles, they are more likely able and willing to invest those energies in the service of their work role performances.

Role overload   Role overload occurs when employees have too much work to do in the time available for its completion (Beehr, Walsh, and Taber, 1976). Although a challenging workload has potential to raise expectations and enhance work meaningfulness as we have previously argued, there comes a point where work demands can overwhelm individuals' capacity and trigger negative emotions (e.g. fear, anxiety, anger) that make them feel unable to adequately deal with these demands (Crawford et al., 2010; Lazarus and Folkman, 1984). This makes them feel less capable of having the physical, cognitive, and emotional energy available to invest in their role performances (Kahn, 1990). Empirical research provides support for this reasoning. For example, Britt, Thomas, and Dawson (2006) found that Reserved Officer Training Corps (ROTC) cadets who felt their skill level was overwhelmed by the level of their task demands reported significantly decreased levels of engagement. Similarly, Bakker et al. (2006) found that constabulary officers who believed their tasks were too complex given their level of skill and education were also more likely to report decreased engagement. Both Hakanen et al. (2006) and Lorente et al. (2008) found that teachers reported decreased engagement when they felt constantly overwhelmed by unfinished work tasks. Finally, in a heterogeneous sample of both blue and white collar workers, Korunka, Kubicek, Schaufeli, and Hoonakker (2009) found that workers who felt overloaded also reported decreased levels of engagement. Crawford et al. (2010) estimated the relationship between role overload and engagement to be –.20 based on five studies and a combined sample of over 6,000 individuals. Thus, while a challenging workload can be beneficial for employee engagement, evidence suggests that workloads that overwhelm the capacity of the individual to deal with them become detrimental.

Work-role conflict   One type of conflict that can harm individuals' psychological availability is work-role conflict, which occurs when employee behaviors expected by superiors, coworkers, or clients are inconsistent (Rizzo, House, and Lirtzman, 1970). Role conflict damages psychological availability because it leads employees to believe that they cannot simultaneously satisfy conflicting demands with any amount of effort (Kahn, 1990; LePine et al., 2005). In line with this thinking, Hallberg and Schaufeli (2006) found that employees that reported receiving incompatible requests from two or more people at work exhibited sharply lower levels of engagement. Similarly, Lorente et al. (2008) found that teachers who felt that their work was acceptable to some but not to others also reported decreased levels of engagement. Hakanen and colleagues' work with samples of dentists has shown that having to cope with conflicting demands of maintaining a comfortable and relaxed atmosphere for patients while simultaneously having to inflict pain to deliver treatment can have a dampening effect on their engagement (Hakanen et al., 2005; Hakanen, Schaufeli, et al., 2008). Crawford et al. (2010) estimated the relationship between role conflict and engagement to be –.24 based on 12 studies and a combined sample of over 3,600 individuals. These findings confirm that if organizations wish to avoid damaging employee engagement, one way they can do so is to minimize work-role conflicts.

Family–work conflict   Another type of conflict that harms individuals' psychological availability is family–work conflict that occurs when the role pressures from the work and family domains are mutually incompatible in some respect (Greenhaus and Beutell, 1985). Although researchers have made a distinction between family–work conflict in which the demands, time, and strain involved with family roles interfere with performing work related responsibilities; and work–family conflict in which the demands, time, and strain created by the job interfere with performing family related responsibilities (Netemeyer, Boles, and McMurrian, 1996), for simplicity's sake in this chapter we do not maintain the distinction. Family–work conflict should reduce psychological availability because conflicting events in work and non-work lives distract employees to the point that they have reduced energy to invest in role performances (Kahn, 1990). Studies investigating this reasoning, however, have provided mixed results. For example, although several researchers have found evidence of significant negative associations between family–work conflict and engagement (Mauno et al., 2007; May et al., 2004; Peeters, Wattez, Demerouti, and de Regt, 2009), others have failed to find evidence of a significant relationship (Little, Simmons, and Nelson, 2007; Montgomery, Peeters, Schaufeli, and Den Ouden, 2003; Simbula, 2010; Vansteenkiste et al., 2007). Additionally, in one study engagement exhibited strong positive relationships with family–work conflict (Halbesleben, Harvey, and Bolino, 2009), leading these researchers to suggest that perhaps the causal ordering of these two variables should be reversed. That is, they suggested that employees who are too highly engaged in their work may be creating their own source of interference with their ability to function in their family roles. These conflicting findings point to the need for additional research to clarify these relationships before significant conclusions can be reached on how family–work conflict can be managed to enhance engagement.

Resource inadequacies   Resource inadequacies refer to situations where work tasks are made harder because of problems caused by missing or defective equipment or by missing or outdated information (Sonnentag, 2003; Zapf, 1993). Resource inadequacies decrease psychological availability because they sap physical and emotional energy that could otherwise be used for productive self-investment in work role performances (Kahn, 1990). Consistent with this notion, several studies have shown that working in unfavorable or difficult physical environments that place undue physical strain on the body is associated with decreased levels of engagement (Bakker et al., 2006; Britt and Bliese, 2003; Hakanen et al., 2005; Hakanen et al., 2006; Hakanen, Schaufeli, et al., 2008). Sonnentag (2003) found that situational constraints involving a lack of appropriate information or materials to do the job were negatively associated with engagement in a sample of public service workers. Bakker et al. (2003) found that customer service employees working in a call center that experienced significant computer problems and malfunctions also reported decreased levels of engagement. Rothmann and colleagues' research on police service and emergency response personnel showed that resource inadequacies such as a lack of officers to handle specific tasks or inadequate and poor quality equipment were associated with decreased engagement (Mostert and Rothmann, 2006; Naudé and Rothmann, 2006). Crawford et al. (2010) estimated the relationship between engagement and resource inadequacies to be $-.18$ based on 11 studies and a combined sample of nearly 12,000 individuals. Taken together, these results indicate that organizations can eliminate one of the distractions limiting employees' engagement by ensuring they have resources sufficient to do their jobs.

Time urgency   Time urgency refers to the processing speed required for employees to complete work tasks (Zapf, 1993). Pressure to complete tasks within a given time frame taxes employees' energy and capabilities (Zapf, 1993), but it also focuses their attention and effort such that by coping with this demand they can experience a sense of personal accomplishment (LePine et al., 2005). Time urgency can increase people's psychological availability because it helps to eliminate distractions that would otherwise occupy their time and attention (Kahn, 1990). Empirical evidence supports this reasoning that time urgency at work is associated both with increased engagement as well as increased strain. For example, Beckers et al. (2004) found that having to work very fast exhibited significant positive relationships with engagement as well as with fatigue. This finding was later replicated as both Bakker et al. (2006) and Schaufeli, Taris, and van Rhenen (2008) found that having to work very fast had significant positive relationships with engagement as well as exhaustion. Though they did not examine strain, Mauno et al. (2007) did find that time urgency was positively related to engagement. Other studies have failed to replicate this result, however, finding weak or insignificant relationships between time urgency and work engagement (Sonnentag, 2003; Sonnentag, Mojza, Binnewies, and Scholl, 2008). Meta-analytic estimates, which account for lack of significant results due to sampling error, are helpful to clarify these results. Crawford et al. (2010) estimated the relationship between time urgency and engagement to be .21 based on nine studies with a combined sample of over 6,500 individuals. Importantly, the credibility interval for this estimate excludes zero, indicating that most observed relationships in studies of time urgency and engagement should be positive. However, caution should be applied before organizations raise time pressure simply for the sake of increasing engagement given that time pressure is also associated with increased exhaustion and fatigue. This suggests that organizations may have to identify additional resources that can be made available to employees to cope with the strains involved with increased time urgency (Crawford et al., 2010).

Off-work recovery   An intriguing factor predicting engagement at work is employee's ability to disengage when not at work. A stream of research by Sonnentag and colleagues provides increasing support for the notion employees' ability to psychologically detach and recover during off-work periods improves their ability to re-engage at work in subsequent periods (Sonnentag, 2003; Sonnentag, Binnewies, and Mojza, 2010; Sonnentag et al., 2008). This is consistent with Kahn's (1990) reasoning that recharging physical and emotional resources is a prerequisite for feeling psychologically available for work role performances. Research on shift work has shown that employee alertness improves as the number of days since the last shift worked increases (Totterdell, Spelten, Smith, Barton, and Folkard, 1995). The Crawford et al. (2010) meta-analytic estimate for the relationship between off-work recovery and engagement is .29 based on three studies with a combined sample of 350 individuals. Additional findings indicate that off-work recovery may also be just the resource to cope with the strain of time pressure demands discussed above. For example, work by Kinnunen and colleagues indicate that off-work recovery periods for employees that work with time pressure are associated with decreased exhaustion as well as increased engagement (Kinnunen, Mauno, and Siltaloppi, 2010; Siltaloppi et al., 2009). Thus, a benefit of ensuring that employees disengage from work during off-work periods is that it helps ameliorate accumulated fatigue from time urgency at work and it allows them recharge their resources to be ready to re-engage when they return.

Dispositions   In line with Macey and Schneider (2008), we refer to dispositions as personality characteristics or general tendencies to experience affective states over time. In relation to engagement, the most frequently studied dispositions include conscientiousness, and positive and negative affectivity (see also Chapter 2 of this volume). Conscientiousness refers to behavioral tendencies toward achievement striving, dependability, orderliness, duty, and deliberation (Barrick, Mount, and Judge, 2001; McCrae and Costa, 1987). Conscientious individuals are hard-working and tend to stay focused while eliminating distractions from work tasks (Witt, Burke, Barrick, and Mount, 2002). Positive affectivity refers to the dispositional tendency to feel enthusiastic, active, and alert. Positive affect broadens people's momentary thought-action repertoires and builds their physical, cognitive, and emotional resources (Fredrickson, 2001). Negative affectivity refers to the dispositional tendency to feel anger, disgust, guilt, fear, and nervousness (Watson, Clark, and Tellegen, 1988). Negative affect leads to a tightening of mental processes and hinders mobilization of cognitive resources and behavioral options (Bledow, Schmitt, Frese, and Kühnel, 2011). Thus, these dispositions are likely to affect engagement by virtue of their preconditioning the level of psychological availability an individual is likely to experience (Kahn, 1990; Macey and Schneider, 2008).

Findings are generally supportive of this reasoning. In three separate samples Halbesleben et al. (2009) found that conscientiousness exhibited significant positive relationships with engagement. Conscientiousness was also positively related to engagement in samples of police personnel (Mostert and Rothmann, 2006) and sandwich shop employees (Kim, Shin, and Swanger, 2009). Christian et al. (2011) estimated the relationship between conscientiousness and engagement to be .42 based on 12 studies with a combined sample of over 5,800 individuals. Several studies have shown simultaneously that positive affect is associated with increased engagement while negative affect is associated with decreased engagement (Balducci, Fraccaroli, and Schaufeli, 2010; Sonnentag et al., 2008; Williams et al., 2009). Several other studies examining negative affect in isolation have found it is associated with decreased levels of engagement (Halbesleben et al., 2009; Parker, Jimmieson, and Amiot, 2010; Sonnentag et al., 2010). Christian et al. (2011) estimated the relationship between positive affect and engagement to be .43 based on 14 studies with a combined sample of over 6,700 individuals. No published meta-analytic estimate is available for negative affect. In sum, these results suggest that one way organizations can increase engagement is to select individuals with dispositional tendencies towards conscientiousness and positive affectivity. Furthermore, the extent to which individuals can be induced to experience positive moods at work may also improve engagement levels, though more research is still needed to understand the intricacies of such a process.

Personal resources   Personal resources are aspects of the self that are generally linked to resiliency and refer to individuals' own sense of ability to control and impact their environment successfully (Hobfoll, Johnson, Ennis, and Jackson, 2003; Xanthopoulou et al., 2007). The personal resources most frequently studied in relation to engagement have been general self-efficacy, organization-based self-esteem, and optimism. General self-efficacy refers to a person's belief in their own competence to respond effectively across a wide variety of achievement situations (Chen, Gully, and Eden, 2001). It fosters greater availability because it directly affects people's sense of confidence and security that they have the abilities necessary to successfully negotiate their work role performances (Kahn, 1990). Organization-based self-esteem is the degree to which members believe they can satisfy their needs by participating in roles within the context of an organization (Pierce, Gardner, Cummings, and Dunham, 1989). It enhances availability because it increases people's certainty regarding their desires to be a part of their organizational systems and contribute to its end goals (Kahn, 1990). Optimism refers to people's general tendency to believe that things will go their way and good things will happen to them in life (Scheier and Carver, 1985). It improves availability because it helps people feel secure concerning their selves and their work status, reduces anxiety, and frees up energy that would otherwise be preoccupied from being invested in personal engagement (Kahn, 1990).

Empirical studies examining personal resources and engagement have generally found that they are positively related. For example, Mauno et al. (2007) found that health care personnel with high levels of organization-based self-esteem reported elevated levels of engagement in a follow-up survey two years later. Hakanen and Lindbohm (2008) found that optimism was a key factor in predicting increased engagement among currently employed cancer survivors. Both general self-efficacy and optimism were significant predictors of increased engagement among Dutch public and private employees (van den Heuvel, Demerouti, Schreurs, Bakker, and Schaufeli, 2009). Xanthoupoulou and colleagues have found all three types of personal resources to have strong positive relationships with engagement in samples of electronics company employees (Xanthopoulou et al., 2007; Xanthopoulou, Bakker, Demerouti, and Schaufeli, 2009a), flight attendants (Xanthopoulou, Bakker, Heuven, Demerouti, and Schaufeli, 2008), and fast-food workers (Xanthopoulou et al., 2009b). Although no published meta-analytic estimate for the relationship between personal resources and engagement is available, these findings clearly indicate that employees with greater reserves of personal resources are likely to exhibit higher levels of engagement.

Summary   The third key driver of engagement, psychological availability or the sense that one is ready to personally engage at a particular moment, looks inward from the organizational or job to peoples' experiences of themselves within these systems. Among the studies we have reviewed, we find that individuals' reservoirs of personal resources in the form of general self-efficacy, organization-based self-esteem, and optimism, and personal dispositions in the form of conscientiousness, positive affectivity, and negative affectivity have strong influence over their personal readiness to engage. We find that time urgency acts as a catalyst for encouraging individuals to apply their resources in focused, dedicated work periods. However, individuals are not machines that can endlessly apply their energy, and once exhausted, they require periods of off-work psychological detachment to rest and recharge. Indeed we find that individuals who are overwhelmed or overloaded begin to lose capacity to engage. Resource inadequacies as well as conflicts between work roles or between work and home domains complicate individuals' readiness to engage with most results suggesting these conflicts are detrimental. Additional primary studies or meta-analyses that help to clarify family–work conflict and engagement relationships and the moderating conditions under which the relationship is negative, positive, or non-existent would be welcome. Also meta-analyses summarizing the relationships of various types of personal resources and relationships with engagement would be useful. From a practical perspective, organizations may find they can leverage engagement levels by paying attention to individual differences such as conscientiousness during selection, and by adopting scheduling practices that account for the flexibility and detachment employees may need to accommodate working in fast-paced or high-pressure environments.

Inter-relationships of antecedent factors

Up to this point, we have highlighted the relationships between engagement and its most often-studied antecedent factors that could be organized under one of three psychological conditions – meaningfulness, safety, and availability. In doing so, we have generally focused on bivariate relationships to the exclusion of examining relationships with engagement when these antecedent factors are included together as predictors. Returning for a moment to Kahn's original theory, he stated that '[t]he extent to which individuals experience the three conditions, taken together, influences how psychologically present (and behaviorally engaged) they are in particular work situations' (1992, p. 340). Thus, according to Kahn's theory, antecedents that fall under each of the three psychological conditions should have a unique relationship with engagement, even when considered together. He was less explicit, however, regarding the exact nature of how the three psychological conditions combine to influence moments of personal engagement, suggesting that they may combine additively or even interactively. Below we consider each of these two ways of understanding the inter-relationships among antecedent factors – first by understanding their unique influences when investigated together, and second, by considering the synergistic, buffering, or more general interactive effects of these antecedents.

Unique influences   In one of the first studies to investigate the unique roles of various drivers of engagement, May et al. (2004) found that, when included together, psychological meaningfulness, safety, and availability were significant independent predictors of engagement. When they considered a more distal set of antecedent factors to predict engagement, they found similar results, with proxies of meaningfulness (job challenge and work role fit), along with proxies of safety (climate) and availability (self-consciousness) having strong significant relationships with engagement. Similarly, Xanthopoulou et al. (2009a) found that when two antecedent factors were considered together – namely, job resources (measured as a mix of psychological meaningfulness and safety factors) and personal resources (measured with availability factors of self-efficacy, organization-based self-esteem, and optimism) – each had unique and equally strong relationships with engagement.

This general pattern where multiple antecedent factors included together still have strong unique relationships with engagement has continued to hold as more research accumulates. Siltaloppi et al. (2009) found that autonomy (meaningfulness), organizational justice (safety), and recovery (availability), each uniquely related to engagement in sample of 484 participants across five organizations. Similarly, Rich et al. (2010) found that value congruence (meaningfulness), perceived organizational support (safety), and core self-evaluations (availability), each uniquely influenced job engagement in a sample of fire-fighters. In the most extensive examination of these unique effects to date, Christian et al. (2011) conducted a meta-analytic path analysis to simultaneously estimate the influence of several antecedent variables on engagement. When considered together, they found that task variety and significance (meaningfulness), transformational leadership (safety), as well as conscientiousness and positive affect (availability), each uniquely influenced work engagement. In sum, the limited amount of evidence accumulated to date supports Kahn's original theorizing that, when taken together, antecedent factors that mirror these three psychological conditions appear to collectively, and uniquely, drive engagement.

Interactive influences A few scholars have begun to explore the notion that these three conditions may actually interact, and therefore influence experiences of engagement in a nonlinear manner, which is quite different than what would be expected under a more basic additive approach. Hakanen et al. (2005) found evidence of an important interaction between meaningfulness and availability factors in a sample of nearly 2,000 dentists randomly split into two groups for analysis. In this study, both beneficiary contact (an antecedent factor that impacts meaningfulness; Grant, 2012) and task variety (also a meaningfulness factor) buffered the effects of work–role conflict (an availability factor) on engagement, such that the relationship between role conflict and engagement was less negative when beneficiary contact or task variety were high. Beneficiary contact also appeared to buffer the negative effect of resource inadequacies (another availability factor) on engagement. While this study also found significant interactions between safety factors (e.g. social support and climate) and availability factors (e.g. role conflict and resource inadequacies), these were not replicated across the two groups of dentists, and as such, should be interpreted with caution.

Zhu et al. (2009) identified a synergistic relationship between transformational leadership (safety) and follower characteristics (an availability factor self-reported by followers as having more general positive attributes), such that when these follower characteristics were high, the positive relationship between transformational leadership and engagement was stronger. Kinnunen et al. (2010) found a similar interactive relationship with distinctly different predictors. They found that off-work recovery (availability) significantly weakened the negative relationship between job insecurity (safety) and engagement. It is interesting to note here that we were unable to find any studies that had looked at an interactive relationship between meaningfulness and safety factors. It seems that, up to this point, availability factors have been the key focus in theorizing about nonlinear relationships among engagement antecedents. This is one area in need of additional theory and research in order to more clearly understand the full magnitude of the potential influence that these three types of antecedent factors have on driving engagement.

Antecedents spanning multiple conditions We acknowledge that certain variables discussed above may actually directly influence more than one of the psychological conditions. For example, we have up to this point suggested that transformational leadership is a driver of psychological safety. This categorization was guided by Kahn's (1990) theory that argued that supervisor behaviors are a key determinant of psychological safety. However, it is likely that transformational leaders could directly influence all three psychological conditions. Regarding psychological meaningfulness, some have argued explicitly that transformational leaders give meaningfulness to work by infusing work and organizations with moral purpose and commitment (Shamir, House, and Arthur, 1993). Similarly, transformational leaders that communicate high performance expectations and confidence in their followers' knowledge, skills and abilities, will, in turn, enhance the degree to which their followers believe they have the resources necessary to accomplish their tasks (Walumbwa, Avolio, and Zhu, 2008). Zhu et al. (2009) argued that transformational leaders would influence work engagement through all three psychological conditions but did not include those variables in the empirical study. Future studies examining the ways in which antecedents such as transformational leadership simultaneously influence multiple psychological conditions are warranted.

Case study: Employee engagement at Shands Healthcare

Shands HealthCare is the teaching hospital of the University of Florida College of Medicine. Employing over 1,500 physicians, 12,000 staff members and more than 1,000 volunteers, Shands has developed a reputation for quality care and service in more than 100 specialty and subspecialty medical areas including cancer, heart care, neuromedicine, women and children's services, and transplant services. Shands is a leader in the health care industry, embracing an innovative multidisciplinary team approach to patient care customized to each patient's needs through diagnosis, treatment and recovery. The Human Resource Department at Shands recognizes that their employees are their greatest asset and therefore the development and measurement of employee engagement is one of the organization's top priorities.

To assess levels of employee engagement, Shands conducts annual employee surveys that measure attitudes and perceptions of its staff. Recent survey results indicated that employees who felt that they were supported by management and had cooperative and trusting interpersonal relationships with other employees in the organization had higher levels of engagement. Additionally, employees who perceived that their personal goals and values were in alignment with those of the organisation were also more likely to report higher levels of engagement. Furthermore, those employees who felt they were capable of handling their workload reported higher levels of engagement.

As a result of these findings senior human resource managers and other managers across the business divisions decided to conduct interviews and focus groups with employees to ascertain where these drivers could be leveraged to improve overall employee engagement. Based on these interviews and focus groups the following factors were identified as impacting engagement including:

- Interpersonal challenges faced by employees working in a large diverse organization.
- Uncertainty about the organization's core values or what was expected of employees.
- Demands of working in a high-pressure and fast-paced environment.
- Working relationships between physicians and staff were not optimal, and at times strained.
- Poor communication between departments slowed interactions and processes.
- The hospital staff placed great value on continuous quality improvement efforts.
- The organization's necessity of promoting a collaborative work environment.

Based on these findings, management developed a multifaceted action plan to address these issues. Included in this plan were onboarding initiatives in the form of employee mentoring and socialization programs that would communicate organizational values and introduce employees to their roles and responsibilities within this network. Programming was also created to teach employees about conflict resolution, teamwork, interpersonal skills development and leadership. The performance management system was enhanced to provide developmental feedback and recognition to its employees. Departmental staffing levels were also reviewed to ensure that adequate personnel were in place.

Through these efforts Shands was able to increase the level of value alignment between its employees and the organization while also developing a supportive, collaborative, and trusting culture where its employees were able to meet the demands of their job. Recognizing the importance of employee engagement, Shands continues to monitor its success to ensure that its human resource practices are aligned with the mission and values of the organization.

References

Aryee, S., Walumbwa, F. O., Zhou, Q., and Hartnell, C. A. (2012). Transformational leadership, innovative behavior, and task performance: Test of mediation and moderation processes. *Human Performance*, 25, 1–25.

Babcock-Roberson, M. E., and Strickland, O. J. (2010). The relationship between charismatic leadership, work engagement, and organizational citizenship behaviors. *Journal of Psychology*, 144, 313–26.

Bakker, A. B., and Bal, P. M. (2010). Weekly work engagement and performance: A study among starting teachers. *Journal of Occupational and Organizational Psychology*, 83, 189–206.

Bakker, A. B., and Demerouti, E. (2008). Towards a model of work engagement. *Career Development International*, 13, 209–23.

Bakker, A. B., Demerouti, E., and Schaufeli, W. B. (2003). Dual processes at work in a call centre: An application of the job demands–resources model. *European Journal of Work and Organizational Psychology*, 12, 393–417.

Bakker, A. B., Demerouti, E., and Schaufeli, W. B. (2005). The crossover of burnout and work engagement among working couples. *Human Relations*, 58, 661–89.

Bakker, A. B., Hakanen, J. J., Demerouti, E., and Xanthopoulou, D. (2007). Job resources boost work engagement, particularly when job demands are high. *Journal of Educational Psychology*, 99, 274–84.

Bakker, A. B., and Leiter, M. P. (2010). *Work engagement: A handbook of essential theory and research*. New York: Psychology Press.

Bakker, A. B., Schaufeli, W. B., Leiter, M. P., and Taris, T. W. (2008). Work engagement: An emerging concept in occupational health psychology. *Work & Stress*, 22, 187–200.

Bakker, A. B., van Emmerik, H., and Euwema, M. C. (2006). Crossover of burnout and engagement in work teams. *Work & Occupations*, 33, 464–89.

Balducci, C., Fraccaroli, F., and Schaufeli, W. B. (2010). Psychometric properties of the Italian version of the Utrecht Work Engagement Scale (UWES-9): A cross-cultural analysis. *European Journal of Psychological Assessment*, 26, 143–9.

Barling, J., Weber, T., and Kelloway, E. K. (1996). Effects of transformational leadership training on attitudinal and financial outcomes: A field experiment. *Journal of Applied Psychology*, 81, 827–32.

Barrick, M. R., Mount, M. K., and Judge, T. A. (2001). Personality and performance at the beginning of the new millennium: What do we know and where do we go next? *International Journal of Selection and Assessment*, 9, 9–30.

Bass, B. M. (1997). Does the transactional-transformational leadership paradigm transcend organizational and national boundaries? *American Psychologist*, 52, 130–9.

Beckers, D. G. J., van der Linden, D., Smulders, P. G. W., Kompier, M. A. J., van Veldhoven, M. J. P., and van Yperen, N. W. (2004). Working overtime hours: Relations with fatigue, work motivation, and the quality of work. *Journal of Occupational & Environmental Medicine*, 46, 1282–9.

Beehr, T. A., Walsh, J. T., and Taber, T. D. (1976). Relationship of stress to individually and organizationally valued states: Higher order needs as a moderator. *Journal of Applied Psychology*, 61, 41–7.

Bion, W. R. (1961). *Experiences in groups*. New York: Basic Books.

Bledow, R., Schmitt, A., Frese, M., and Kühnel, J. (2011). The affective shift model of work engagement. *Journal of Applied Psychology*, 96, 1246–57.

Britt, T. W. (1999). Engaging the self in the field: Testing the triangle model of responsibility. *Personality and Social Psychology Bulletin*, 25, 696–706.

Britt, T. W. (2003). Aspects of identity predict engagement in work under adverse conditions. *Self & Identity*, 2, 31–45.

Britt, T. W., and Bliese, P. D. (2003). Testing the stress-buffering effects of self engagement among soldiers on a military operation. *Journal of Personality*, 71, 245–66.

Britt, T. W., Castro, C. A., and Adler, A. B. (2005). Self-engagement, stressors, and health: A longitudinal study. *Personality and Social Psychology Bulletin*, 31, 1475–86.

Britt, T. W., Thomas, J. L., and Dawson, C. R. (2006). Self-engagement magnifies the relationship between qualitative overload and performance in a training setting. *Journal of Applied Social Psychology*, 36, 2100–14.

Britt, T. W., Dickinson, J. M., Greene-Shortridge, T. M., and McKibben, E. S. (2007). Self-engagement at work. In D. L. Nelson and C. L. Cooper (eds), *Positive organizational behavior* (pp. 143–58). Thousand Oaks, CA: SAGE Publications.

Burns, J. M. (1978). *Leadership*. New York: Harper & Row.

Cavanaugh, M. A., Boswell, W. R., Roehling, M. V., and Boudreau, J. W. (2000). An empirical examination of self-reported work stress among U.S. Managers. *Journal of Applied Psychology*, 85, 65–74.

Chambel, M. J., and Oliveira-Cruz, F. (2010). Breach of psychological contract and the development of burnout and engagement: A longitudinal study among soldiers on a peacekeeping mission. *Military Psychology*, 22, 110–27.

Chen, G., Gully, S. M., and Eden, D. (2001). Validation of a new general self-efficacy scale. *Organizational Research Methods*, 4, 62–83.

Christian, M. S., Garza, A. S., and Slaughter, J. E. (2011). Work engagement: A quantitative review and test of its relations with task and contextual performance. *Personnel Psychology*, 64, 89–136.

Cohen, D. J. (2007). The very separate worlds of academic and practitioner publications in human resource management: Reasons for the divide and concrete solutions for bridging the gap. *Academy of Management Journal*, 50, 1013–19.

Cole, M. S., Walter, F., Bedeian, A. G., and O'Boyle, E. H. (2012). Job burnout and employee engagement: A meta-analytic examination of construct proliferation. *Journal of Management*, 38, 1550–81.

Colquitt, J. A., Conlon, D. E., Wesson, M. J., Porter, C. O. L. H., and Ng, K. Y. (2001). Justice at the millenium: A meta-analytic review of 25 years of organizational justice research. *Journal of Applied Psychology*, 86, 425–45.

Crawford, E. R., LePine, J. A., and Rich, B. L. (2010). Linking job demands and resources to employee engagement and burnout: A theoretical extension and meta-analytic test. *Journal of Applied Psychology*, 95, 834–48.

Dienesch, R. M., and Liden, R. C. (1986). Leader-member exchange model of leadership: A critique and further development. *Academy of Management Review*, 11, 618–34.

Eden, D. (1990). Pygmalion without interpersonal contrast effects: Whole groups gain from raising manager expectations. *Journal of Applied Psychology*, 75, 394–8.

Eisenberger, R., Huntington, R., Hutchison, S., and Sowa, D. (1986). Perceived organizational support. *Journal of Applied Psychology*, 71, 500–7.

Fredrickson, B. L. (2001). The role of positive emotions in positive psychology – the broaden-and-build theory of positive emotions. *American Psychologist*, 56, 218–26.

Freud, S. (1922). *Group psychology and the analysis of the ego* (vol. 18). London: International Psychoanalytic Press.

Glick, W. H. (1985). Conceptualizing and measuring organizational and psychological climate pitfalls in multilevel research. *Academy of Management Review*, 10, 601–16.

Goffman, E. (1961a). *Asylums*. New York: Doubleday Anchor.

Goffman, E. (1961b). *Encounters: Two studies in the sociology of interaction*. Oxford, England: Bobbs-Merrill.

Gorter, R. C., te Brake, J. H. M., Hoogstraten, J., and Eijkman, M. A. J. (2008). Positive engagement and job resources in dental practice. *Community Dentistry and Oral Epidemiology*, 36, 47–54.

Graen, G. B., and Uhl-Bien, M. (1995). Relationship-based approach to leadership: Development of leader-member exchange (LMX) theory of leadership over 25 years: Applying a multi-level multi-domain perspective. *Leadership Quarterly*, 6, 219–47.

Grant, A. M. (2012). Leading with meaning: Beneficiary contact, prosocial impact, and the performance effects of transformational leadership. *Academy of Management Journal*, 55, 458–76.

Greenhaus, J. H., and Beutell, N. J. (1985). Sources of conflict between work and family roles. *Academy of Management Review*, 10, 76–88.

Hackman, J. R., and Oldham, G. R. (1975). Development of the job diagnostic survey. *Journal of Applied Psychology*, 60, 159–70.

Hackman, J. R., and Oldham, G. R. (1980). *Work redesign*. Reading, MA: Addison-Wesley.

Hakanen, J. J., Bakker, A. B., and Demerouti, E. (2005). How dentists cope with their job demands and stay engaged: The moderating role of job resources. *European Journal of Oral Sciences*, 113, 479–87.

Hakanen, J. J., Bakker, A. B., and Schaufeli, W. B. (2006). Burnout and work engagement among teachers. *Journal of School Psychology*, 43, 495–513.

Hakanen, J. J., and Lindbohm, M.-L. (2008). Work engagement among breast cancer survivors and the referents: The importance of optimism and social resources at work. *Journal of Cancer Survivorship*, 2, 283–95.

Hakanen, J. J., Perhoniemi, R., and Toppinen-Tanner, S. (2008). Positive gain spirals at work: From job resources to work engagement, personal initiative and work-unit innovativeness. *Journal of Vocational Behavior*, 73, 78–91.

Hakanen, J. J., Schaufeli, W. B., and Ahola, K. (2008). The job demands–resources model: A three-year cross-lagged study of burnout, depression, commitment, and work engagement. *Work & Stress*, 22, 224–41.

Halbesleben, J. R. B., Harvey, J., and Bolino, M. C. (2009). Too engaged? A conservation of resources view of the relationship between work engagement and work interference with family. *Journal of Applied Psychology*, 94, 1452–65.

Hallberg, U. E., Johansson, G., and Schaufeli, W. B. (2007). Type a behavior and work situation: Associations with burnout and work engagement. *Scandinavian Journal of Psychology*, 48, 135–42.

Hallberg, U. E., and Schaufeli, W. B. (2006). 'Same same' but different? Can work engagement be discriminated from job involvement and organizational commitment? *European Psychologist*, 11, 119–27.

Harter, J. K., Schmidt, F. L., and Hayes, T. L. (2002). Business-unit-level relationship between employee satisfaction, employee engagement, and business outcomes: A meta-analysis. *Journal of Applied Psychology*, 87, 268–79.

Hobfoll, S. E., Johnson, R. J., Ennis, N., and Jackson, A. P. (2003). Resource loss, resource gain, and emotional outcomes among inner city women. *Journal of Personality and Social Psychology*, 84, 632–43.

Hornung, S., Rousseau, D. M., Glaser, J., Angerer, P., and Weigl, M. (2010). Beyond top-down and bottom-up work redesign: Customizing job content through idiosyncratic deals. *Journal of Organizational Behavior*, 31, 187–215.

Inoue, A., Kawakami, N., Ishizaki, M., Shimazu, A., Tsuchiya, M., Tabata, M., Kuroda, M. (2010). Organizational justice, psychological distress, and work engagement in Japanese workers. *International Archives of Occupational and Environmental Health*, 83, 29–38.

Ironson, G. H., Brannick, M. T., Smith, P. C., Gibson, W. M., and Paul, K. B. (1989). Construction of a job in general scale – a comparison of global, composite, and specific measures. *Journal of Applied Psychology*, 74, 193–200.

Jackson, L. T. B., Rothmann, S., and Van de Vijver, F. J. R. (2006). A model of work-related well-being for educators in South Africa. *Stress & Health: Journal of the International Society for the Investigation of Stress*, 22, 263–74.

Kahn, W. A. (1990). Psychological conditions of personal engagement and disengagement at work. *Academy of Management Journal*, 33, 692–724.

Kahn, W. A. (1992). To be fully there: Psychological presence at work. *Human Relations*, 45, 321–49.

Kim, H. J., Shin, K. H., and Swanger, N. (2009). Burnout and engagement: A comparative analysis using the big five personality dimensions. *International Journal of Hospitality Management*, 28, 96–104.

Kinnunen, U., Mauno, S., and Siltaloppi, M. (2010). Job insecurity, recovery and well-being at work: Recovery experiences as moderators. *Economic and Industrial Democracy*, 31, 179–94.

Korunka, C., Kubicek, B., Schaufeli, W. B., and Hoonakker, P. (2009). Work engagement and burnout: Testing the robustness of the job demands–resources model. *The Journal of Positive Psychology*, 4, 243–55.

Kristof-Brown, A. L., Zimmerman, R. D., and Johnson, E. C. (2005). Consequences of individual's fit at work: A meta-analysis of person-job, person-organization, person-group, and person-supervisor fit. *Personnel Psychology*, 58, 281–342.

Lazarus, R. S., and Folkman, S. (1984). *Stress, appraisal, and coping*. New York: Springer Pub. Co.

LePine, J. A., Podsakoff, N. P., and LePine, M. A. (2005). A meta-analytic test of the challenge stressor-hindrance stressor framework: An explanation for inconsistent relationships among stressors and performance. *Academy of Management Journal*, 48, 764–75.

Levinson, H. (1965). Reciprocation: The relationship between man and organization. *Administrative Science Quarterly*, 9, 370–90.

Lewin, K. (1945). The research center for group dynamics at massachusetts institute of technology. *Sociometry*, 8, 126–36.

Lisbona, A., Morales, J. F., and Palací, F. J. (2009). El engagement como resultado de la socialización organizacional. *International Journal of Psychology & Psychological Therapy*, 9, 89–100.

Little, L. M., Simmons, B. L., and Nelson, D. L. (2007). Health among leaders: Positive and negative affect, engagement and burnout, forgiveness and revenge. *Journal of Management Studies*, 44, 243–60.

Llorens, S., Bakker, A. B., Schaufeli, W., and Salanova, M. (2006). Testing the robustness of the job demands–resources model. *International Journal of Stress Management*, 13, 378–91.

Locke, E. A., and Latham, G. P. (1990). *A theory of goal setting & task performance*. Englewood Cliffs, NJ, US: Prentice-Hall, Inc.

Lorente, L., Salanova, M., Martínez, I. M., and Schaufeli, W. B. (2008). Extension of the job demands-resources model in the prediction of burnout and engagement among teachers over time. *Psicothema*, 20, 354–60.

Macey, W. H., and Schneider, B. (2008). The meaning of employee engagement. *Industrial and Organizational Psychology*, 1, 3–30.

Macey, W. H., Schneider, B., Barbera, K. M., and Young, S. A. (2009). *Employee engagement: Tools for analysis, practice, and competitive advantage*. West Sussex, UK: Wiley-Blackwell.

Mauno, S., Kinnunen, U., Mäkikangas, A., and Nätti, J. (2005). Psychological consequences of fixed-term employment and perceived job insecurity among health care staff. *European Journal of Work & Organizational Psychology*, 14, 209–37.

Mauno, S., Kinnunen, U., and Ruokolainen, M. (2007). Job demands and resources as antecedents of work engagement: A longitudinal study. *Journal of Vocational Behavior*, 70, 149–71.

May, D. R., Gilson, R. L., and Harter, L. M. (2004). The psychological conditions of meaningfulness, safety and availability and the engagement of the human spirit at work. *Journal of Occupational and Organizational Psychology*, 77, 11–37.

McCrae, R. R., and Costa, P. T. (1987). Validation of the five-factor model of personality across instruments and observers. *Journal of Personality and Social Psychology*, 52, 81–90.

Merton, R. K. (1957). *Social theory and social structure*. New York: Free Press of Glencoe.

Montgomery, A. J., Peeters, M. C. W., Schaufeli, W. B., and Den Ouden, M. (2003). Work–home interference among newspaper managers: Its relationship with burnout and engagement. *Anxiety, Stress & Coping*, 16, 195–211.

Moss, S. (2009). Cultivating the regulatory focus of followers to amplify their sensitivity to transformational leadership. *Journal of Leadership & Organizational Studies*, 15, 241–59.

Mostert, K., and Rothmann, S. (2006). Work-related well-being in the South African police service. *Journal of Criminal Justice*, 34, 479–91.

Nahrgang, J. D., Morgeson, F. P., and Ilies, R. (2009). The development of leader–member exchanges: Exploring how personality and performance influence leader and member relationships over time. *Organizational Behavior and Human Decision Processes*, 108, 256–66.

Naudé, J. L. P., and Rothmann, S. (2006). Work-related well-being of emergency workers in Gauteng. *South African Journal of Psychology*, 36, 63–81.

Nembhard, I. M., and Edmondson, A. C. (2006). Making it safe: The effects of leader inclusiveness and professional status on psychological safety and improvement efforts in health care teams. *Journal of Organizational Behavior*, 27, 941–66.

Netemeyer, R. G., Boles, J. S., and McMurrian, R. (1996). Development and validation of work–family conflict and family–work conflict scales. *Journal of Applied Psychology*, 81, 400–10.

Noe, R. A., Hollenbeck, J. R., Gerhart, B., and Wright, P. M. (2010). *Human resource management: Gaining a competitive advantage* (7th edn). New York, NY: McGraw-Hill/Irwin.

Parker, S. L., Jimmieson, N. L., and Amiot, C. E. (2010). Self-determination as a moderator of demands and control: Implications for employee strain and engagement. *Journal of Vocational Behavior*, 76, 52–67.

Peeters, M., Wattez, C., Demerouti, E., and de Regt, W. (2009). Work–family culture, work–family interference and well-being at work: Is it possible to distinguish between a positive and a negative process? *Career Development International*, 14, 700–13.

Pierce, J. L., Gardner, D. G., Cummings, L. L., and Dunham, R. B. (1989). Organization-based self-esteem – construct definition, measurement, and validation. *Academy of Management Journal*, 32, 622–48.

Rhoades, L., Eisenberger, R., and Armeli, S. (2001). Affective commitment to the organization: The contribution of perceived organizational support. *Journal of Applied Psychology*, 86, 825–36.

Rich, B. L., LePine, J. A., and Crawford, E. R. (2010). Job engagement: Antecedents and effects on job performance. *Academy of Management Journal*, 53, 617–35.

Rizzo, J. R., House, R. J., and Lirtzman, S. I. (1970). Role conflict and ambiguity in complex organizations. *Administrative Science Quarterly*, 15, 150–62.

Rothbard, N. P. (2001). Enriching or depleting? The dynamics of engagement in work and family roles. *Administrative Science Quarterly*, 46, 655–84.

Rothmann, S., and Joubert, J. H. M. (2007). Job demands, job resources, burnout and work engagement of managers at a platinum mine in the North West province. *South African Journal of Business Management*, 38, 49–61.

Russell, S. S., Spitzmuller, C., Lin, L. F., Stanton, J. M., Smith, P. C., and Ironson, G. H. (2004). Shorter can also be better: The abridged job in general scale. *Educational and Psychological Measurement*, 64, 878–93.

Ryan, R., and Deci, E. (2000). Self-determination theory and the facilitation of intrinsic motivation, social development, and well-being. *American Psychologist*, 55, 68–78.

Saks, A. M. (2006). Antecedents and consequences of employee engagement. *Journal of Managerial Psychology*, 21, 600–19.

Salanova, M., Agut, S., and Peiró, J. M. a. (2005). Linking organizational resources and work engagement to employee performance and customer loyalty: The mediation of service climate. *Journal of Applied Psychology*, 90, 1217–27.

Salanova, M., and Schaufeli, W. B. (2008). A cross-national study of work engagement as a mediator between job resources and proactive behaviour. *International Journal of Human Resource Management*, 19, 116–31.

Schaufeli, W. B., and Bakker, A. B. (2004). Job demands, job resources, and their relationship with burnout and engagement: A multi-sample study. *Journal of Organizational Behavior*, 25, 293–315.

Schaufeli, W. B., and Salanova, M. (2007). Work engagement: An emerging psychological concept and its implications for organizations. In S. W. Gilliland, D. D. Steiner and D. P. Skarlicki (eds), *Research in social issues in management: Managing social and ethical issues in organizations* (vol. 5, pp. 135–77). Greenwich, CT: Information Age Publishing.

Schaufeli, W. B., Taris, T. W., and van Rhenen, W. (2008). Workaholism, burnout, and work engagement: Three of a kind or three different kinds of employee well-being? *Applied Psychology: An International Review*, 57, 173–203.

Scheier, M. F., and Carver, C. S. (1985). Optimism, coping, and health – assessment and implications of generalized outcome expectancies. *Health Psychology*, 4, 219–47.

Schneider, B., Macey, W. H., Barbera, K. M., and Martin, N. (2009). Driving customer satisfaction and financial success through employee engagement. *People & Strategy*, 32, 22–7.

Schneider, B., and Reichers, A. E. (1983). On the etiology of climates. *Personnel Psychology*, 36, 19–39.

Shamir, B., House, R. J., and Arthur, M. B. (1993). The motivational effects of charismatic leadership – a self-concept based theory. *Organization Science*, 4, 577–94.

Siltaloppi, M., Kinnunen, U., and Feldt, T. (2009). Recovery experiences as moderators between psychosocial work characteristics and occupational well-being. *Work & Stress*, 23, 330–48.

Simbula, S. (2010). Daily fluctuations in teachers' well-being: A diary study using the job demands-resources model. *Anxiety, Stress & Coping*, 23, 563–84.

Slater, P. E. (1966). *Microcosm*. New York: Wiley.

Smith, K. K., and Berg, D. N. (1987). *Paradoxes of group life: Understanding conflict, paralysis, and movement in group dynamics*. San Francisco: Jossey-Bass.

Sonnentag, S. (2003). Recovery, work engagement, and proactive behavior: A new look at the interface between nonwork and work. *Journal of Applied Psychology*, 88, 518–28.

Sonnentag, S., Binnewies, C., and Mojza, E. J. (2010). Staying well and engaged when demands are high: The role of psychological detachment. *Journal of Applied Psychology*, 95, 965–76.

Sonnentag, S., Mojza, E. J., Binnewies, C., and Scholl, A. (2008). Being engaged at work and detached at home: A week-level study on work engagement, psychological detachment, and affect. *Work & Stress*, 22, 257–76.

Sosik, J. J. (2006). Full range leadership: Model, research, extensions, and training. In C. L. Cooper and R. J. Burke (eds), *Inspiring leaders*. New York, NY: Routledge.

Sverke, M., Hellgren, J., and Naswall, K. (2002). No security: A meta-analysis and review of job insecurity and its consequences. *Journal of Occupational Health Psychology*, 7, 242–64.

Tims, M., Bakker, A. B., and Xanthopoulou, D. (2011). Do transformational leaders enhance their followers' daily work engagement? *Leadership Quarterly*, 22, 121–31.

Totterdell, P., Spelten, E., Smith, L., Barton, J., and Folkard, S. (1995). Recovery from work shifts – how long does it take. *Journal of Applied Psychology*, 80, 43–57.

Van den Broeck, A., Vansteenkiste, M., De Witte, H., and Lens, W. (2008). Explaining the relationships between job characteristics, burnout, and engagement: The role of basic psychological need satisfaction. *Work & Stress*, 22, 277–94.

van den Heuvel, M., Demerouti, E., Schreurs, B. H. J., Bakker, A. B., and Schaufeli, W. B. (2009). Does meaning-making help during organizational change? Development and validation of a new scale. *Career Development International*, 14, 508–33.

Vance, R. J. (2006). *Employee engagement and commitment: A guide to understanding, measuring and increasing engagement in your organization.* Alexandria, VA: Society for Human Resource Management Foundation.

Vander Elst, T., Baillien, E., De Cuyper, N., and De Witte, H. (2010). The role of organizational communication and participation in reducing job insecurity and its negative association with work-related well-being. *Economic and Industrial Democracy*, 31, 249–64.

Vansteenkiste, M., Neyrinck, B., Niemiec, C. P., Soenens, B., De Witte, H., and Van Den Broeck, A. (2007). On the relations among work value orientations, psychological need satisfaction and job outcomes: A self-determination theory approach. *Journal of Occupational & Organizational Psychology*, 80, 251–77.

Walumbwa, F. O., Avolio, B. J., and Zhu, W. (2008). How transformational leadership weaves its influence on individual job performance: The role of identification and efficacy beliefs. *Personnel Psychology*, 61, 793–825.

Watson, D., Clark, L. A., and Tellegen, A. (1988). Development and validation of brief measures of positive and negative affect: The PANAS scales. *Journal of Personality and Social Psychology*, 54, 1063–70.

Whitford, T., and Moss, S. A. (2009). Transformational leadership in distributed work groups: The moderating role of follower regulatory focus and goal orientation. *Communication Research*, 36, 810–37.

Williams, S. A., Wissing, M. P., Rothmann, S., and Temane, Q. M. (2009). Emotional intelligence, work, and psychological outcomes in a public service context. *Journal of Psychology in Africa*, 19, 531–40.

Witt, L. A., Burke, L. A., Barrick, M. A., and Mount, M. K. (2002). The interactive effects of conscientiousness and agreeableness on job performance. *Journal of Applied Psychology*, 87, 164–9.

Xanthopoulou, D., Bakker, A. B., Demerouti, E., and Schaufeli, W. B. (2007). The role of personal resources in the job demands–resources model. *International Journal of Stress Management*, 14, 121–41.

Xanthopoulou, D., Bakker, A. B., Demerouti, E., and Schaufeli, W. B. (2009a). Reciprocal relationships between job resources, personal resources, and work engagement. *Journal of Vocational Behavior*, 74, 235–44.

Xanthopoulou, D., Bakker, A. B., Demerouti, E., and Schaufeli, W. B. (2009b). Work engagement and financial returns: A diary study on the role of job and personal resources. *Journal of Occupational and Organizational Psychology*, 82, 183–200.

Xanthopoulou, D., Bakker, A. B., Heuven, E., Demerouti, E., and Schaufeli, W. B. (2008). Working in the sky: A diary study on work engagement among flight attendants. *Journal of Occupational Health Psychology*, 13, 345–56.

Zapf, D. (1993). Stress-oriented analysis of computerized office work. *European Work and Organizational Psychologist*, 3, 85–100.

Zhu, W., Avolio, B. J., and Walumbwa, F. O. (2009). Moderating role of follower characteristics with transformational leadership and follower work engagement. *Group & Organization Management*, 34, 590–619.

4 Relational contexts of personal engagement at work

William A. Kahn and Emily D. Heaphy

The various definitions of employee engagement on which scholars base their work tend to focus on the degree of intensity with which employees approach their jobs. Rothbard (2001) emphasizes the extent to which employees think about and become absorbed in their roles. Maslach, Schaufeli and Leiter (2001) define engagement in terms of energy and involvement, while Schaufeli and Bakker (2004) point to vigor and dedication. These definitions offer the portrait of the engaged employee as engrossed in his or her work, intensely absorbed and dedicated to the completion of tasks and performance of roles. One can imagine such an employee in motion, as he or she moves between the focused research and writing of a report, to an impassioned and reasoned argument supporting a change in strategy, to educating others about a new protocol, to perfecting a laboratory technique, to editing a manuscript, to double-checking the logistics for a meeting, *ad infinitum*. In writing about such engagements, scholars attend less to the details of the particular settings – the board room, computer screen, conference call, library – than to the intensity of the dedication and vigor that employees demonstrate.

We write this chapter in order to pay close attention to a particular dimension of engagement that is routinely undervalued. Our focus is on how engagement thrives in the context of some relationships and wilts in others. We take seriously the notion that organizations are defined by sets of relationships among people who coordinate their activities in the service of tasks, goals, and missions (Gittell, Seidner and Wimbush, 2010; Kahn, 1998). Relationships affect how work gets done – how individuals and teams coordinate, share knowledge and accomplish tasks (Bechky, 2006). Relationships are, metaphorically, the nervous system of the organization, the source of complex social interactions, rapid coordination of systems, and integrated processing of concurrent signals. Relational contexts include co-workers and partnerships, groups and teams, departments and divisions, hierarchical and peer relations. We suggest here that these contexts invariably shape the extent to which people engage.

Existing research on employee engagement does not explicitly examine relational contexts, even as those contexts become the stages upon which engagement is enacted. Employee engagement theory and research focus on job-level features, such as job design (Fleck and Inceoglu, 2010), job demands and resources (Bakker and Demerouti, 2007), and empowerment and control (Bakker and Demerouti, 2008). Other factors, such as supportive environments and organizational climates (Meyer, Gagne and Parfyanova, 2010) and leadership (Bakker and Schaufeli, 2008) imply but do not explore the particular importance of relationships to engagement. The research on the relation between trust and engagement (Schneider, Macey, Barbera and Young, 2010) offers the most pointed focus on relational dimensions of engagement, but the particular nature of that connection remains abstract. The relational contexts of engagement are often assumed to exist, but interchangeably and in the background.

In this chapter we bring relationships to the foreground of an understanding of the nature and causes of engagement. The consideration of relationships enables us to revisit the original conceptualization of engagement as *personal engagement* rather than as work engagement or employee engagement. The nomenclature is important; it signals that the core of engagement is the individual as a person rather than as a worker or employee. The initial scholarly work focused on personal engagement, defined in terms of individuals harnessing their *selves* to their work roles (Kahn, 1990). Personally engaged individuals employ and express their selves physically, cognitively, and emotionally during role performances. The combination of employing and expressing one's preferred self yields behaviors that bring alive the relation of self-in-role, with neither being sacrificed for the other (Kahn, 1990; 1992). Self and role thus exist in some dynamic, negotiable relation in which the person both drives personal energies into role behaviors (self-employment) and displays the self within the role (self-expression). Current conceptualizations of employee or work engagement emphasize self-employment at the expense of self-expression (see Macey and Schneider, 2008). A renewed focus on personal engagement attends to self-expression – and to the relational contexts that shape how, when, and to what effect people disclose and express their selves in the course of role performances.

This chapter is structured according to how relational contexts affect the three psychological conditions initially identified as shaping personal engagement (Kahn, 1990). The three psychological conditions – *meaningfulness*, *safety*, and *availability* – together shape how people inhabit their roles. It is as if organization members ask themselves (though not consciously) three questions in each situation, and personally engage or disengage depending on the answers. The questions are: (1) How meaningful is it for me to bring myself into this performance; (2) How safe is it to do so?; and (3) How available am I to do so? In this chapter, we suggest ways in which the answers to these questions are shaped by relational contexts.

Relational dimensions of meaningfulness

Psychological meaningfulness is feeling a sense that one's physical, cognitive, or emotional energies matter (Kahn, 1990). People experience such meaningfulness when they feel worthwhile, useful, and valuable – as though they make a difference and are not taken for granted. They feel able to give themselves to others and to their work. The lack of meaningfulness is connected to feeling that little is asked or expected of one's self, and that there is little room to give or to receive in work role performances (Kahn and Fellows, 2012).

We suggest here that a significant component of people's experiences of meaningfulness derives from the relationships that they create in the context of their work. While work relationships are implicit factors in, for example, how much room people have to give or to receive in work role performances, or able to wield influence, their true impact on felt meaningfulness at work remains undervalued. We focus here on two particular ways in which relationships shape felt meaningfulness and thus personal engagement: they deepen people's experiences of the purposes of their work and heighten their sense of belongingness at work.

Deepened purposes

A key source of meaning at work is the nature of the purposes of that work (Kahn and Fellows, 2012). When people occupy roles and perform tasks that culminate in purposes that they define as important, above and beyond instrumental rewards, they are more likely to define their work as meaningful. The sense of meaning derives from their feeling part of enterprises larger than themselves; they feel joined and connected to others in the pursuit of encompassing purposes that give their own individual efforts larger meaning. The relational aspects of such deepened purposes are key to joining people to these larger enterprises. We briefly suggest three contexts in which connections that deepen purposes and meaningfulness occur: groups and teams; leader–follower relations; and relations with beneficiaries.

First, people join collective efforts in the context of groups, teams, task forces, coalitions, and alliances. Such collectives vary widely, of course, in the extent to which they are settings for people to experience deepened senses of purpose and meaning. Groups can be places in which members feel that the meaning of their work is lessened, due to unclear missions and uncertain authorizations, political maneuverings and subsequent lack of resources, unworked differences and unmanageable conflicts, and weak leadership (Smith and Berg, 1987). Yet groups can also be settings in which the meaning of one's efforts becomes enlarged, and enlivened, as members join together to create, discover, learn, and achieve what none of them could do alone (Senge, 1990).

In engaged work teams (Richardson and West, 2010), for example, such joining together occurs as members interact frequently, share information, influence decisions, and provide mutual support. Similarly, in what Leavitt and Lipman-Blumen (1995) term 'hot groups' – lively, high-achieving, dedicated groups whose members are turned on to exciting and challenging tasks – members are intensely absorbed and preoccupied with missions. The meaningfulness (and intense pleasure) of their efforts derives both from what they achieve and how they join together to do so. In a different context, Meyerson (2001) wrote of 'tempered radicals', people who are both inside organizations, occupying work roles, yet outside them as well, through their commitment to certain agendas or ideals that drive them to make change, often quite slowly, in their organizations. Meyerson found that tempered radicals built networks over time of people with similar values, through hiring, working hard to retain these hires, and cultivating shared values and identities within the organization over extended periods of time. These tempered radicals slowly created for themselves alliances that both furthered their agendas and, through their relationships, affirmed and deepened their purposes.

Second, as people attach to leaders and the missions those leaders pursue and embody, the purposes of work are enlarged and made more meaningful. Transformational leaders create connections with followers in the context of shared missions that enlarge the meaning of their collective efforts (Bass, 1985). Bass (1990) identified four elements of transformational leadership: individualized consideration (leaders attend to, communicate with, and challenge individual followers); intellectual stimulation (leaders challenge assumptions, take risks, solicit followers' ideas, and develop others' independent thinking); inspirational motivation (leaders articulate visions that are appealing and inspiring to followers); and idealized influence (leaders provide role models for high ethical behavior, instill pride, gain respect and trust). As leaders perform these behaviors, they create relationships that usher followers into deeper levels of connectivity, not simply with the leaders themselves but with the work, with colleagues, and ultimately, with the selves that they discover and bring forth through their efforts.

Third, people deepen the meaning of their work through meaningful contact with beneficiaries of that work. Research on prosocial motivation shows that when jobs are designed such that the employees are able to have contact with those whom they are helping, their work takes on more meaning and they become more motivated to make a difference at work (Grant, 2007). This motivation results in greater effort, persistence and helping behaviors at work, as well as in workers' experiences of themselves as competent and worthy. Grant writes that 'the more frequent, extended, physically proximate, expressive, and broad the contact with beneficiaries [of their work], the more meaningful the contact is to employees' (2007: 398). Indeed, when individuals feel they are making a difference on others (both coworkers and beneficiaries) they feel more capable of effecting positive change – and experience greater meaningfulness in their work (Grant, 2008).

Workers have at least some control over the extent to which they experience their work as meaningful. Wrzesniewski and Dutton (2001) argue that people can change the quality and/or amount of interaction with others on the job, and that this changes the meaning of the work. As an example of such 'job crafting', they describe hospital cleaners who actively engage in caring relationships with patients and families, and integrate themselves into the work of the units. As a result, their work becomes more meaningful, as they come to see themselves as helpers of the sick, part of an integrated whole of which they are a vital part. Wrzesniewski and Dutton (2001) argue that by changing the nature of relationships, people can reframe the purpose of and experience their work more meaningfully. In so doing, job crafters seek out audiences who can help them sustain desirable identities. The meaningfulness of their work is thus a product of their relations with both those who benefit from that work and those who confirm its importance. The relation between job crafting and engagement is thus quite clear (Bakker, 2010).

These three contexts – various formal and informal groups, leader–follower relations, and close connections with the beneficiaries of work – each have the potential to deepen the meaningfulness that people experience in their roles. At the core of the sense of meaningfulness is the belief that one's efforts truly and deeply matter. Each of these contexts has the potential to affirm such mattering, as people join with others on missions and feel that they are making a difference in ways important to them.

Heightened belongingness

Relationships deepen and affirm the meaningfulness of work partly through a process of social identification, in which people's preferred identities (i.e. how they wish to see themselves) are reflected and confirmed by their participation in desirable relationships (Bartel, 2001). Meaningfulness is thus heightened by the extent to which their roles enable people to see themselves in preferred ways routinely confirmed by others' positive reactions. Social identification not only provides positive confirmation of a preferred identity, however; it also enables people to feel the sense of belongingness key to their experience of community (Block, 2008). The sense of belongingness comprises a second relational dimension of meaningfulness.

Work relationships provide varying levels of feelings of belongingness. When people are part of desirable groups with whom they identify, and which affirm their own preferred identities, they experience a sense of shared fate or humanity with others (Rosso, Dekas and Wrzesniewski, 2010). They find meaningfulness in the context of their belongingness. Belongingness occurs not simply through the mechanism of social identification but more familiarly through interpersonal connectedness, generated in certain interactions through which people feel supported (Rosso et al., 2010). We focus on three relational settings in which such interpersonal connectedness translates into heightened belongingness (and thus meaningfulness). The settings are high-quality connections, relations of compassion, and facilitative leader–follower relations.

Research into high-quality connections is based on the idea that the quality of connections (and relationships) varies, with high quality connections being life-giving and low-quality connections being life-depleting (Dutton and Heaphy, 2003). Several dimensions that create high-quality connections are particularly relevant to understanding their relation to belongingness and meaningfulness (see Dutton and Heaphy, 2003). One dimension is *positive regard*, in which one's self is viewed positively by another. A second dimension is *felt mutuality*, in which individuals are being fully met and engaged with by the other person in the interaction. Finally, the *capacities* of individuals embedded in high-quality connections to process and constructively express positive and negative emotions helps create authentic relations that allow for genuine intimacy. Each of these dimensions enables individuals to feel, through their connections to others, that they are not alone in their journeys. High-quality connections anchor people to others, attachments that offer a genuine sense of meaningfulness.

Compassion at work offers another mechanism by which people feel a sense of meaningfulness via heightened belongingness. Acts of compassion involve caring for others, physically and emotionally, enabling them to feel personally connected to, cared for, and invested in by others (Kahn, 1993). Compassion occurs in the context of various sorts of relationships among organization members (Kahn, 1993), including peers and work groups (Lawrence and Maitlis, 2012), leaders and followers (Kahn, 2001), and organizational communities (Dutton, Worline, Frost and Lilius, 2006). Compassionate acts bridge gulfs between people, reaching out to attach and hold them within the bounds of a caring relationship or social system. When people at work are treated with compassion, their belongingness is heightened; they feel more meaningfully connected to others and to their collective work.

Leader–follower relationships can offer a sense of connectedness as well as a place of attachment to purposes and missions. Such relationships are facilitative in nature: the leader's focus is not simply instrumental, in terms of motivating employees to work hard and well, but expressive, focused on the individuality of people and what they need in order to fulfill themselves in the conduct of their roles (Bass, 1990). Facilitative leaders create relationships in which followers feel connected to leaders whom they work with as well as work for; along with direction comes mentoring, coaching, and development. Berg, Wrzesnewski and Dutton (2010), for example, describe how certain leaders create the space enabling lower ranking employees to craft their jobs. Such leadership not only enabled workers to reshape their work roles and relationships, but heightened their sense of belongingness and felt meaningfulness at work.

Relational dimensions of safety

Psychological safety is feeling able to show and employ one's self without fear of negative consequences to self-image, status, or career (Kahn, 1990). This reflects a tenet of clinical work stating that therapeutic relationships (Sandler, 1960), families (Minuchin, 1974), groups (Smith and Berg, 1987), and organizations (Schein, 1987) create contexts in which people feel more or less safe in taking the risks of self-expression and engaging in the processes of change. Such self-expression is apparent as individuals use or suppress their authentic voices at work. People vary widely in their abilities and willingness to do so – to voice concerns or conflicting views, to give voice to difficult experiences and conversations, to be vocal about what is most crucial for them to say and others to hear. Voice is thus part of engagement (Beugré, 2010), in that engaged people safely express rather than withdraw their selves from view (Kahn, 1990).

Psychological safety is intimately linked to the nature of work relationships, as the contexts in which individuals feel able to express themselves, with all of the vulnerability and exposure that self-expression implies. Such relationships occur in interpersonal relations, in groups and teams, and in organizations more generally, with co-workers of varying closeness and with leaders. Each of these types of relationships creates the context in which safety, and thus engagement, can be enhanced or undermined. We focus here on how people construct safe places – conceptualized here as holding environments – and engage in certain key patterns of group-level interactions that ultimately enable their personal engagements.

Holding environments

The holding environment concept was developed by British psychoanalyst D. W. Winnicott (1965) to describe the nature of effective caregiving relationships between mothers and infants. Winnicott's insight was that 'good-enough mothering' involves physically holding infants, whose subsequent experiences of feeling safely encompassed enable the initiation and movement of developmental processes. Winnicott and others further used the holding environment concept to describe the analytic setting (Modell, 1976; Winnicott, 1965), in which patients are enabled to temporarily regress without fear of impingement. Subsequent applications of the concept broaden the notion that holding environments can occur in work organizations of various types (Shapiro and Carr, 1991).

The holding process occurs when organizational members experience potentially disabling anxiety at work (Kahn, 2001). It occurs among adults who generally function at reasonably high levels, and throughout organizational life, although it is not usually labeled as such. Pieces of the holding environment concept are scattered across various literatures that document holding within mentoring (Kram, 1983), leader–member relations (Berg, 1998), as well as in group (Bolton and Roberts, 1994) and co-worker (Lyth, 1988) relationships. In their most effective moments, such settings are temporary holding environments, in which people floundering in anxiety are caught up and secured by others – calmed, appreciated, understood, helped – until they are able to regain their equilibrium and continue on their way.

Holding environments have integrity when there exists a sense of safety, created through a series of acts, which one party (individual, group) performs on behalf of others (Winnicott, 1965). These acts fall into three categories (Kahn, 2001). *Containment* involves making oneself accessible, actively attending to the other, inquiring into the other's experiences, and receiving those experiences with compassion and acceptance. *Empathic acknowledgement* involves curiously exploring others' experiences, empathetically identifying with others as a source of insight, and validating others. *Enabling perspective* involves helping others make sense of their experiences, using self-reflection as a source of information about others, orienting others toward work task requirements, and negotiating interpretations of anxiety-arousing situations. These three types of behaviors enable workers to feel safe enough to share their experiences and gain insight and support.

Recent research has identified several additional mechanisms important to the creation of psychological safety. One such mechanism is identity affirmation. Relationships that enable individuals to feel affirmed as they are acting authentically likely create the safety necessary for people engage their selves at and in work (Rosso et al., 2010). A second mechanism is trust. In trusting relationships, people are more likely to feel safe to engage themselves fully (Schneider et al., 2010). Recent research suggests that high quality connections enable trust via the ability of people to have emotional carrying capacity, which occurs when relationship partners constructively express more of their emotions, positive and negative

(Stephens, Heaphy, Carmeli, Spreitzer and Dutton, forthcoming). These mechanisms – identity affirmation (enabling authenticity) and emotional carrying capacity (enabling trust) – help create the sense of safety necessary to create and sustain holding environments.

In practice, the creation of holding environments requires organizational members to turn from a focus on the work itself and toward a focus on the self of the worker. This process requires members to create reflective spaces in which they can accept, contain, and give meaning to anxiety and distress (Hinshelwood, 2001). Such spaces enable members to temporarily shift from encountering one another in instrumental ways to doing so in expressive ways. For example, Kellogg's (2011) ethnography of surgical units attempting to move to an 80-hour work week found that relational spaces, defined as areas of isolation, interaction and inclusion, allowed middle managers (surgeons) and subordinates (residents) safe spaces in which to form new identities, frames, and relationships that supported their actions to create counter-cultural change. As organization members create temporary spaces in which to turn toward one another in ways characterized by openness and supportiveness, they feel increasingly safe to personally engage with one another.

Group patterns of interaction

Holding environments can be created in group as well as interpersonal settings. Groups offer a particular set of dynamics that are important to understand, in terms of facilitating or undermining psychological safety. Safety in the context of one-on-one high-quality relationships is a function of the trust, respect, honesty and openness, and appreciation that people are able to give and receive to one another. As those conditions are created, individuals are able to become more authentic, to present their selves and thus engage more deeply (Kahn, 1992). Creating and sustaining these conditions in the context of groups is a more complex matter.

Theorists and researchers who focus on the capability of teams to learn from experience have mapped some of this complexity. Senge (1990) notes that teams learn about themselves when members engage in authentic dialogue, suspending assumptions and entering into genuine thinking together. They thus move away from affixing blame and toward discovering together. As members go on the quest together to discover how they can work more effectively, they invariably strengthen their relationships and engender trust and safety (Kahn, 2010). The relation between psychological safety and team learning was explicitly examined by Edmondson (1999) in her study of manufacturing teams. The research indicated that when members of a team shared the belief that the team was a safe place for interpersonal risk-taking, they engaged in the dialogues necessary for them to learn, individually and collectively, about their teams and how to improve processes and outcomes. Their increasingly high-quality relationships promoted safety and subsequent learning through dialogue (Carmeli and Gittell, 2009).

Psychological safety in groups is also influenced by the various informal roles that individuals assume. Group dynamics are often marked by unconscious 'plays' that characterize the more conscious workings of organizations (Bion, 1966). Social systems have a 'mentality' beyond that of individual members, connecting group members by processes of unconscious alliance and collusion (Wells, 1980). In the context of the work group, members collude to act out plays that allay anxieties. Such plays revolve, for example, around plots dealing with authority, competition, or sexuality; they depend on organization members to play the informal (i.e. unconscious) roles that such plots demand. Once cast into these roles, members vary in how much room they have to safely bring their selves into work role performances

(Kahn, 1990). The point here is that informal roles vary greatly in terms of whether they offer safe havens from which to personally engage, depending on how much respect and authority those characters are given (Kahn, 1992).

Relational dimensions of availability

Psychological availability occurs when people have the physical, emotional, or psychological resources to personally engage at particular points in time (Kahn, 1990). It is a readiness statistic of how available people are amidst distractions. Personal engagement requires physical, cognitive, and emotional resources that may or may not be scarce, given the competing demands of other aspects of people's work and non-work lives. Such resources are affected – positively and negatively – by the nature of the relationships that organizational members create and maintain. Relational contexts can provide relief for individuals or reduce the slack that they have in their work lives, add or drain energy, and support or undermine the boundaries necessary to remain available at work. We describe these processes in the contexts of energizing and enervating interactions, and emotional relief and depletion.

Energizing and enervating interactions

The relationships that organization members develop at work have the potential to provide or deplete them of positive energy. An early scholarly example was Roy's (1959) account of how a group of machine operators kept away the boredom of monotonous work by routinely engaging in horseplay, pranks, and jokes. These rituals provided a source of energy amidst what would have otherwise been numbing boredom. It was in their relations with one another that the workers, deadened by their tasks, came alive; they became lively, animated, interested, and interesting (Roy, 1959). Roy's article offered the first scholarly research that took seriously the idea that work relationships, and not simply the work tasks themselves, are powerful sources of meaning, energy, and satisfaction. Since then it has become clear that work relationships can also drain meaning, energy, and satisfaction from work as well. Bullies (Beasley and Rayner, 1997), demeaning and abusive leaders (Tepper, 2000), and ultra-competitive co-workers (Fletcher, Major and Davis, 2008) create relational contexts that drain energy from workers, leading them to defend rather than make their selves available in the workplace.

Dutton (2003) argues that high-quality connections are crucial to building and sustaining energized workplaces. Indeed, she identifies respectful engagement – defined as being present to others, affirming them, and communicating and listening in a way that communicates regard and an appreciation of another's worth – as central to creating work relationships that connect and energize individuals at work. Such connections can occur irrespective of the particular tasks on which people work; while highly collaborative tasks require more and more intensive interactions than highly individual tasks, all organization members are embedded in relational networks of some sort (Kahn, 1998) and thus are influenced by the restorative or draining nature of those networks. When those relationships are positive (i.e. respectful, caring, playful, and the like), people can think and problem-solve more quickly (Baker, Cross and Wooten, 2003), have more physical energy (Heaphy and Dutton, 2008), and feel more deeply (Hinshelwood, 2001) than when embedded in relationships in which they need to make their selves less available.

Energizing and enervating interactions occur between individuals and within groups. The primary action of interpersonal replenishment or depletion occurs in conversations, which vary in terms of what they convey to participants about how cared about, respected, appreciated, heard, and valued they are by others (Kahn, 1993). Energy is similarly generated or depleted in groups through the patterns of interactions that members create over time as they assume leader and follower roles, divide labor, integrate efforts, identify and correct strategies and tactics, and work toward their collective goals (Smith and Berg, 1987). As team members pursue these activities, they create relational patterns that shape how available they become to one another and to the work itself. For example, how teams distribute the workload leads members to feel energized by being part of a true collective effort or enervated by their collusion with an unbalanced 'free rider' effect (Kerr and Bruun, 1983). Similarly, how teams understand and react to the problems they experience – as a matter of joint responsibility or by scapegoating individuals – similarly leads members to make their selves more or less available to one another (Smith and Berg, 1987).

Emotional relief and depletion

Organization members can be more of less psychologically available according to how much emotional capacity they have to empathize with and connect to others (Kahn, 1992). When individuals are themselves emotionally overwhelmed, for whatever reasons, they tend to protect themselves from the possibility of exposure to further emotional material (Kahn, 2005). The underlying imagery here is that of a container: as individuals become filled with emotions triggered by certain situations or individuals, their own capacities to feel on behalf of themselves or others becomes increasingly diminished (Kahn, 2005). Unless these individuals are able to close themselves off from taking on further emotion, they are likely to experience the depersonalization – the emotional removal of one's self from others – endemic to burnout (see Maslach et al., 2001). This 'closing off' from others is a retreat of the authentic self, a making of that self unavailable in the performance of the given role (Kahn, 1992).

It is thus worth considering the relational contexts that render people more emotionally available to personally engage. In terms of the container imagery, caring interactions with others enables people to release some of the emotions triggered by painful interactions. Research with trauma victims (Herman, 1992) has shaped scholarly understanding of the importance of caring interactions that enable traumatized people to share their experiences, and in so doing, release the painful emotions lodged within them by traumatic events that were making the people unavailable to themselves and others. In organizational contexts, Frost (2003) studied how 'toxic handlers' – leaders and managers who deal with others' emotional pain in the workplace – provide co-workers with a relational context in which their pain can be heard, and sometimes released or transformed, rendering them more available. This work fits with research that suggests how relationships create the emotional capacity necessary for engagement by generating positive emotions (Loehr and Schwartz, 2001).

Interactions and relationships that shape organization members' emotions, and thus their availability for engagement, occur not simply with co-workers, but in some professions, with clients, patients, and care-receivers. Various caregivers (e.g. social workers, therapists, pastors, nurses, welfare workers) are less available emotionally due to compassion fatigue, the negative emotional effects of working with distressed populations (Figley, 1995). Compassion fatigue sharply reduces caregivers' willingness and abilities to perform tasks that bring them into further and more intense contact with distressed clients, reflecting the natural inclination of emotionally depleted or overwhelmed caregivers to distance themselves from further exposure (Figley, 1995). It is also possible for caregivers to experience moments of compassion satisfaction, defined in terms of the pleasure of helping others (Stamm and Figley, 2009). Connections with clients and patients thus have the potential to be enriching as well as depleting (Lilius, 2012); they can enhance or diminish how available people are to personally engage in their roles.

We began this chapter by suggesting that relationships shapes the answers to the three key questions of personal engagement: (1) How meaningful is it for me to bring myself into this performance; (2) How safe is it to do so?; and (3) How available am I to do so? We drew on a broad range of literatures to identify the mechanisms through which relationships influence personal engagement. Relationships influence the meaningfulness of work through providing a deeper sense of meaning about the tasks one engages in, and by creating an amplified sense of belongingness in their work environment. The safety necessary for personal engagement is created when two or more people come together to create holding environments, which are safe spaces in which identities can be affirmed, enhanced, or developed, emotions worked through, and psychological safety constructed. One's availability for personal engagement is shaped by the energetic content of relationships (e.g. whether they are energizing or enervating), whether relationships provide emotional relief and depletion, by the relationships outside of work. We illustrate the relational contexts of personal engagement with the following case study.

Case study

Miles Frommer is a pharmacy technician employed in a large teaching hospital in Boston. Miles has worked at the hospital pharmacy since graduating from a pharmacy training program five years earlier. The role of pharmacy technician includes preparation of first doses, restocking the pharmacy's automated dispensing cabinets, unit dose compounding, answering and triaging telephone calls, and preparing and distributing reports for pharmacists. Miles has always enjoyed the technical aspects of handling and understanding medicines and their complex interactions with one another. In the last year, however, Miles has found himself tired of spending hours alone in the back room of the pharmacy, compounding medicines, filling dosages, and filing reports. His interactions with the clinical pharmacists are few and fleeting, he does not work jointly with other technicians, and he rarely sees the department manager who spends much of her time in meetings. It has gotten to the point where he is beginning to dread going into work.

This state of affairs begins to shift when a senior clinical pharmacist approaches Miles to ask him about a prescription that Miles had filled the day before. The pharmacist is confused about a particular aspect of the order. Miles explains. The pharmacist nods in understanding, and tells Miles that she herself would never have caught the potential danger in how she had written the order, given the rare drug interactions that Miles had noticed while filling the order. Miles grinned shyly at the compliment before turning back to his work. Later that day his supervisor asked to see him at the end of his shift. She had been impressed by Miles' work with the senior clinical pharmacist, and told Miles that it was time for him to expand his role in the department and contribute more. They spent an hour together, with the supervisor asking Miles about his interests and the areas in which he thinks the department could improve. Miles felt great walking out of the hospital that day and was excited about what his new role might look like.

Miles then became involved in several initiatives. He was asked to create a working group with several senior pharmacy technicians that would recommend key changes to how orders were processed. The working group met weekly, with lots of follow-up conversations between meetings, and its members came to trust and respect one another as they brainstormed ideas, created innovative solutions, and rallied the rest of the department on several key changes. Miles was also placed on a hospital-wide committee whose task was to look closely at the safety issues related to medication errors. His role was to act as a reliable bridge between the committee and the department, working with each group to develop the most credible understandings of the safety problems and potential solutions.

Over the course of this work, Miles developed a sense of his self as useful, valued, and sought out by others. He developed closer relationships with co-workers in the pharmacy department, his supervisor, and members of other departments. He spent time with physicians, nurses, and patients, as he worked to figure out the source of medication errors. He found many of these interactions respectful, given that they were all working toward the same goal of error reductions. He became closer to the senior clinical pharmacist, to whom he turned when he ran into roadblocks or was confused or upset by an event. As the months passed, Miles found it difficult to believe that he had felt bored, lonely, and unhappy at work. He looked forward to going to work each day, knowing that he would be able to say what he thought and felt, and thus truly contribute to the hospital, its workers, and its patients.

Conclusion

The relational context of personal engagement is a crucial, if overlooked, dimension of engagement. Indeed, work tasks cannot be cleanly separated from work relationships. When organization members are doing their work – by themselves, developing presentations and preparing reports, or with others, discussing ideas and making decisions – their choices about how to perform their tasks are shaped by their relationships. Further, shifts in the design of jobs bring shifts in relational possibilities; these latter shifts are mostly ignored in analyses of the factors of engagement. In the case study above, Miles' job was re-designed to involve him in expanded tasks that embedded him in larger aspects of the department and the hospital. Such job design efforts are often undertaken in order to enhance engagement (see Bakker, 2010). We would argue, however, that the real shift was not in the new tasks that Miles performed but in the relationships that those new tasks enabled him to create. It was in the context of those relationships that Miles felt more fully engaged: he developed a heightened sense of meaningfulness, as he joined with and attached to others to do important work together; a deeper sense of safety, as he felt embraced and affirmed by key individuals and his working groups; and more fully available, through interactions that provided energy and emotional relief.

The relational context comes into sharper focus when linked to *personal* engagement rather than the more abstract, generalized 'employee engagement'. When workers are considered as persons, not just employees, relationships assume greater prominence: it is in the context of relationships that people make choices about bringing their selves fully into their work. Taking this notion seriously means examining more closely the nature of the relationships that facilitate or undermine personal engagement. In the case study above, for example, a cursory explanation of Miles' movement toward being more fully engaged would be that he was able to interact with more people in working groups that had meaningful purposes and goals. This would be an accurate but incomplete explanation. It is the *nature* of those relationships – the behaviors and experiences that they enabled – that matters most in terms of personal engagement or disengagement. Miles was able to experience himself as connected and attached to others, to feel valued by them and to value himself in return, to feel appropriately cared for by others, and to feel joined with others in the service of shared purposes. As a result, he was able to bring himself fully into the performances of his role: saying what he thought and felt, in order to make the work better; working hard and energetically; seeking to provide and receive feedback, in order to learn as much as possible to help his department, organization, and patients.

Placing relationships in the foreground rather than the background raises awareness of the interventions that can heighten the conditions for personal engagement. Human Resource professionals have unique opportunities to use the ideas discussed in this chapter to help facilitate organization members' personal engagements. They can raise awareness of the centrality of certain types of relationships – high-quality connections that enable members to attach to and support one another in the context of supervision and leadership, peers, and working groups – to such engagements. They can encourage leaders to help their employees engage in job crafting activities through which the positive relational components of their work with co-workers, clients, patients and consumers become a prominent source of engagement. More generally, they can help develop, support, reward, and hold accountable leaders for facilitating members' personal engagements through the relationships that they create with those members. To the extent that human resource professionals are mindful of the centrality of the relational contexts of engagement, they can develop interventions in dysfunctional relationships (within and across groups) that focus in creating conditions in which organization members experience the appropriate sense of meaningfulness, safety, and availability.

References

Baker, W., Cross, R. and Wooten, M. (2003). 'Positive organizational network analysis and energizing relationships'. In K. S. Cameron, J. E. Dutton and R. E. Quinn (eds), *Positive organizational scholarship: Foundations of a new discipline*, San Francisco: Berrett-Koehler, pp. 328–42.

Bakker, A. B. (2010). 'Engagement and "job crafting": Engaged employees create their own great place to work'. In S. Albrecht (ed.), *The handbook of employee engagement: Perspectives, issues, research and practice*. Edward Elgar: Cheltenham, pp. 229–44.

—— and Demerouti, E. (2007) 'The job demands–resources model: State of the art'. *Journal of Managerial Psychology*, 22, pp. 309–28.

—— and Demerouti, E. (2008) 'Towards a model of work engagement'. *Career Development International*, 13, pp. 209–23.

—— and Schaufeli, W. B. (2008) 'Positive organizational behavior: Engaged employees in flourishing organizations'. *Journal of Organizational Behavior*, 29, pp. 147–54.

Bartel, C. A. (2001) 'Social comparisons in boundary-spanning work: Effects of community outreach on members' organizational identity and identification'. *Administrative Science Quarterly*, 46(3), pp. 379–413.

Bass, B. M. (1985). *Leadership and performance beyond expectation.* New York: Free Press.

—— (1990). 'From transactional to transformational leadership: Learning to share the vision'. *Organizational Dynamics*, pp. 19–31.

Beasley, J. and Rayner, C. (1997). 'Bullying at work'. *Journal of Community and Applied Social Psychology*, 7(3), pp. 177–80.

Bechky, B. A. (2006) 'Gaffers, gofers, and grips: Role-based coordination in temporary organizations'. *Organization Science*, 17(1), pp. 3–21.

Berg, D. N. (1998). 'Resurrecting the muse: Followership in organizations'. In E. Klein, F. Gabelnick and P. Herr (eds), The psychodynamics of leadership. Madison, CT: Psychosocial Press, pp. 27–52.

Berg, J. M., Wrzesniewski, A. and Dutton, J. E. (2011) 'Perceiving and responding to challenges in job crafting at different ranks: When proactivity requires adaptivity'. *Journal of Organizational Behavior*, 31, pp. 158–86.

Beugré, C. (2010). 'Organizational conditions fostering employee engagement: The role of voice'. In S. Albrecht (ed.), *The handbook of employee engagement: Perspectives, issues, research and practice*, pp. 174–81.

Bion, W. R. (1961). *Experiences in groups*. New York: Basic Books.

Bolton, W. and Roberts, V. Z. (1994). 'Asking for help: Staff support and sensitivity groups re-viewed'. In A. Obholzer and V. Z. Roberts (eds), *The unconscious at work*. London: Routledge.

Block, P. (2008) *Community: The structure of belonging*. San Francisco, CA: Berrett-Kohler.

Carmeli, A. and Gittell, J. H. (2009). 'High-quality relationships, psychological safety, and learning from failures in work organizations'. *Journal of Organizational Behavior*, 30, pp. 709–29.

Dutton, J. E. (2003). *Energizing your workplace: Building and sustaining high quality relationships at work*. San Francisco, CA: Jossey Bass.

—— and Heaphy, E. (2003) 'The power of high quality connections'. In K. Cameron, J. E. Dutton and R. E. Quinn (eds), *Positive organizational scholarship*, San Francisco: Berrett-Kohler, pp. 263–78.

——, Worline, M. C., Frost, P. J. and Lilius, J. (2006). 'Explaining compassion organizing'. *Administrative Science Quarterly*, 51(1), pp. 59–96.

Edmondson, A. (1999). 'Psychological safety and learning behavior in work teams'. *Administrative Science Quarterly*, 44, pp. 350–83.

Figley, C. R. (1995) 'Compassion fatigue as secondary traumatic stress disorder'. In C. R. Figley (ed.), *Compassion fatigue* Florence, KY: Brunner/Mazel, pp. 1–20.

Fleck, S. and Inceoglu, I. (2010) 'A comprehensive framework for understanding and predicting engagement'. In S. Albrecht (ed.), *The handbook of employee engagement: Perspectives, issues, research and practice*, pp. 31–42.

Fletcher, T. D., Major, D. A. and Davis, D. D. (2008). 'The interactive relationship of competitive climate and trait competitiveness with workplace attitudes, stress, and performance'. *Journal of Organizational Behavior*, 29(7), pp. 899–922.

Frost, P. (2003) *Toxic emotions at work*. Boston, MA: Harvard Business School Press.

Gittell, J. H., Seidner, R. and Wimbush, J. (2010). 'A relational model of how high-performance work systems work'. *Organization Science*, 21(2), pp. 490–506.

Grant, A. M. (2007). ' Relational job design and the motivation to make a prosocial difference'. *Academy of Management Review*, 32, pp. 393–417.

—— (2008). 'The significance of task significance: Job performance effects, relational mechanisms, and boundary conditions'. *Journal of Applied Psychology*, 93, 108–24.

Heaphy, E. D., and Dutton, J. E. (2008). 'Integrating organizations and physiology: Getting started'. *Academy of Management Review*, 33(4), pp. 1009–11.

Herman, J. (1992). *Trauma and recovery*. New York: Basic Books.

Hinshelwood, R. D. (2001). *Thinking about institutions*. London: Jessica Kingsley Publishers.

Kahn, W. A. (1990) 'Psychological conditions of personal engagement and disengagement at work'. *Academy of Management Journal*, 33(4), pp. 692–724.

—— (1992) 'To be fully there: Psychological presence at work'. *Human Relations*, 45(4), pp. 321–49.

—— (1993) 'Caring for the caregivers: Patterns of organizational caregiving'. *Administrative Science Quarterly*, 38(4), pp. 539–63.

—— (1998) 'Relational systems at work. *Research in organizational behavior*, 20, pp. 39–76. Greenwich, CT: JAI Press.

—— (2001) Holding environments at work'. *Journal of Applied Behavioral Science*, 37(3), pp. 260–79.

—— (2005). *Holding fast*. London: Brunner-Routledge.

—— (2010) 'The essence of engagement: Lessons from the field'. In S. Albrecht (ed.), *The handbook of employee engagement: Perspectives, issues, research and practice*, pp. 20–30.

—— and Fellows, S. (2012). 'Employee engagement and meaningful work'. In B. Dik, Z. Byrne and M. Steger (eds), *Purpose and meaning in the workplace*. Washington, DC: APA Books.

Kellogg, K. C. (2011). *Challenging operations: Medical reform and resistance in surgery*. Chicago, IL: University of Chicago Press.

Kerr, N. L. and Bruun, S. E. (1983). 'Dispensability of member effort and group motivation losses: Free-rider effects'. *Journal of Personality and Social Psychology*, 44(1), pp. 78–94.

Kram, K. E. (1983). 'Phases of the mentor relationship'. *Academy of Management Journal*, 26(4), pp. 608–25.

Lawrence, T. B. and Maitlis, S. (2012). 'Care and possibility: Enacting an ethic of care through narrative practice'. *Academy of Management Review*, 37(4), pp. 641–63.

Leavitt, H. J. and Lipman-Blumen, J. (1995) *Hot groups*. London: Oxford University Press.

Lilius, J. M. (2012) 'Recovery at work: Understanding the restorative side of "depleting" client interactions'. *Academy of Management Review*, 37(4), pp. 569–88.

Loehr, J., and Schwartz, T. (2001). 'The making of a corporate athlete'. *Harvard Business Review*, 79(1), pp. 120–9.

Lyth, I. M. (1988) *Containing anxiety in institutions*. London: Free Association Books.

Macey, W. H. and Schneider, B. (2008) ' The meaning of employee engagement'. *Industrial and Organizational Psychology*, 1, pp. 131–42.

Maslach, C., Schaufeli, W. B. and Leiter, M. P. (2001). 'Job burnout'. *Annual Review of Psychology*, 52, pp. 397–422.

Meyer, J. P., Gagne, M. and Parfyonova, N. M. (2010) 'Toward an evidence-based model of engagement: What we can learn from motivation and commitment research'. In S. Albrecht (ed.), *The handbook of employee engagement: Perspectives, issues, research and practice*, pp. 62–73.

Meyerson, D. (2001) *Tempered radicals*. Boston, MA: Harvard Business School Press.

Minuchin, S. (1974) *Families and family therapy*. Cambridge, MA: Harvard University Press.

Modell, A. (1976). 'The holding environment and the therapeutic action of psychoanalysis'. *Journal of the American Psychoanalytic Association*, 24, pp. 285–307.

Richardson, J. and West, M. A. (2010). ' Engaged work teams'. In S. Albrecht (ed.), *The handbook of employee engagement: Perspectives, issues, research and practice*, pp. 323–40.

Rosso, B. D., Dekas, K. H. and Wrzesniewski, A. (2010) 'On the meaning of work: A theoretical integration and review'. *Research in Organizational Behavior*, 30, pp. 91–127.

Rothbard, N. P. (2001). 'Enriching or depleting? The dynamics of engagement in work and family roles'. *Administrative Science Quarterly*, 46, pp. 655–84.

Roy, D. F. (1959). 'Banana time: Job satisfaction and informal interaction'. *Human Organization*, 18, pp. 158–68.

Sandler, J. (1960) 'The background of safety'. *International Journal of Psychoanalysis*, 41, pp. 352–6.

Schaufeli, W. B. and Bakker, A. B. (2004). 'Job demands, job resources, and their relationship with burnout and engagement: a multi-sample study'. *Journal of Organizational Behavior*, 25, pp. 293–315.

Schein, E. H. (1987) *Process consultation* (vol. 2). Reading, MA: Addison-Wesley.

Schneider, B., Macey, W. H., Barbera, K. M. and Young, S. A. (2010). 'The role of employee trust in understanding employee engagement'. In S. L. Albrecht (ed.), *The handbook of employee engagement: Perspectives, issues, research and practice*, pp. 159–73.

Senge, P. (2010) *The fifth discipline*. New York: Random House.

Shapiro, E. R. and Carr, A. W. (1991). *Lost in familiar places*. New Haven, CT: Yale University Press.

Smith, K. K. and Berg, D. N. (1987). *Paradoxes of group life*. San Francisco, CA: Jossey-Bass.

Stamm, B. H. and Figley, C. R. (2009). 'Advances in the theory of compassion satisfaction and fatigue and its measurement with the ProQOL 5'. *International Society for Traumatic Stress Studies*. Atlanta, GA.

Stephens, J. P., Heaphy, E. D., Carmeli, A., Spreitzer, G. S., Dutton, J. E. (in press) 'Relationship quality and virtuousness: Emotional carrying capacity as a source of individual and team resilience'. *Journal of Applied Behavioral Science*.

Tepper, B. J. (2000). 'Consequences of abusive supervision'. *Academy of Management Journal*, 43, pp. 178–90.

Wells, L. Jr. (1980). 'The group-as-a-whole: A systemic socio-analytic perspective on interpersonal and group relations'. In C. P. Alderfer and C. L. Cooper (eds), *Advances in experiential social processes* (vol. 2). New York: Wiley, pp. 50–85.

Winnicott, D. W. (1965). *The maturational processes and the facilitating environment.* New York: International University Press.

Wrzesniewski, A. and Dutton, J. E. (2001). ' Crafting a job: Revisioning employees as active crafters of their work'. *Academy of Management Review*, 26, pp. 179–201.

Part 2

Employee engagement

The HRM implications

5 Strategic HRM and employee engagement

Paul Sparrow

Introduction

This chapter analyses the purposes to which HR functions put employee engagement strategies, and how these strategies should fit into the total HR strategy. It analyses the assumptions that are being made in practice, both about the nature of employee engagement, and about the ways in which it contributes to organizational performance. It identifies the challenges and directions being taken by organizations when they use employee engagement as a basis for HR strategy, and argues that we should use the engagement strategy as the unit of analysis, rather than individual levels of engagement. It discusses the challenges involved in explaining employee engagement as a strategic narrative, principally by examining the 'performance recipes' involved in the delivery of two high-level strategic drivers – innovation and lean management. It considers how the delivery of these outcomes might be associated with employee engagement, and finally considers the implications of the analysis for HR practice.

We must acknowledge that many practitioners and academics now take conflicting views about the utility of engagement strategies. Different constituencies are more or less likely to be persuaded that the dictates of practice and the need for action (of any kind) might override some of the growing caution, the competing intellectual inheritance and the ongoing debate that surrounds the topic. Others might agree with the diagnosis put forward in this chapter, but not the prognosis. It is necessary, therefore, to begin by restating some of the principles of my work in this field – to lay out my own observations, beliefs and assumptions – before then moving to the main argument, which is that we are seeing a maturation of work on employee engagement that is leading HR functions to think carefully about the performance claims that they make and, hopefully, about the most appropriate engagement strategies and structures to put in place.

Categorising engagement strategies

The first key finding from recent work is that many HR Directors use their engagement strategies to serve many masters, without being explicit about the performance assumptions that are built into their strategy. In a critical evaluation of the body of research surrounding engagement and HR strategy, we identified three different streams of management thinking that underpin engagement strategies (Sparrow and Balain, 2010). Each stream, whilst arguing that employee engagement is a foundation for HR strategy, is based on a different implicit argument about *how engagement contributes to performance*. Understandably, HR Directors are attracted to different elements of and performance claims within each of the three agendas that we have identified.

The first stream of engagement initiatives are based on a line of management thinking that draws on a strategy of *process improvement.* Social exchange theory positions engagement as an antecedent bond, from which proximate performance outcomes result (Saks, 2008). Engagement, as part of an exchange relationship, provides the organization with a stock of human capital – a blanket of trust – whereby motivated employees pay back organizational investments by in turn taking care of the organization and its customers. This line of thinking argues that engagement naturally involves a number of related constructs such as satisfaction, involvement, commitment, citizenship behaviours and desire to stay with an organization (Macey and Schneider, 2008). All these constructs tend to have an emotional, cognitive and intentional element, hence the natural overlap between them (Rich, Lepine and Crawford, 2010). The performance claim is relatively 'soft', and based on effects that are very proximate to the role holder:

> people can use varying degrees of their selves, physically, cognitively, and emotionally, in the roles they perform, even as they maintain the integrity of the boundaries between who they are and the roles they occupy. *Presumably* [my italics], the more people draw on their selves to perform their roles within those boundaries, the more stirring are their performances and the more content they are with the fit of the costumes they don.
>
> (Kahn, 1990: 692)

The HR strategy therefore assumes that motivated employees, when also encouraged to act as good citizens, will self-manage and take the initiative to improve on business processes. The performance claim, then, is not that engagement improves bottom-line (or what I later note is called distal) performance, but rather that it acts as an 'efficiency multiplier' – a necessary ingredient for, or precursor of, subsequent effective business performance. The performance effect is thus to reduce the background noise and drag on general task performance that is created by a poor exchange relationship.

A second stream of engagement initiatives is based on a strategy which considers engagement to be *predictive of corporate performance.* In these initiatives, HR strategy is influenced by the human relations movement (Judge et al., 2001) and more recently by the marketing literature, which argues that attitudes facilitate and guide behaviour. Positive attitudes serve to energize positive feelings which, in turn, serve to strengthen identification with the job, unit or organization, heightening motivation, which then serves as a component, or consequence of commitment. The HR strategy also draws strongly on assumptions drawn from the customer services literature, which in turn includes insights from models such as emotional contagion theory (Hatfield, Cacioppo and Rapson, 1993); service-profit chain theory (Heskett, Sasser and Schlesinger, 1997); and service climate theory (Schneider, 1990).

All of these models suggest a direct and causal engagement–service–profit chain, whereby raised levels of employee engagement yield higher levels of business unit performance. Three key links are assumed in this relationship: an association between employee satisfaction and customer satisfaction; an association between employee perceptions of organizational climate (especially its focus on service) and customer satisfaction levels, and also between these favourable climates and levels of employee satisfaction and commitment; and, finally, an association between customer satisfaction and financial performance. Specific HRM practices therefore have the power to positively influence important employee behaviours, such as customer orientation, a behaviour which is further considered to be linked to organizational performance.

Finally, a third stream of engagement initiatives is based on a line of management thinking which draws upon assumptions about *internal marketing*, or more recently what is being called a *strategic narrative*. Here, the HR strategy (Sparrow and Balain, 2010) targets specific communications that resonate with the unique needs of key communities (employee segments) to develop a shared mental model of what is required of both the organization and the employee. It then assesses the extent to which both sides are delivering this 'deal', with engagement surveys deployed both as an employee feedback mechanism and as a management control device to assess how well the organization is doing with regard to the implementation of strategy and how the employees (as internal customers) feel about the proposition. The performance claim, then, is that engagement speeds the execution of a desired strategy, or a business transformation, by matching the sent message to the desires and drivers of important employee segments, and that this more focused line of sight and communication will have indirect financial and quality benefits.

Implicit theories of performance

Laying out the implicit management thinking that underpins these different engagement strategies is important. Each involves different assumptions about:

- what needs to be measured under the label 'engagement'
- what the consequence of positive or negative scores on such measurements will be, and
- what remedial action the organization needs to make dependent on that measurement.

The second key finding from an analysis of engagement strategies is that both the main (competing) academic engagement constructs in play, and the more applied research, have within them implicit theories of performance that make very different assumptions about the *fulcrum performance variables around which practitioner interventions should be designed* (Sparrow, 2013). These theories of performance in practice involve making predictions about the range of effects. There are three different and increasingly more complex performance outcomes across the implied performance range:

1   Proximal performance outcomes, e.g. task performance, contextual performance, commitment, satisfaction, turnover intentions.
2   Intermediate performance outcomes that capture the delivery of a strategy, e.g. customer service or value proposition, innovative behaviour, understanding of a broader business model and performance context.
3   Distal or organizational performance outcomes, e.g. measures of quality or financial performance.

A central argument in this chapter is that there remains a missing level of research (akin to the 'black box' issue within the HR practices–performance debate), which is the need to link engagement to the more managerially useful intermediate performance outcomes, such as innovative behaviour, customer centricity, lean and efficient management (Sparrow, 2013).

The engagement–performance debate: the need to accept more nuanced performance claims

This moves us onto the third key finding from our existing analysis of engagement strategies, which is that, whilst still supporting the proposition that engagement can contribute usefully to performance, HR Directors need to be much more realistic about the way in which such a link is engineered, and the basis upon which they argue that engagement delivers organizational performance. They need to avoid being seduced by the rhetoric, and they need to temper the clearly supported view that engagement can be correlated (politely called 'linkage studies') with useful performance outcomes (which it can be) with a much more business-relevant explanation of why engagement is useful. In short, having put in place measurement systems and human capital analytics, the challenge now is to link this to something more useful in the organization than inflated correlations. Where measurement begins, insight must follow.

To provide such insight, Sparrow and Balain (2010) argued that a more mature approach needs to be taken to HR strategies. With regard to the evidence suggesting a link between engagement and organizational performance, notwithstanding helpful reviews of the practitioner evidence (Rayton and Dodge, 2012), the answer must remain that 'it depends'.

There are five nuances to performance that engagement research still needs to address. It is important to be open about these nuances, because the more 'business-savvy' line manager (or Operations Director, or Capability Director, or CEO) who may nevertheless be somewhat sceptical about engagement is otherwise likely to use their own insight into organizational effectiveness to argue that HR seems to be making rather naive claims:

1   Sometimes being in a well-performing unit makes employees engaged, not the other way round. There are competing views about whether job attitudes cause performance, the extent of reverse causation, or the presence of bi-directional influences (Schneider, Hanges, Smith and Salvaggio, 2003; Riketta, 2008; Harter, Schmidt, Asplund, Killham and Agrawal, 2010; Winkler, König and Kleinmann, 2012), but the balance of evidence suggests bi-directional pathways. Hence the comment that linkage studies over-inflate the performance effects of high levels of engagement.

2   The idea that employees are either engaged or not, and that once engaged, the impact on performance is linear (a bit more engagement equals just that bit more performance) seems overly simple. Sometimes performance effects may only begin at very extreme levels of engagement, and this level of 'engagement sensitivity' may also change over time. As an asset, engagement might sometimes be rather blunt, whereas in other contexts and at other levels of intensity, it may have a very powerful leveraging effect and value.

3   Sometimes engagement might be able to create useful performance effects through intermediate outcomes typically measured at the individual level – such as satisfaction, commitment or loyalty. Other times, it works through the creation of a long causal chain of necessary conditions, for example, when engagement flows into the right strategic behaviours (such as customer orientation), and only if the employee has the resources they need to channel engaged behaviour into end-service. An engaged but ill-equipped employee is a happy nuisance to many a customer. Or an engaged but still incompetent employee may be seen as well-intentioned but irrelevant (think of a 2 x 2 matrix of high–low engagement and high–low competence). The reality is that it only takes one or two events outside the influence of HR, or the employee, to break the whole chain. Organizational effectiveness is only achieved if a whole collection of performance promises coincide – the engagement promise needs to be supported by the brand promise and by the organizational capability promise. So, good work by HR can soon get dissipated.

4   Sometimes engagement may only work when it creates a collective capability – employees as a team display certain behaviours and emotions and understand how to

correct their unit's performance. One unhappy person amongst a group of happy people can destroy unit performance, so average engagement benchmarks are problematic. An engagement strategy, in trying to create multi-level outcomes that range from individual engagement through to much more collective conditions, in reality may have to cope with the fact that there may be different antecedents to the creation of individual engagement as compared with collective engagement.

5　Finally, employees respond in a variety of ways to the same work context and conditions, with such differences reflected in the way they answer survey questions. Therefore, the extent to which behavioural and survey responses will subsequently predict performance will depend on many other characteristics, such as tenure, age, gender, hours of work and pay patterns, what country they work in, whether they work for a core or a more peripheral organizational unit (for example one that is outsourced), or whether they come from a particular organizational constituency (employee segment).

The caution expressed a few years ago remains in force today: 'when analysed at the individual level, engagement is just too complex and too big a concept to be able to consistently and reliably explain much organizational performance. Organizations are measuring the symptoms of performance, not the causes' (Sparrow and Balain, 2010: 288).

Searching for a simple elixir of strategic life – that engagement equals organizational performance – undervalues the realities of HR strategy and the different purposes to which an engagement strategy is typically put to use. Organizations in practice build complex service models that attempt to bring together a range performance factors. These include, for example, internal service quality, customer expectations, organizational image or brand, perceived product or service quality, external service value, customer satisfaction, customer loyalty, and customer advocacy. These models, which are embedded within a firm's organizational capabilities and business approach mean that, when viewed across different organizational settings, only a general relationship should be assumed between employee engagement and strategic outcomes.

For instance, we should expect there to be different levels of sensitivity or influence that employee engagement will have over any organization performance event. The 'recipe' linking engagement to organizational performance should not be blandly copied, but be understood to require unique solutions across different service (industry) models, and indeed across sectors such as manufacturing, engineering, the public sector, etc. Further, multi-sector studies are needed that unravel the implicit 'performance recipe' being pursued in order to understand other causal factors. Future studies therefore need to measure engagement alongside parallel work perceptions and, if we attempt prediction, it is likely that different work perceptions will in fact predict different elements of the service model.

The possibility of such studies seems unlikely for several reasons. Longitudinal data make directional linkage more plausible, but still do not prove causation, and studies are very rare. Even where we have more robust data, authors have argued different directional paths; positive effects one way or another are likely time dependent and erode with unknown loss of intensity. The tight experimental controls that might shed light on the processes involved are difficult to introduce into applied organizational settings.

Engagement as strategic narrative

Of the three strategies outlined earlier in the chapter, the third (internal marketing) is beginning to become more important, but rather than being seen perhaps in the more negatively perceived language of internal marketing (which makes it sound as if the organization is using marketing techniques to sell its wares to a workforce, whether the workforce really needs this product or not!), the language of 'strategic narrative' is now taking hold.

This is a positive development, but the more nuanced articulation of engagement as a narrative creates a new set of demands for the HR strategy. If engagement is seen as being underpinned by a strategic narrative, then the utility of engagement has to lie in the association of this strategic narrative with a believable performance recipe, or a performance belief (Sparrow and Balain, 2010). The language of engagement in effect has to serve the purpose of focusing attention on the centrality of human action for the strategic mission of an organization or community – laying out *what* it is that *engagement has to be directed towards*.

At a practical level, the Engage for Success movement in the UK has long argued that engagement is best seen as the creation of a strategic narrative (see also Chapters 11 and 12). More recently, Engage for Success has argued that this narrative can be seen in either transactional or transformative terms. The view emerging from practice can broadly be summarized as follows. A transactional strategic narrative strategy tends to involve the use of surveys, data collection and targeting of engagement scores linked to a change programme, often also associated with a process plan. It risks creating short-term halo effects around being seen to have moved engagement scores up by a few notches, but also being seen as something that is done to employees, rather than involving employees in the narrative.

Organizations will always need a transactional element to their strategic narrative – tracking and targeting interventions based on data. Transactional is not bad, it is just deficient, a necessary but not a sufficient component. Such strategies are useful, but employees may not care that much about them. Given the degree of discomfort about the pursuit of transactional approaches to engagement strategy, practitioners often define what is implied by a more desirable transformational approach to strategic narrative, not by defining what is meant by 'transformational', but by saying what it is not!

Ideas about transformational strategic narratives are often a reaction to a perception of 'old school' management models. They are seen as *not being about* a 'command and control' approach to strategy, nor about top down communication and internal marketing of a strategy. Even though it could be argued that a command and control strategic narrative may still work and deliver productivity and engagement in an emerging market such as India or China (see Chapters 9 and 10 for more insights on this), in a Western context, these strategies are deemed not to be an efficient or effective route towards engagement (although such approaches may be still capable of delivering performance outcomes such as productivity).

So, a transformational strategic narrative contains assumptions about cultural fit – it is based around assumptions about what engages 'us, and in our times', with all the contemporary demands we have in a low-trust environment for more sharing of and transparency in strategies. Transformational engagement strategies therefore have to involve a degree of shared beliefs in order to work. They inevitably have to lay out a series of emotional behaviours that employees need to 'lock onto'.

Practitioners argue that it is this transformational element to a strategic narrative that allows an organization to 'raise the bar'. 'Raising the bar' in turn means that people (all the people of an organization, or of its mission) are more mindful, attentive and attached to the goal. It is about building a picture so that people collectively understand and believe what is important in a strategy. People have to be able to relate to the strategic narrative, identify with it, and find meaning in this narrative. This is not the marketing of a strategy – it is about the creation of meaningfulness and authenticity of a strategy. A transformational strategic narrative lays out the committing act, and also the contribution to an ongoing story – the ability for people to be able to add to the narrative.

However, this pragmatic articulation of what a transformational strategic narrative is, also makes it patently clear that *any narrative is only useful at a certain point in time* – by laying out the 'engage with what . . .?' picture (the strategy), there is a secondary process of understanding why, and in what ways, at this point on the strategic journey, does engagement with this narrative serve a purpose?

So what might we learn from research about the use of engagement to create strategic narratives? We can usefully look to the body of research on strategic change. Traditionally, this field has focused on the privileged role of senior managers in formulating appropriate strategy, and to a lesser degree, on the role of middle managers in interpreting such strategy during implementation. It has until recently paid little attention to the role of employees and their engagement with the strategy during the execution of change (Bartunek et al., 2006; Maitlis and Sonenshein 2010). Rather than assuming a traditional 'employee resistance' lens, a number of academics have recently looked at how employees can be encouraged to be open and ready for change, and may construct positive interpretations of and engagement with change. This work (Sonenshein and Dholakia, 2012:1): 'focuses on a set of dispositional and contextual antecedents that can facilitate employee engagement with change, and not the interpretive variety in reactions to change'.

Sonenshein and colleagues (Sonenshein, 2010; Sonensheim and Dholakia, 2012), in addressing this challenge, have drawn attention to a stream of research that has highlighted the important psychological resources (such as commitment, identification and a sense of efficacy) that lead to useful outcomes including: readiness for organizational change (Armenakis et al., 1993); extra-role effort in support of workplace change (Morrison and Phelps, 1999); cognitive, affective and behavioural responses to strategic change (Smollan, 2006); employee reactions to change content (Self et al., 2007); commitment to strategic change (Herold et al., 2007); and meaning making and employee adjustment to stressful change (Park, 2010).

In drawing attention to this literature, Sonenshein and Dholakia (2012) have examined how front-line employees in a retail organization undertake strategic change implementation, and make sense of the worldview inherent in the strategy (sensemaking) and perceived benefits. In doing so, they help organizations understand that they need to broaden out their engagement strategies into ones that, rather than measuring the state of individual engagement as some form of human capital to be built up and then spent, focuses instead on communicating the necessary meaning of change, but in ways that enable employees to bring to bear more positive psychological resources (Sonenshein and Dholakia, 2012: 2):

> the basic model of meaning-making by social psychologists – that, regardless of objective circumstances, individuals are more likely to positively adapt to major life changes by explaining those changes within a dominant worldview (understanding) and finding more benefits versus downsides to these changes (benefits finding) – provides a foundation to explain the conditions under which employees can overcome difficulties in implementing change and work to make change successful.

These positive psychological resources are predicated on a number of collective communications – managerial communication, collegial communication, a strategy worldview and the finding of benefits.

Engagement and intermediate strategic outcomes

It is not surprising, then, that I argue that any strategic narrative for engagement has to be based on creating, in the eyes of the 'non-believers' (the more cynical or hard-pressed line manager or business director), a clearer line of sight between engagement and their pursuit of a specific strategic outcome. This outcome, as noted earlier, can be viewed as an intermediate performance outcome, such as customer centricity, innovative behaviour, intelligent but lean organizational processes or effective globalization of the business model.

In the following sections, I take two typically important intermediate performance outcomes, and without too much recourse to the HR literature, lay out the 'total' performance recipe that seems necessary to deliver that strategic outcome. I begin by considering the role of engagement in relation to the intermediate performance outcome of lean management. It should become apparent that it is easier to see how engagement might become important in the delivery of this as a strategic outcome (other HR strategies also still remain necessary). Then I shall consider the intermediate performance outcome of innovation. By contrast, it should become apparent that solving the second performance problem is far more complex, and requires many more strategic HR interventions, than the former.

In both instances, however, the formal research has not yet been carried out, and I use this chapter to signal that mapping out the respective dependency of each performance recipe on employee engagement remains a vitally important research and practitioner task.

A lean management performance recipe (or strategic narrative)

Traditional concerns with efficiency and effectiveness have now led to what has been called 'the new lean' – attempts to create fast and frugal organization processes that do not, however, fall into the trap of being driven just by cost cutting, as seen in many previous philosophies, such as business process re-engineering.

In a post credit-crunch world, lean is gaining renewed attention. The conditions which spawned the birth of lean management – a shortage of both capital and resources in Japan after the Second World War – have become features once more in the new context of an 'age of austerity'. Efficiency and effectiveness, coupled with attention to quality, are major drivers of change.

A variety of methodologies are available for process improvement (Gershon, 2010). These include Six Sigma, Lean Management, Lean Six Sigma, Agile Management, Business Process Reengineering (BPR), Total Quality Management (TQM), Just-In-Time (JIT), Kaizen, Hoshin Planning, Poka-Yoka, Design of Experiments and Process Excellence. Of these, Lean Management and Six Sigma have arguably become the dominant regimes. They are both quality/cost improvement approaches that focus on business processes and on business needs as defined by the customer, use multi-disciplinary teams to address business problems and utilize specified creative, technical and change management toolsets aimed at moving from operational chaos to operational excellence (Antony, 2011).

Of course, productivity or efficiency can be thought about in different ways – how busy and utilized people and resources are – or more constructively, how fast value can be delivered to customers. Lean thinking – originally associated with product development and production systems at Toyota and popularized by researchers at MIT who compared production at Toyota to mass production systems (Womack, Jones and Roos, 1990; Womack and Jones, 1996) has come to represent a philosophy associated with sustainable and long-term performance. Sustainable performance – seen as the focus of responsible management and the global system goal – concerns the flow of value to the customer without delay through the removal of non-value-adding activity (a better definition than waste). This definition is itself broken down to imply the shortest lead time, best quality and value (to people and society), the most customer delight, at lowest cost, with high morale, and driven by safety. It argues such a performance outcome requires competition based on the ability to adapt, avoid inventory, and work in very small units – removing bottlenecks to create faster throughput of value to customers rather than simply locally optimizing and maximizing utilization of employees or machines. It has now been applied to a wide range of issues, spanning management, design and delivery issues in functions such as product development, service, sales, HR and production.

Early research examining lean manufacturing argued that it leads to work intensification and represents 'management by stress' (Delbridge, Turnbull and Wilkinson, 1992; Anderson-Connolly, Grunberg, Greenberg and Moore, 2002). Reflecting back on the 'lean is mean' debate, Pepper and Spedding (2010:141) observe:

> The view that lean is pro-company, not pro-employee, has some validity, and cannot be dismissed. For example, it is said that employees feel a sense of insecurity, perceiving lean as a redundancy threat . . . that management avoid accountability when problems arise, letting it filter downwards onto the lower levels of hierarchy . . . [but] this is to miss the fundamental underpinning of empowerment and cultural change, resulting from a failure by management to approach lean with the correct goals. Lean requires and relies on a review of organizational values, which in itself is key to sustainability of lean. Without this we see an adverse effect on morale, increasing levels of worker unhappiness and withdrawal, ultimately leading to operational failures.

Lean management involves several well-known but potentially mechanistic management tools, such as Kanban, root-cause analysis, removing waste or queue management. But it is not the tools that are key, nor some of the more ritualistic values and behaviours that are often prescribed, but rather the fundamental principles of 'building people, then building products' by educating them to become skilful systems thinkers, harnessing their intellect and then building a culture of 'challenge the status quo' or continuous improvement (called *Kaizen*): 'The essence of [the Toyota system] is that each individual employee is given the opportunity to find problems in his own way of working, to solve them and to make improvements' (Hino, 2006).

Consider 'what' it is that organizations driven by strategic imperatives of lean management are asking employees (and managers and leaders) to engage *with*. There are different ways in which lean may be executed – poorly, as an exercise of cost control and reduction – or more positively, as a new mode of working based on engagement and commitment. So, consider where the pursuit of this strategic imperative might be dependent upon engagement, and what the strategic narrative has to be?

Whilst there are many different prescribed sets of 'principles' or 'pillars' as the thinking has been refined and exported, at the highest level, there are two pillars:

- Respect for people (whoever are the consumers of your work) by developing people through skills to make problems visible and then solvable, eradicating wasteful work, enabling teams and individuals to evolve their own practices and improvements, and building partners with stable relationships based on trust and responsibility for actions.
- Kaizen or continuous improvement and challenging the status quo.

Lean management focuses on efficiency – defined as minimal waste and elimination of non-valued added activities – in order to improve speed and increase productivity. The aim is to produce products and services at the lowest cost and as fast as possible. Lean principles are based on qualitative models developed from years of experience – i.e. the formalization and codification of experience and judgement. Lean also generally requires the engagement of people at the grass root level through a range of creative and continuous improvement activities. The latter, in turn, have to be delivered through a range of quite formalized mechanisms, to which the employee must engage. How engaging are the following mechanisms?:

- Go See (called *genchi genbutsu*) by going to the place of real work – i.e. the physical front line place of value work, where hands-on workers operate to find facts and build consensus
- Out-learning the competition, through generating more useful knowledge
- Using this knowledge, remembering it effectively, and spreading it horizontally by letting knowledge unfold (called *yokoten*, similar to a community of practice)
- Mastering standardized work to provide a baseline (set by the team itself and not a central benchmark) to improve against and to decide what is 'common-cause' or 'special cause' variability
- Stopping to find and fix the root cause of problems
- Learning how to solve problems through hands-on experiments, applying this to new domains through small steps
- Using 'retrospectives' – frequent events to analyse and design activities
- Making decisions slowly by consensus, thoroughly considering options, but implementing them rapidly
- Developing root cause analysis skills and value stream mapping and taxonomies of non-value adding activities
- Removing waste caused by variability in processes (called *mura*) by varying things like cycle lengths, work packages, team sizes, delivery or request times, defects and overburden (caused by things like arbitrary overtime or specialist bottlenecks)
- Maximizing 'pull' systems (responding only to customer signals or downstream requests), and finally
- Minimizing 'push' systems (inventory) by pursuing the 'perfection challenge'.

The research literature can make quite a powerful case that the intermediate performance outcome of lean management is likely well served by attention to employee engagement.

In addition to engagement, another critical component for success is top leadership support. A recent review of case studies in the area by non-HR academics identified several success factors, which were mainly people-related. The prerequisites for effective implementation are: 'top management commitment, cultural change in organizations, good communication down the hierarchy, new approaches to production and to servicing customers and a higher degree of training and education of employees' (Antony, 2011: 186). Despite continued debate over the precise meaning and execution of lean management, for De Menezes, Wood and Gelade (2010), it has

> commonly been taken to involve techniques concerned with production, work organization, quality management, logistics, supply chain, customer satisfaction, efficient delivery and continuous improvement methods. In other words, the adoption of lean

production implies integration in the use of operation (OM) and human resource management (HRM) practices.

(p. 455)

Two performance studies – by Wood, Stride, Wall and Clegg (2004) and Birdi, Clegg, Patterson, Robinson, Stride, Wall and Wood (2008) – have used data from the Modern Management Practices Survey Series. These studies have included four operations management practices (total quality management, just-in-time procedures, integrated computer-based technology and supply-chain partnering) and three associated HRM practices (a learning culture through extensive training, empowerment and teamwork). These studies found that the operations management practices on their own, and also the combination of the four, were not linked to performance. However, when seen in combination with the HRM practices, various linkages emerged as important. Teamwork interacted with most practices, and these combined effects were positively linked to productivity, and supply-chain partnering enhanced the effect of all the other operations management practices. Adopting empowerment and extensive training was the key to productivity.

The existing research on the pursuit of lean management has led to the following conclusions:

- The operations management and the human resource management practices that together represent a lean philosophy have a synergistic effect on performance, i.e. both are needed before performance benefits may be sustained (Scherrer-Rathje, Boyle and Deflorin, 2009).
- Successful implementation of lean management, even within the traditional areas of manufacturing and engineering, requires the creation of change in both technical and culture aspects of the organization (Hines, Holweg and Rich, 2004; Holweg, 2006; Hines, Found and Harrison, 2008; Radnor, 2010). Radnor (2010: 423), drawing upon the studies by Hines and colleagues, summarized these as the 'enabling elements of strategy and alignment, leadership and behaviour and engagement'.
- The pursuit of lean management can on the one hand reduce or offset stress for employees through the elimination of rework and improved quality of processes, but on the other hand might increase stress through the intensification of the work process or perceived loss of control often involved (De Treville and Antonakis, 2006).
- Through the enhancement of the problem solving capability of people, this makes employees 'more valuable to themselves and to the organization they belong, both current and future' (Antony, 2011: 189).
- The outcomes indeed do depend on the quality and integrity of implementation by managers: 'favourable aspects of high-level implementation – such as continuous improvement projects, improved quality, more orderly work places and more predictable flow – can compensate for stressful high intensity and repetitiveness' (Conti, Angelis, Cooper, Faragher and Gill, 2006: 1026) and the 'results indicate that LP [lean production] is not inherently stressful and worker well-being is not deterministic. It depends heavily on management choices in designing and operating lean systems' (p. 1031).
- A number of important supporting conditions are necessary to create positive outcomes (such as engagement) in lean, which include the level of team working, skill utilization, autonomy, social climate and participation: 'lean manufacturing can have both motivational and demanding implications for job design, which will determine psychosocial

outcomes through both their direct effects and interaction with one another' (Cullinane, Bosak, Flood and Demerouti, 2012: 16).

The delivery of lean as an intermediate performance outcome becomes very dependent on managers acting as teachers of thinking skills, or as coaches and mentors. The success, or not, of such a strategic outcome is rooted in the qualities or capabilities of the managers themselves, and the philosophical integrity among the management team. Managers have to be hands-on masters themselves of what they teach – walking the talk – seen to mirror lean principles in their own actions and decisions. Their time is spent teaching and not managing – training people to think for themselves.

Seen this way, engagement is of course a potential outcome from the pursuit of lean management – flowing from appropriate and effective implementation – rather than an input. Yet, the above analysis also signals points at which engagement acts as a necessary input to the activities required. From a business and strategic perspective, an important but under-researched question then is, in which ways does engagement act as a necessary *input* to, or *output* from, the successful pursuit of a lean management strategy? Are there specific practices and values that employees must engage *with*? Is there a need for employees to identify with both the end customer and the nature of the work process? Does a generic positive sense of engagement sustain and generalize – or not – into engagement with the strategic activities and pursuits implicit within a lean strategy?

An innovation performance recipe (or strategic narrative)

What does the picture look like, however, if innovation lies at the heart of the strategic narrative, what are the component HR strategies necessary to deliver innovation, and in what way are these component strategies in turn underpinned by employee creation?

Despite numerous studies carried out in economics, organizational theory, strategic management and marketing, and examinations of the role played by structure, climate and culture, group and organizational behaviour and individual psychology, it seems there is no one set of antecedent variables that has emerged that differentiates between successful innovators and those that struggle. It is a multi-layered performance problem.

Meta-analyses of the possible determinants and moderators of innovation have long shown that there are several different types of innovation in terms of scale and scope (incremental or radical changes in either products, processes, practices, technology or business model), each bringing a different set of challenges to manage (Damanpour, 1991). Performance is only developed through a mix of the investment of substantial resources from the organization, the interplay between years of experience but also rapid insight amongst a small number of individuals, the broader intrinsic motivation of employees, the marshalled time effort of multiple people and groups, the management of uncertainty and risk and the politics of persuasion (Anthony, Johnson and Sinfield, 2008).

It revolves around four political resource investments and risks: reconciling the tension between creativity and control to increase the speed of the innovation; managing routes to commercialization with high risks of failure and the management of complex but appropriate organizational behaviours; risks of conflict with interests in the current business model or other ongoing strategic initiatives in which sales and market positions may be cannibalized by the new operations and historical competence destroyed; and resource allocations based on uncertainty are claimed as future revenue earning escalators (Freeman and Engel, 2007).

It may be delivered through different organizational models – designed to enable people to collaborate at lower cost, reduce unproductive search and co-ordination costs, create clear boundaries around different kinds of risk, place the testing of new ideas within boundaries, apply scarce resources through discretionary spending, manage what talent focuses on, and place the voice of the user in internal management processes. The organization design choice is central to subsequent performance, and might involve building units that are specialized to the creative portion of the innovation problem; using fluid, lateral modes of co-ordination (teams) with joint decision making rights at the front end (in time) of the innovation process; building external venture capital models to acquire and then internalize the running of entrepreneurial start-up operations; developing an internal venture capital/entrepreneurial model ('professional entrepreneur' model) to build businesses that are born to be sold, and place investment bets in the units in return for offering a brokerage service to resources; or creating cross-organization and open innovation models that leverage the one-on-one interpersonal relationships between entrepreneurs and the development of co-operative capabilities.

Common to all these organization design choices is the need to make subtle use of incentive and contractual systems to engineer appropriate behaviour between investors, innovators and employees, build generic management skills in the innovative units, and threaten old power structures as expertise is made obsolete, new career trajectories are initiated, and cultural fit is questioned as management skills and business models become redundant. The HR function also has to understand skill formation strategies and long-term organizational capability; look to the crucial skill ingredients which include advanced technological skills resident in a handful of highly-talented employees, taking bets or 'options' on such talent to ensure the success of the business model; decode business dialogues to articulate a new capability or provide insight into a hybrid skill; and manage the transformation/evolution of the existing skill/ knowledge base into new mindsets that 'glue' together the business model.

The technical literature on innovation tells us that: 'financial resources are probably the most necessary, if not sufficient, element in ensuring the translation of creative ideas into new processes, products or services' (Hewrold, Jayaraman and Narayanaswamy, 2006: 372). The (non-HR) management literature also tells us that an innovation strategy that is concerned principally with the ways the organization combines and transfers knowledge across talent, creates the right incentives, and eliminates other strategic distractions, represents necessary but insufficient interventions (Barsh, 2008; Hamel and Breen, 2007).

The performance recipe therefore needs a macro-level HR strategy for innovation focused on the challenge of business model innovation, the organizational and structural alternatives necessary to develop it, and the challenges of institutionalizing an innovation culture. And it needs a micro-level HR strategy that addresses the messages for leadership, creates a culture or climate for innovation at team level and shapes the creativity and innovation of people through the management and selection of individual talent.

Engagement can play an important part in getting people into the broad frame of mind to accept the complex performance challenge, but it does not guarantee the delivery of the recipe. There is surely still some kind of central strand of activity – especially around the encouragement of people to give of their creativity – that employee engagement should serve well. But the performance recipe is also surely one that places employee engagement in a much more nuanced role.

Implications for practice: a maturation of engagement strategies

In reading the above two example performance recipes necessary for the delivery of intermediate strategic outcomes – innovation or lean but effective organization – ask yourself:

- Would I be persuaded by a claim – or risk my reputation on making a claim – that if x per cent of my workforce complete a survey to say they are engaged (as typically measured by employee surveys) that this in itself causes y per cent (usually figures in the 40 to 60 per cent range are claimed by linkage studies) in end financial performance?
- Would I bet my mortgage on the belief that notching the engagement scores up a few more percentage points was job done and performance outcome guaranteed?
- Would I design my HR intervention around the monitoring and tracking of such data, as opposed to the many other component HR strategies involved?

The answer might still be 'yes' for some, but would be 'no' for others, or at least they might take out a more bounded option and hedged bet.

By asking these questions, it becomes evident that I believe it would be unwise to make generic statements that employee engagement delivers high levels of organizational performance. This is not to say that I believe that engagement is not an important component of delivering business performance. It evidently is. But it is not a goal in itself. Nor is it that engagement per se is sufficient to deliver the performance. Rather, it is the application of engagement to other things that makes engagement of any value (just being engaged is insufficient). It is the '*engagement with what?*' question that HR has to manage.

And this requires a continued process of maturation within engagement strategies. Exactly how these strategies should evolve is still open to debate, and most certainly should be the subject of ongoing research. For Sparrow and Balain (2010), the time came a while back for the HR profession to de-layer the concept of engagement. In rebuilding it:

> if engagement is to be a meaningful concept for HR Directors, then it has to be designed to work at the level of strategic business units or the team. It has to work at this level – business unit rather than individual – because HR Directors need to 'reverse engineer' the sorts of performance that are required by the particular service model that their organization pursues. They need to understand the logic that suggests why a particular range of employee attributes (whether you call them engagement or not) must serve a central purpose in delivering that type of performance.
>
> (Sparrow and Balain, 2010: 291)

> we . . . now have a useful understanding (if not a manageable one) of how engagement works as a psychological process. But from a strategic perspective, engagement is a rather sterile concept unless we know what it is that employees are expected to engage with.
>
> (Sparrow and Balain, 2010: 292)

> HR functions need to articulate whatever it is that they want their employees to engage with [and] ask the harder questions – do employees believe in the strategy and the assumptions that the organization makes about the necessary performance? What are the probabilities of success that their beliefs are based on?
>
> (Sparrow and Balain, 2010: 294)

Given this academic inheritance, then, we should accept that the direct causal lines between engagement (however measured and operationalized) and performance are complex and subject to considerable situational variation. Whilst in some sectors there remains immense opportunity to link employee attitudes (including engagement) directly to organizational effectiveness and performance outcomes, in others, the relationship is more complex.

Moreover, given both the shift towards the development of a strategic narrative around employee engagement outlined earlier, and the reality that in many instances performance is engendered at a team or more collective level, it would be far better if HR directs its measurement to what we (Sparrow and Balain, 2010: 293) called a 'Performance Belief':

> This is the shared belief of a team that it has the required ability, resources, goal clarity and leadership attributes to achieve the desired performance outcomes. The performance belief is the cause, and being engaged to perform is the effect.

As a strategic function, HR should be most concerned about how it should manage engagement – how it gets employees to believe in the vision of performance that the organization offers. The inescapable reality, however, is that in shifting attention to how engagement is managed, it becomes clear that what you measure also has to change. So too must our level of analysis. If engagement strategies are directed towards the goal of creating organizational effectiveness, then the role of both individual and collective constructs of engagement need now to be examined, and in each instance, we need to link them into a clear logic of how they tie into performance – both as inputs and outputs from that performance.

References

Anderson-Connolly, R., Grunberg, L., Greenberg, E. S. and Moore, S. (2002) Is lean mean?: Workplace transformation and employee well-being, *Work, Employment and Society*, 16: 389–413.

Anthony, S. D., Johnson, M. W. and Sinfield, J. V. (2008) Institutionalizing Innovation, *MIT Sloan Management Review*, 2008(4): 45–53.

Antony, J. (2011) Six Sigma versus Lean: Some perspectives from leading academics and practitioners, *International Journal of Productivity and Performance Management*, 60(2): 185–90.

Armenakis, A. A., Harris, S. G. and Mossholder, K. W. (1993) Creating readiness for organizational change, *Human Relations*, 46(6): 681–703.

Barsh, J. (2008) Innovative management: a conversation with Gary Hamel and Lowell Bryan. *The McKinsey Quarterly*, 2008(1): 1–10.

Bartunek, J. M., Rousseau, D. M., Rudolph, J. and DePalma, J. (2006) On the receiving end: sensemaking, emotion, and assessments of an organizational change initiated by others, *Academy of Management Review*, 42(2): 182–206.

Birdi, K., Clegg, C., Patterson, M., Robinson, A., Stride, C. B., Wall, T. D. and Wood, S. J. (2008) The impact of human resource and operational management practices on company productivity: a longitudinal study, *Personnel Psychology*, 61: 467–501.

Conti, R., Angelis, J., Cooper, C., Faragher, B. and Gill, C. (2006) The effects of lean production on worker job stress, *International Journal of Operations and Production Management*, 26(9): 1013–38.

Cullinane, S.-J., Bosak, J., Flood, P. and Demerouti, E. (2012) Job design under lean manufacturing and its impact on employee outcomes, *Organizational Psychology Review*, 3(1): 41–61.

Damanpour, F. (1991) Organizational innovation: a meta-analysis of effects of determinants and moderators, *Academy of Management Journal*, 34(3), 555–90.

De Menezes, L. M., Wood, S. and Gelade, G. (2010) The integration of human resource and operation management practices and its link with performance: A longitudinal latent class study, *Journal of Operations Management*, 28: 455–71.

De Treville, S. and Antonakis, J. (2006) Could lean production job design be intrinsically motivating? Contextual, configurational, and levels-of-analysis issues, *Journal of Operations Management*, 24: 99–123.

Delbridge, R., Turnbull, P. and Wilkinson, B. (1992) Pushing back the frontiers: Management control and work intensification under JIT/TQM regimes, *New Technology Work and Employment*, 7: 97–106.

Freeman, J. and Engel, J. S. (2007) Models of innovation: start-ups and mature corporations, *California Management Review*, 50(1): 94–119.

Gershon, M. (2010) Choosing which process improvement methodology to implement, *Journal of Applied Business and Economics*, 10(5): 61–70.

Hamel, G. and Breen, B. (2007) *The Future of Management*. Cambridge, MA: Harvard Business School Press.

Harter, J. K., Schmidt, F. L., Asplund, J. W., Killham, E. A. and Agrawal, S. (2010) Causal impact of employee work perceptions on the bottom line of organizations, *Perspectives on Psychological Science*, 5: 378–89.

Hatfield, E., Cacioppo, J. T. and Rapson, R. I. (1993) Emotional contagion, *Current Directions in Psychological Science*, 2(3): 96–9.

Herold, D. M., Fedor, D. B. and Caldwell, S. D. (2007) Beyond change management: A multilevel investigation of contextual and personal influences on employees' commitment to change, *Journal of Applied Psychology*, 92(4): 942–51.

Heskett, J. L., Sasser, W. E. and Schlesinger, I. A. (1997) *The service profit chain*. New York: Free Press.

Hewrold, D. M., Jayaraman, N. and Narayanaswamy, C. R. (2006) What is the relationship between organizational slack and innovation?, *Journal of Managerial Issues*, 18(5): 372–92.

Hines, P., Found, P. and Harrison, R. (2008) *Staying lean: Thriving, not just surviving*, Lean Enterprise Research Centre, Cardiff University, Cardiff.

Hines, P., Holweg, M. and Rich, N. (2004) Learning to evolve: A review of contemporary lean thinking, *International Journal of Operations and Production Management*, 24(10): 994–1011.

Hino, S. (2006) *Inside the mind of Toyota: Management principles for enduring growth*. New York: Productivity Press.

Holweg, M. (2006) The genealogy of Lean production, *Journal of Operations Management*, 25: 420–37.

Judge, T. A., Thoresen, C. J., Bono, J. E. and Patton, G. K. (2001) The job satisfaction–job performance relationship: A qualitative and quantitative review, *Psychological Bulletin*, 127: 376–407.

Kahn, W. A. (1990) Psychological conditions of personal engagement and disengagement at work, *Academy of Management Journal*, 33: 692–724.

Macey, W. H. and Schneider, B. (2008) The meaning of employee engagement, *Industrial and Organizational Psychology*, 1(1): 3–30.

Maitlis, S. and Sonenshein, S. (2010) Sensemaking in crisis and change: Inspiration and insights from Weick 1988, *Journal of Management Studies*, 47(3): 551–80.

Morrison, E. W. and Phelps, C. C. (1999) Taking charge at work: Extrarole efforts to initiate workplace change, *Academy of Management Journal*, 42(4): 403–19.

Park, C. L. (2010) Making sense of the meaning literature: An integrative review of meaning making and its effects on adjustment to stressful life events, *Psychological Bulletin*, 136(2): 257–301.

Pepper, M. P. J. and Spedding, T. A. (2010) The evolution of lean Six Sigma, *International Journal of Quality and Reliability Management*, 27(2): 138–55.

Radnor, Z. (2010) Transferring lean into government, *Journal of Manufacturing Technology*, 21(3): 411–28.

Rayton, B. and Dodge, T. (2012) *The evidence: Employee engagement task force 'nailing the evidence' workgroup*. London: Engage for Success.

Rich, B. L., LePine, J. A. and Crawford, E. R. (2010) Job engagement: Antecedents and effects on job performance, *Academy of Management Journal*, 53(3): 617–35.

Riketta, M. (2008) The causal relation between job attitudes and performance: A meta-analysis of panel studies, *Journal of Applied Psychology*, 93: 472–81.

Saks, A. M. (2008) The meaning and bleeding of employee engagement: How muddy is the water?, *Industrial and Organizational Psychology*, 1: 40–3.

Scherrer-Rathje, M., Boyle, T. A. and Deflorin, P. (2009) Lean, take two! Reflections from the second attempt at lean implementation, *Business Horizons*, 52(1): 79–88.

Schneider, B. (1990) *Organizational Climate and Culture*. San Francisco, CA: Jossey-Bass.

——, Hanges, P. J., Smith, D. B. and Salvaggio, A. N. (2003) Which comes first: Employee attitudes or organizational financial and market performance?, *Journal of Applied Psychology*, 88(5), 836–51.

Self, D., Armenakis, A. A. and Schraeder, M. (2007) Organizational change content, process, and context: A simultaneous analysis of employee reactions, *Journal of Change Management*, 7(2): 211–29.

Smollan, R. K. (2006) Minds, hearts and deeds: Cognitive, affective and behavioural responses to change, *Journal of Change Management*, 6(2): 143–58.

Sonenshein, S. (2010) We're changing – or are we? Untangling the role of progressive, regressive, and stability narratives during strategic change implementation, *Academy of Management Journal*, 53(3): 477–12.

—— and Dholakia, U. (2012) Explaining employee engagement with strategic change implementation: a meaning-making approach. *Organization Science*, 23(1): 1–23.

Sparrow, P. R. (2013) Engagement and performance. In P. Flood and Y. Freeney (eds) *Wiley Encyclopedia of Management, Volume 11 Organizational Behavior*. Cheltenham: Wiley, pp. 000–000.

—— and Balain, S. (2010) Engaging HR strategists: Do the logics match the realities? In Albrecht, S. (ed.) *The handbook of employee engagement: Models, measures and practice.* London: Edward-Elgar., pp. 263–96.

Winkler, S., König, C. J. and Kleinmann, M. (2012) New insights into an old debate: investigating the temporal sequence of commitment and performance at the business unit level, *Journal of Occupational and Organizational Psychology*, 85: 503–22.

Womack, J. and Jones, D. T. (1996) *Lean thinking*, New York: Free Press.

Womack, J., Jones, D. T. and Roos, D. (1990) *The machine that changed the world*. New York: Harper Perennial.

Wood, S. J., Stride, C. B., Wall, T. D. and Clegg, C. W. (2004) Revisiting the use and effectiveness of modern management practices, *Human Factors and Ergonomics in Manufacturing*, 14(4): 415–32.

6 Human resource development and employee engagement

Brad Shuck and Tonette S. Rocco

In recent decades, the experiences of work and the performance outcomes associated with work have been loosely, yet gradually connected in research and practice (Adler, 2001; Chalofsky and Krishna, 2009; Cho, Cho and McLean, 2009). This connection is reflective of the increasing humanization of the workplace, the globalization of work, and the unification of human development and organizational structures (Chalofsky, 2010; Kuchinke, 2010). Interestingly, increasing research in the field of human resource development (HRD) is moving toward the intersection of such connections.

Traditional models of management, which customarily focus on performance as the singular lens from which work can be examined, connote a rigid, hard, calculative approach (Sambrook, 2012). For example, *hard* approaches consider human resource functions that legislate performance through control over and of human capital. This often involves leveraging longstanding structures, processes, and procedures for capitalistic gain where employees are managed and expended in the same fashion as raw materials and equipment. Specific examples include selection, appraisal, and reward functions that emphasize performance outcomes without consideration for context or condition. On the other hand, relatively new and emerging softer approaches consider a more humanistic approach yet also maintain a focus toward performance. For example, *soft* approaches involve leveraging more meaningful and democratic forms of work and capitalizing on workplace learning in association with performance as a means to significant human development (Chalofsky, 2010; Kuchinke, 2010; Sambrook, 2012). Selection, appraisal, and reward functions are still leveraged, yet consideration for context and condition are reflected in this approach.

At present, the field of HRD aligns both 'hard' and 'soft' approaches (Sambrook, 2012), simultaneously considering the performance requirement of an organization alongside applications of human development. Through HRD, meaningful learning and work become possible within efficient, profitable, and performance driven organizational systems. This is the hallmark and central focus of HRD.

Of recent interest in HRD has been the focus toward employee engagement and its unique application as a 'soft-hard approach' (Sambrook, 2012). While research has considered engagement in a variety of contexts, its use, understanding, and application in HRD is only now gaining serious momentum. Building on this momentum, this chapter is focused on the perspective and breadth of research around employee engagement in the context of HRD. This chapter unfolds in four main sections: (a) overview of HRD, (b) examination of HRD and engagement literature, (c) strategies for developing engagement from an HRD context, and (d) emerging avenues for HRD and engagement.

Overview of the HRD field

Some debate continues on the defining parameters and boundaries of the HRD field (Blake, 1995; Lee, 2001). Roth (2004) suggested that HRD and other related disciplines have at times developed at arms' length from one another rather than exploring the utility and practicality of fertile ground between collaborative disciplines and approaches. This has resulted perhaps in some confusion about what HRD is and its application in both theory and practice to individual and organizational performance. Thus, when attempting to define HRD, there are several definitions from which to choose (see Roth, 2004 for a comprehensive overview). One particularly inclusive and comprehensive definition was offered by McLean and McLean (2001), who suggested that HRD could be defined as:

> A process or activity that, either initially or over the long term, has the potential to develop adults' work-based knowledge, expertise, productivity, and satisfaction, whether for personal or group/team gain, or for the benefit of an organization, community, and nation, or ultimately, the whole of humanity.
>
> (p. 322)

This definition echoes Kuchinke (2010) who suggested HRD was not only focused toward selection, appraisal, and reward functions but equally toward 'improving health, education, welfare, security, and social justice around the world' (p. 578). HRD then is in service to individuals and organizations as a function of human capital development but also to other 'considerations not typically perceived as manpower planning' (i.e., community building, culture development, and health promotion; McLean, 2004: 269). The simultaneous development of both human and social capital is a critical focus of emerging HRD and a central tenet in HRD's expanding role in research and practice.

For example, drawing from Sen's (Alkire, 2002) capability approach, Kuchinke (2010) argued for the discipline of HRD to focus more broadly as a means to better develop and balance the capability of individuals. From this lens, individuals could be employees within an organizational system, or citizens of a country with their own unique social, political, economic, and psychological circumstances. Sambrook (2012) noted this as a *soft-hard* approach, most closely aligned with the ideas of human development where HRD balances the need for performance alongside the need for better communities. HRD's primary focus using this approach is 'personal or group/team gain for the benefit of an organization, community, nation, or ultimately, the whole of society' (McLean and McLean, 2001: 322).

Thus, HRD is by all accounts an applied field of study focused on individuals and organizations. Some scholars would agree that HRD, as a discipline, is rooted in the epistemological underpinnings of more mature fields such as psychology, sociology, adult learning, economics, and organizational behavior (Roth, 2004; Swanson and Holton, 2009). The benefit of such underpinnings for HRD is the interplay and connectedness of each field to performance, the historical footing on which each stands, and each field's unique application to large, complex, and interconnected systems. HRD utilizes these epistemological underpinnings as frameworks, associations, and principles with flexibility, applying knowledge from these fields toward a myriad of different opportunities and challenges, from the largest organization to the individual employee.

Given the scholarly and practical flexibility of HRD and its focus toward individual and organizational performance, some scholars in HRD have recently turned their focus toward understanding the relation between employee engagement and HRD. The interest in engagement for HRD lies at the crossroads between performance improvement and the individual experience of work. The unique contribution of HRD is to not only look at *how much* performance can be leveraged, but also, *how* performance can be leveraged through experiences that enhance the meaning of work.

HRD and engagement: an overview of the literature

In the context of engagement, researchers in HRD have drawn heavily on the writings of seminal scholars such as Kahn (1990), Schaufeli, Bakker, and Salanova (2006), and Macey and Schneider (2008). These scholars have been instrumental in progressing research on and around engagement, overcoming such challenges as how to conceptualize engagement and what antecedents and outcomes can be expected as engagement is leveraged within organizations. In advancing these ideas, scholars in HRD are drawing on the theoretical depth of the field to develop a coherent, and deepening stream of research within the bounds of theory and practice.

HRD research on employee engagement has emerged primarily only within the past decade. Some of the earliest HRD engagement research appeared quietly in the *Academy of Human Resource Development's* annual conference proceedings (AHRD) in 2008, 2009, and 2010. Authors such as Berry and Morris (2008), Shuck and Albornoz (2008), Bonebright (2009), Shuck, Wollard, and Reio (2009) and Joo, Jeung and Shim (2010) provided early conceptual frameworks to the application of engagement within the HRD field. In 2009, the first HRD-related article (Chalofsky and Krishna, 2009) containing the term *employee engagement* (or any combination of the engagement construct; i.e. work engagement, job engagement, and so forth) appeared in a special issue of *Advances in Developing Human Resources* on the subject of meaningful work.

In their article, Chalofsky and Krishna (2009) explored the intersection of engagement and commitment as facets of meaningful work and its growing importance in understanding and shaping the experiences of work. In many ways, this piece was the impetus for Chalofsky's later work in 2010, which focused specifically on the development of meaningful workplaces and the application of engagement to meaningful work development. Building from the meaningful work context, Shuck, Rocco, and Albornoz (2011) utilized a case study design method to explore the phenomenon of engagement using a qualitative lens within a large, multinational service corporation. Findings suggested that perceptions of the environment and management as well as individual personality factors such as one's capacity to engage and intrinsically rooted motivation ultimately influenced the development of engagement through the framework of meaningful work. Paralleling and advancing this work, Fairlie (2011) provided evidence of the empirical linkage between meaningful work (e.g. intrinsic rewards) and engagement (utilizing the Utrecht Work Engagement Scale [UWES] as the operationalization of engagement). Fairlie proposed that by measuring meaningful work, variables such as self-actualization, social impact, feelings of personal accomplishment, and perceived ability to meet one's highest career goals could be leveraged within an organization.

In 2010, Shuck and Wollard (2010) provided an overview of the engagement literature using a historical analysis methodology. From their review of 159 articles, a definition of employee engagement was specifically offered for the HRD field, whereby engagement was defined as the cognitive, emotional, and behavioral energy an employee directs toward positive organizational outcomes. This definition used the multidimensional framework espoused by Saks (2006) and was careful to be inclusive of early research on engagement

(Kahn, 1990; Maslach et al., 2001; Schaufeli et al., 2002) as well as grounded in frameworks of the time (Macey and Schneider, 2008; Macey et al., 2009; Saks, 2006). The definition continues to be used in emerging HRD research. For example, using this framework, Shuck, Reio, and Rocco (2011) provided empirical evidence that job fit, affective commitment, and psychological climate were all significantly related to the development of employee engagement and further, that engagement was significantly related to discretionary effort and intention to turnover.

Advancing their earlier work, Shuck and Reio (2011) proposed a conceptual framework for engagement developed from cognitive, emotional, and behavioral phenomena reflective of an individual employee's response to a series of rational, contextually grounded judgment appraisals. Cognitive engagement revolved around how an employee thought about and reflected on their job, company, and culture. Emotional engagement revolved around the emotional bond one felt toward one's place of work and represented an overall willingness to involve personal, individually controlled resources such as pride, belief, and knowledge. Finally, behavioral engagement was operationalized as the physical and overt manifestation of cognitive and emotional engagement often tangibly identified as increased effort, performance, or productivity. This framework was offered as a foundational starting point for reflection, dialogue, and future scholarly inquiry (Shuck and Reio, 2011).

In more specific domains of applied practice such as leadership, several authors have examined the construct of engagement. Hoon Song, Kolb, Lee, and Kim (2012) were the first to examine implicit knowledge creation as a facet of engagement within HRD. Findings from their work suggested that transformational leadership style was significantly related to engagement and that engagement mediated the relation between leadership style and knowledge creation. Further, Shuck, and Herd (2012) proposed a holistic conceptual model of leadership and engagement that explored connections between employees' needs, motivation contexts, and levels of engagement. This model considered style and outcome as interconnected and further explored leadership behavior as a differentiator of high levels of engagement. In a more HRD-centric context, Rurkkhum and Bartlett (2012) empirically examined the relation between organizational citizenship behavior (OCB), HRD practices, and engagement.

Several authors have explored promising new avenues of research alongside engagement. For example, in 2011 Zigarmi and Nimon conceptually introduced the notion of employee work passion. Their work presented the construct of work intention as potential evidence of being engaged and proposed employee intentionality as a potentially powerful indicator of behavior. Reio and Sanders-Reio (2011) examined the relation between supervisor and coworker incivility and engagement. As a rather unsettling finding, empirical evidence from their work suggested a large majority of participants had experienced uncivil behavior at some point in their career. Levels of incivility were shown to share a negative statistical relation with engagement (e.g. higher levels of incivility resulted in lower levels of reported employee engagement). HRD practice was introduced as a means for reducing workplace incivility and increasing engagement through the implementation of training and development activities such as diversity awareness, conflict management, and program interventions. In looking at the other side of engagement, Wollard (2011) called attention to the 70 per cent of employees who report non-engagement or disengagement (as suggested by the Gallup studies). To guide future research and practice, Wollard presented a process model of disengagement and provided readers with an alternative perspective of the contemporary engagement literature. HRD was presented as a means to reduce the likelihood of an employee being disengaged.

Finally, HRD and engagement are not without criticism, as discussed further in Part 3 of this volume. In 2011, Newman, Joseph, Sparkman, and Carpenter (2011) provided sharp critique to the engagement construct in response to empirical work by Nimon, Zigarmi, Houson, Witt, and Diehl (2011). Specifically, Newman et al. (2011) called the engagement construct into serious question and rehighlighted the nomological confusion between engagement and other well-researched job factors such as satisfaction and commitment. Shuck, Ghosh, Zigarmi, and Nimon (2013) responded further by proposing differentiation through a series of diagrams, research questions, and propositions all using an HRD context for reference. For example, in the context of job satisfaction Shuck et al. (2013) agreed that employee engagement and satisfaction were similar in that they both measured a comparable dimension of a motivation-related nomological dimension (e.g. employee engagement and job satisfaction both sought to measure a work-related attitude); however, the authors further proposed conceptually that engagement was in fact distinct, measuring a dynamic, in-the-moment expression of energy directed toward organization outcomes, whilst satisfaction measured more general, global, and static expressions of an overall work-related attitude.

As a supplement to advancing research, situating the construct of engagement within the primary tools of the HRD field seems sound. In the next section we discuss engagement and organizational development, workplace learning, and career development.

Strategies for developing employee engagement from the HRD context

In this section we present strategies for developing employee engagement through the use of organizational development, workplace learning, and career development interventions. Organizational development is discussed as: (a) a data management and utilization issue, (b) a communication issue, and (c) an organizational accountability issue. Workplace learning suggests two fundamental areas for increasing engagement: (a) employee development and (b) management training. Finally, career development is considered separately from organizational development and workplace learning as an opportunity to increase engagement through career-related development activities and positive reinforcement of employee strength.

Organizational development

As organizational development focuses toward wide-ranging, change-related movements that can affect engagement levels, entire human resource functions are incorporated into long-term strategies. These strategies are often some of the most common, familiar interventions available. For example, organizational interventions such as change management, process improvement, and strategic planning often fall under the guise of organizational development (McLean, 2006). An examination of engagement and organizational development can be categorized into three main themes: (a) collecting and utilizing employee engagement data progressively for both economic and systems gain, (b) communication strategies that promote meaning, and (c) promoting employee accountability through inclusive performance and development systems.

Collecting and utilizing employee engagement data progressively for both economic and systems gain. Collecting data on engagement occurs when an organization assembles information on levels of engagement. Many organizations currently collect data (i.e. culture survey, satisfaction survey, work engagement survey, and so forth). While this is quite commonplace, and could seem obvious to include, the data are often poorly collected and inadequately analyzed. While scholars might debate definitions and measurement tools, practitioners often do not, as is explored further in Chapter 15. This trend produces data that may not measure what the practitioner set out to measure, resulting in potential data misinterpretation and misapplication. Further complicating the issue of engagement in practice is that organizations do not often employ statisticians or engagement experts in their employee ranks. Increasingly, they lean toward third party, for-profit consulting firms to tell them what engagement is and how to best measure the construct.

Notwithstanding, several consulting firms have well-documented products that seem to align with engagement, but often such products are unidimensional, have little variation from organization to organization, and even fewer utilize modeling techniques beyond correlational analysis (often referred to as a *driver analysis*). More unsettling is the lack of basic reliability and validity information made available to clients regarding measurement tools that purport to measure the construct of engagement. Finally, few organizations have the expertise to use the data once the results are in. This lack of expertise contributes to a scarcity of data-driven strategic planning, inefficient use of data, and wasted resources applied to organizational systems that may not need improvement.

Clearly, collecting data is a critical factor in creating interventions, which is a first step to increasing engagement. The conversations, decisions, and opportunities to invite employees into the process can be just as important as the data collected and fall within the expertise of HRD. A suggestion for better practice would be to partner with an engagement consortium or research group or to choose consulting firms who are just as willing to work with the organization as the organization is to work with them. Conversations about what engagement is, how to best capture it, and what processes can be employed are often enhanced when done in conjunction with revising or developing vision and mission statements. Cultural building and change through engagement initiatives gives substantive focus and strategy to organizational development interventions as an outcome of the engagement process; these processes lie uniquely within the field of HRD. Further, after collection, data can be used to align human resource functions more strategically, using the outcomes to support human resource alignment with the planned objectives of the organization. Collecting some data, using it to understand the organizational narrative, and making evidence-based decisions can be powerful for developing engagement.

Communication strategies that promote meaning. Communication strategies include attempts made by the organization to connect with their employees using a variety of media. Much research mentions communication as a strategy for developing and maintaining employee engagement, making up a significant portion of the known literature on engagement and organizational development. Communication is employed to (a) help employees relate to the organization through an understanding of how they contribute to the organization and (b) provide fair and accurate feedback as a means of helping employees find solutions to work challenges (Catteeuw et al., 2007; Razi, 2006; Shaw, 2005). Through this understanding, clear links exist between creating meaningful work, engagement, and communication (Fairlie, 2011). As communication with employees is regular, consistent, and non-threatening, employees may report feeling more a part of the organization and developing higher levels of trust in their leadership.

Communication is often delivered through existing formal systems such as performance reviews, goal setting sessions, departmental meetings, orientation processes, and weekly employee–manager conversations as well as informal methods that are more fleeting and conversational than structured (Catteeuw et al., 2007). The key success factor for communication is the consistency and quality of the communication, the strategy employed, and the intent of the message (Razi, 2006). Communication is vital for developing engagement and must be carefully considered as a tool when developing engagement strategies, particularly as a means for strategic, transparent, and positive organizational development. At times, communication might go beyond traditional corporate strategies to more authentic and organic opportunities to connect; this however takes presence of mind and a sense of genuine care – a unique facet of the soft-hard approach – where a focus on psychological and systems mechanisms can ultimately drive economic levers. Employees can sense a disingenuous message, and will react accordingly, which could produce a backlash and decrease engagement.

Promoting employee accountability through inclusive performance and development systems. Accountability is a result of identifying significant performance metrics around engagement and developing strategies for holding leaders, managers, and employees responsible for positive performance. Perhaps as an unusual approach, the focus toward accountability for the HRD practitioner is developmentally focused toward growth, not rooted in deficit or weakness. Examples of these measures include results on annual culture/engagement surveys, overall retention rates, or other hard performance metrics that are shown to be important linkages between engagement and organization functioning. Involving leaders and managers in identified areas as stakeholders and strategy owners helps drive the accountability theme and is a subtle, but important component of developing engagement. In this case, as the saying goes, what gets measured gets done and becomes a primary focus for strategy development. Holding leaders and managers responsible for *how much* work gets done alongside *how* work gets done can be a formidable approach.

For HRD, this aligns with how performance is leveraged through experiences that enhance the meaning of work. For example, as we see in Chapter 8 of this volume, scholars agree that leaders and managers have an enormous influence on the development of employee engagement with tremendous latitude to positively affect engagement. The experience of work that is influenced by a manager or leader can cast a long shadow. What a leader actually does in relation to how their employees perceive their wellbeing matters. 'Managers and supervisors are key levers of engagement . . . they must be aware of not just what they do but how they do it' (Catteeuw et al., 2007: 155) and they must be invested in the outcome of any engagement process. Holding leaders, managers, and even perhaps employees accountable for levels of engagement can be powerful and empowering simultaneously. Developing accountable practices that help managers become better managers, and leaders become better leaders, is essential. As a word of caution to the accountability theme, accountability should not become a punishment tool, and when presented as such, responsibility and accountability are rejected and resisted. Conversely, inclusive practices that invite participation and promote employee voice allow organizational and individual outcomes to flourish.

One strategy HRD practitioners often utilize includes the integration of strategies into existing organizational systems. Examples of this include recognition systems, team development, culture building, and systems training that might already be in place within organizational processes and structures and that promote a dimension of accountable practice.

Workplace learning

The HRD literature on employee engagement and workplace learning is focused in two areas: (a) individual employee development and (b) management training.

Individual employee development   Workplaces provide opportunities for learning in formal and informal ways by providing direct and indirect support and resources (Billet, 2001).

Learning and work cannot be separated (Lave, 1993). Environment and resources at work including those that support learning have the potential to influence employee engagement. Researchers have suggested that direct and indirect support for learning is viewed through the lens of social exchange theory as a reciprocally focused process (Lee and Bruvold, 2003). As an organization invests in the employee, the employee invests back into the organization (Lee and Bruvold, 2003).

Using this framework, researchers have suggested that the choice to be involved in workplace learning practices (such as those involving training and development) is a critical component of an organization's success when it comes to the development of employee engagement (Ferris, Hochwarter, Buckley, Harrell-Cook, and Frink, 1999). Several scholars have suggested that high commitment to employee development practices such as a commitment to HRD activities significantly affects important organizational outcomes such as turnover, organizational commitment, job satisfaction, and organizational citizenship behaviors (Arthur, 1994; Huselid, 1995; Lee and Bruvold, 2003; Whitener, 2001). Such commitment of organizations towards their employees sends a powerful message about the personal and professional growth of the employee and their value to the organization (Lee and Bruvold, 2003). This value translates into engagement as an employee feels supported, invested in, and a part of the organization's future.

Through the connection of organizational support, workplace learning in the areas of essential skills (i.e. coaching, communication, supervision), designing learning with a focus on engagement as an outcome (Czarnowsky, 2008), and linking training to organizational goals (Catteeuw et al., 2007; Mathieson, 2006) are ways workplace learning and engagement can be conceptualized in practice. Wildermuth and Pauken (2008) caution, however, that 'engagement will [never] be impacted by a single training program regardless of its quality. Enhancing engagement is a long-term proposition', that requires a wider organizational perspective inclusive of the HRD function (p. 210). In the literature, workplace learning and employee engagement are linked as (a) a means to support wider organizational initiatives (Catteeuw et al., 2007), (b) a recruitment and retention strategy (Woodruffe, 2006), and (c) as a process for developing organizational buy-in (Mathieson, 2006).

Management training   Management training is discussed in the HRD literature as any workplace learning initiative geared toward managers for the specific purpose of training knowledge, skills, and abilities that foster development. Frontline managers do much of the engagement work as a first line of contact between an employee and the organization (Shuck, Rocco, and Albornoz, 2011). Further, some have suggested that employees often view their organization from the same perspective in which they view their managers (Galford and Drapeau 2003). This makes management training important on two fronts: (a) managers as employees increase their own level of engagement in relation to their development and (b) managers as overseers and representatives of the organizational persona foster engagement in those they manage through their actions and attitudes. Consequently, learning opportunities around techniques that managers can use to increase engagement remain vital. Underscoring the importance of workplace learning initiatives around management development can be best captured in the saying, 'the root of employee disengagement is [often] poor management' (Gopal, 2003).

Specific strategies such as training managers in the areas of coaching (Czarnowsky, 2008; Woodruffe, 2006) and communication (Catteeuw et al., 2007; Shaw, 2005) are often mentioned as approaches. Involving management in the development of training via focus groups (Mathieson, 2006) and in the defining of employee engagement strategies for the organization are other potential strategies. One promising approach was introduced by Kroth and Keeler

(2009) who proposed *care* as a management strategy framework. Kroth and Keeler (2009) went on to suggest that an ethos of care had the potential to affect employee perceptions of their work as well as their productivity. Connected to this was Kahn's (1993) suggestion that managers as caregivers protected and served as guides during an employee's journey toward growth and engagement while providing the emotional, technical, and physical resources needed.

The common theme throughout the literature suggested that a focus toward management development is essential for an engagement-driven culture. Helping managers understand the need for consistent communication, the delivery of clearly defined expectations, and feedback are of paramount importance, however, few managers may understand this role. Bogged down with day-to-day administrative tasks, the literature suggested that few managers may feel they have the time or skills to fully engage their staff (Woodruffe, 2006). Ironically, only 47 per cent of organizations reportedly have a new supervisor-training program in place and even when in place, few measure the program's effectiveness (Czarnowsky, 2008). As a result, only 15 per cent of employees report feeling that their current manager had the skills to engage them (Czarnowsky, 2008).

Career development

According to Hall (2002) a career is advancement in a profession, a lifelong sequence of jobs, and a series of role-related experiences. Career development can be best understood as someone in an authority position intentionally assisting an employee to understand his or her career goals, path, and development. From this HRD angle, talking with employees about career goals and their advancement opportunities helps add a sense of meaningfulness to an employee's position (Wildermuth and Pauken, 2008). Woodruffe (2006) suggested that career development programs can be of mutual benefit to both the employee and employer, building a sense of significance into one's job, which in turn builds a sense of engagement (Fornes et al., 2008). Engagement then builds out of a circular model where meaning development happens in reciprocal perspectives. For example, employees are able to add value and significance to what they are doing through meaningful work as well as receive feedback that they are valuable and significant to the organization (Fairlie, 2011; Shuck and Reio, 2011).

Within the HRD literature, one strategy includes the embracement of the *Strengths* philosophy (Buckingham and Clifton, 2001; Clifton and Harter, 2003; Woodruffe, 2006). A *strength* was defined as 'consistent near perfect performance in an activity' (Buckingham and Clifton, 2001: 25) and is developed from productively applied reoccurring patterns of thought, feeling, or behavior. It is assumed that each employee's strengths are unique to the context of his or her life roles and that these roles intersect at work. Strengths can evolve into competencies that are possible to further develop and nurture. The authors of this philosophy (Buckingham and Clifton, 2001) assert, 'we must find the best fit possible of people's strengths and the roles we are asking them to play at work. Only then will we be as strong as we should be' (p. 245). The philosophy of Strength is rooted in positive psychology and fits well within the emerging appreciative inquiry framework, which looks to emphasize the positive and manage weakness (Grant and Humphries, 2006). Rather than a deficit-based approach, appreciative inquiry focuses toward a 'proactive, positive approach emphasizing strengths, rather than continuing in the downward spiral of negativity trying to fix weaknesses' (Luthans, 2002: 695). This approach is gaining increasing conceptual momentum in HRD.

Helping an employee develop the talents that come naturally to them, reinforcing talents through purposeful development, or simply having conversations about the unique value and talents an employee brings to the organization plays a significant role in the development of employee engagement through career development. For some, simply having a conversation with their manager about their career can be a daunting, yet deeply sought-after opportunity. This area of HRD is strikingly undervalued, underrepresented, and thus amazingly cost effective. Having conversations with employees about talent development, competency building, and career progression, versus constantly identifying deficits and areas of shoring up can be an enabling experience that builds good will toward a manager, an organization, and thereby increases engagement. So often, leaders, managers, and employees can go months without a conversation regarding career pathing or development, let alone positive feedback regarding their performance.

Emerging avenues for HRD and engagement: final remarks

While the history of HRD and engagement is brief, the future seems increasingly promising and robust. Because of the epistemological flexibility of HRD, new areas of exploration can be examined without violating the bounds of the field.

Most notably, future research will focus on explicit empirical linkages between HRD practice and engagement using advanced statistical modeling techniques and experimental design in partnership with willing organizations. For example, because of the relevant newness of engagement and HRD, few studies have examined how HRD activities impact learning, performance, and engagement simultaneously. This is a ripe area for inquiry and exploration with strong benefits to the science and practice of engagement. Moreover, longitudinal research seems a prudent step in establishing a deeper understanding between the intersections of the experiences of work and performance outcomes associated with work rather than momentary snapshots of involvement. As suggested in this chapter, engagement and HRD share an important relationship; uncovering specific leverage points that direct practitioners toward evidence-based models that improve performance and the experience of work simultaneously seems a likely and advantageous focus.

Further, alongside research on HRD practice, areas of corporate social responsibility and sustainability are on the forefront of the HRD agenda (Scully-Russ, 2012). As practitioners consider the role of engagement within their places of work, sustainable efforts that transcend culture, continent, and context are an exciting focal point. Engagement is becoming less of a corporate event and more of a sustainable strategy. These areas of inquiry have received little attention in HRD, or within any major academic field, and represent opportunities for researchers who often work in disparate fields, and who unfortunately at times work at odds, to join together for real advancement toward a promising idea. Perhaps one encouraging development is the application of a social ecological framework where individual systems of influence are considered alongside meso- and macro-systems simultaneously (Weinstein and Shuck, 2011). Consequently, the social ecological framework broadens the conversation beyond the finite work context of employee engagement and considers engagement in relation to a person's immediate environment, family, community, nationality, and global context all within philosophical, social, spiritual, and emotional dimensions. Engagement then becomes broad and explanatory as a framework from which to understand a human being rather than regaled only as an outcome of work. This kind of work requires the melding of various academic and practitioner partnerships; a truly beneficial opportunity.

Finally, compassion and passion represent two constructs in early phases of theoretical development but with some suggested relation to engagement (Zigarmi and Nimon, 2011; Nimon and Zigarmi, 2011). Both represent more emotional and heightened levels of individual awareness; passion being focused on the peak experiences of being human and compassion being more attuned to benevolence toward those around us. These ideas represent the forward thinking of the HRD field as well as the introspective, more individually focused perspective the field is increasingly taking along other more positively focused constructs such as hope, resiliency, and optimism (Luthans, 2012).

In closing, we remain excited about the development of engagement within the HRD field, and are encouraged by the science-driven application of engagement across various fields of inquiry. HRD will be at the forefront of knowledge development and the soft-hard science of performance and human development in an increasingly complex and humane context.

Case study: Yum! Brands, Inc.: The soft side

Kathleen Gosser
Director, HR, KFC/YUM! Brands

YUM! Brands, Inc., based in Louisville, Kentucky, is the world's largest restaurant company, with nearly 38,000 restaurants (*Kentucky Fried Chicken*, *Pizza Hut*, and *Taco Bell*), locations in over 120 countries and almost 1 million employees. YUM! Brands, Inc. is a Fortune 500 company and recognized as a global leader for their *Famous Recognition Culture*, which drives their rich culture of engagement. Building, executing, and maintaining such a culture is, however, no easy task. David Novak, recently chosen as CEO of the year by *Chief Executive* (Donlon, 2012), leads YUM! Brands, Inc. globally with strong leadership and a dedication to role modeling from the top.

Recent research conducted at YUM! offers strong supporting evidence of the relation between a culture characterized by engagement and recognition and performance outcomes. In a study of 935 team members across one of the major YUM! Brands, results revealed that recognition and being treated with kindness and respect by one's manager were critical to hourly team members in relation to their levels of engagement – even more important than pay. Through this research, team members were asked about their intent to stay with the organization along with their levels of satisfaction across a number of key areas including organizational justice and socialization (Gosser, 2011). Issues of organizational justice, such as when employees felt they had a voice in a process or when they believed decision outcomes and the distribution of resources were fairly allocated across the organization, were significantly related to intent to stay, particularly around areas of work load distribution, recognition, and being treated with kindness and respect. These results provided support for the rich culture that Yum! Brands intentionally builds worldwide. For YUM!, building a culture where people enjoy work and feel as if they are a part of the process is the foundation to achieving high levels of performance.

YUM! Brands builds this kind of culture with intentionality and focus throughout each of their restaurants across the globe. For example, when David Novak became president of *Kentucky Fried Chicken* (USA), he developed a personal recognition award, a plastic toy floppy chicken, on which he would write a personal message of encouragement and recognition to associates within the company. As a result, floppy plastic chickens became very popular inside YUM! – having one was a high status commodity as it was recognition that you had done something well; it also sent a strong message of organizational support in that someone took time to notice and reinforce good work. As a way to cascade the recognition culture throughout the organization, Novak insisted that each associate be able to provide a similar award on a smaller scale when they caught someone doing something great at work. Associates across the organization began handing out their personal awards such as a toy navigational compass for a job well done. For another YUM! recognition award, Novak uses a set of oversized walking teeth – called the *Walk the Talk* award. This award is used to recognize employees for excellent performance such as exceeding sales, launching a new product, leading a new process, or any individual contribution of outstanding work that contributes to business performance.

As Novak has stated regarding his work with YUM!, 'culture is no accident' (Novak, 2012: 152). The standard line at YUM! is 'Why would you want to work anywhere else?' As a result of their focus on recognition and the intentional creation of a culture rich in recognition, YUM! continues to be a global leader in the restaurant business. Novak suggests, 'Numbers don't run a business – people do' (2012: 148). Building the 'know how' for creating a culture rich in recognition is the first step; execution follows only after you take care of your people.

References

Adler, P. S. (2001) 'Market hierarchy, and trust: The knowledge economy and the future of capitalism', *Organization Science*, 12: 215–234.

Alkire, S. (2002) *Valuing freedoms: Sen's capability approach and poverty reduction,* Oxford: Oxford University.

Arthur, J. B. (1994) 'Effects of human resource systems on manufacturing performance and turnover', *Academy of Management Journal,* 37(3): 670–87. doi: 10.2307/256705

Berry, M. L. and Morris, M. L. (2008) 'The impact of employee engagement factors and job satisfaction on turnover intent', paper presented at Academy of Human Resource Development Annual Conference in Panama City, FL, February.

Billet, S. (2001) *Learning in the workplace: Strategies for effective practice*, Crows Nest: Allen & Unwin.

Blake, R. R. (1995) 'Memories of HRD', *Training and Development*, 49(3): 22–8.

Bonebright, D. (2009) 'The relationship between employee engagement and workplace training: A proposed model', paper presented at Academy of Human Resource Development Annual Conference in Washington, DC, February.

Buckingham, M. and Clifton, D. O. (2001) *Now, discover your strengths*, New York: The Free Press.

Catteeuw, F., Flynn, E. and Vonderhorst, J. (2007) 'Employee engagement: Boosting productivity in turbulent times', *Organizational Development Journal*, 25(2): 151–8.

Chalofsky, N. E. (2010) *Meaningful Workplaces: Reframing how and where we work,* Hoboken, NJ: John Wiley & Sons.

Chalofsky, N. and Krishna, V. (2009) 'Meaningfulness, commitment, and engagement: The intersection of a deeper level of intrinsic motivation', *Advances in Developing Human Resources*, 11(2):189–203. doi: 10.1177/1523422309333147

Cho, Y., Cho., E. and McLean, G. N. (2009) 'HRD's role in knowledge management', *Advances in Developing Human Resource Development*, 11(3): 263–72. doi: 10.1177/1523422309337719

Clifton, D. O. and Harter, J. K. (2003) 'Investing in Strengths', in K. S. Cameron, J. E. Dutton and R. E. Quinn (eds) *Positive organizational scholarship: Foundations of a new discipline*, San Francisco: Berrett-Koehler Publishers.

Czarnowsky, M. (2008) *Learning's role in employee engagement: An ASTD research study,* Alexandria, VA: ASTD.

Donlon, J. P. (2012) *CEO of the year David Novak: The recognition leader*. Available at http://chiefexecutive.net/ceo-year-david-novak-the-recognition-leader [accessed 19 December 2012].

Fairlie, P. (2011) 'Management tools: The meaning of work', *HR Magazine*, 56(1): pgs. doi: 10.1177/1523422311431679

Ferris, G. R., Hochwarter, W. A., Buckley, M. R., Harrell-Cook, G. and Frink, D. D. (1999) 'Human resources management: Some new directions', *Journal of Management*, 25(3): 385–415. doi: 10.1177/014920639902500306

Fornes, S. L., Rocco, T. R. and Wollard, K. K. (2008) 'Workplace commitment: A conceptual model developed from integrative review of the research', *Human Resource Development Review*, 7(3): 339–57. doi:10.1177/1534484308318760

Galford, R. and Drapeau, A. (2003) *The trusted leader: Bringing out the best in your people and your company*, New York: The Free Press.

Gopal, A. (2003) *Disengaged employees cost Singapore $4.9 billion.* Available at http://gmj.gallup. com/content/default.aspx?ci=1207> [accessed 20 July 2006].

Gosser, K. (2011) 'Predictors of intent to stay for hourly employees in the fast food industry', doctoral dissertation, University of Louisville.

Grant, S. and Humphries, M. (2006) 'Critical evaluation of appreciative inquiry: Bridging an apparent paradox', *Action Research*, 4(4): 401–18. doi: 10.1177/1476750306070103

Hall, D. T. (2002) *Careers in and out of organizations,* Thousand Oaks, CA: Sage Publications.

Hoon Song, J., Kolb, J. A., Hee Lee, U. and Kyoung Kim, H. (2012) 'Role of transformational leadership in effective organizational knowledge creation practices: Mediating effects of employees' work engagement', *Human Resource Development Quarterly*, 23(1): 65–101. doi: 10.1002/hrdq. 21120

Huselid, M. (1995) 'The impact of human resource management practices on turnover, productivity, and corporate financial performance', *Academy of Management Journal*, 38(3): 635–72. doi: 10.2307/256741

Joo, B., Jeung, C. and Shim, J. (2010) 'Antecedents of employee engagement: The roles of psychological empowerment and transformational leadership', paper presented at Academy of Human Resource Development Annual Conference in Knoxville, TN, February.

Kahn, W. (1990) 'Psychological conditions of personal engagement and disengagement at work', *Academy of Management Journal*, 33(4): 692–724. doi: 10.2307/256287

—— (1993) 'Caring for the caregivers: Patterns of organizational caregiving,' *Administrative Science Quarterly*, 38(4): 539–63. doi:10.2307/2393336

Kroth, M. and Keeler, C. (2009) 'Caring as a managerial strategy', *Human Resource Development Review*, 8(4): 506–31. doi: 10.1177/1534484309341558

Kuchinke, K. P. (2010) 'Human development as a central goal for human resource development', *Human Resource Development International*, 13(5): 575–85. doi: 10.1080/13678868.2010. 520482

Lave, J. (1993) 'The practice of learning', in S. Chaiklin and J. Lave (eds) *Understanding Practice: Perspectives on Activity and Context*, Cambridge, UK: Cambridge University Press.

Lee, M. (2001) 'A refusal to define HRD', *Human Resource Development International*, 4(3): 327–41. doi:10.1080/13678860110059348

Lee, C. H. and Bruvold, N. T. (2003) 'Creating value for employees: Investment in employee development', *The International Journal of Human Resource Management*, 14(6): 981–1000. doi:10.1080/0958519032000106173

Luthans, F. (2002) 'The need for and meaning of positive organizational behavior', *Journal of Organizational Behavior*, 23(6): 695–706. doi:10.1002/job.165

—— (2012) 'Psychological capital: Implications for HRD, retrospective analysis, and future directions', *Human Resource Development Quarterly*, 23: 1–8. doi: 10.1002/hrdq.21119

Macey, W. and Schneider, B. (2008) 'The meaning of employee engagement', *Industrial and Organizational Psychology,* 1: 3–30. doi:10.1111/j.1754-9434.2007.0002.x

——, Schneider, B., Barbera, K. M. and Young, S. (2009) *Employee engagement: Tools for analysis, practice, and competitive advantage*, Malden, MA: Wiley Blackwell.

Maslach, C., Schaufeli, W. B. and Leiter, M. P. (2001) 'Job burnout', *Annual Review of Psychology*, 52(1): 397–422. doi:10.1146/annurev.psych.52.1.397

Mathieson, M. (2006) 'Improving organizational performance through developing our people', *Industrial and Commercial Training*, 38: 70–7. doi:10.1108/00197850610653135

McLean, G. N. (2004) 'National human resource development: What in the world is it?', *Advances in Developing Human Resources*, 6(3): 269–75. doi: 10.1177/1523422304266086

McLean, G. (2006) *Organization development: Principles, processes, performance*, San Francisco, CA: Berrett-Koehler.

—— and McLean, L. (2001) 'If we can't define HRD in one country, how can we define it in an international context?', *Human Resource Development International*, 4(3): 313–26. doi: 10.1080/13678860110059339

Newman, D. A., Joseph, D. L., Sparkman, T. E. and Carpenter, N. C. (2011) 'Invited reaction: The work cognition inventory: Initial evidence of construct validity', *Human Resource Development Quarterly*, 22(1): 37–47.

Nimon, K. and Zigarmi, D. (2011) 'The assessment of a multinational using the employee work passion model', *Advances in Developing Human Resources*, 13(4): 494–507. doi: 10.1177/1523422311431681

——, Zigarmi, D., Houson, D., Witt, D. and Diehl, J. (2011) 'The work cognition inventory: Initial evidence of construct validity,' *Human Resource Development Quarterly*, 22(1): 7–35. doi:10.1002/hrdq.20064

Novak, D. (2012) *Taking people with you*, New York, NY: Penguin Group.

Razi, N. (2006) 'Employing OD strategies in the globalization of HR', *Organization Development Journal*, 24(4): 62–8.

Reio, T. G. and Sanders-Reio, J. (2011) 'Thinking about workplace engagement: Does supervisor and coworker incivility really matter?', *Advances in Developing Human Resources*, 13(4): 462–78. doi: 10.1177/1523422311430784

Roth, G. L. (2004) 'CPE and HRD: Research and practice within systems and across boundaries', *Advances in Developing Human Resources*, 6(1): 9–19. doi: 10.1177/1523422303260417

Rurkkhum, S. and Bartlett, K. R. (2012) 'The relationship between employee engagement and organizational citizenship behaviour in Thailand', *Human Resource Development International*, 15(2): 157–74. doi:10.1080/13678868.2012.664693

Saks, A. M. (2006) 'Antecedents and consequences of employee engagement', *Journal of Managerial Psychology*, 21(7): 600–19. doi:10.1108/02683940610690169

Sambrook, S. (2012) 'Human and resource development is hard', *Human Resource Development International*, 15(2): 135–9. doi:10.1080/13678868.2012.663189

Schaufeli, W. B., Bakker, A. B. and Salanova, M. (2006) 'The measurement of work engagement with a short questionnaire: A cross-national study', *Educational and psychological Measurement*, 66(4): 701–16. doi: 10.1177/0013164405282471

——, Salanova, M., González-Romá, V. and Bakker, A. B. (2002) 'The measurement of engagement and burnout: A two sample confirmatory factor analytic approach', *Journal of Happiness Studies*, 3(1): 71–92. doi:10.1023/A:1015630930326

Scully-Russ, E. (2012) 'Human resource development and sustainability: Beyond sustainable organizations', *Human Resource Development International*, 15(4): 399–415. doi: 10.1080/13678868.2012.707529

Shaw, K. (2005) 'Getting leaders involved in communication strategy: Breaking down barriers to effective leadership communication', *Strategic Communication Management*, 9, 14–17.

Shuck, B. and Albornoz, C. (2008) 'Employee engagement: Under the salary line', paper presented at Academy of Human Resource Development Annual Conference in Panama City, FL, February.

—— and Herd, A. M. (2012) 'Employee engagement and leadership: Exploring the convergence of two frameworks and implications for leadership development in HRD', *Human Resource Development Review*, 11(2): 156–81. doi: 10.1177/1534484312438211

—— and Reio, T.G. (2011) 'The employee engagement landscape and HRD: How do we link theory and scholarship to current practice?', *Advances in Developing Human Resources*, 13(4): 419–28. doi: 10.1177/1523422311431153

——, Ghosh, R., Zigarmi, D. and Nimon, K. (2013) 'The jingle jangle of employee engagement: Further exploration of the emerging construct & implications for workplace learning and performance', *Human Resource Development Review*, 12(1): 11–35. doi: 10.1177/1534484312463921

——, Reio, Jr, T. G. and Rocco, T. S. (2011) 'Employee engagement: An examination of antecedent and outcome variables', *Human Resource Development International*, 14(4): 427–45. doi: 10.1080/13678868.2011.601587

——, Rocco, T. and Albornoz, C. (2011) 'Exploring employee engagement from the employee perspective: Implications for HRD', *Journal of European Industrial Training*, 35(4): 300–25. doi: 10.1108/03090591111128306

—— and Wollard, K. (2010) 'Employee engagement and HRD: A seminal review of the foundations', *Human Resource Development Review*, 9(1): 89–110. doi: 10.1177/1534484309353560

——, Wollard, K. K. and Reio, T. G. (2009) 'Positive psychology and employee engagement: What are organizations doing and why should HRD professionals care? An Innovative session', paper presented at Academy of Human Resource Development Annual Conference in Washington, DC, February.

Swanson, R. A. and Holton, E. F. (2009) *The process of framing research in organizations,* San Francisco, CA: Berrett-Koehler Publishers.

Weinstein, M. G. and Shuck, B. (2011) 'Social ecology and worksite training and development: Introducing the social in instructional system design', *Human Resource Development Review*, 10(3): 286–303. doi: 10.1177/1534484311411074

Whitener, E. M. (2001) 'Do "high commitment" human resource practices affect employee commitment? A cross-level analysis using hierarchical linear modeling', *Journal of Management*, 27(5): 515–35. doi: 10.1177/014920630102700502

Wildermuth, C. and Pauken, P. D. (2008) 'A perfect match: Decoding employee engagement – Part II: Engaging jobs and individuals', *Industrial and Commercial Training*, 40(4): 206–10. doi: 10.1108/00197850810876253

Wollard, K. K. (2011) 'Quiet desperation: Another perspective on employee engagement', *Advances in Developing Human Resources*, 13(4): 526–37. doi: 10.1177/1523422311430942

Woodruffe, C. (2006) 'The crucial importance of employee engagement', *Human Resource Management International Digest*, 14: 3–5. doi: 10.1108/09670730610643891

Zigarmi, D. and Nimon, K. (2011) 'A cognitive approach to work intention: The stuff that employee work passion is made of?', *Advances in Developing Human Resources*, 13(4): 447–61. doi: 10.1177/1523422311431152

7 Job design and employee engagement

Maria Tims and Arnold B. Bakker

Introduction

A well-designed job may foster employee well-being and engagement (Bakker and Demerouti, 2013; Hackman and Oldham, 1980; Parker and Wall, 1998). It is therefore not surprising that researchers have aimed to examine which job characteristics contribute to employee well-being and engagement, and which are likely to increase job stress. Together, the characteristics of the job comprise the design of the job.

More specifically, job design describes how 'jobs, tasks, and roles are structured, enacted, and modified and what the impact of these structures, enactments, and modifications are on the individual, group, and organizational outcomes' (Grant and Parker, 2009, p. 5). For more than 60 years, job design theories have guided scholars and practitioners to describe, explain, and change the work experiences and behaviors of employees. Job design is usually approached as a top-down process in which the organization creates jobs and, in turn, selects people with the right knowledge, skills, and abilities for these jobs. When employee experiences (e.g. work engagement) and behaviors (e.g. performance) tend to decrease, management may redesign the jobs of their employees. For example, one reason for job redesign may be that management notices that absenteeism among certain employees is relatively high. After talking to the employees, company doctors and HR professionals may find out that the job is too demanding for the employees and needs to be changed. Another reason for job redesign may be the introduction of a new machine that (partly) replaces the work of employees. The jobs of these employees may then be redesigned to include other tasks such as maintaining the machines.

The way a job is (re)designed strongly influences how employees perceive their job and, in turn, how they perform their tasks. Managers and researchers started to focus their attention on the influence of job design on employees' behaviors and attitudes when it was found that changes in the work environment were accompanied with changes in employee attitudes and motivation. For example, over a century ago, the scientific management approach (Taylor, 1911) and the introduction of the assembly line at Ford in 1914, strongly promoted job simplification. Employees' jobs changed from, for example, building a complete car to assembling only parts of the car, and this job change had a considerable impact on employee motivation. The early empirical research that focused on the psychological consequences of such repetitive jobs confirmed that simplified jobs were boring, tiring, and dissatisfying as well as potentially damaging to mental health (see Parker, Wall, and Cordery, 2001). The idea of increasing employees' efficiency and productivity by making their jobs as small and simple as possible had overlooked the person's sense of self-worth and well-being. Therefore, attention needed to be paid to find a way in which the design of jobs contributed to employee performance and employee well-being and motivation simultaneously.

During the past decades, a lot of research has shown a strong link between job design and employee engagement. In this chapter, we evaluate this research and discuss what the implications are for the HRM professional in terms of how to design jobs effectively to raise levels of engagement. The chapter starts off with an overview of various job design theories that focus on the effect of job design on employee well-being. Next, the job characteristics that particularly influence employee engagement are presented and the mechanisms through which job characteristics may lead to employee engagement are addressed. The closing section attempts to integrate the various research findings in order to provide useful insights for HRM professionals. However, the focus will not only be on how organizations should (re)design jobs for their employees. We will also discuss how employees may influence their own job characteristics and levels of work engagement through job crafting.

Review of job design literature

The view on how to design a job has changed considerably over the years, which has resulted in various job design theories. We provide an overview of the most important job design theories and perspectives that emerged over the last 60 years and that aimed to increase employee well-being or engagement. Note that, originally, most job design theories focused on job satisfaction or motivation. Employee engagement only recently gained the attention of researchers with the growing focus on positive organizational scholarship (Cameron, Dutton, and Quinn, 2003) and positive organizational behavior (Nelson and Cooper, 2007). For the purpose of this chapter, we will review not only theories that focus specifically on employee engagement (e.g. job demands–resources model – JD–R) but we will also describe influential job design theories that have contributed to the evolution of the job demand-resources theory (Bakker and Demerouti, 2013).

Employee engagement, in this chapter, is defined as a positive, fulfilling, work-related state of mind that is characterized by vigor, dedication, and absorption (Schaufeli, Bakker, and Salanova, 2006). Vigor refers to high levels of willingness to invest energy into work, and to persevere even in the case of difficulties. Dedication is defined as the involvement in one's work and the experience of significance, inspiration, pride, and challenge. Absorption constitutes the third and final component of employee engagement and refers to being fully concentrated in work and finding it difficult to divert attention from work (Schaufeli et al., 2006). Employee engagement has attracted considerable interest from researchers and practitioners, most likely because it has been shown to influence employee job performance and organizational productivity (Christian, Garza, and Slaughter, 2011; Demerouti and Cropanzano, 2010; Harter, Schmidt, and Hayes, 2002). It is therefore interesting to find out how engagement may be increased when designing jobs for employees.

In this chapter, we discuss five job design models that have all been or still are very influential. The models we review are: (1) sociotechnical systems theory; (2) two-factor theory; (3) job characteristics model; (4) demand-control model; and (5) job demands–resources theory. Each theory is examined for its ability to explain how work design contributes to employee engagement (or job satisfaction) and is shown to offer a different perspective on the design of work. The five job design theories cover the 1960s up to now. However, before discussing the first theory, we briefly go back in time once more to see how jobs were designed at the turn of the nineteenth century since this influenced the way job design theories were designed in later years.

Early job design approaches

Taylor (1911) redesigned jobs in a way that employees performed the simplest tasks possible in a prescribed, 'scientific' way. Close supervision and bureaucratic rules dehumanized employees; there was no room for suggestions or experiments, and employees had to do what they were told to do in a specified way and time (Littler, 1978). Even though Taylor reported the successful implementation of scientific management in many companies, mainly in industrial settings, it soon appeared that employees were not satisfied with their jobs and this actually negated the efficiencies implemented in their jobs. One can imagine the employees were not engaged in their work as there was simply no room for engagement: tasks were so simple and repetitive that losing oneself in the task at hand and feeling dedicated because the task was meaningful was not possible. The human relations movement (Mayo, 1933; Roethlisberger and Dickson, 1939) emerged to include the human aspects of work and led to improved personnel policies. However, this movement was not able to counter the work alienation that was evident at that time (Walker and Guest, 1952). This was likely due to the fact that the structure of jobs had not changed (Trist, 1981). The job design theories that followed the human relations movement focused explicitly on the design of jobs to show which job characteristics should be managed such that employee motivation and satisfaction would increase.

Sociotechnical systems theory

Sociotechnical systems (STS) theory was conceptualized by Eric Trist during his work at the Tavistock Institute for Human Relations in London (Trist and Bamforth, 1951). STS theory focuses on the interdependencies between people, technology, and the work environment (Emery and Trist, 1965). This theory thus combines the social and technical systems to increase productivity and job satisfaction, rather than focusing on only one of these aspects, which was prevalent in earlier theories. The technological system consists of the equipment and methods that are used to transform materials into products, whereas the social system refers to the work structure that relates people to the technology and each other. The main goal of this approach is the joint optimization of the social and technical aspects of work that may be achieved by changing the technology (e.g. equipment), the work structure (e.g. work roles), or both (Cummings, 1978; Emery and Trist, 1965).

A new feature of STS is that it focused on group rather than individual job design (Parker et al., 2001). Autonomous work groups, in which teams work on a whole and meaningful task, develop skills relevant to their tasks, and have discretion over their tasks, are seen as a concrete outcome of this theory (Cummings, 1978). As a result of the self-regulation of the team, there would be higher productivity and job satisfaction among employees and lower supervision costs. Presumably, the most famous example of sociotechnical redesign is that undertaken at Volvo's Kalmar and Uddevalla car plants (Walker, Stanton, Salmon, and Jenkins, 2008). The plants were changed from hierarchical organizations to organizations based on smaller groups. The production line was replaced by autonomous work groups. Both plants proved to be productive and human-oriented (although they were closed within five years after their opening as a result of a global production strategy decision) (Sandberg, 1995).

Nonetheless, STS theory has been shown to have its weak points. One weakness refers to the 'joint' optimization of the social and technical systems. It has been argued that sociotechnical redesign is often focused on only one of the systems and not on optimizing both (Matthews, 199/). And, more importantly, an explicit specification of how the technical and social systems affect each other is missing (Hackman and Oldham, 1976). In addition, technology is often approached as a given, such that the social system is designed around the technology. As a result, information on how to design and optimize the technical system is lacking (De Sitter, Den Hertog, and Dankbaar, 1997). Also, the basis for the theory, production organizations and the preference for autonomous work groups, complicate application of the STS principles to a broader range of organizations (Kompier, 2003).

Two-factor theory

Around the same time, Herzberg (1966) introduced the two-factor theory of motivation and satisfaction that focused on the design of individual jobs. The theory states that some aspects of the work and work environment influence employee satisfaction while other aspects merely influence employee *dis*satisfaction. Motivator factors (i.e. intrinsic aspects of the job) such as interesting tasks and recognition, were hypothesized to influence employee satisfaction but would have little impact on dissatisfaction. In contrast, hygiene factors (i.e. extrinsic aspects of the job) such as pay and company policy, were hypothesized to have little effect on satisfaction but would cause dissatisfaction when absent (Herzberg, Mausner, and Snyderman, 1967). As can be seen from this hypothesis, Herzberg did not define satisfaction and dissatisfaction as opposites on the same continuum. Rather, he argued that the opposite of satisfaction is no satisfaction, and not dissatisfaction. Similarly, the opposite of dissatisfaction is no dissatisfaction, not satisfaction. Furthermore, the theory postulates that a lack of motivating factors in a job tends to draw peoples' attention to hygiene factors, with the result that more and more hygiene (e.g. pay) must be provided to obtain the same level of performance.

Even though the two-factor theory, or motivation-hygiene theory, was influential, it has been criticized as a theory that is induced from the data. That is, the results may have been found due to the method Herzberg used in his research, namely the critical incident technique (e.g. Dunnette, Campbell, and Hakel, 1967; House and Wigdor, 1970). Indeed, the two factors are not replicated well when other methods are used (Behling, Labovitz, and Kosmo, 1968; Miner, 2005). Moreover, the theory assumes that the motivating factors potentially increase the work motivation of all employees. Yet some individuals are much more likely to respond positively to an enriched, complex job than are others (Hulin, 1971). Thus, the theory provides no guidance in determining how individual differences should be dealt with in work settings (Hackman and Oldham, 1976).

However, an important contribution of the two-factor theory, that is still relevant today (Parker et al., 2001), is the idea of job enrichment, although it only relates to the first part of the theory (motivation factors). Job enrichment comprises building motivator factors into employees' jobs such as more opportunities for personal achievement and challenging work while at the same time improving task efficiency and satisfaction (Paul, Robertson, and Herzberg, 1969). For example, Parker and Wall (1998) reviewed the job design literature and concluded that unenriched jobs can lead to psychological depression and cardiovascular disease whereas adding motivator factors to such jobs can lead to increased employee well-being.

Job characteristics model

A very influential job design model emerged during the 1970s, when Hackman and Oldham (1976) introduced the Job Characteristics Model (JCM). In this model, it was argued that five core characteristics of jobs (i.e. skill variety, autonomy, feedback, task significance, and task identity) influence three critical psychological states (i.e. experienced meaningfulness of work, experienced responsibility for work outcomes, and knowledge of results), which, in turn, enhance internal work motivation, growth and job satisfaction, performance, and reduce absenteeism (Hackman and Lawler, 1971). It is further suggested that strong growth needs, the requisite knowledge and skills, and reasonable levels of satisfaction with the work context moderate the relationship between the five core job characteristics and the critical psychological states; and the relationship between the critical psychological states and the work outcomes (Fried and Ferris, 1987). Finally, the overall motivating potential of the job can be calculated by averaging employees' scores on skill variety, task identity, and task significance and multiplying this score with their scores on autonomy and feedback. The additive relationships for the first three characteristics indicate that they can compensate for lack of another, whereas the multiplicative function indicates that autonomy and feedback are important: a zero value for either of them will also render the MPS (motivating potential score) as zero.

The JCM has become a dominant model of work design, as its variables are relatively easy to measure using the Job Diagnostic Survey (Hackman and Oldham, 1980) that measures all the relevant variables (Miner, 2005). Studies have supported the assumption that job characteristics influence work-related psychological well-being, including job satisfaction (De Jonge, Dormann, Janssen, Dollard, Landeweerd, and Nijhuis, 2001). However, with regard to the other propositions, the evidence has been more equivocal. For example, the formula to calculate the motivating potential score is found to work less well in predicting outcomes than simply adding the five core job characteristics (Hinton and Biderman, 1995). Another criticism is that the JCM includes only a subset of the job characteristics that influence employees' experiences and behaviors (Bakker and Demerouti, 2013), and that causality of the proposed model is not clearly supported (Algera, 1991). With respect to the moderating role of growth needs, the empirical support has been inconsistent (Hogan and Martell, 1987; Johns, Xie, and Fang, 1992), and the same holds for the mediating role of the critical psychological states (e.g. Behson, Eddy, and Lorenzet, 2000). Thus, even though the effectiveness of the model is generally supported (Fried and Ferries, 1987), the JCM is also not without its critics.

Demand-control model

The demand-control model (DCM), posited as a stress-management model of job strain, predicts that mental strain results from the interaction of job demands and job decision latitude (Karasek, 1979). More specifically, the DCM postulates that psychological strain results from the joint effects of the demands of a work situation and the range of decision-making freedom (discretion) available to the worker facing those demands. Put simply, job stress will increase when demands increase but decrease when job control increases. The combination of high (low) demands with low (high) control results in higher (lower) levels of stress than would be expected on the basis of the main effects of demands and control (Taris, 2006).

A major implication of Karasek's (1979) work is that job redesign interventions should include increases in decision latitude to reduce mental strain, thus not necessarily affecting the job demands. This implication is interesting for organizations as it may suggest that the job demands, which may be associated with organizational productivity, do not have to be decreased. Important to note here is that there is a limit to increasing job control. The increase in job control may be used to eliminate unnecessary constraints on decision-making but, generally, increasing control may actually lead to higher levels of strain. Similarly, increasing employees' control while there is no room to use it may also have a negative effect on employee well-being (Bazerman, 1982; Cordery, 1997).

Like the JCM, the DCM has attained a prominent position in the job design literature. The empirical evidence for the demand-control model has also been inconsistent (De Jonge and Kompier, 1997; De Lange, Taris, Kompier, Houtman, and Bongers, 2003; Van der Doef and Maes, 1999). Studies have supported the additive effects (i.e. main effects) of job demands and job control on employee well-being and motivation, but the status of the interaction effects proposed by the model is reported to be weak (Taris, 2006). The most common conceptual criticism is that the DCM is too simplistic and fails to capture the complexity of work environments. Johnson and Hall (1988) have argued that job control is not the only resource available for coping with job demands and proposed that social support from colleagues or superiors may also play an important role. Some studies have indeed confirmed this hypothesis (see De Lange et al., 2003; Van der Doef and Maes, 1999), while others have included occupation-specific demands in the DCM in addition to workload (e.g. De Croon, Blonk, De Zwart, Frings-Dresen, and Broersen, 2002). This shortcoming of the DCM and other job design models in capturing the complexity of work environments constituted the starting point of the job demands-resources model (Bakker and Demerouti, 2007, 2013; Demerouti, Bakker, Nachreiner, and Schaufeli, 2001).

Job demands–resources model

The only job design model that specifically postulates that job characteristics may influence employee engagement is the job demands–resources (JD–R) model (Demerouti et al., 2001). In this heuristic model, two types of job characteristics are distinguished that are labeled job demands and resources. Job demands consume psychological and physical energy and when there is prolonged exposure to high job demands, employees may experience psychological and physical costs. Burnout, for example, may be the result of (prolonged exposure to) excessive job demands. Common job demands include workload and emotional job demands. Job resources, on the other hand, are the psychological, social, organizational, and physical resources that (1) enable goal achievement, (2) reduce or buffer against job demands, and (3) enable growth and development (Bakker and Demerouti, 2007; Schaufeli and Bakker, 2004). As can be seen from this description, the JD–R model incorporates aspects of the job that may lead to job stress (i.e. job demands) and to increased engagement (i.e. job resources). The model states that job demands initiate a health-impairment process while job resources instigate a motivational process. Specifically, high levels of job demands may exhaust employees' physical and mental resources and may lead to an increase in energy and health problems. In contrast, high levels of job resources are motivational and may lead to employee engagement, goal-directed behaviors, and well-being (Bakker and Demerouti, 2007). The JD–R model does not specify beforehand which job characteristics may be most likely to influence outcomes, which makes the model flexible in its use (Bakker and Demerouti, 2013).

Recently, a distinction in types of job demands has been made by LePine, Podsakoff, and Lepine (2005) in an attempt to clarify inconsistencies found regarding the influence of job demands on job stress. That is, even though job demands seem to be associated with job stress, some demands also relate positively to motivation. The demands that also relate to motivation are called challenging job demands, whereas the demands that relate to job stress are called hindering job demands (Cavanaugh, Boswell, Roehling, and Boudreau, 2000).

Challenging job demands stimulate employees to develop their knowledge and skills or to attain more difficult goals (LePine et al., 2005). These demands also offer mastery experiences (Gorgievski and Hobfoll, 2008). Hindering job demands unnecessarily thwart personal growth and goal attainment and are therefore associated with stress and burnout. A meta-analysis conducted by Crawford, LePine, and Rich (2010) indeed found that challenging job demands were positively related to employee engagement even though they can also be appraised as stressful. This distinction between hindering and challenging demands should be incorporated in future studies using the JD–R model (Van den Broeck, De Cuyper, De Witte, and Vansteenkiste, 2010). Another point of criticism is that the JD–R model does not focus on the process through which job resources, for example, may lead to employee engagement. This point will be addressed later in the chapter.

Effects of job characteristics on employee engagement

The previous discussion of job design theories suggests that employee engagement is aligned with the way a job is designed and can thus be facilitated through job design (Christian et al., 2011). This section of the chapter will deal with empirical studies that have shown which job characteristics specifically relate to employee engagement.

Prior studies have consistently shown that job resources such as social support from colleagues and supervisors, performance feedback, skill variety, autonomy, and learning opportunities are positively associated with employee engagement (Bakker and Demerouti, 2007). A meta-analysis of 53 articles providing 74 unique samples (total $N = 45,683$) revealed that job resources are positively related to employee engagement (Halbesleben, 2010). For example, Schaufeli and Bakker (2004) found a positive relationship between employee engagement and the job resources performance feedback, social support, and supervisory coaching, among employees from four different Dutch service organizations: an insurance company, a pension fund company, an Occupational Health and Safety Service, and a home-care institution. The same relationship was tested in a Finnish sample of over 2,000 teachers (Hakanen, Bakker, and Schaufeli, 2006) while using the following job resources: job control, information, social climate, supervisory support, and innovative climate. Again, all job resources were positively related to employee engagement.

Conceptually similar findings have been reported by Llorens, Bakker, Schaufeli, and Salanova (2006) in a Spanish context while including the resources job control, performance feedback, and social support. In addition, Koyuncu, Burke, and Fiksenbaum (2006) found that particularly control, reward and recognition, and value fit were predictive of employee engagement in a Turkish context. There are numerous other studies that provide additional support for the relationship between job resources and employee engagement (e.g. Rich, LePine, and Crawford, 2010; Salanova and Schaufeli, 2008; Salanova, Agut, and Peiro, 2005; see also Bakker, 2010, 2011).

Longitudinal study designs have also confirmed the positive relationship between job resources and employee engagement. Mauno, Kinnunen, and Ruokolainen (2007) employed a two-year longitudinal design to investigate employee engagement and its antecedents among Finnish health care personnel. Job resources predicted work engagement better than job demands; job control and organization-based self-esteem in particular proved to be the best lagged predictors of the three dimensions of employee engagement (i.e. vigor, dedication, and absorption). Further, in their study among managers and executives of a Dutch telecom company, Schaufeli, Bakker, and Van Rhenen (2009) found that changes in job resources were predictive of engagement over a period of one year. Specifically, results showed that increases in social support, autonomy, opportunities for development, and performance feedback were positive predictors of Time 2 employee engagement after controlling for baseline engagement. Finally, Xanthopoulou, Bakker, Demerouti, and Schaufeli (2009) found that job resources including autonomy, social support, supervisory coaching, performance feedback, and opportunities for professional development, were positively associated with engagement approximately 18 months later.

In addition, researchers have tested the interaction effects proposed by the JD-R model. Hakanen, Bakker, and Demerouti (2005) tested whether job resources (job control, innovativeness, skill variability, peer contact, and patient contact) are most beneficial in maintaining employee engagement under conditions of high job demands (e.g. workload, unfavorable physical environment). These authors found that job resources buffered the negative effect of qualitative workload on employee engagement. Comparable findings have been reported by Bakker, Hakanen, and Demerouti (2007). In their study among Finnish teachers they observed that job resources mitigated the negative relationship between pupil misbehavior and employee engagement. In addition, they found that job resources such as supervisor support and appreciation particularly influenced employee engagement when teachers were confronted with high levels of pupil misconduct.

Other job resources such as reward and recognition, and innovativeness have been less often included in studies but are also found to be positively associated with employee engagement (Hakanen et al., 2005; Koyuncu et al., 2006). The same holds for fairness, which is the extent to which decisions at work are perceived as being fair. For example, Moliner, Martínez-Tur, Ramos, Peiró, and Cropanzano (2008) found positive correlations between procedural and interactional justice and employee engagement. Together, these results confirm the importance of high, or at least sufficient, job resources for employee engagement to exist. But why are these resources so important for employee engagement?

Mechanisms through which job characteristics lead to employee engagement

In this section, several mechanisms are proposed that may explain *why* job characteristics may be related to employee engagement. The only job design theory that incorporates mechanisms through which job characteristics may affect outcomes is the job characteristics model. Accordingly, job characteristics influence work motivation and job satisfaction through the three psychological states of meaningfulness, responsibility, and knowledge of results. Experienced meaningfulness of the work relates to the degree to which the individual experiences the job as one that is generally meaningful, valuable, and worthwhile. Experienced responsibility for work outcomes refers to the degree to which the employee feels personally accountable and responsible for the results of the work he or she does, and knowledge of results is defined as the degree to which the individual knows and understands how effectively he or she is performing the job (Hackman and Oldham, 1976). In short, these psychological states may be related to employee engagement to the extent that employees know that they personally performed well on a task they cared about. However, as stated earlier, evidence for the mediating role of the three psychological states remains scarce (Behson et al., 2000).

Kahn (1990) also proposed that psychological meaningfulness would be related to employee engagement as well as psychological safety and availability. May, Gilson, and Harter (2004) tested these assumptions and found that job enrichment (measured as the five core job characteristics) and work role fit were both positively related to meaningfulness. In addition, they found that meaningfulness mediated the relationship between job enrichment and work role fit, and employee engagement. With regard to psychological safety and availability, the results were less convincing for the hypothesized relationships: job resources were related to psychological safety and availability but there was weak evidence for the mediating role of these states.

Interestingly, Albrecht (in press) argued that satisfaction of the need for meaningful work would be a mediator in the relationship between job resources and engagement. Albrecht and Su (2012) addressed this idea and found that the job resource performance feedback was related to engagement through fulfilling employees' need for meaningful work. Extending this research, Albrecht (in press) found that satisfaction of the need for meaningful work had significant direct effects on engagement and also mediated the influence of job resources (job feedback and skill development) on employee engagement. Thus, there is some support for the contention that employees will feel engaged in their work when their work is meaningful.

Another theory that has been proposed to explain why job resources are related to employee engagement is social exchange theory (Emerson, 1976; see Saks, 2006). This theory states that when employees receive resources (either economic resources such as pay or socio-emotional resources such as recognition) from their organization they feel obliged to repay the organization with greater levels of engagement (Saks, 2006). For example, employees who have higher perceived organizational support might become more engaged in their job as part of the reciprocity norm of social exchange theory in order to help the organization reach its objectives (Rhoades, Eisenberger, and Armeli, 2001).

Furthermore, an interesting mechanism that may explain how job resources promote employee engagement is basic need fulfillment. According to Deci and Ryan's (1985) self-determination theory (SDT), people have three universal psychological needs – the need for autonomy, belongingness, and competence (ABC). The need for autonomy is defined as the desire to experience ownership of behavior and to act with a sense of volition (Deci and Ryan, 2000). The need for autonomy is thus different from the job resource autonomy (Van den Broeck, Vansteenkiste, De Witte, and Lens, 2008). The need for belongingness or relatedness is defined as the need to form close relationships with others and the desire to achieve a sense of belongingness (Baumeister and Leary, 1995). For example, employees with high social support experience positive interactions with others and are therefore more likely to have their need for belongingness fulfilled than employees who feel lonely at work. Finally, the need for competence represents individuals' desire to feel capable of mastering the environment, to bring about desired outcomes, and to manage various challenges (White, 1959).

There is indeed some evidence that these needs may mediate the relationship between job resources and employee engagement. Van den Broeck and colleagues (2008) examined the effect of the job resources autonomy, skill utilization, and positive feedback on the vigor component of work engagement and whether this effect was mediated through the fulfillment of the three basic needs. They found that need satisfaction, a combined score of the needs for ABC, partially explained the positive relationship between the job resources and vigor.

Finally, personal resources have been found to mediate the relationship between job resources and employee engagement (Xanthopoulou, Bakker, Demerouti, and Schaufeli, 2007). Personal resources refer to one's sense of being able to control and impact the environment successfully (Hobfoll, Johnson, Ennis, and Jackson, 2003). In their study, Xanthopoulou and colleagues included self-efficacy, organizational-based self-esteem, and optimism as personal resources. On the basis of a literature review, these authors found that job resources activate personal resources, which, consequently, fuel engagement. More specifically, job resources activate employees' self-efficacy, self-esteem, and optimism and make them feel more capable of controlling their work environment. As a result, they may have been more confident and proud of the work they did, found meaning in it, and, in turn, stayed engaged (Xanthopoulou et al., 2007). In a later study, these authors were able to extend these findings to the day-level, by showing that on days that employees were exposed to more job resources they were more self-confident and, in turn, more engaged than on days without job resources (Xanthopoulou et al., 2009).

Practical implications for the HRM professional

Organizational job (re)design

As has become evident from the previous paragraphs, it is important that managers and HRM professionals are mindful of the characteristics that make up the job when assigning employees to tasks and jobs. A high availability of job resources that foster meaningfulness or lead to the satisfaction of basic human needs may lead to the desired state of employee engagement. Interventions to redesign jobs should therefore focus mostly on the job resources that are available in the work environment. However, job demands that are challenging may also increase employee engagement (Van den Broeck et al., 2010). Thus, management should offer their employees sufficient job challenges and job resources that enable employees to perform their job tasks in a healthy and interesting way. The specific job resources and challenging demands should be determined on the basis of the particular organization although social support, feedback, skill variety, autonomy, and learning opportunities are seen as relevant to most jobs (Hackman and Oldham, 1980; Lee and Ashforth, 1996).

Even though supervisory coaching and support have been included in the JD–R model as job resources, more formally, leaders may also play a crucial role in fostering the engagement of their employees. Leaders who are high in task behavior and support have been shown to be particularly effective in promoting employee engagement (Schaufeli and Salanova, 2008). Transformational leaders (Bass, 1985) provide support, inspiration, and quality coaching, which makes it likely that their employees experience work as more challenging, involving and satisfying, and consequently, become more engaged with their job tasks (Tims, Bakker, and Xanthopoulou, 2011). Zhu, Avolio, and Walumbwa (2009) demonstrated that managers' perceptions of the transformational leadership qualities of their executive leaders were positively associated with the managers' own engagement. Moreover, transformational leaders may be effective in promoting employees' personal resources or job resources which in turn may enhance their employee engagement (Tims et al., 2011). Research has shown that transformational leadership can be trained (Barling, Weber, and Kelloway, 1996; Dvir, Eden, Avolio, and Shamir, 2002). For example, Barling and colleagues designed a transformational leadership training in which they first teach managers about transformational leadership and then individually train them. Managers who received the training were rated as more transformational five months after the training compared to two weeks before the training and compared to the no-training control group. This indicates that leaders can develop their transformational leadership behavior in a relatively short period of time, and this development is also noticeable to their followers.

As observed by Gruman and Saks (2011), many practices for assessing and then improving employee engagement involve the use of an employee engagement survey to assess engagement levels and the work environment factors that may be related to engagement (e.g. job resources). The results of these employee surveys are then used to identify interventions to improve engagement levels in the organization. However, the aggregate levels of job resources may not be indicative for an individual employee's needs. That is, individual preferences for specific job resources may be overlooked by a one-size-fits-all redesign approach (Grant and Parker, 2009). For example, not all employees may value additional support as some of them already experience enough support from their supervisors. Allowing employees to have a say in the design of their work may therefore be effective in increasing employee engagement because employees are then able to increase the fit between their skills, needs, and values and the job which may promote psychological meaningfulness (Gruman and Saks, 2011; May et al., 2004). However, it has been observed that employees can change their job characteristics on their own initiative such that the job aligns with their individual values, skills, and needs. This is called job crafting, to which we turn now.

Individual job redesign: job crafting

Job crafting may include changing what one does as a part of the job, how one approaches work, or how one interacts with others. According to Wrzesniewski and Dutton (2001), job crafting allows employees to change the meaning of their work by modifying characteristics of the job and the social work environment. This makes job crafting an interesting strategy that employees may use to stay or become engaged in their work. There is indeed accumulating evidence that job crafting is positively related to employee engagement (Bakker, Tims, and Derks, 2012; Petrou, Demerouti, Peeters, Schaufeli, and Hetland, 2012; Tims, Bakker, and Derks, 2012, 2013). According to Tims and colleagues (Tims and Bakker, 2010; Tims et al., 2012), individual job crafting entails proactively increasing structural and social job resources (e.g. autonomy and feedback, respectively), increasing challenging job demands (i.e. start new projects), and decreasing hindering job demands (i.e. cognitive and emotional demands). These researchers developed and validated a scale with 21 items to measure the four dimensions of job crafting (Tims et al., 2012).

Studies using this job crafting scale have shown that the crafting of job resources and challenging job demands related positively to employee engagement (Bakker et al., 2012; Tims et al., 2012). Moreover, using a three-wave design with one month between the measurements, Tims et al. (2013) found that employees who crafted their social and structural job resources between T1 and T2, showed an increase in these job resources T1 and T3, and this increase in job resources mediated the relationship between job crafting and increases in employee well-being over two months (increased levels of work engagement, job satisfaction, and decreased levels of burnout). The job crafting dimension of 'decreasing hindering job demands' was found to relate negatively to work engagement (Tims et al., 2012; Petrou et al., 2012). It seems that employees decrease their hindrance demands as a strategy to reduce stress and not necessarily to increase their engagement. Taken together, when employees proactively increase their job resources and challenging job demands they may be successful in increasing their own work engagement.

Practically, this means that job crafting should be acknowledged by the management of organizations. To our knowledge, in none of the studies conducted so far was job crafting part of an intervention: employees engaged in job crafting on their own initiative. It is even suggested and found that job crafting takes place in many types of jobs, even in those with relatively low levels of autonomy (Berg, Wrzesniewski, and Dutton, 2010; Wrzesniewski and Dutton, 2001). This implies that managers should work with job crafting in such a way that it also aligns with the organizational goals. A clear communication and agreement of goals that are in line with organizational objectives should be able to guide job crafting towards positive individual and organizational outcomes, as it may lead to work engagement. Communicating about job crafting also provides employees with the confidence to engage in it on their own initiative. Employees may perceive that they are allowed to change their job characteristics such that they are able to perform their job in an effective and meaningful way.

Conclusion

A lot of research has shown that there is much that employers can do to raise the levels of employee engagement. The JD–R model in particular provides useful guidelines on how to design a job in such a way that employee engagement increases. It all boils down to increasing employees' job resources, providing them with challenging job demands, and building their personal resources. In addition, employees may also craft their own job demands and resources, which results in increased engagement. Employee engagement thus seems highest when organizations provide the necessary preconditions for engagement in which employees are also allowed to craft those specific job characteristics they value or prefer. With this combined top-down and bottom-up approach, all employees have the potential to become engaged in their work.

Case study: Job crafting in a chemical plant

Increasingly, organizations expect their employees to take responsibility for their own work-related well-being. One such organization is a multinational based in the Netherlands. The occupational health doctor of this company used to focus on healing employees and conducting health examinations. However, recently, the focus of the occupational doctor has changed from a doctor who cures diseases to a health-supporting professional. In line with the broader goals of the management, the occupational doctor now aims to advance work engagement in a personal manner by taking the personal differences between employees into account. Job crafting has captured his attention because employees then proactively alter their job characteristics to create a better alignment between the job and themselves, which likely results in more engaged employees. The question is, how can employees be encouraged to craft their own jobs and, as such, work on their own engagement?

To this end, the authors have developed an individual, online feedback intervention that uses surveys and personal feedback. The feedback intervention consists of three phases. In the first phase, the reflection phase, employees report their current levels of job demands (e.g. workload, emotional demands), job resources (e.g. autonomy, supervisory coaching), and well-being (e.g. work engagement). After completing the survey, employees receive personal feedback, generated by the software program, showing their average scores on each job demand and resource and the score of a benchmark group on these job characteristics. The feedback serves two goals. The first goal is to create awareness among employees of how they experience their work and how relevant others (the benchmark) experience their work. The second goal of the feedback is to provide employees with suggestions of how to alter specific levels of job demands and resources. The job crafting suggestions are by no means obligatory; the employee has to decide whether and how job crafting may be used to optimize personal levels of job demands and resources. Employees then report their job crafting intentions.

The second phase, the crafting phase, consists of four weeks in which employees can craft their jobs. A time lag of four weeks has been chosen because intentions predict behavior best when the time lag is not too long (Ajzen and Fishbein, 1980). Moreover, job crafting has been shown to occur at the day-level (Petrou et al., 2012), thus a month between the measurements should be sufficient to capture job crafting activities. After this month, job crafting activities are measured. The third phase, the follow-up phase, consists of the same survey as used in the first phase and enables researchers to examine changes in these variables over time.

Employees from all departments, ranging from administration, research and development, and plant maintenance, have been invited to participate in the feedback intervention. The panel group consists of 288 employees. Most of them are male (83 per cent) with a mean age of 45.2 years. On average, employees' work experience was 23.7 years, of which they worked 18.3 years for the present organization. The percentage of employees who actually crafted their jobs was considerable: At least 66.3 per cent of the employees regularly increased their structural job resources; 33.4 per cent of the employees increased their challenging job demands; 11.9 per cent regularly increased their social job resources; and 6.1 per cent decreased their hindering job demands. Thus, there was evidence that job crafting occurs regularly. Especially increasing job resources and challenging job demands leads to higher levels of work engagement and job satisfaction, and lower levels of burnout, indicating that employees are able to influence their well-being through personally crafting their jobs.

References

Ajzen, I., and Fishbein, M. (1980). *Understanding attitudes and predicting social behaviour.* Englewood Cliffs, NY: Prentice-Hall.

Albrecht, S. L. (in press). Work engagement and the positive power of meaningful work. In A. B. Bakker (ed.), *Advances in Positive Organizational Psychology*. Bingley: Emerald.

——, and Su, J. M. (2012). Job resources and employee engagement in a Chinese context: The mediating role of job meaningfulness, felt obligation and positive mood. *International Journal of Business and Emerging Markets*, 4, 277–92.

Algera, J. A. (1991). Analyse van arbeid vanuit verschillende perspectieven [Job analysis from different perspectives]. Amsterdam: Swets & Zeitlinger.

Bakker, A. B. (2010). Engagement and 'job crafting': Engaged employees create their own great place to work. In S. L. Albrecht (ed.), *Handbook of employee engagement: Perspectives, issues, research and practice* (pp. 229–44). Glos., UK: Edward Elgar.

—— (2011). An evidence-based model of work engagement. *Current Directions in Psychological Science, 20*, 265–269.

——, and Demerouti, E. (2007). The job demands–resources model: State of the art. *Journal of Managerial Psychology*, 22, 309–328.

——, and Demerouti, E. (2013). Job demands–resources theory. In C. Cooper, and P. Chen (eds), *Wellbeing: A complete reference guide*. Chichester: Wiley-Blackwell.

——, Hakanen, J. J., Demerouti, E., and Xanthopoulou, D. (2007). Job resources boost work engagement, particularly when job demands are high. *Journal of Educational Psychology*, 99, 274–84.

Barling, J., Weber, T., and Kelloway, E. K. (1996). Effects of transformational leadership training on attitudinal and financial outcomes: A field experiment. *Journal of Applied Psychology*, 81, 827–32.

Bass, B. M. (1985). *Leadership and performance beyond expectations*. New York: Free Press.

Baumeister, R. F., and Leary, M. R. (1995). The need to belong: Desire for interpersonal attachment as a fundamental human motivation. *Psychological Bulletin*, 117, 497–529.

Bazerman, M. H. (1982). Impact of personal control on performance: Is added control always beneficial? *Journal of Applied Psychology*, 67, 472–9.

Behling, O., Labovitz, G., and Kosmo, R. (1968). The Herzberg controversy: A critical reappraisal. *The Academy of Management Journal*, 11, 99–108.

Behson, S. J., Eddy, E. R., and Lorenzet, S. J. (2000). The importance of the critical psychological states in the job characteristics model: A meta-analytic and structural equations modelling examination. *Current Research in Social Psychology*, 5, 170–89.

Berg, J. M., Wrzesniewski, A., and Dutton, J. E. (2010). Perceiving and responding to challenges in job crafting at different ranks: When proactivity requires adaptivity. *Journal of Organizational Behavior*, 31, 158–86.

Broeck, A., Van den, De Cuyper, N., De Witte, H., and Vansteenkiste, M. (2010). Not all job demands are equal: Differentiating job hindrances and job challenges in the job demands–resources model. *European Journal of Work and Organizational Psychology*, 19, 735–59.

——, Vansteenkiste, M., De Witte, H., and Lens, W. (2008). Explaining the relationships between job characteristics, burnout and engagement: The role of basic psychological need satisfaction. *Work & Stress*, 22, 277–94.

Cameron, K. S., Dutton, J. E., and Quinn, R. E. (2003). An introduction to positive organizational scholarship. In K. S. Cameron, J. E. Dutton, and R. E. Quinn (eds), *Positive Organizational Scholarship* (pp. 3–13). San Fransisco: Berret-Koehler.

Cavanaugh, M. A., Boswell, W. R., Roehling, M. V., and Boudreau, J. W. (2000). An empirical examination of self-reported work stress among U.S. managers. *Journal of Applied Psychology*, 85, 65–74.

Christian, M. S., Garza, A. S., and Slaughter, J. E. (2011). Work engagement: A quantitative review and test of its relations with task and contextual performance. *Personnel Psychology*, 64, 89–136.

Crawford, E. R., LePine, J. A., and Rich, B. L. (2010). Linking job demands and resources to employee engagement and burnout: A theoretical extension and meta-analytic test. *Journal of Applied Psychology*, 95, 834–48.

Cordery, J. (1997). Reinventing work design theory. *Australian Psychologist*, 22, 185–9.

Croon, E. M. de, Blonk, R. W. B., Zwart, B. C. H. de, Frings-Dresen, M. H. W., and Broersen, J. P. J. (2002). Job stress, fatigue, and job dissatisfaction in Dutch lorry drivers: Towards an occupation specific model of job demands and control. *Occupational and Environmental Medicine*, 59, 356–61.

Cummings, T. G. (1978). Self-regulating work groups: A socio-technical synthesis. *Academy of Management Review*, 3, 625–34.

Deci, E. L., and Ryan, R. M. (1985). *Intrinsic motivation and self-determination in human behavior.* New York: Plenum.

——, and Ryan, R. M. (2000). The 'what' and 'why' of goal pursuits: Human needs and self-determination of behavior. *Psychological Inquiry*, 11, 319–38.

Demerouti, E., Bakker, A. B., Nachreiner, F., and Schaufeli, W. B. (2001). The job demands–resources model of burnout. *Journal of Applied Psychology*, 86, 499–512.

——, and Cropanzano, R. (2010). From thought to action: Employee work engagement and job performance. In A. B. Bakker, and M. P. Leiter (eds), *Work engagement: A handbook of essential theory and research* (pp. 147–63). New York: Psychology Press.

Doef, M., van der, and Maes, S. (1999). The job demand-control (-support) model and psychological well-being: A review of 20 years of empirical research. *Work & Stress*, 13, 87–114.

Dunnette, M. D., Campbell, J. P., and Hakel, M. D. (1967). Factors contributing to job satisfaction and job dissatisfaction in six occupational groups. *Organizational Behavior and Human Performance*, 2, 143–74.

Dvir, T., Eden, D., Avolio, B. J., and Shamir, B. (2002). Impact of transformational leadership on follower development and performance: A field experiment. *Academy of Management Journal*, 45, 735–44.

Emerson, R. M. (1976). Social exchange theory. *Annual Review of Sociology*, 2, 335–62.

Emery, F. E., and Trist, E. L. (1965). The causal texture of organizational environments. *Human Relations*, 18, 21–32.

Fried, Y., and Ferris, G. R. (1987). The validity of the job characteristics model: A review and meta-analysis. *Personnel Psychology*, 40, 287–322.

Gorgievski, M. J., and Hobfoll, S. E. (2008). Work can burn us out or fire us up: Conservation of resources in burnout and engagement. In J. R. B. Halbesleben (ed.), *Handbook of stress and burnout in health care*. Hauppauge, NY: Nova Science Publishers.

Grant, A. M., and Parker, S. K. (2009). Redesigning work design theories: The rise of relational and proactive perspectives. *Academy of Management Annals*, 3, 317–75.

Gruman, J. A., and Saks, A. M. (2011). Performance management and employee engagement. *Human Resources Management Review*, 21, 123–36.

Hackman, J. R., and Lawler, E. E. (1971). Employee reactions to job characteristics. *Journal of Applied Psychology*, 55, 259–86.

——, and Oldham, G. R. (1976). Motivation through the design of work: Test of a theory. *Organizational Behavior and Human Performance*, 16, 250–79.

——, and Oldham, G. R. (1980). *Work redesign*. Reading, MA: Addison-Wesley.

Hakanen, J. J., Bakker, A. B., and Demerouti, E. (2005). How dentists cope with their job demands and stay engaged: The moderating role of job resources. *European Journal of Oral Sciences*, 113, 479–87.

——, Bakker, A. B., and Schaufeli, W. B. (2006). Burnout and work engagement among teachers. *Journal of School Psychology*, 43, 495–513.

Halbesleben, J. R. B. (2010). A meta-analysis of work engagement: Relationships with burnout, demands, resources, and consequences. In A. B. Bakker, and M. P. Leiter (eds), *Work engagement: A handbook of essential theory and research* (pp. 102–17). New York: Psychology Press.

Harter, J. K., Schmidt, F. L., and Hayes, T. L. (2002). Business-unit-level relationships between employee satisfaction, employee engagement, and business outcomes: A meta-analysis. *Journal of Applied Psychology*, 87, 268–79.

Herzberg, F. (1966). *Work and the nature of man*. Oxford, England: World.

——, Mausner, B., and Snyderman, B. S. (1959). *The motivation to work*. New York: Wiley.

Hinton, M., and Biderman, M. (1995). Empirically derived job characteristics measures and the motivating potential score. *Journal of Business and Psychology*, 9, 355–64.

Hobfoll, S. E., Johnson, R. J., Ennis, N., and Jackson, A. P. (2003). Resource loss, resource gain, and emotional outcomes among inner city women. *Journal of Personality and Social Psychology*, 84, 632–43.

Hogan, E. A., and Martell, D. A. (1987). A confirmatory structural equations analysis of the job characteristics model. *Organizational Behavior and Human Decision Processes*, 39, 242–63.

House, R. J., and Wigdor, L. A. (1970). Herzberg's dual-factor theory of job satisfaction and motivation: A review of the evidence and a criticism. *Personnel Psychology*, 20, 369–89.

Hulin, C. L. (1971). Individual differences and job enrichment – The case against general treatment. In J. Maher (ed.), *New perspectives in job enrichment*. New York: Van Nostrand-Reinhold.

Johns, G., Xie, J. L., and Fang, Y. (1992). Mediating and moderating effects of job design. *Journal of Management*, 18, 657–77.

Johnson, J. V., and Hall, E. M. (1988). Job strain, work place social support, and cardiovascular disease: A cross-sectional study of a random sample of the Swedish working population. *American Journal of Public Health*, 78, 1336–42.

Jonge, J. de, Dormann, C., Janssen, P. P. M., Dollard, M. F., Landeweerd, J. A., and Nijhuis, J. N. (2001). Testing reciprocal relationships between job characteristics and psychological well-being: A cross-lagged structural equation model. *Journal of Occupational and Organizational Psychology*, 74, 29–46.

——, and Kompier, M. A. J. (1997). A critical examination of the demand-control-support model from a work psychological perspective. *International Journal of Stress Management*, 4, 235–58.

Kahn, W. A. (1990). Psychological conditions of personal engagement and disengagement at work. *Academy of Management Journal*, 33, 692–724.

Karasek, R. A. (1979). Job demands, job decision latitude, and mental strain: Implications for job redesign. *Administrative Science Quarterly*, 24, 258–308.

Kompier, M. (2003). Job design and well-being. In M. J. Schabracq, J. A. M. Winnubst, and C. L. Cooper (eds), *The Handbook of Work and Health Psychology* (pp. 429–54). West Sussex: John Wiley & Sons Ltd.

Koyuncu, M., Burke, R. J., and Fiksenbaum, L. (2006). Work engagement among women managers and professionals in a Turkish bank: Potential antecedents and consequences. *Equal Opportunities International*, 25, 299–310.

Lange, A. H. de, Taris, T. W., Kompier, M. A. J., Houtman, I. L. D., and Bongers, P. M. 2003. 'The *very* best of the millennium': Longitudinal research and the demand-control-support model. *Journal of Occupational Health Psychology*, 8, 282–305.

Lee, R. T., and Ashford, B. E. (1996). A meta-analytic examination of the correlates of the three dimensions of job burnout. *Journal of Applied Psychology*, 81, 123–33.

LePine, J. A., Podsakoff, N. P., and LePine, M. A. (2005). A meta-analytic test of the challenge stressor–hindrance stressor framework: An explanation for inconsistent relationships among stressors and performance. *Academy of Management Journal*, 48, 764–75.

Littler, G. R. (1978). Understanding Taylorism. *British Journal of Sociology*, 29, 185–202.

Llorens, S., Bakker, A. B., Schaufeli, W. B., and Salanova, M. (2006). Testing the robustness of the job demands–resources model. *International Journal of Stress Management*, 13, 378–91.

Matthews, J. A. (1997). Introduction to the Special Issue. *Human Relations*, 50, 487–96.

Mauno, S., Kinnunen, U., and Ruokolainen, M. (2007). Job demands and resources as antecedents of work engagement: A longitudinal study. *Journal of Vocational Behavior*, 70, 149–71.

May, D. R., Gilson, R. L., and Harter, L. M. (2004). The psychological conditions of meaningfulness, safety and availability and the engagement of the human spirit at work. *Journal of Occupational and Organizational Psychology*, 77, 11–37.

Mayo, E. (1933). *The human problems of an industrial civilization.* New York: Macmillan.

Miner, J. B. (2005). *Essential theories of motivation and leadership.* Sharpe, London.

Moliner, C., Martínez-Tur, V., Ramos, J., Peiró, J. M., and Cropanzano, R. (2008). Organizational justice and extrarole customer servisse: The mediating role of well-being at work. *European Journal of Work and Organizational Psychology*, 17, 327–48.

Nelson, D., and Cooper, C. L. (eds). (2007). *Positive organizational behavior: Accentuating the positive at work.* Thousand Oaks, CA: Sage.

Parker, S. K., and Wall, T. D. (1998). *Job and work design: Organizing work to promote well-being and effectiveness.* San Francisco, CA: Sage.

——, Wall, T. D., and Cordery, J. L. (2001). Future work design research and practice: Towards an elaborated model of work design. *Journal of Occupational and Organizational psychology*, 74, 413–40.

Paul, W. J., Robertson, K. B., and Herzberg, F. (1968). Job enrichment pays off. *Harvard Business Review*, 47, 61–78.

Petrou, P., Demerouti, E., Peeters, M. C. W., Schaufeli, W. B., and Hetland, J. (2012). Crafting a job on a daily basis: Contextual correlates and the link to work engagement. *Journal of Organizational Behavior*, 33, 1120–41.

Rhoades, L., Eisenberger, R., and Armeli, S. (2001). Affective commitment to the organization: The contribution of perceived organizational support. *Journal of Applied Psychology*, 86, 825–36.

Rich, B. L., LePine, J. A., and Crawford, E. R. (2010). Job engagement: Antecedents and effects on performance. *Academy of Management Journal*, 53, 617–35.

Roethlisberger, F. J., & Dickson, W. J. (1939). *Management and the worker.* Boston, MA: Harvard University Press.

Saks, A. M. (2006). Antecedents and consequences of employee engagement. *Journal of Managerial Psychology*, 21, 600–619.

Salanova, M., and Schaufeli, W. B. (2008). A cross national study of work engagement as a mediator between job resources and proactive behaviour. *International Journal of Human Resource Management*, 19, 116–31.

——, Agut, S., and Peiro, J. M. (2005). Linking organizational resources and work engagement to employee performance and customer loyalty: The mediation of service climate. *Journal of Applied Psychology*, 90, 1217–27.

Sandberg, A. (ed.) (1995). Enriching production: Perspectives on Volvo's Uddevalla plant as an alternative to lean production. Avebury, UK: Aldershot.

Schaufeli, W. B., and Bakker, A. B. (2004). Job demands, job resources, and their relationship with burnout and engagement: A multi-sample study. *Journal of Organizational Behavior*, 25, 293–315.

——, Bakker, A. B., and Salanova, M. (2006). The measurement of work engagement with a short questionnaire: A cross-national study. *Educational and Psychological Measurement*, 66, 701–16.

——, Bakker, A. B., and Rhenen, W., van. (2009). How changes in job demands and resources predict burnout, work engagement, and sickness absenteeism. *Journal of Organizational Behavior*, 30, 893–917.

Sitter, L. U., de, Hertog, J. F., de, and Dankbaar, B. (1997). From complex organizations with simple jobs to simple organizations with complex jobs. *Human Relations*, 50, 497–534.

Taris, T. W. (2006). Bricks without clay: On urban myths in occupational health psychology. *Work & Stress*, 20, 99–104.

Taylor, F. W. (1911). *The principles of scientific management.* New York: W. W. Norton.

Tims, M., and Bakker, A. B. (2010). Job crafting: Towards a new model of individual job redesign. *SA Journal of Industrial Psychology*, 36, 1–9.

——, Bakker, A. B., and Derks, D. (2012). Development and validation of the job crafting scale. *Journal of Vocational Behavior*, 80, 173–86.

——, Bakker, A.B., and Derks, D. (2013). The impact of job crafting on job demands, job resources, and employee well-being. *Journal of Occupational Health Psychology*, 18, 230–40.

——, Bakker, A. B., and Xanthopoulou, D. (2011). Do transformational leaders enhance their followers' daily work engagement? *Leadership Quarterly*, 22, 121–31.

Trist, E. (1981). The evolution of socio-technical systems theory: A conceptual framework and an action research program. In A. Van De Ven & W. Joyce (eds), *Perspective on organizational design and behavior* (pp. 19–75). New York: Wiley.

——, and Bamforth, K. W. (1951). The social and psychological consequences of the longwall method of coal-getting: An examination of the psychological situation and defences of a work group relation to the social structure and technological content of the work system. *Human Relations*, 4, 3–38.

Walker, C. R., and Guest, R. H. (1952). *The man on the assembly line.* Cambridge, MA: *Harvard University Press.*

Walker, G. H., Stanton, N. A., Salmon, P. M., and Jenkins, D. P. (2008). A review of sociotechnical systems theory: a classic concept for new command and control paradigms. *Theoretical Issues in Ergonomics Science*, 9, 479–99.

White, R. (1959). Motivation reconsidered: The concept of competence. *Psychological Review*, 66, 279–333.

Wrzesniewski, A., and Dutton, J. E. (2001). Crafting a job: Revisioning employees as active crafters of their work. *Academy of Management Review*, 26, 179–201.

Xanthopoulou, D., Bakker, A. B., Demerouti, E., and Schaufeli, W. B. (2007). The role of personal resources in the job demands-resources model. *International Journal of Stress Management*, 14, 121–41.

——, Bakker, A. B., Demerouti, E., and Schaufeli, W. B. (2009). Work engagement and financial returns: A diary study on the role of job and personal resources. *Journal of Occupational and Organizational Psychology*, 82, 183–200.

Zhu, W., Avolio, B. J., and Walumbwa, F. O. (2009). Moderating role of follower characteristics with transformational leadership and follower work engagement. *Group and Organization Management*, 34, 590–619.

8 Leadership and employee engagement

Emma Soane

Leaders play a pivotal role in creating the environment within which employees can engage with their work. There is a wealth of theoretical and empirical research that has demonstrated associations between strong leadership and a range of desirable outcomes such as high performance, commitment, creativity and well-being. In recent years, there has been a focus on engagement both as a valuable outcome of effective leadership and as a catalyst for other positive attitudes and behaviours. However, the processes by which leaders achieve engagement have received relatively little direct attention. This chapter will examine how leaders can stimulate and promote engagement by considering leaders as individuals embedded within a social organizational context, and leadership for engagement as a malleable process that can be enhanced through mindful interventions.

The discussion that follows draws together empirical and theoretical research from published studies. Original data, gathered as part of a larger project (Alfes, Truss, Soane, Rees and Gatenby, 2010), are used to illustrate some of the theoretical concepts and the relationships between leadership and engagement. The organization in focus here is a plastic bottle manufacturer, referred to as PlasticCo, that has been through a period of change designed to enhance engagement and performance. Thirty-four managers were interviewed and were asked a number of questions about leadership processes and their outcomes.

The chapter is organized thus: first, I consider the nature of leadership and examine current approaches to understanding leaders, the leadership process and implications for engagement. I move on to examine three strands of theory and research, each of which contributes important insights into leading for engagement (inspiration for engagement, the relational context for engagement, the emotional landscape and engagement). I consider the nature of jobs and the extent to which leadership can overcome some job design challenges. I then reflect upon the impact of negative forms of influence and poor management practices. An overarching theme of all the discussion is that leaders and leadership can be developed, hence I present a method for assessing engaging leadership and suggest applications. The chapter concludes by summarizing five key points that leaders seeking to enhance engagement can apply to their everyday practices.

The nature of leadership

Leaders make the difference between work as a mundane grind, devoid of meaning and purpose, and work as an enriching and fulfilling experience that provides an essential source of identity which infuses all aspects of being. The notion that good leadership provides opportunities for positive experiences of work has considerable intuitive appeal, and matches the experience of much day-to-day work. Yet, understanding how leaders can truly contribute to employees' engagement with work requires attention to a number of aspects of both leaders and leadership.

In this chapter, I consider a leader as 'a person who influences individuals and groups within an organization, helps them in establishing goals, and guides them toward achievement of those goals, thereby allowing them to be effective' (Nahavandi, 2009: 4). This definition emphasizes the dynamic nature of leadership, and the significance of aligning individual and organizational goals. Such processes are at the core of many leadership endeavours. Positive forms of influence are also implicit in the definition since a leader is enabling others to be effective. Current thinking about leadership focuses on means as well as ends and draws upon notions of positive psychology, discussed elsewhere in this book, as well as recognition that changing models of organizations require new models of leadership (see Chapter 2). Thus developing truly effective leaders requires attention to how organizations can build upon individual attributes to develop successful leadership. Moreover, attaining and sustaining effective leadership remains one of the most important organizational goals.

Leading for engagement

The focus in this section is on how positive forms of leadership will stimulate engagement. As interest in engagement has grown in recent years, so definitions of engagement have proliferated. Kahn's (1990) foundational research described engagement as the harnessing of the self to work, and as a state arising from the experience of self-in-role requiring meaning, safety and psychological availability. Drawing on Kahn's (1990) work, I have defined engagement as 'being positively present during the performance of work by willingly contributing intellectual effort, experiencing positive emotions and meaningful connections to others' (Alfes et al., 2010: 5). I have proposed that engagement has three facets: intellectual, social and affective engagement (Soane, Truss, Alfes, Rees and Gatenby, 2012). Intellectual engagement is the extent to which one is intellectually absorbed in work. Social engagement is the extent to which one is socially connected with the working environment and shares common values with colleagues. Affective engagement is the extent to which one experiences a state of positive affect relating to one's work role. Leaders and leadership can influence each facet of engagement through a range of processes. I consider three main sets of theoretical frameworks that describe and explain how to enhance engagement.

Inspiration for engagement

Leaders can inspire and motivate employees through their leadership, and these processes can influence the experience of engagement just as they can enhance performance. The transformational leadership framework can aid understanding of how this can occur. The concept of transformational leadership was developed by Bass and Avolio (1990, 2000). The model was derived by coalescing theoretical research and empirical data about leadership processes. The resulting taxonomy comprises four components that, collectively, increase the likelihood of high performance and other positive outcomes.

Idealized influence is the extent to which leaders instil a sense of pride, go beyond self-interest, display power and confidence, talk about values, beliefs and ethics, and emphasize the collective mission. These factors inspire followership and collective effort. An important aspect of idealized influence is role modelling. This was acknowledged by the PlasticCo CEO in our research:

> Promoting the behaviour on an ongoing basis. You can't talk this and then not have the behaviour to back it up. So, you know, in any interaction you have with individuals, trying to practise hard to be in the mode of promoting.

Idealized influence can also have a role in increasing engagement, particularly via the impact of charisma. Charisma is a compelling ingredient of transformational leadership. It is the articulation of vision, and the projection of strength and confidence that draws followers toward the organizational mission (Conger and Kanungo, 1988). Charisma can also function to increase perceived meaningfulness of work. In general, employees are highly motivated to find meaning in their work (Frankl, 1992), and meaningfulness is an antecedent of engagement (May, Gilson and Harter, 2004). This link is explained in terms of the intrinsic worth and value that needs to be attached to work for an employee to invest their psychological and physical energy in their task. Meaningful work is a critical factor that seems to contribute to engagement and positive responses to work in the form of a general sense of positive well-being as well as successful skill development and application (Thomas and Velthouse, 1990). While some employees might be adept at finding meaning in their work (Cohen, 2008), an important aspect of the manager's role could be to assist employees who do not tend to see how their work fits with the broader purpose of the organization. A complementary aspect of managers' work is creating an environment where meaning is present. As the PlasticCO CEO noted:

> Well, they've been made aware that I'm going around sites asking people ... the opportunity to sit with the Managing Director and ask questions, so that's one way. We're trying to get managers to be a little bit more open about the business itself. I think what we find, and you may well find the same when you go round the sites, that people are really interested in what's going to impact on them directly. So if they work in Manchester they are really interested in what the impact is going to be on them day to day rather than a wider business scope.

Inspirational motivation involves talking optimistically and enthusiastically about the future and what needs to be accomplished, articulating a compelling vision of the future, and expressing confidence that goals will be achieved. These actions help people to believe in possibilities. The PlasticCo CEO acknowledged the importance of motivation:

> Every manager who has got people working for them, it's how effective they are at motivating people. You know I think, if there's one thing I say to a lot of people in our business, is we can invest in the highest state-of-the-art machinery and spend millions and millions of pounds on it, but at the end of the day it's always going to come down to people are going to be to make that kit work and therefore the relationships we have with our subordinates. We like to motivate people and make them feel valued and rewarded and I think that's a huge, huge impact for leaders in our business, something I personally spend a lot of time on.

Intellectual stimulation requires leaders to encourage followers to examine critical assumptions, seek differing perspectives, and to suggest new ways of looking at how to perform tasks. This aspect of leadership encourages high-quality decision making and innovation. Empirical research has tested the link between transformational leadership and creativity. For example, Ul Haq, Ali et al. (2010) examined this relationship among employees of two insurance companies in Pakistan. Survey data confirmed the link, and supported the view that transformational leaders encourage followers to feel free to explore and to express their ideas, thus enabling creativity. A senior manager in the manufacturing company in our research talked about how he approaches the decision making process:

> I like to get the team involved, and I would rather give them a problem and they give me the answer than me giving them the problem and the answer. They need to be able to think for themselves. So there's no point in me saying that there's a problem on such and such a machine and this is how you fix it. As long as they give me the end result, how they get there is entirely up to them. I like them to be free thinking and be able to develop themselves. I believe in minimum supervision of the engineers I've got. It's only if I've got a problem with somebody that I'll actually help . . . I work on them and also if I've got a problem with one of my engineers I bring them in and chat to them and make sure we get the problem resolved. So I don't have any issues there, about communicating that way. Also keeping them informed of any new developments, any new recruitments coming in, you know and that kind of thing and I want to try and get them to develop the plant to make the plant a better place.

Individualized consideration involves teaching and coaching, attention to individual-level needs, abilities and aspirations, and a focus on helping others to develop their strengths. This contributes to individual and team growth. The leadership and development manager in the manufacturing company discussed how to permeate a culture of individualized consideration through the business:

> Some of that's about the leadership in the business, the management style. Some of it's down to the individuals themselves and some people don't see work as important to them, people see work as just a means of getting income so they can run their life around it, and I think those individuals are going to be very difficult to take to another level because that's their priority, which we do respect. But others it can . . . you know I think how they're treated, how they're encouraged, how they're led, management style, leadership style plays an important part I think.

The second component of the model is transactional leadership. Contingent reward involves giving followers rewards for fulfilling obligations; discussing who is responsible for what targets; making clear what to expect when goals are achieved. Contingent reward shows recognition and is motivating.

At the ineffective and passive end of the transactional leadership model are potentially negative aspects of leadership: management by exception active (error monitoring), management by exception, passive (dealing with errors when brought to the leader's attention) and laissez faire leadership (withdrawal from leadership responsibilities). Positive forms of transactional leadership are necessary in organizations; however, if not combined with transformational leadership, performance tends to be limited to the achievement of expected levels of individual and organizational performance.

Transformational leadership increases the likelihood and frequency of high performance because it raises the level of awareness of followers about the importance of achieving valued outcomes, a vision and the required strategy. Transformational leadership also encourages followers to transcend their own self-interest for the sake of the team, organization or larger collective. Moreover, the process can expand followers' portfolio of needs by raising their awareness to improve themselves and what they are attempting to accomplish (Bass, 1985).

When considered within the context of engagement, it is clear that transformational leadership can provide some of the conditions required for employees to engage with their work. Research by Tims, Bakker and Xanthopoulou (2011) has shown that transformational leaders offer opportunities to develop mastery, and generate optimism about possibilities. These factors then contribute to increased levels of engagement. The difference between non-transformational management and a more transformational style of leadership was summed up by the PlasticCo CEO:

> I think the old style of management was very much about getting things done – look, just do it, just do it – is probably the best way I could put it. Now what we are trying to say is, look, you know, we need to be a bit more engaging, we need to listen to people, we need to allow them to make some decisions and try things out for themselves . . . I think you just need to give people the opportunity to grow and make a difference. Therefore style of management is more about leadership than management I think, under the new culture. We've been a very management culture which for me is about doing, leadership culture is more strategic, it's more empowering, it's participative, engaging, listening.

In summary, the relationship between transformational leadership and effective leadership outcomes has theoretical and empirical support. There are also indications that transformational leadership is likely to enhance engagement. In particular, the combined effects of idealized influence, inspirational motivation, individualized consideration and intellectual stimulation, could increase overall engagement through unleashing inspired effort focused on achieving individual and organizational goals.

The relational context for engagement

Leadership and followership are embedded within the social fabric of an organization. Some perspectives on leadership have characterized the relationship as a one-way, downward flow of information. An alternative approach is to de-emphasize the hierarchical boundaries between leaders and followers, and to consider leadership as a relational construct that requires an understanding of followers and the followership process (Awamleh and Gardner, 1999). Just as leadership is concerned with connectedness, social embeddedness is fundamental to engagement (discussed further in Chapter 4). William Kahn's 1990 work on engagement remains the lodestone for the field. Kahn (1990) suggested that the experience of connectedness with others is critical to the expression of self-in-role that forms the basis of engagement. Conversely, lack of social connectedness can be associated with disengagement. For example, Kahn quotes a camp counsellor who said: 'I was really shut down, not letting loose or being funny or letting them get close to me by talking more about myself. I just didn't let them in, I guess' (Kahn, 1990: 702). For Kahn, there is clearly a social dimension to engagement that is linked up with connectedness and empathy, a willingness to share views and to work collaboratively.

Social Exchange Theory (SET, Blau, 1964) provides a theoretical framework for Kahn's observations. SET emphasizes the fundamental nature of social reciprocation. Applications of SET to the work context support the notion that many organizational behaviours rely upon meaningful social exchange. Studies have examined a range of contexts including information sharing (Kankanhalli, Tan and Kwok-Kee, 2005), the outcomes of working partnerships (Lee and Kim, 1999) and relationships between leaders and followers (Hooper and Martin, 2008; Nelson and Dyck, 2005). Focusing on engagement, Saks (2006) suggested that SET can explain how individuals respond to work conditions with differing levels of engagement depending on norms of reciprocity and interdependence. Although most published measures of engagement do not specify a social dimension, I have suggested that the social dimension is critical to the conceptualization and operationalization of engagement for the reasons outlined above.

Building on our construction of engagement, and Social Exchange Theory (Blau, 1964), we can extend frameworks of leadership to encompass the relational exchanges between leaders and followers. Leader-Member Exchange Theory (LMX, Graen and Cashman, 1975) is a relevant framework. LMX proposed that interactions between leaders and members influence the development of mutual relationships, and that the quality of relationship between leader and member may differ from one member to another. High-quality relationships are underpinned by liking, trust and mutual respect. Development of high quality relationships is beneficial to both parties. As the norm of reciprocity (Gouldner, 1960) suggests, followers feel empowered in the light of a strong relationship with their leader and this builds a sense of obligation to reciprocate through high levels of effort and attainment (Graen and Uhl-Bien, 1995).

LMX theory has been tested in numerous empirical studies, and there is support for the influence of positive LMX on beneficial outcomes (e.g. Liden, Sparrowe and Wayne, 1997). However, there is little research that provides a direct test of the association between LMX and engagement. Although not an examination of work engagement in the terms defined in this chapter, recent research has shown that LMX is important to engagement in learning activities, particularly when leaders are also effective in setting clear and challenging goals (Bezuijen, van Dam, van den Berg and Thierry, 2010). Given the theoretical construction, and drawing together strands of previous empirical research, it seems reasonable to propose that focusing on developing high quality LMX relationships is likely to yield engagement with work.

The data from organizations in our research indicates that the social environment is considered to be an important aspect of the engagement process. As the PlasticCo CEO explained:

> I think historically we've been a top-down led business so it's been very much driven from the top. A small number of people telling the majority what to do and how to do it. We are now trying to change that strategy around which says that there's an opportunity for everybody to get involved if they want to.

He continued by discussing how to go about promoting engagement through consideration of the social environment:

> Well that's through this type of work which is engaging with and listening to people and place a lot of emphasis of that, about listening. Doing a lot more listening and talking and then giving feedback against some of the things they raise because not everything that's raised we can address, it's just not going to be viable. I think what's important is that we give answers back as to why we can't do that and the things that we can we must do them and let people see that things are changing and – oh yes, management seem

to listen but actually they've done something about it so they have now listened. So the words are only of very little value unless you back it up with action.

In the organizations that we have studied, this facet of engagement tends to be less well developed than the other facets. However, as we have seen from the above theoretical and empirical research, generating and sustaining social engagement is an essential component of engaging leadership. An increased emphasis on the significance of the social environment, not just in terms of warmth and openness, but also as the context for developing shared values and nurturing innovation, is likely to lead to valued organizational goals.

The emotional landscape for engagement

Positive affect (emotion) is fundamental to the experience of engagement (Soane et al., 2012) and a range of other outcomes. Affect has a motivational function (Clore, 1994) that influences attitudes and behaviour. For example, the positive affect associated with the experience of interest promotes exploration, seeking new experiences and self-development (e.g. Csikszentmihalyi, 1990). Phelps (2006) suggested that affect is relevant to performance due to the interaction between affective and cognitive systems. Under conditions of positive affect, this interaction benefits high performance behaviours due to enhanced access to information stored in memories (Mayer, Gayle, Meehan and Haarman, 1990), effective use of information aided by emotional cues for choice making (Bechara and Damasio, 2005; Finucane, Alhakami, Slovic and Johnson, 2000) and greater responsiveness to feedback (Ilies and Judge, 2005). High performance behaviours can lead to a reinforcing cycle of positive individual-level responses and the development of further high performance behaviour via good feedback from the task itself (e.g. in manufacturing products) or other people (e.g. customers and line managers).

The broaden-and-build theory (Frederickson, 1998, 2002) can be considered as a frame-work for drawing together various components of affect research and underpinning the engagement process. Broaden-and-build theory proposes that positive affect both broadens the frequency and quality of associations between thoughts and actions, and builds personal resources. The broadening and building effects of positive emotions contrasts with the focusing effect of negative emotions which functions to protect, evade and survive. Given that engagement encompasses positive affect, and broaden-and-build processes explain how positive affect influences beneficial outcomes, the two approaches together can aid understanding of how leaders can enhance engagement through managing the emotional landscape and employee experiences.

Prior research has shown that positive affect is more susceptible to situational influence than is negative affect and, when managed well, is associated with presence at work and performance (George, 1990). Feeling positive about work increases interest in social interaction through an enhanced need to affiliate with others (Pelled and Xin, 1999). Positive affect can also arise through perceptions that managers, and the organization more generally, are supportive of employee efforts. For example, Eisenberger, Fasolo and Davis-LaMastro (1990) found links between perceived organizational support and innovation. Perceptions of being valued and respected led to willingness to innovate and actual innovation for the organization without additional formal reward. They concluded that emotion-based approaches are critical to understanding employees' responses to work. As a manager of traders in financial markets noted, his role can be seen as a 'director of emotions' (Fenton-O'Creevy et al., 2011: 1054). He talked about how trading in financial markets was a fundamentally emotional process. Traders need to understand and manage their own emotions in order to make good decisions, and they also need to bring their own emotional understanding to bear on insights into others' decision process to improve their comprehension of market movements.

Discussions in PlasticCo also highlighted the importance of emotion management. For example, a quality control manager in PlasticCo acknowledged the beneficial impact of supervisory support to her job satisfaction:

> I love my job, I do love my job . . . I'm constantly getting encouragement from my boss and things like that so I mean . . . I do, like I say, as far as job satisfaction is concerned I do like it.

She went on to discuss the stronger focus on a positive working environment that was being introduced as part of the organizational change process:

> I mean every company's the same, every company wants to improve, don't they, but they want the staff, you know showing that . . . like this year, they really want the staff to be happy and create a better atmosphere in the workforce and they want to understand the problems. So to me that's a really good thing.

The leadership and development manager also recognized the significance of emotion management and its impact on the business:

> I think quite a lot of them are committed, yes. If you're in a role that you don't feel you've got much of a voice or much of an influence as much as you're committed, if you come across the same problems day in and day out and you don't feel you're being given the resources to do your job properly, that probably affects your motivation and energy levels. So there might be peaks or troughs in terms of how energetic people are or how emotionally committed they are and I think you know, it's like everything else you know, the manager steps down and gives you a bit of time and talks stuff through with you and you get some feedback, you are more emotionally in tune with what is going on.

The theoretical and empirical research reviewed above, illustrated by the quotations from PlasticCo, show that there is clear evidence that positive affect leads to worthwhile individual and organizational outcomes, and that affect is central to the engagement process. Leaders have a key role in increasing the frequency and intensity of positive affective experiences. One way that leaders can do so is through individual-level interactions that focus on shaping emotional tone and affective responses to situations. Leaders can work with individuals to guide them through the process of making appropriate emotional responses to situations, to help individuals to manage their own emotions and improve their insights into others' feelings. Such learning could contribute to the broadening of related thought processes as well as building of personal resources, such as a sense of self-efficacy that arises from dynamic, affirmative input-output cycles.

The working environment

The interactions between leaders and employees represent a significant source of engagement. However, a discussion of the role of leaders would not be complete without consideration of the job context since work roles are the channel for engagement. Prior research has identified several components of the working environment that are worthy of leaders' attention. The Job Demands-Resources Model (Bakker and Demerouti, 2007; Demerouti and Bakker, 2011) proposed that individual-level job resources direct and motivate effort towards performing work that, in turn, leads to high levels of effort, absorption and attainment. This framework contributes to understanding of assured, constructive responses to demanding jobs via development and deployment of personal resources such as skills, resilience and self-efficacy (Hobfoll, 2002). Conversely, low levels of demands can be insufficiently motivating to trigger enactment of resources, and low levels of personal resources with little supervisory support can result in seemingly overwhelming demands or even burnout. Since engagement is a positive state resulting from experiences of self-in-role, perceived fit with work is important.

Leaders can approach engagement through ensuring a fit between employees and their roles and a match between demands and resources that can take personal growth into account. One way to achieve this fit is through consideration of objective fit, i.e. the match between skills required by the job and skills possessed by an employee, and subjective fit, i.e. beliefs about fit (Resick et al., 2007). In practical terms, these factors map onto selection and development, respectively. One of the site managers at PlasticCo discussed the importance of training in the performance management process:

> There's always a training need. You have got to start with whether that person has a training need, and then establish whether further training . . . look at whether they're the right person for the role, it may be that they really don't want to be in that role and they would be more than happy doing another role with less money and less responsibility and so there are a lot of options before you look at disciplinaries.

Overall, setting motivational challenges that are matched with skill development opportunities will provide a context for engagement. Leaders need to have a clear view on the aspects of work that can be developed, such as reorganization of tasks or roles, and ensure that two-way dialogue can support the growth of engagement.

Non-leadership and poor management

Thus far, I have focused on leaders' abundant potential to create a positive working environment that promotes engagement and a host of other beneficial outcomes. Conversely, everyday experience shows us that evidence of non-leadership and bad management is all too inherent within organizational life. Given the definition of leadership and the association between leadership and positive forms of influence, I do not consider the flipside to be bad leadership. Rather, it is the passive lack of leadership or active instigation and promulgation of poor practices that are the obverse of true leadership. Not only do such practices make high performance difficult for even the most dedicated individuals, they also raise the probability of employee retaliation. Recent theoretical and empirical developments have examined a number of negative workplace behaviours, including counterproductive work behaviours, alienation, burnout and turnover. While there are frequently some individual differences in play here, managers have a role in making normally unacceptable behaviours seem like acceptable responses to poor practices. These outcomes could arise from two foci: managers themselves or the work context, and these are considered in turn.

The leadership theories discussed so far in this chapter have rested on the premise that leaders are benign in their attempts to influence employees, and that they are authentic – that is, genuine in their intentions and behaviour. However, this perspective does not have universal application. There is a wide literature on Machiavellianism and the preponderance of some managers to present tough challenges with active attempts to derail others' performance while avoiding personal detriment (Wilson, Near and Miller, 1996). Machiavellian managers could have a direct impact on disengagement through their hard-ball tactics – why would employees engage with their work if it is a constant fight to achieve any recognition or intrinsic reward? Machiavellian managers might also have a more indirect impact. Recent research by Den Hartog and Belschak (2012) showed that Machiavellian managers might feign a transformational style in order to achieve their desired outcomes, however, such attempts are usually transparent and can ultimately have a negative impact on engagement. True authenticity and genuinely positive values are therefore important attributes of leaders.

Similarly, the charisma component of transformational leadership could also be manipulated for personal gain. Since charisma is compelling and draws followers toward a leader's vision, it is critical that the vision is derived appropriately. Vision driven by personal need and egregious ambition is more accurately described as pseudo-transformational leadership (Bass and Steidlmeier, 1999). Charismatic leaders can also be narcissistic, they can generate a cult of personality and create difficulties for succession (Conger, 1989). Thus senior leaders need to attend to questions such as how to separate the right kind of charisma, focused on the greater good, from the misuse of power; how to employ appropriate risk-taking behaviours without venturing into dangerous territory; and how to derive a vision from organizational strategy and stakeholder interests. Such questions can only be addressed through frequent, open discussions about values, mission and objectives. Such discussions will have the additional benefits of aligning interests and fostering engagement.

The work context also has relevance. Although some jobs might seem inherently more engaging than others, there can be wide differences in individual-level perception and these perceptions have an important influence on engagement and performance behaviours. For example, Shantz and Alfes (2011) found that employees with low levels of engagement could still perform to a high level if they believed that the organization supported their efforts. In a related study, Shantz et al. (2013) showed that high levels of task variety, autonomy, feedback from the job, task identity and task significance (all components of the Job Characteristics Model, Hackman and Oldham, 1980) were associated with engagement and performance. However, when levels of engagement were low, the likelihood of deviant behaviours, such as turning up to work late without permission, increased. Consequently, the role of leaders becomes critical in either shaping optimal working environments or, at least, buffering the potentially negative impact of a more challenging job context.

Achieving engaging leadership

The theories reviewed in this chapter provide some guidance concerning how leaders and leadership processes can function to enhance engagement and increase the likelihood of other significant outcomes such as high performance. As with other aspects of leadership, developing engaging leadership requires thoughtful, reflective practice and attention to the engagement process. One way to achieve such personal development is to use a psychometric assessment. The definition of engagement presented earlier in this chapter has been operationalized in the ISA Engagement Scale (Soane et al., 2012). This scale is a nine-item measure that can assess overall engagement as well as each facet (intellectual, social and affective engagement). Our data indicate that the scale is a valid measure of engagement, and that it can be used to understand engagement within wider frameworks, such as the engagement–performance relationship.

Building on the research to date, the ISA Engagement Scale can be adapted to function as a measure of engaging leadership, and our preliminary work with executives has supported this adaptation. Thus the ISA Engagement Scale for Leaders can be used to assess the extent to which leaders encourage and assist employees to engage with their work. The scale can be used as part of leadership development programmes or wider employee attitude survey to measure engagement levels. The scale can also be used to consider how engagement is related to other factors in the working environment such as communication or job design which can be measured using other, valid question sets.

In order to evaluate the strength of engaging leadership, leaders answer nine questions on a seven-point scale from 'strongly disagree' to 'strongly agree'. This will give an overall engaging leadership score, and a score for each of three facets of engaging leadership as follows:

Intellectual engagement (questions 1–3): this measures the extent to which leaders encourage intellectual absorption in work, or thinking hard about work. Calculate the total score for the three questions.

Social engagement (questions 4–6): this measures the degree to which leaders encourage social connections in their work environment, and shared values among colleagues. Calculate the total score for the three questions.

Affective engagement (questions 7–9): this measures the extent to which leaders encourage employees to have positive and energizing feelings about their work. Calculate the average score for the three questions.

The maximum score for each facet is 21, and the maximum score for the scale overall is 63. Leaders will generally aim for a score of 18 or above for each facet and for a score of 54 or above for the overall scale.

Engaging leadership scale

Please answer each of the following questions using the following response scale: 1 strongly disagree, 2 disagree, 3 somewhat disagree, 4 neither disagree nor agree, 5 somewhat agree, 6 agree, 7 strongly agree.

As a leader, I encourage my direct reports to. . .

1 Focus hard on their work
2 Concentrate on their work
3 Pay a lot of attention to their work
4 Share the same work values as their colleagues
5 Share the same work goals as their colleagues
6 Share the same work attitudes as their colleagues
7 Feel positive about their work
8 Feel energetic in their work
9 Be enthusiastic in their work

Data from the ISA Engaging Leadership Scale can provide a snapshot of current perspectives. As such, the scale could be a useful addition to regular developmental activity. Furthermore, the scale could be supplemented by qualitative conversations between leaders and employees.

These conversations have dual functionality – they serve both to provide feedback about the extent of engaging leadership as well as to provide an opportunity to enhance the components of engagement through discussion.

Conclusion

This chapter has examined how leaders can create a positive working environment within which employees can engage with their work. Here, I highlight five critical ingredients of engaging leadership. First, leaders must have an unwavering focus on positive forms of influence and true transformational leadership. Superficial attempts to gain personal support through charisma or self-serving vision must be surfaced and eradicated.

Second, leaders need to consider how to evolve from manager to engaging leader. While there are many routes to the development of leaders and leadership skills, a clear link between attitudes, actions and engagement can be attained through a focus on the aspects of engagement itself. Thus I recommend the use of measures such as the ISA Engaging Leadership Scale. When considered within a wider framework of individual development and reflective practice, this focused activity could assist growth of engagement-specific skills.

Third, leaders need to create a forum for intellectual debate. Open discussion about leadership and the nature of work can stimulate both engagement and innovation. Although changes to practices can have a short-term cost because of the additional time required to generate and review ideas, making such practices routine is likely to have significant long-term advantages.

Fourth, leaders must value and promote a socially engaging environment where values are shared, employees feel socially embedded, and there are frequent opportunities for the open discussion of ideas. This socially engaging context will also contribute to attainment of the broader goals summarized here.

Fifth, leaders need to actively manage the emotional landscape. Although negative experiences can provide some useful information that promotes learning, leaders should emphasize, and set the stage for, positive affect. Enthusiasm engenders engagement as well as commitment, satisfaction, invention and performance.

To conclude, leaders have a duty to create optimal working environments. The theoretical and empirical evidence reviewed in this chapter has highlighted a number of ways that leaders can surface tacit assumptions about how and why employees might engage with their work. Focused attention on actions linked to personal development, and the conditions for intellectual, social and affective engagement will contribute to the growth and sustenance of employee engagement and high-performance organizations.

References

Alfes, K., Truss, C., Soane, E. C., Rees, C. and Gatenby, M. (2010) *Creating an engaged workforce.* London: CIPD.

Awamleh, L. and Gardner, W. L. (1999) 'Perceptions of leader charisma and effectiveness: The effects of vision content, delivery, and organizational performance', *Leadership Quarterly*, 10(3): 345–73.

Babcock-Roberson, M. E. and Strickland, O. J. (2010) 'The relationship between charismatic leadership, work engagement and organizational citizenship behaviors', *Journal of Psychology*, 144(3): 313–26.

Bakker, A. B. and Demerouti, E. (2007) 'The Job Demands–Resources model: State of the art', *Journal of Managerial Psychology*, 22: 309–28.

Bass, B. (1985). *Leadership and performance beyond expectations*. New York: Free Press.

—— and Avolio, B. (1990) 'The implications of transactional and transformational leadership for individual, team, and organizational development', *Research in Organizational Change and Development*, 4: 231–72.

—— and Avolio, B. (2000) *MLQ Multifactor Leadership Questionnaire technical report*. Redwood City, CA: Mind Garden Inc.

Bass, B. and Steidlmeier, P. (1999) 'Ethics, character, and authentic transformational leadership behavior', *Leadership Quarterly*, 10: 181–217.

Bechara, A. and Damasio, A. R. (2005) 'The somatic marker hypothesis: A neural theory of economic decision', *Games and Economic Behavior*, 52: 336–72.

Blau, P. M. (1964) *Exchange and power in social life*. New York: Wiley.

Conger, J. A. and Kanungo, R. N. (1998) *Charismatic leadership in organizations*. Thousand Oaks, CA: Sage.

Bezuijen, X. M., van Dam, K., van den Berg, P. T. and Thierry, H. (2010) 'How leaders stimulate employee learning: A leader-member exchange approach', *Journal of Occupational and Organizational Psychology*, 83: 673–93.

Clore, G. L. (1994) Why emotions vary in intensity. In P. Ekman and R. J. Davidson (eds), *The nature of emotion: Fundamental questions* (pp. 386–93). New York: Oxford University Press.

Cohen, G. M. (2008) 'Connecting with the larger purpose of our work', *Journal of Pharmaceutical Sciences*, 97: 1041–6.

Csikszentmihalyi, M. (1990) *Flow. The psychology of optimal experience*. New York: Harper.

Demerouti, E. and Bakker, A. (2011) 'The Job Demands–Resources model: Challenges for future research', *South African Journal of Industrial Psychology*, 37: 1–9.

Den Hartog, D. and Belschak, F. D. (2012) 'Work engagement and Machiavellianism in the ethical leadership process', *Journal of Business Ethics*, 107: 35–47.

Eisenberger, R., Fasolo, P. and Davis-LaMastro, V. (1990) 'Perceived organizational support and employee diligence, commitment, and innovation' *Journal of Applied Psychology*, 75: 51–9.

Fenton-O'Creevy, M., Soane, E, Nicholson, N. and Willman, P. (2011) 'Thinking, feeling and deciding: The effects of emotions on the decision making of traders in financial markets', *Journal of Organizational Behavior*, 32: 1044–61.

Finucane, M. L., Alhakami, A., Slovic, P. and Johnson, S. M. (2000) 'The affect heuristic in judgments of risks and benefits' *Journal of Behavioral Decision Making*, 13: 1–17.

Frankl, V. (1992) *Man's search for meaning: An introduction to logotherapy*. Boston, MA: Beacon.

Fredrickson, B. L. (1998) 'What good are positive emotions?' *Review of General Psychology*, 2(3): 300–319.

—— (2001) 'The role of positive emotions in positive psychology', *American Psychologist*, 56(3): 218–26.

George, J. M. (1990) 'Personality, affect, and behavior in groups', *Journal of Applied Psychology*, 75(2): 107–16.

Gouldner, A. W. (1960) 'The norm of reciprocity: A preliminary statement', *American Sociological Review*, 25: 161–77.

Graen, G. and Cashman, J. E. (1975) 'A role-making model of leadership in formal organizations: A development approach'. In J. G. Hunt and L. L. Larson (eds), *Leadership frontiers* (pp. 143–65). Kent, OH: Kent State University Press.

—— and Uhl-Bien, M. (1995) 'Relationship-based approach to leadership: Development of leader-member exchange (LMX) theory of leadership over 25 years: Applying a multi-level multi-domain perspective', *Leadership Quarterly*, 6: 219–47.

Hackman, J. R. and Oldham, G. R. (1980) *Work redesign*. Reading, MA: Addison-Wesley.

Hobfoll, S. E. (2002) 'Social and psychological resources and adaptation', *Review of General Psychology*, 6: 307–24.

Hooper, D. and Martin, R. (2008) 'Beyond personal Leader-Member Exchange (LMX) quality: The effects of perceived LMX variability on employee reactions', *Leadership Quarterly*, 19: 20–30.

Illes, R. and Judge, T. A. (2005) 'Goal regulation across time: The effects of feedback and affect', *Journal of Applied Psychology*, 90: 453–67.

Kahn, W. A. (1990) 'Psychological conditions of personal engagement and disengagement at work', *Academy of Management Journal*, 33: 692–724.

Kankanhalli, A., Tan, B. C. Y. and Kwok-Kee, W. (2005) 'Contributing knowledge to electronic knowledge repositories: An empirical investigation', *Management Information Systems Quarterly*, 29: 113–43.

Lee, J.-N. and Kim, Y.-G. (1999) 'Effect of partnership quality on IS outsourcing success: Conceptual framework and empirical validation', *Journal of Management Information Systems*, 15: 29–61.

Liden, R. C., Sparrowe, R. T. and Wayne, S. J. (1997) 'Leader-member exchange theory: The past and potential for the future', *Research in Personnel and Human Resources Management*, 15: 47–119.

May, D. R., Gilson, R. L. and Harter, L. M. (2004) 'The psychological conditions of meaningfulness, safety and availability and the engagement of the human spirit at work', *Journal of Occupational & Organizational Psychology*, 77: 11–37.

Mayer, J. D., Gayle, M., Meehan, M. E. and Haarman, A.-K. (1990) 'Toward better specification of the mood-congruency effect in recall', *Journal of Experimental Social Psychology*, 26: 465–80.

Nahavandi, A. (2009) *The Art and Science of Leadership* (5th edn). New York: Pearson Education International.

Nelson, G. and Dyck, J. (2005) 'Forbearance in leadership: Opportunities and risks involved in cutting followers some slack', *Leadership Quarterly*, 16: 53–70.

Pelled, L. H. and Xin, K. R. (1999) 'Down and out: An investigation of the relationship between mood and employee withdrawal behavior', *Journal of Management*, 25(6): 875–95.

Phelps, E. A. (2006) 'Emotion and cognition: Insights from studies of the human amygdala', *Annual Review of Psychology*, 57: 27–53.

Resick, C. J., Baltes, B. B. and Shantz, C. W. (2007) 'Person-organization fit and work-related attitudes and decisions: Examining interactive effects with job fit and conscientiousness', *Journal of Applied Psychology*, 92(5): 1446–55.

Saks, A. M. (2006) 'Antecedents and consequences of employee engagement', *Journal of Managerial Psychology*, 21: 600–619.

Shantz, A. and Alfes, K. (2011) *Supporting employees with low levels of engagement: Performance implications*. Unpublished paper presented at The Employee Engagement Conference, Kent, UK.

——, Alfes, K., Truss, K. and Soane, E. (2013) 'The role of employee engagement in the relationship between job design and task performance, citizenship and deviant behaviours', *International Journal of Human Resource Management*, 24(13): 2608–27.

Soane, E., Alfes, K., Truss, K., Rees, C. and Gatenby, M. (2012) 'Employee engagement: Measure validation and associations with individual level outcomes', *Human Resource Development International*. 15(5): 529–47.

Tims, M., Bakker, A. and Xanthopoulou, D. (2011) 'Do transformational leaders enhance their followers' daily work engagement?' *The Leadership Quarterly*, 22: 121–31.

Thomas, K. W. and Velthouse, B. A. (1990) 'Cognitive elements of empowerment: An "interpretive" model of intrinsic task motivation', *Academy of Management Review*, 15: 666–81.

Wilson, D. S., Near, D. and Miller, R. R. (1996) 'Machiavellianism: A synthesis of evolutionary and psychological literatures', *Psychological Bulletin*, 119(2): 285–99.

Ul Haq, I., Ali, A., Azeem, M. U., Hijazi, S. T., Qurashi, T. M. and Quyyum, A. (2010) 'Mediation role of employee engagement in creative work process on the relationship of transformational leadership and employee creativity', *European Journal of Economics, Finance and Administrative Sciences*, 25: 94–101.

9   Employee engagement in a cultural context

Sebastiaan Rothmann

Introduction

Employee engagement is an important concept for researchers, practitioners and managers for various reasons. First, interest in employee engagement emerged with the shift in focus in psychology from weaknesses, malfunctioning and damage towards happiness, human strengths and optimal functioning (Seligman and Csikszentmihayi, 2000). Second, the needs of businesses to maximise the inputs of employees have contributed to the interest in engagement. Studies have shown that employee engagement predicts productivity, job satisfaction, motivation, commitment, low turnover intention, customer satisfaction, return on assets, profits and shareholder value (Bakker, Demerouti and Schaufeli, 2003; Bakker, Schaufeli, Leiter and Taris, 2008; Harter, Schmidt and Hayes, 2002; May, Gilson and Harter, 2004; Schaufeli and Bakker, 2004). Third, engagement affects the mindset of employees, and relates to personal initiative and learning (Sonnentag, 2003). Furthermore, it fuels discretionary efforts and concerns for quality (Salanova, Llorens, Cifre, Martinez and Schaufeli, 2003).

This chapter takes a cross-cultural perspective on employee engagement. First, relevant concepts are defined. Second, considerations regarding a cross-cultural perspective on employee engagement are outlined. Third, the measurement of employee engagement from a cross-cultural perspective is discussed. Fourth, causes of employee engagement in different cultures are described. Last, implications of a cross-cultural perspective on employee engagement are discussed.

Definition of concepts

The frameworks of Kahn (1990) and Schaufeli, Salanova, González-Romá and Bakker, (2002) have been used in research regarding employee engagement in various countries. Kahn (1990: 694) defined engagement as the 'harnessing of organizational members' selves to their work role by which they employ and express themselves physically, cognitively and emotionally during role performance'. Furthermore, Schaufeli et al. (2002) defined employee engagement as a positive, fulfilling, work-related state of mind characterised by vigour, dedication and absorption. Both the frameworks distinguish between three components of employee engagement, namely a physical component (being physically involved in a task and showing vigour and a positive affective state), a cognitive component (being alert at work and experiencing absorption and involvement) and an emotional component (being connected to the job/others while working and showing dedication and commitment).

For the reasons mentioned above, employee engagement would seem an important construct for different countries and cultures. While research is needed to investigate why engagement matters and how it can be optimised, cross-cultural research regarding employee engagement is necessary, especially with increasing globalisation, immigration, diversity and multiculturalism (Berry, Poortinga, Segall and Dasen, 2002: 375; Shimazu, Schaufeli, Miyanaka and Iwata, 2010). Next, these concepts are defined to show why a cross-cultural approach to employee engagement is necessary.

- Globalisation is defined as the process of increasing the connectivity and interdependence of the world's markets and businesses. Globalisation leads to multinational organisations and expanded markets: a business that had previously only sold its goods domestically can start selling products to other countries. It also leads to a global workforce, i.e. an international pool of immigrant workers employed by multinational organisations. Globalisation results in an increase in cross-cultural contacts, but may be accompanied by a decrease in the uniqueness of communities isolated in the past.
- Immigration refers to the action of coming to live permanently in a foreign country. Surveys in 2012 by Gallup have shown that approximately 640 million adults would want to migrate to another country in the world permanently if they were afforded the opportunity (http://www.gallup.com/poll/153992/). More than 150 million adults worldwide reported that they would like the United States as their desired future residence, while 7 per cent of respondents chose the United Kingdom. Other desired destination countries included Canada, France, Saudi Arabia, Australia, Germany and Spain.
- Diversity refers to the multitude of individual differences and similarities that exist among people. It includes the mixture of many dimensions which make people unique and different from one another.
- Multiculturalism refers to the orientation that accepts both the maintenance of cultural identity and characteristics of all ethno-cultural groups and the contact and participation of all groups in the larger plural society. Multiculturalism is valued in countries like Canada and South Africa.

It is clear from the abovementioned definitions that a cross-cultural perspective on employee engagement is necessary. However, practical interest in employee engagement has increased faster than the research evidence regarding the construct, its antecedents and outcomes (Burke, Koyuncu, Tekinkus, Bektas and Fiksenbaum, 2012). Furthermore, as is the case with other research on motivational processes in work organisations, most studies regarding employee engagement have been conducted in the United States, Spain, Portugal, the Netherlands and the United Kingdom (Deci, Ryan, Gagné, Leone, Usunov and Kornazheva, 2001; Shimazu et al., 2010). Studies have mainly been done in countries that have democratic governments, privately owned companies and a relatively strong emphasis on individualism. Therefore, the question arises whether the dynamics highlighted by employee engagement research are applicable to other cultures with economic systems, governments and cultural values different from those in the United States and Europe.

According to Arnett (2008), psychological research published in journals of the American Psychological Association focuses too narrowly on Americans, who comprise less than 5 per cent of the world's population. Applied to employee engagement, this might result in an understanding that is incomplete and does not adequately represent humanity. Many researchers and practitioners assume that people anywhere can be taken to represent people everywhere (Arnett, 2008: 610). However, understanding employee engagement across national and cultural boundaries allows researchers and practitioners to investigate how engagement might be cultivated in a wide variety of settings (Klassen et al., 2012).

Culture is defined as the shared life of a group of people (Berry et al., 2002). It refers to the collective mental programming of the human mind which distinguishes one group of people from another. This affects the patterns of thinking which are reflected in the meaning people attach to various aspects of life and which become crystallised in the institutions of a society. However, everyone in a given society is not programmed in the same way: there are differences between individuals.

According to Mathews (2012: 304), culture has traditionally been defined as 'the way of life of people in a given society'. Globalisation and developments in information technology, mass media and transport have led to more exposure from people in one culture to the way of life of people in other cultures. People choose aspects of their culture from the 'global cultural supermarket', which influence their ways of living. Therefore, some aspects of a specific culture could be unique, while other aspects are the same as in other cultures.

While this chapter argues in favour of a cross-cultural perspective on employee engagement, the importance of culture should not be overstated. Mathews (2012: 304) states that

> it has become increasingly apparent to anthropologists in recent decades that societies do not have walls around them. There is no absolutely separate set of values distinguishing all those who are Japanese or German or Brazilian from all those who are not; rather there are so many borderlands and other impressions that all such cultural comparison becomes questionable.

This does not mean that the concept of culture should be dismissed; some elements of separate cultures remain. The cultural supermarket is strongly affected by factors such as education, wealth and individuals' social and national worlds.

A cross-cultural perspective on employee engagement

Various considerations are relevant when employee engagement is studied from a cross-cultural perspective.

Etic versus emic perspectives

Two perspectives, namely an etic and emic perspective, are relevant for the study of constructs in cross-cultural context. An *etic* construct is defined similarly across cultures. The etic approach addresses the comparability of variables across cultures and requires that the measurement equivalence of imported assessment tools be studied (Cheung, Van de Vijver and Leong, 2011). An *emic* construct is defined differently across cultures and requires that a specific construct be studied in a specific culture. In the emic approach sensitivity to the family, social, cultural and ecological contexts is incorporated. Cultural variables, such as the world view of participants, acculturation level and racial identity, might influence the assessment of a construct. When imported measurement instruments are used, emic aspects of a construct will be hidden. An emic analysis focuses on a single culture and employs descriptive and qualitative methods to study the behaviour of interest.

Cheung et al. (2011) suggest that a combined etic and emic approach be used, which combines methodological rigour and cultural sensitivity. Such an approach is helpful in delineating the universal and culture specific aspects of constructs. Employee engagement must be understood not only in universal terms (i.e. an etic perspective), but also in terms of each culture (an emic perspective). Mathews (2012) argues in favour of a combined etic and emic approach towards subjective well-being (and this includes employee engagement) to enable cultural understanding. The cultural context of employee engagement has to be unpacked in a given society to fully understand the measurement of engagement in that society.

Difficulties might arise when comparing constructs (e.g. employee engagement) across cultural bounds (Kahneman and Krueger, 2006; Mathews, 2012). For example, concerning self-reports of subjective well-being, North Americans may engage in self-serving biases such as self-enhancement more than East Asians (Diener, Oishi and Lucas, 2003). In East Asian societies such as Japan, personal modesty and suppression of positive affect are key social values and one should not boast one's success or declare one's well-being too strongly (Mathews, 2012). According to Shimazu et al. (2010), a common bias exists in the comparison of mental health and other psychological conditions due to the wording of items, particularly regarding responses to positive terms (which are included to measure employee engagement).

Cultural dimensions

The cultural dimensions theory of Hofstede (Hofstede, Hofstede and Minkov, 2010) distinguishes between five cultural dimensions, namely individualism, power distance, uncertainty avoidance, masculinity and long-term orientation.

Individualism refers to a loosely knit social framework in which people are supposed to look after their own interests and those of their immediate family. Collectivism is characterised by a tight social framework in which people expect others in groups to which they belong (such as an organisation) to look after them and protect them when they are in trouble. In exchange for this security, they feel they owe loyalty to the group. The degree of individualism in a country is closely related to that country's wealth. Rich countries, like the United States, Great Britain and the Netherlands are very individualistic, while poor countries, like Colombia and Pakistan, are very collectivistic. In these societies the needs of the group are more important than those of the individual (Smith and Bond, 1993; Triandis, 1994). However, variation exists within broad cultural categories (e.g. 'Western' or 'non-Western' or 'Asian'), and also within countries. For example, residents of Hong Kong rate higher on individualism than residents of other regions in China. Countries within broad heterogeneous regions (such as Asia) may share similarities on cultural dimensions in spite of differences in religion, economics and history (Hofstede et al., 2010).

Power distance is a measure of the extent to which a society accepts the fact that power in institutions is distributed unequally. A high power-distance society accepts wide differences in power in organisations. Titles, rank and status carry a lot of weight. Countries high in power distance include the Philippines and India. In contrast, a low power-distance society plays down inequalities as much as possible. Superiors still have power, but subordinates are not fearful of their managers. Denmark, Israel and Austria are examples of countries with low power-distance scores.

Members of societies which have low *uncertainty avoidance* accept uncertainty, are relatively comfortable with risks and are relatively tolerant of behaviour and opinions which differ from their own, because they do not feel threatened by them. Countries which fall into this category include Singapore, Switzerland and Denmark. A society high in uncertainty avoidance is characterised by a high level of anxiety among its people, which manifests in nervousness, stress and aggression. Because people feel threatened by uncertainty and ambiguity in these societies, mechanisms are created to provide security and reduce risk. Organisations are likely to have more formal rules, there will be less tolerance for deviant ideas and behaviour, and members will strive to believe in absolute truths. Employees in countries with high uncertainty avoidance demonstrate relatively low job mobility and lifetime employment. Countries in this category include Japan, Portugal and Greece.

Some cultures (e.g. Japan and Austria) emphasise *masculinity*. That is, they value *quantity* of life, assertiveness and the acquisition of money and material things. Other cultures (e.g. Norway, Sweden and Denmark) emphasise *femininity*. That is, they value *quality* of life, relationships, sensitivity and concern for the welfare of others.

Long-term orientation was found in a study among students in 23 countries around the world and deals with virtue (www.geerthofstede.com/dimensions.html). Values which are associated with long-term orientation are persistence, ordering relationships by status and having a sense of shame. A strong long-term orientation was found in China, Hong Kong, Japan and Taiwan. Values which are connected with short-term orientation are respect for tradition, fulfilling social obligations and protecting one's 'face'. A strong short-term orientation was found in Nigeria, Ghana, the United Kingdom and United States.

Measurement issues in cross-cultural contexts

The question of measuring employee engagement in general terms is addressed in more detail in Chapter 15. Here, we focus on the measurement of engagement across cultural settings. Various measurement issues exist which can make it impossible to compare employee engagement scores in and across different cultural groups. These issues include lack of standardisation, scaling issues and response bias which might affect the scores of employees on engagement measures. Concerning standardisation, measures which lack adequate representation of multicultural or cross-cultural groups in normative samples should not be used to assess employee engagement. The levels of employee engagement of different cultural groups can only be compared if the measuring instrument of engagement is unbiased and equivalent (invariant) for all groups, and if representative samples were used in determining norms for the measuring instrument.

Scaling issues (e.g. Likert versus forced choice scales) should be considered when employee engagement is measured. Individuals may interpret and use response categories differently. Response bias occurs when cultural groups rate emotions or perceptions at the extreme or midpoints of the scale. Social desirability might also play a role in responding (Kahneman and Kruger, 2006). Individuals may respond to items in the way that they think the investigator might want them to respond.

Equivalence and bias are specifically important concepts concerning measurement in cross-cultural contexts. Employee engagement tools should be equivalent and unbiased (in addition to the usual requirements of reliability and validity) before direct comparisons can be drawn between cultural groups. Bias and equivalence are often treated as antonyms (Van de Vijver, 2003). Bias occurs when score differences in the indicators of a particular construct do not correspond with differences in the underlying construct (Van de Vijver and Tanzer, 1997). Bias refers to the presence of nuisance factors, which impact on the scores obtained with some instrument, while equivalence is the concept used to describe the consequence of the nuisance factors on the comparability of scores across cultures.

Equivalence

Equivalence refers to the comparability of questionnaire scores obtained in different cultural groups; it involves the question as to whether scores obtained in different cultures can be meaningfully compared. Equivalence of measures is also referred to as measurement invariance. Equivalence and bias are related (Van de Vijver and Rothmann, 2004). If scores are unbiased (free from nuisance factors), they are equivalent and (assuming that they are metrical) can be compared across cultures.

Van de Vijver and Leung (1997) distinguish between three types of equivalence:

- *Construct (structural) equivalence*, which is the most common type of equivalence which has to be assessed in cross-cultural studies, indicates the extent to which the same construct is measured across all cultural groups studied, irrespective of whether or not the measurement of the construct is based on identical instruments across cultures. It implies the universal validity of the underlying psychological construct.

    Construct equivalence can be investigated with several techniques, such as factor analysis, cluster analysis and multidimensional scaling or other dimensionality-reducing techniques (Van de Vijver and Leung, 1997). The idea behind the application of these techniques is to obtain a structure of a construct (e.g. employee engagement) in each culture, which can then be compared across all cultures involved. For example, Rothmann (2013) analysed the construct equivalence of the Orientations to Happiness Questionnaire (Peterson, Park and Seligman, 2005). The engagement subscale showed unacceptable structural equivalence in the South African and Namibian samples compared to the United States sample. Exploratory and confirmatory factor analyses are the most frequently employed techniques for studying construct equivalence. Confirmatory factor analysis is used when information is available about the com-position of the instrument (on the basis of previous studies). Exploratory factor analysis is used when no information about the composition of a measuring instrument is available.
- *Measurement unit equivalence* can be obtained when two metric measures have the same measurement unit, but different origins. In this case no direct score comparisons can be made across cultural groups unless the size of the offset (i.e. the difference in scale origin) is known.
- *Scalar equivalence* can be obtained when two metric measures have the same mea-surement unit and the same origin.

Equivalence cannot be assumed, but should be established and reported in each study (Van de Vijver and Leung, 1997). Structural, measurement unit and scalar equivalence are hierarchically ordered. The third presupposes the second, which presupposes the first. As a consequence, higher levels of equivalence are more difficult to establish. It is easier to verify that an instrument measures the same construct in different cultural groups (structural equivalence) than to identify numerical comparability across cultures (scalar equivalence).

Bias

Bias refers to the presence of nuisance factors in cross-cultural measurement (Van de Vijver and Rothmann, 2004). The psychological meaning of biased scores is not invariant across cultures and differences between cultural groups in assessment outcome are influenced by cultural or measurement artefacts. Bias has to do with the characteristics of an instrument in a specific cross-cultural comparison rather than with its intrinsic properties (Van de Vijver and Tanzer, 1997). The question as to whether an instrument is biased cannot be answered in general terms, but can be addressed when an instrument is biased in a specific comparison.

A distinction can be made between two different forms of bias, namely internal and external bias. Internal bias focuses on the relationship between an observed score and a latent trait variable. Internal bias refers to the presence of nuisance factors that play a differential role in different cultures (Van de Vijver and Leung, 1997). For example, scores of an employee engagement questionnaire may be more influenced by social desirability in one culture than in another. Internal bias challenges the validity of comparisons of constructs or scores obtained in different cultural groups. External bias (also known as predictive bias or differential prediction) focuses on the relationship between two observed variables – a predictor (e.g. employee engagement) and a criterion (e.g. job performance).

Van de Vijver and Rothmann (2004) identified three different types of internal bias, namely construct bias, method bias and item bias:

- *Construct bias* occurs when the construct measured is not identical across groups or when behaviours that constitute the domain of interest from which items sampled, are not identical across cultures. An example of construct bias is when the definition of a construct shows an incomplete overlap across cultures.
- *Method bias* includes all sources of bias emanating from the method and procedure of a study, including sample incomparability, instrument differences, tester and interviewer effects and the mode of administration. Method bias can be caused by confounding sample differences (e.g. effects of schooling confound differences between cultures), differences in the procedures or mode used to administer an instrument and general features of an instrument (e.g. individuals from different cultures might not deal in the same way with Likert rating scales).
- *Item bias* occurs when persons with the same standing on the underlying construct (e.g. they are equally engaged), but coming from different cultural groups do not have the same average score on the item. An item is biased when its psychological meaning is not identical across cultures. The item is biased because it favours one cultural group across all test score levels. Sources of item bias include poor item translation, ambiguities in the original item, low familiarity or appropriateness of the item content in certain cultures and the influence of cultural specifics such as nuisance factors or connotations associated with the item wording. Uniform bias occurs when the influence of bias on an item is consistent for all the score levels of that particular item. Non-uniform bias occurs when significantly larger differences in terms of a particular item exist in one group when compared to the other group across the different score levels for the specific item.

Measuring employee engagement in different cultures

As discussed elsewhere in this volume, one of the popular tools which measures employee engagement is the Gallup Survey. This survey, which uses 12 items to assess employee engagement, is administered in various countries. Based on the results of this survey, it was found that the global average engaged employees are 11 per cent. In China, the results of a 2012 survey showed that 6 per cent of employees were engaged, while 68 per cent and 26 per cent were not engaged and actively disengaged respectively (www.gallup.com/poll/ 160190). In the United States, 29 per cent of employees were engaged in 2011, while 52 per cent and 19 per cent were not engaged and actively disengaged respectively (www.gallup.

com/poll/150383). However, despite the usefulness of the Gallup Survey, an analysis of the items shows that it measures the work environment rather than employee engagement. It is also not clear whether bias and equivalence of the survey were assessed prior to comparing different cultures in terms of levels of 'employee engagement'.

Before practitioners and researchers can investigate employee engagement, equivalence and bias should be tested for in contexts where differences in scores could be attributed to cultural influences in terms of item meaning and understanding, rather than differences resulting from the measuring of the constructs (Poortinga, 1989; Van de Vijver and Leung, 1997). If cultural influences are not accounted for, invalid conclusions regarding the constructs under study could be made.

Shimazu et al. (2010) studied the measurement of employee engagement with the Utrecht Work Engagement Scale (UWES) in the Netherlands and Japan. They found that the Japanese version had difficulty in differentiating respondents with extremely low work engagement, whereas the original Dutch version had difficulty in differentiating respondents with high employee engagement. The measurement accuracy of the two versions was not similar. Suppression of positive affect among Japanese people and self-enhancement (the general sensitivity to positive self-relevant information) among Dutch people may have caused decreased measurement accuracy (Shimazu et al., 2010). In a comparison of 16 countries, the authors found that Japan had the lowest employee engagement scores, while Germany had the highest score. However, Shimazu et al. (2010) warned that low engagement scores among Japanese as well as high engagement scores among Western employees should be interpreted with caution.

A study of the psychometric properties of the UWES for police members in South Africa confirmed the equivalence of three dimensions (i.e. vigour, dedication and absorption) for different cultural groups (Storm and Rothmann, 2003). No evidence was found for uniform or non-uniform bias of the items of the UWES for different race groups. In another South African study, Naudé and Rothmann (2004) found that some of the items of the UWES are problematic, resulting in unacceptable construct equivalence for different cultural groups. For example, the item 'Time flies when I'm working' (which uses a metaphor quite common in the English language as an indicator of cognitive engagement), should not be used when the goal is to compare employee engagement scores in different cultural groups, because African cultures attach a different meaning to 'time flies'. According to Van de Vijver and Leung (1997), metaphors should be avoided in questionnaires.

Employee engagement measures should be administered in the preferred language of the individual being assessed. Instruments are often administered in English, which is a third or even fourth language of respondents in many countries. Problems with bias and equivalence arise when respondents are not fluent in a specific language (e.g. English). Furthermore, problems of translation equivalence also exist, which means that it is sometimes difficult to find equivalent concepts in different languages when translating measures (see Valchev et al., 2011). For example, some English words might be difficult to understand in South Africa, where there are a number of languages and English is a second language for most people. The use of metaphors and uncommon words such as 'resilience', 'immersed' and 'engrossed' in instruments which measure employee engagement could contribute to mis-understandings. Although it is often argued that questionnaires should be administered in English because it is regarded as the 'business language', the best strategy to endure construct equivalence of the measures might be to translate them into the mother tongue of employees.

Klassen et al. (2012) investigated the validity of the UWES in a sample of 853 teachers in Australia, Canada, China, Indonesia and Oman. They found that a three-factor model of employee engagement (consisting of physical, emotional and cognitive components) was acceptable in countries like Australia and Indonesia, while a one-factor model (where all the items of the UWES formed part of a single employee engagement factor) was acceptable within countries like Canada and China. Although the UWES was invariant (equivalent) in Western and non-Western groups (i.e. either a three-factor or one-factor model of engagement was supported in cultural groups), invariance did not exist across the cultural groups (i.e. scores could not be compared across cultural groups because of three-factor structures in some cultures versus one-factor structures in others). Furthermore, although a one-factor model of employee engagement might be preferable to use across cultures (Shimazu et al., 2010), the dimensions of engagement (e.g. the emotional versus the cognitive component versus the physical component) might show differential in predicting the value of individual and organisational outcomes.

Balducci, Fraccaroli and Schaufeli (2010) studied the construct equivalence (also referred to as factorial invariance) of the UWES for samples in the Netherlands and Italy. They reported factorial and covariance invariance of a one-factor model of employee engagement samples of white collar workers. Studies in South Africa confirmed the structural equivalence of two scales of the UWES for emergency medical technicians in two cultural groups (Naudé and Rothmann, 2004).

To summarise, it is important to consider the construct equivalence (measurement invariance) and bias of employee engagement measures in addition to the usual requirements of construct validity (does the questionnaire measure what it is supposed to measure) and reliability (does the questionnaire provide a consistent measure of the construct). In most cross-cultural studies of employee engagement, the UWES has been used. Research is needed regarding the equivalence and bias of questionnaires measuring employee engagement (and antecedents and outcomes thereof) before they are used for measurement and decision making purposes across different cultures. In some studies, employee engagement could be best described in terms of a single dimension, while in others three dimensions (cognitive, physical and emotional engagement) reflected employee engagement best.

Causes of employee engagement in different cultures

Employee engagement might take different forms around the world. Therefore, a one-size-fits-all approach will be doomed to failure. It becomes increasingly difficult to determine what the causes of employee engagement are as workforces become more culturally diverse.

This section deals with the antecedents of employee engagement in different cultures. First, three models which have been tested in different cultures are discussed, followed by an overview of the causes of employee engagement in different cultures.

Antecedents of employee engagement: models and theories

Three models and theories which have been tested cross-culturally show promising results in understanding and predicting employee engagement, namely the personal engagement model of Kahn (1990), the job demands–resources model (Schaufeli and Bakker, 2004) and self-determination theory (Deci et al., 2001). Given the possibility that cultural differences might exist in specific antecedents of employee engagement, it is advisable to approach the antecedents from models and theories. For example, according to the job demands–resources model, the availability of resources (relatively to demands) affects employee engagement, but it allows for cultural differences in the sense that a specific resource (e.g. supportive supervisor relations) might be more important in one culture compared to another culture. Similarly, according to self-determination theory, satisfaction of the psychological needs for autonomy, competence and relatedness affects employee engagement, but it allows for the possibility that different factors might contribute to psychological need satisfaction in different cultures. Therefore, the three models and theories which could explain employee engagement are discussed.

The personal engagement model

According to the personal engagement model of Kahn (1990), various antecedents contribute to individuals attaching themselves to their roles. The perception of job context affects employees' psychological responses, which affect their engagement. Kahn (1990) concluded from a qualitative study that various job contextual factors impact employee engagement via the experience of three psychological conditions, namely psychological meaningfulness, psychological availability and psychological safety.

Psychological meaningfulness relates to the value individuals attach to a work goal compared to their own personal goals (Kahn, 1990; May et al., 2004). Psychological safety is defined as the experience of being able to act in a way that is natural and to be able to use and employ all skills and knowledge in a role without having to fear being ridiculed or experiencing negative consequences. Psychological availability is defined by Kahn (1990) as the ability to engage as a result of having the cognitive, emotional and physical resources. Psychological meaningfulness and psychological availability were found to be important predictors of employee engagement in the United States (May et al., 2004), Israel (Steger, Littman-Ovadia, Miller, Menger and Rothmann, in press), South Africa (Rothmann and Rothmann, 2010) and Namibia (Rothmann and Welsh, 2013). The reliability and validity of a measure of psychological safety which was developed by May et al. (2004) in the United States could not be confirmed in the South African and Namibian studies.

A study by May et al. (2004) showed that work role fit, good relations with co-workers and job enrichment contributed to psychological meaningfulness and employee engagement. Supportive supervision contributed to psychological safety, while the availability of physical, cognitive and emotional resources contributed to psychological availability and employee engagement. In a study in Namibia it was found that work role fit and job enrichment showed the strongest relationships with psychological meaningfulness and employee engagement (Rothmann and Welsh, 2013). Rewards, co-worker relations, resources, supervisor relations and organisational support showed moderate relationships with psychological availability and employee engagement. A study in South Africa showed that work role fit was the best predictor of psychological meaningfulness and employee engagement (Olivier and Rothmann, 2007).

The job demands–resources model

Research on engagement as an experience of work activity has utilised the job demands–resources (JD–R) model (Demerouti, Bakker, Nachreiner and Schaufeli, 2001; Hakanen, Schaufeli and Ahola, 2008) and the conservation of resources (COR) theory (Hobfoll, 1989, 1998 – see also Chapter 7 of this volume). Bakker et al. (2008) regard job and personal resources as important factors associated with employee engagement.

The JD–R model assumes that it is possible to model work characteristics associated with well-being in two broad categories, namely job demands and job resources (Demerouti et al., 2001). Job demands refer to the physical, psychological, social or organisational aspects of the job that require sustained physical and/or psychological effort and that are therefore associated with certain physiological and/or psychological costs (e.g. work pressure, role overload and emotional demands). Job resources refer to the physical, psychological, social or organisational aspects of the job that may be functional in achieving work goals, reducing job demands and stimulating personal growth and development. Resources may be located at the level of the organisation (e.g. salary, career opportunities, job security), interpersonal and social relations (e.g. supervisor support, co-worker support and team climate), the organisation of work (e.g. role clarity, and participation in decision-making), and the level of the task (e.g. performance feedback, skill variety, task significance, task identity and autonomy).

Various studies have shown that job resources, including social support from supervisors and colleagues, and the intrinsic nature of the job (e.g. skill variety, autonomy and learning opportunities) are positively associated with employee engagement (Bakker et al., 2008; Schaufeli and Bakker, 2004). In a longitudinal study, Mauno, Kinnunen and Ruokolainen (2007) found that job resources predicted employee engagement better than job demands. Hakanen et al. (2008) found that job resources predicted future engagement. In a South African study which included various occupations, it was found that job resources at the level of interpersonal and social relations, the organisation of work and the task were strong predictors of employee engagement (Rothmann and Rothmann, 2010).

In a study of eight European countries, Taipale, Selander, Anttila and Nätti (2011) found that job demands reduced employee engagement, while autonomy and support increased employee engagement. However, their study showed differences in the level of demands, autonomy and social support. Demands were high in Finland, Sweden and the United Kingdom and lower in the Netherlands and Germany. Demands were also high in Bulgaria, Portugal and Hungary. Autonomy was high in the Swedish sample, but also in Portugal. Only Sweden registered a higher level of support than other countries. In Sweden employees have better opportunities to participate in decision-making.

Self-determination theory

Deci and Ryan developed the self-determination theory (SDT) (1985, 2011) which propagates that human behaviour is motivated by three innate, essential and universal needs, namely autonomy, competence and relatedness (Deci and Ryan, 2008). Deci et al. (2001) regard psychological need fulfilment as paramount for employee engagement. Autonomy refers to people feeling that they direct and determine their own behaviour. Competence requires succeeding at optimally challenging tasks, attaining desired outcomes and feeling efficient. Relatedness means standing in relation to others, showing concern for others, experiencing acceptance by others and being satisfied with the social world.

Within the SDT framework, it is the satisfaction of the three needs rather than the strength of the desire that is important in predicting employee engagement. The needs for autonomy, competence and relatedness are universal, but individuals differ in terms of the degree to which they are able to satisfy the needs (Deci and Ryan, 2011). SDT differentiates between autonomous and controlled motivation. Autonomous motivation predicts perseverance and adherence (Deci and Ryan, 2008) and relates to psychological well-being. The psychological needs for autonomy, competence and relatedness complement autonomous motivation. Autonomous motivation elicits behaviour by choice and volition; whereas controlled motivation acts to forces external to the self, under pressure and demand.

Deci et al. (2001) found support for the cross-cultural applicability of SDT in a study in the United States and Bulgaria. They found that autonomy-supported behaviour predicted satisfaction of the intrinsic needs for autonomy, competence and relatedness, which predicted task motivation (including task engagement). In a study in Belgium, Van den Broeck, Vansteenkiste, De Witte and Lens (2008) found that job demands and resources indirectly affect employee engagement via satisfaction of the psychological needs for autonomy, competence and relatedness. In a study of managers in South Africa, it was found that task characteristics, supervisor relations and personal resources indirectly affected employee engagement via psychological need satisfaction (Swart, 2012).

Antecedents of employee engagement: the results of surveys

Employee surveys have shown that employee perceptions about work experience differ by country (Sanchez and McCauley, 2006). These surveys did not employ a specific model or theory of employee engagement, although it is possible to apply the three models and theories discussed in this chapter to understand the effects of the work environment on employee engagement.

The following global engagement drivers were identified by Sanchez and McCauley (2006:45): (a) the work itself, and opportunities to develop; (b) confidence and trust in leadership; (c) recognition and rewards; and (d) organisational communication.

Regarding antecedents of employee engagement in specific countries, research showed that most of the important causes of engagement were the same for the United Kingdom and China, while the drivers of engagement in the United States were different from these countries (Sanchez and McCauley, 2006). The most important drivers of employee engagement in the United States were confidence in achieving career objectives, a sense of personal accomplishment, confidence that the organisation will be successful, quality as a high priority in the organisation, opportunity for growth and development and information and assistance in managing careers. In the United Kingdom and China the most important drivers of employee engagement were a sense of personal accomplishment, confidence in senior management, training opportunities, a fair pay and receiving performance feedback. For employees in the United Kingdom and the United States, respect matters. In France and India, employees care about the type of work that they are doing, while in Germany the type of people employees work with matters (Sanchez and McCauley, 2006).

It seems that employees in emergent economies (e.g. India, Mexico and China) are more positive regarding their work experiences than employees in more mature economies (e.g. the United States, United Kingdom and Australia). In a country like Japan, respect is an important value in the society, and it is therefore less important as a driver of employee engagement. Pay was an important driver of employee engagement in Japan, while benefits were important in China. Work–life balance was a less important driver of employee engagement in China and India.

Lu, Siu, Chen and Wang (2011) found that family mastery (defined as the extent to which individuals control their families' lives) strongly affects the engagement of employees in China. They argue that family is a major source of ego strength for individuals in collectivistic cultures. According to Lu et al. (2011), a sense of mastery of family life would make people experience more positive affect (e.g. satisfaction with family roles) and psychological well-being. These positive psychological experiences (also kinds of resources) could be employed by the individuals to help them stay highly engaged in their work.

A study by Cohen (2007) found that work commitment was related to cultural values (e.g. individualism, power distance and masculinity) for educators in Israel. Based on studies of Western and Asian countries, Klassen et al. (2012) reported that educators' work-related beliefs vary with cultural beliefs (i.e. level of collectivism) and country. They reported that widely shared cultural values within a country influence the ways that workplace motivation beliefs operate for educators and other workers. They argued that motivation beliefs that focus on the individual (e.g. engagement) would show lower levels of reliability and construct validity in collectivist settings compared to individualistic settings. Burke et al. (2012), who conducted a study on the antecedents and outcomes of engagement of nurses in Turkey, cautioned against the application of Western human resource practices to Turkish organisations.

Implications

Employee engagement in organisations could be influenced by cultural factors. This has various implications for managers and human resource practitioners. Increased contact between people of different cultures, wealth and education reduce cross-cultural differences. Whilst the importance of culture should not be overstated, some aspects of cultures could be unique, and should be considered to understand and influence employee engagement.

Assessment and promotion of employee engagement in different cultures require the consideration of etic and emic aspects of cultures, standardisation of measures, language differences, scaling and response bias and cultural variables. Bias and equivalence should be considered before scores are compared. Given the fact that assessment instruments were often imposed upon people in the past, it is necessary that the cultural context be considered. It is necessary to take a combined etic and emic approach towards the assessment and promotion of employee engagement. This will combine the scientific rigour of an etic approach with the cultural sensitivity of an emic approach (Cheung et al., 2012). Unique cultural behaviour can be detected when an emic approach is used.

Cultural or measurement artifacts may contribute to constructs not being invariant between cultures. Therefore bias and equivalence should be assessed when measuring instruments are applied cross-culturally. Van de Vijver and Leung (1997) distinguished between construct, method and item bias. Construct bias occurs when the construct measured is not equal across cultural groups; method bias emanates from the methods and procedures used in a study, and item bias occurs when groups with the same standing on a construct do not have the same mean scores on items. It is important to consider the equivalence of employee engagement measures before scores of different cultural groups are compared.

Various methodological questions should be attended to when assessing employee engagement, namely whether respondents are proficient in reading English, the translation of measures was done accurately, the translated measure is equivalent to the original measure, there are cross-cultural differences in the means and distributions of scores and how cross-cultural differences in scores could be interpreted.

It appears that cultural dimensions affect employee engagement. It is crucial for employers expanding their operations around the world to find the drivers of employee engagement in culturally diverse workforces. The cultural dimensions (individualism, power distance, uncertainty avoidance, masculinity and long-term orientation) identified by Hofstede et al. (2010), could be analysed to understand the factors which drive employee engagement.

However, organisational cultures in the United States, Canada, Australia and the United Kingdom are the most individualistic in the world, according to research reported by Hofstede et al. (2010). These cultures reward individual success and self-reliance more than teamwork and collaboration. Individualistic managers try to inject engagement into employees with a stirring vision and volumes of one-way communication rather than involve them in their own thinking.

According to Hofstede et al. (2010), individualistic Anglo-Saxon cultures are mid-way on the masculinity–femininity scale. Japan is the most masculine culture, thus the most assertive and decisive. However, the Anglo-Saxon combination of high individualism (self-reliance) and relatively strong masculinity (assertiveness and decisiveness), which idolise visionary and charismatic leaders, can stifle collaboration and engagement (Hofstede et al., 2010).

The question is whether a global or local strategy or a combination of the two should be used. Research results reported by Sanchez and McCauley (2006: 45) showed that four factors strongly affect employee engagement, regardless of the national culture. These factors are the work itself and opportunities to develop, confidence and trust in leadership, recognition and rewards and organisational culture.

Regarding the work itself and opportunities for development, international studies showed that work role fit and the intrinsic characteristics of a job (including opportunities to accomplish, develop and function autonomously) are important drivers of employee engagement. Employees who experience work role fit can express their beliefs and values at work and they perceive the workplace to be conducive to living out these beliefs and values (May et al., 2004). SDT (Deci et al., 2001), the personal engagement model of Kahn (1990) and the JD–R model (Demerouti et al., 2001), confirm the importance of the work itself for experiences of psychological meaningfulness and satisfaction of the psychological needs for autonomy and competence.

Globally, confidence and trust in supervisors and management are important drivers of employee engagement. Collaborative goal setting, on-going feedback and recognition, managing employee development, discussing performance with employees and building a climate of trust and empowerment contribute to employee engagement (Olivier and Rothmann, 2007). Good supervisor and management relations contribute to psychological safety (Kahn, 1990) and satisfaction of the psychological needs for autonomy and relatedness (Deci et al., 2001), which impact employee engagement. Furthermore, two-way communication, characterised by sharing of information and asking for feedback from all levels of an organisation, drives employee engagement. Recognition and rewards contribute to employee engagement in different cultures. Employees will be more likely to engage at work if they perceive more rewards and recognition for their work, especially when these are linked to personal accomplishment (Kahn, 1990) and satisfaction of the psychological need for competence (Deci et al., 2001). However, organisations should also recognise the influence of regional or national cultures on employee engagement. In line with an emic perspective, cultural differences should be identified and taken into account when initiatives are implemented to increase engagement of the workforce.

References

Arnett, J. J. (2008) 'The neglected 95%: Why American psychology needs to become less American', *American Psychologist*, 63: 602–14.

Bakker, A. B., Demerouti, E. and Schaufeli, W. B. (2003) 'Dual processes at work in a call centre: An application of the job demands–resources model', *European Journal of Work and Organizational Psychology*, 12: 393–417.

Bakker, A. B., Schaufeli, W. B., Leiter, M. P. and Taris, T. W. (2008) 'Work engagement: An emerging concept in occupational health psychology', *Work and Stress*, 22: 187–200.

Balducci, C., Fraccaroli, F. and Schaufeli, W. B. (2010). 'Psychometric properties of the Italian version of the Utrecht Work Engagement Scale: A cross-cultural analysis', *European Journal of Psychological Assessment*, 26: 143–49.

Berry, J. W., Poortinga, Y. P., Segall, M. H. and Dasen, P. R. (2002) *Cross-cultural Psychology: Research and Applications*, Cambridge: Cambridge University Press.

Burke, R. J., Koyuncu, M., Tekinkus, M., Bektas, C. and Fiksenbaum, L. (2012) 'Work engagement among nurses in Turkish hospitals: Potential antecedents and outcomes', *IS GUC Industrial Relations and Human Resources Journal*, 14(1): 7–24.

Cheung, F. M., Van de Vijver, F. J. R. and Leong, F. T. L. (2011) 'Toward a new approach to the study of personality in culture', *American Psychologist*, 66: 593–603.

Cohen, A. (2007) 'An examination of the relationship between commitments and culture among five cultural groups of Israeli teachers', *Journal of Cross-Cultural Psychology*, 38: 34–49.

Deci, E. L. and Ryan, R. M. (1985) *Intrinsic Motivation and Self-determination in Human Behavior*, New York: Plenum Books.

—— and Ryan, R.M. (2008) 'Self-determination theory: A macro-theory of human motivation, development, and health', *Canadian Psychology,* 49(3): 182–5.

—— and Ryan, R. M. (2011) 'Levels of analysis, regnant causes of behaviour and well-being: The role of psychological needs', *Psychological Inquiry,* 22: 17–22.

——, Ryan, R. M., Gagné, M., Leone, D. R., Usunov, J. and Kornazheva, B. P. (2001). 'Need satisfaction, motivation, and well-being in the work organizations of a former Eastern Bloc country', *Personality and Social Psychology Bulletin*, 27: 930–42.

Demerouti, E., Bakker, A. B., Nachreiner, F. and Schaufeli, W. B. (2001) 'The Job Demands–Resources model of burnout', *Journal of Applied Psychology*, 86: 499–512.

Diener, E., Oishi, S. and Lucas, R. E. (2003) 'Personality, culture and subjective well-being: Emotional and cognitive evaluations of life', *Annual Review of Psychology*, 54: 403–25.

Harter, J. K., Schmidt, F. L. and Hayes, T. L. (2002) 'Business-unit-level relationship between employee satisfaction, employee engagement and business outcomes: A meta-analysis', *Journal of Applied Psychology*, 87: 268–79.

Hakanen, J. J., Schaufeli, W. B. and Ahola, K. (2008) 'The Job Demands–Resources model: A three-year cross-lagged study of burnout, depression, commitment, and work engagement', *Work and Stress*, 22: 224–41.

Hobfoll, S. E. (1989) 'Conservation of resources: A new attempt at conceptualizing stress', *American Psychologist*, 44: 513–24.

—— (1998) *The Psychology and Philosophy of Stress, Culture, and Community*, New York: Plenum Books.

Hofstede, G., Hofstede, G. J. and Minkov, M. (2010) *Cultures and Organizations: Software of the Mind*, 3rd edn, New York: McGraw-Hill.

Jackson, L. T. B., Rothmann, S. and Van de Vijver, A. J. R. (2006) 'A model of work-related well-being for educators in South Africa', *Stress and Health*, 22: 263–74.

Kahn, W. A. (1990) 'Psychological conditions of personal engagement and disengagement at work', *Academy of Management Journal*, 33: 692–724.

Kahneman, D. and Krueger, A. B. (2006) 'Developments in the measure of subjective well-being', *Journal of Economic Perspectives*, 20(1): 3–24.

Klassen, R. M., Aldhafri, S., Mansfield, C. F., Purwanto, E., Siu, A. F. Y., Wong, M. W. and Woods-McConney, A. (2012) 'Teachers' engagement at work: An international validation study', *The Journal of Experimental Education*, 80: 317–37.

Lu, C., Sui, O., Chen, W. and Wang, H. (2011) 'Family mastery enhances work engagement in Chinese nurses: A cross-lagged analysis', *Journal of Vocational Behavior*, 78: 100–9.

Mathews, G. (2012) 'Happiness, culture and context', *International Journal of Well-being*, 2: 299–312.

Mauno, S., Kinnunen, U. and Ruokolainen, M. (2007) 'Job demands and resources as antecedents of work engagement: A longitudinal study', *Journal of Vocational Behavior*, 70: 149–71.

May, D. R., Gilson, R. L. and Harter, L. M. (2004) 'The psychological conditions of meaningfulness, safety and availability and the engagement of the human spirit at work', *Journal of Occupational and Organizational Psychology*, 77: 11–37.

Naudé, J. L. P. and Rothmann, S. (2004) 'The validation of the Utrecht Work Engagement Scale for emergency health technicians in Gauteng', *South African Journal of Economic and Management Sciences*, 7: 459–68.

Olivier, A. L. and Rothmann, S. (2007) 'Antecedents of work engagement in a multinational oil company', *South African Journal of Industrial Psychology*, 33(3): 49–56.

Peterson, C., Park, N. and Seligman, M. E. P. (2005) 'Orientations to happiness and life satisfaction: The full life versus the empty life', *Journal of Happiness Studies*, 6: 25–41.

Rothmann, S. (2013) 'Measuring happiness: Results of a cross-national study', in M. P. Wissing (ed.), *Cross-cultural Advancements in Positive Psychology*, Dordrecht: Springer.

—— and Rothmann, S. (Jr). (2010) 'Factors associated with employee engagement in South African organisations', *SA Journal of Industrial Psychology*, 36(1): 1–12.

—— and Welsh, C. (2013) 'Employee engagement in Namibia: The role of psychological conditions', *Management Dynamics*, 22(1): 14–25.

Salanova, M., Llorens, S., Cifre, E., Martinez, I. and Schaufeli, W. B. (2003) 'Perceived collective efficacy, subjective well-being and task performance among electronic work groups: An experimental study', *Small Group Research*, 34: 43–73.

Sanchez, P. and McCauley, D. (2006) 'Measuring and managing engagement in a cross-cultural workforce: New insights for global companies', *Global Business and Organizational Excellence*, 26(1): 41–50.

Schaufeli, W. B. and Bakker, A. B. (2004) 'Job demands, job resources and their relationship with burnout and engagement: A multi-sample study', *Journal of Organizational Behavior*, 25: 293–315.

——, Salanova, M., González-Romá, V. and Bakker, A. B. (2002) 'The measurement of engagement and burnout: A two sample confirmatory factor analytic approach', *Journal of Happiness Studies*, 3: 71–92.

Seligman, M. E. P. and Csikszentmihalyi, M. (2000). 'Positive psychology: An introduction', *American Psychologist*, 55, 5–14.

Shimazu, A., Schaufeli, W. B., Miyanaka, D. and Iwata, N. (2010) 'Why Japanese workers show low work engagement: An item-response theory analysis of the Utrecht Work Engagement Scale', *BioPsychoSocial Medicine*, 4(17): 1–6.

Smith, P. B. and Bond, M. H. (1993) *Social Psychology across Cultures*, Cambridge, Harvester Wheatsleaf, University Press.

Sonnentag, S. (2003) 'Recovery, work engagement, and proactive behavior: A new look at the interface between non-work and work', *Journal of Applied Psychology*, 88: 518–28.

Steger, M. F., Littman-Ovadia, H., Miller, M., Menger, L. and Rothmann, S. (in press) 'Engaging in work even when it is meaningless: Positive affective disposition and meaningful work interact in relation to work engagement', *Journal of Career Assessment.*

Storm, K. and Rothmann, S. (2003) 'The validation of the Utrecht Work Engagement Scale in the South African Police Services', *South African Journal of Industrial Psychology*, 29(4): 62–70.

Swart, J. P. (2012) 'Antecedents and outcomes of happiness of managers in the agricultural sector in South Africa' unpublished thesis, North-West University, Vanderbijlpark, South Africa.

Taipale, S., Selander, K., Anttila, T. and Nätti, J. (2011) 'Work engagement in eight European countries: The role of job demands, autonomy and social support', *International Journal of Sociology and Social Policy*, 31: 486–504.

Triandis, H. C. (1994) *Cultural and Social Behaviour*, New York: McGraw-Hill.

Valchev, V. H., Van de Vijver, F. J. R., Nel, J. A., Rothmann, S., Meiring, D. and De Bruin, G. P. (2011) 'Implicit personality conceptions of the Nguni cultural-linguistic groups of South Africa', *Cross-cultural Research*, 45: 235–66.

Van de Vijver, F. J. R. (2003) 'Bias and equivalence: Cross-cultural perspectives', in J. A. Harkness, F. J. R. Van de Vijver and P. Ph. Mohler (eds), *Cross-cultural Survey Methods*, New York: Wiley.

—— and Leung, K. (1997) *Methods and Data Analysis for Cross-cultural Research*, Thousand Oaks, CA: Sage.

—— and Rothmann, S. (2004) 'Assessment in multicultural groups: The South African case', *South African Journal of Industrial Psychology*, 30(4): 1–7.

Van den Broeck, A., Vansteenkiste, M., De Witte, H. and Lens, W. (2008) 'Explaining the relationships between job characteristics, burnout, and engagement: The role of basic psychological need satisfaction', *Work & Stress*, 22: 277–94.

10 Employee engagement in multinational organizations

*Clare Kelliher, Veronica Hope Hailey
and Elaine Farndale*

Introduction

Recent years have seen spiralling interest in employee engagement in many economies across the world, from employers, policy organizations and governments. Governments have seen high levels of employee engagement as a means to improve the performance of firms and thereby increase the competitiveness of their national economy.[1] Many employers have developed mechanisms to monitor engagement levels amongst their workforce and have tried to develop policies and practices to foster high levels of employee engagement. Multinational corporations (MNCs), considering employee engagement across their operations, are faced, however, with a more general question of whether employee engagement is a universal concept, similar throughout the world, or whether its meaning and the factors that influence it differ in the different parts of the world in which they operate. As discussed in Chapter 9, cross-national and cross-cultural research would suggest different attitudes to work and different behavioural responses by employees in different parts of the world. Thus, MNCs are faced with the question of whether employee engagement can be measured and compared in a meaningful way across a multinational organization's operations, and whether similar policies and practices are likely to influence levels of engagement similarly in different national contexts.

This chapter is concerned with addressing these questions, by reference to the findings from a study of employee engagement in MNCs operating in the UK, The Netherlands and India.[2] It will explore both the meaning and antecedents of employee engagement in these different national contexts. The chapter first presents a brief overview of some of the contemporary debates in employee engagement (as described in-depth elsewhere in this volume). Second, by reference to models of national culture and institutional contexts, it examines how these might influence the meaning and antecedents of employee engagement. Third, comparative findings from a study of three major MNCs are presented from these three countries. Finally, the findings are discussed and the implications for MNCs attempting to achieve high levels of engagement amongst employees throughout their operations are examined.

In particular, we focus on contrasting MNC operations in India with those in Western nations (the UK and the Netherlands). India has undergone rapid economic growth in the past decade and is of increasing importance in the world economy. Yet India is also known to experience problems in the management of human resources, notably extreme levels of labour turnover (Budhwar and Varma, 2011; Vorhauser-Smith, 2012), potentially indicating problems with employee engagement.

Job and organization engagment

The term 'engagement' has been commonplace in the organizational psychology literature for some time (Macey and Schneider, 2008), however more recently its use has become increasingly widespread in the context of everyday working life (Vance, 2006). Yet, although employee engagement has clear implications for the conduct of human resource management, until recently there has been relatively little research on employee engagement in the HRM field.

The roots of the concept of employee engagement are described in depth in this volume, yet there remain areas which require further conceptual clarification. Kahn (1990) suggests that people occupy roles at work to varying degrees of 'personal' engagement or disengagement, implying that employees extend varying degrees of themselves (cognitively, emotionally and physically) in the way in which they perform their jobs. Job engagement represents the application of high levels of energy, involvement and professional efficacy (Maslach, Schaufeli and Leiter, 2001). Furthermore, job engagement incorporates notions of employee well-being, with high levels of activation and identification, 'a positive, fulfilling, work-related state of mind that is characterized by vigour, dedication, and absorption' (Schaufeli, Martinez, Pinto, Salanova and Bakker, 2002: 72).

Although these definitions of job or work engagement are well known, Saks (2006) notes that employee engagement is 'the extent to which an employee is psychologically present in a particular organizational role' (p. 604). This builds on Kahn's (1990) work, arguing that engagement is role-related, but highlights that a distinction should be made between engagement towards the job and towards the organization, since these reflect important, but different relationships for the employee. In this chapter we focus specifically on these two aspects (job and organization engagement) in our examination of MNCs operating in India, the UK and the Netherlands, exploring the meaning of engagement and its antecedents.

India – institutional and cultural contrasts and comparisons with the UK and the Netherlands

Institutional differences

From an institutional perspective the role of the state in the economy, the structure of finance, the education system, the extent of labour legislation and levels of trade union density, amongst other factors, create a context in which the employment relationship is enacted (Brewster, Sparrow, Vernon and Houldsworth, 2011; Whitley, 1999). India, with a population just over 1.2 billion according to the 2011 Census, is the second largest nation in Asia. As a developing nation it has experienced very significant economic growth in the past decade. Subject to this being sustained, it has been predicted by the World Bank that it will become the fourth largest economy in the world by 2020.

One factor which has contributed to this economic boom has been the continued growth in Foreign Direct Investment (FDI), which in the 2011/12 fiscal year totalled in the region of £29 billion (Syed, 2012). International companies have both invested directly in India with the establishment of operations there and have also off-shored by outsourcing aspects of their operations to Indian companies. Foreign investment has been principally directed towards service industries, telecommunications, computer software and hardware and construction (Syed, 2012) and it is estimated that in the region of 20,000 MNCs operate in India (Budhwar, 2012: 2516). India has a large (in the region of 500 million) and young workforce

(Census, 2011; CIA, World Factbook, 2011). Increasing education levels, coupled with comparatively low wage costs, have attracted MNCs to locate both manufacturing and service operations here (Budhwar and Varma, 2011). In addition, increasingly affluent and sophisticated consumers have resulted in higher levels of domestic demand for services and consumer goods (Syed, 2012). As a consequence, together with increased economic liberalization since the early 1990s, many foreign MNCs have been drawn to India by both an abundant supply of labour and potential customers (The Economist, 2011).

In spite of this growing activity in India, evidence suggests that there remain many challenges for Western MNCs who choose to locate there. These include corruption, high levels of bureaucracy, increasing poverty and the lack of a well-developed infrastructure (Budhwar and Varma, 2011). In HRM terms, the national context such as the culture and dominant institutions, coupled with high levels of competition between employers for skilled employees have presented challenges for MNCs.

Transnational employers face the issue of the extent to which it is desirable and feasible to integrate HRM practices across their operations and/or to tailor practices to local circumstances (Evans, Pucik, and Bjorkman, 2011). In a study of 76 MNCs in India, Bjorkman and Budhwar (2007) found that corporate HRM practices introduced by the overseas parent company were negatively associated with performance, whereas local adaptation of HRM practices showed the reverse pattern. This would suggest a need for local responsiveness in HRM practices, rather than the imposition of Western concepts, such as employee engagement, on a global basis. In the light of this, many companies operating in India have established country-specific headquarters which include an HR function to deal with the local context (Budhwar, 2012). However, other research suggests that, despite considerable diversity among the parent countries of MNCs and India, the Indian context may be receptive to the adoption of some global HRM practices. This has been attributed by some authors to India's long exposure to Western norms and values and the extensive use of the English language for over more than a century (Budhwar and Bhatnagar, 2009).

Turning now to consider the Western countries from an institutional perspective, the UK is classified as a highly developed liberal market economy (LME) (Hall and Soskice, 2001), similar to the USA. In an LME, relationships between firms are largely at arm's length and co-ordinated via the market. Employment relations tend also to be market based and determined at the level of the firm. In the UK 'impatient capital', typical of an LME (Hall and Soskice, 2001), places greater emphasis on performance, particularly in the short-term. By contrast, the Netherlands is again highly developed, but is classified as a co-ordinated market economy (CME). In a CME, relationships between firms are more collaborative and extensive. In the context of the employment relationship, institutions such employers' associations, trade unions and regulatory systems reduce uncertainty and allow a higher degree of co-ordination. In the Netherlands, a more pluralist approach is adopted (Khatri, 2011) and it has been traditionally characterized by a high degree of employee influence, both through trade union representation and through Works Councils, together with a framework of labour legislation, covering employment security and safety (Boselie, Paauwe and Richardson, 2003).

Cultural differences

Studies of national culture have shown Western and Eastern cultures to differ significantly. In particular, differences have been highlighted in relation to the need for organizational hierarchies and the focus on individuals and groups (Hofstede, 1980). Table 10.1 below

Table 10.1 The GLOBE dimensions of culture

	India	UK*	Netherlands
Power distance	*High*	*Medium*	*Low*
Uncertainty avoidance	*Medium*	*Medium*	*Medium-High*
Institutional collectivism	*Medium*	*Medium*	*Medium*
In-group collectivism	*High*	*Low*	*Low*
Gender egalitarianism	*Low*	*High*	*High*
Humane orientation	*Medium-High*	*Medium-Low*	*Medium-Low*
Assertiveness	*Medium-Low*	*High*	*High*
Future orientation	*Medium-High*	*Medium-High*	*High*
Performance orientation	*Medium*	*Medium*	*High*

Note: * GLOBE specifically looked at England, whereas Hofstede states it is the UK.

positions India, the UK and the Netherlands on each of the nine culture dimensions identified in the GLOBE project (House et al., 2004) – a comprehensive research programme designed to study societal and organizational culture across 62 countries.

The UK and the Netherlands show a broad degree of similarity, with some degree of difference identified on power distance, uncertainty avoidance and future and performance orientation. However, there are notable differences between these two European countries and India. In particular, there are differences in relation to power distance, in-group collectivism, gender egalitarianism and assertiveness: India is a more hierarchical, less personally assertive, male-dominated society focused on the importance of in-group membership. This would imply that there are likely to be differences in the way employees respond to the organizations they work for, their managers and the systems in place to manage them.

It is also acknowledged that there is significant diversity within India. India has six main religious groups: Hindus, Muslims, Sikhs, Christians, Jains and Buddhists. There are 179 languages and 544 dialects spoken, although Hindi and English are recognized as the two official languages. The caste system is also powerful and the intertwining of the dominance of Hindu beliefs with caste means that the Indian worker has traditionally been found to be more fearful of people in power. Hence, Indian employees tend to be more compliant and deferential towards hierarchy, tolerant of inequality and conditions of poverty and importantly, more conformist and fatalistic than Western workers (Budhwar and Sparrow, 2002). There are also strong associations with a particular province, or town and people tend to associate themselves with a particular language and a particular religion (Varma, 2007). Hence, in the workplace these characteristics mean that employees tend to seek small groups to identify with and are often mistrustful of other groups, in common with other collectivist societies (House et al., 2004). Family and social relations are also very important.

However, in spite of India's recent, rapid economic growth, it is important to place this in the context of poverty remaining an ever-present feature of everyday life. A recent Oxfam report found that, despite a series of economic reforms from 1991 onwards and a doubling of GDP since that time, 53 million more people than in 1991 were 'going to bed hungry every night' (Narayan, 2011). According to the United Nations Development Programme, 37.2 per cent of India's population still live in poverty and the INGO Action Aid report that more than half of India's children drop out of school before they are 14 years old and more than half of them are female (2012). This context of on-going, significant poverty is likely to affect the way MNCs relate to their employees.

Implications for employee engagement in different country contexts

Recent evidence suggests that, whilst the underlying relationship between employee attitudes and behaviours are fundamentally the same, based on social exchange (Zhang, Tsui, Song and Jia, 2008), the impact of a collectivist, as opposed to individualist society, may affect outcomes such as affective commitment, job satisfaction and turnover intention (Wang, Bishop, Chen and Scott, 2002; Wong, Wong, Hui and Law, 2001). This emerging evidence that employee motivations may differ, particularly between Eastern and Western cultures, requires further research, particularly in this relatively new field of employee engagement (Hui, Lee and Rousseau, 2004).

Engagement has been recognized as fundamentally important to the future successful operation and development of organizations. However, to date much of the debate has been explored in a Western context and relatively little is known about what engagement may mean and what factors are likely to influence it elsewhere, not least in the developing world. It could be argued that the cultural and institutional differences discussed above are likely to have implications for the meaning of employee engagement and the factors which influence it (Schuler and Rogovsky, 1989). Hence this raises the question of whether engagement is a universal concept or simply a Western concept and whether strategies to promote higher levels of engagement can be used across operations in different countries (Khatri, Ojha, Budhwar, Srinivasan and Varma, 2012).

This question is of particular importance for MNCs operating in countries such as India, where rates of labour turnover for some industries run at almost epidemic proportions (cf. Budhwar, 2012: 2521). Companies have experienced difficulties sourcing and retaining appropriately qualified staff, since despite a large workforce, competition for *skilled* human resources is high (Budhwar and Varma, 2011). At least in part because of the rapid economic development, new issues for HRM have emerged in recent years (Budhwar and Varma, 2007). For example, there has been a trend for graduates to go straight into work and not stay on to do higher qualifications, and there is increasing evidence of stress and burnout amongst the workforce. In the IT industry in particular, it has been noted that psychological contracts are changing: the focus is not on a job for life, as there are so many opportunities for employees to be mobile (Krishnan and Singh, 2007). Therefore, retention and motivation of employees has become a major concern for employers in some sectors (Rathi, 2004) and talent management is becoming a key activity (Bhatnagar, 2009). In this context, learning how to engage employees and build loyalty to the organization is likely to be crucial for future success.

Having argued for engagement's critical contribution to organizational performance in MNCs in India, it is worth noting that Blessingwhite (2011) found that the Indian workforce overall exhibits the highest levels of engagement worldwide, with 37 per cent of employees reporting themselves as engaged. They also recorded the highest percentage globally for trust in their organization's senior management, the same level of trust that these employees recorded for their line managers, reflecting perhaps the cultural norm in India of deference towards one's manager. However, unsurprisingly, the same survey reports that engagement levels in India vary greatly according to organization size, gender, workplace structure, generations, role/level and function (p. 54). The primary factor influencing job satisfaction was 'career development opportunities and training', which was also joint first for being the most important factor to increase performance contribution, along with 'greater clarity about what the organization needs me to do and why'. Similarly, the top reason employees consider leaving a job is lack of career opportunities. Furthermore, Blessingwhite (ibid.)

found a positive correlation between engagement and employees' intent to stay in the Indian context.

In contrast, reporting on Europe, the same study found just under 30 per cent of employees were 'engaged', but with little variation across gender, organizational size or structure. Where there were variations it was across generations, role/level and function. The top drivers of job satisfaction in Europe were 'more opportunities to do what I do best' and 'career development opportunities and training'. Asked what would help them increase their performance contribution, 'more resources' was the most important factor (Blessingwhite, 2011: 49). However, answers here did vary across age groups and departments and industries. Only half of the European employees surveyed trusted their senior managers, whereas 74 per cent trusted their immediate boss.

In order to explore further the potential differences in employee engagement between workforces in India, the UK and Netherlands, the following sections describe an empirical study concerned with examining the definitions and drivers of employee engagement in MNCs.

Methods

The purpose of the study was to examine whether the meanings and antecedents of employee engagement varied in different national contexts. Consequently the study was based on MNCs operating in both the developed and developing worlds. By studying companies who operated across these contexts, we were able to compare data from individual companies operating in different countries and therefore were able to limit differences which might be due to different organizational contexts. Findings from three companies are reported here. GKN is a global supplier to the automotive and aerospace industries. It is headquartered in the UK with some 40,000 employees in 30 countries. AkzoNobel is a global paints and coatings company, with its headquarters in the Netherlands. It has operations in more than 80 countries and employs some 57,000 people. Tesco HSC (Hindustan Service Centre) is the global services arm for this major retailer. The retailer is headquartered in the UK and operates in 14 countries, employing approximately 492,000 people. The HSC global services arm provides IT, business and financial services for the company and has over 3,000 employees.

Qualitative data were collected by means of semi-structured interviews with HR and senior managers in each company in both Europe and in India, in order to explore the impact of the different corporate and national contexts studied. The findings reported here are based on a total of 20 interviews (8 in GKN, 8 in AkzoNobel and 4 in Tesco HSC). Interviews lasted 60 to 90 minutes and were audio-recorded and subsequently transcribed. The data were analysed by means of coding the data for each country under the themes of: definitions of engagement, drivers of engagement, managerial practices to create engagement, the impact of economic, social and political context upon that practice, common corporate practices versus local/decentralized practices.

Findings

Perceptions of employee engagement

Corporate centres

In the corporate centres (headquarters) there tended to be a fairly standardized view of what employee engagement entailed, yet, there was an acknowledgement, to varying degrees, that there was a need to take local context into account. For example, in AkzoNobel the corporate centre in the Netherlands focused its thinking around the definition of employee engagement on which the Gallup engagement survey is based (see Chapter 15), and this definition was used as a standardized way of defining and measuring engagement in all its units around the globe. Managers spoke about employee engagement as being an 'emotional connection' with the organization, as distinct from a more 'rational connection such as job satisfaction' (Engagement HR Director – The Netherlands). However, despite having a standardized definition and metrics, HR managers at the centre still saw the drivers of engagement happening primarily at a local level:

> It's a local thing. You can act on it as a local team. So it's not about being satisfied with your company, but it's about your manager and your team members and it's the passion, the energy for work, to go the extra mile.
>
> Employee Engagement Specialist – The Netherlands

For GKN's corporate centre in the UK, the standardized behaviours they expected within every plant around the world were not derived from the concept of employee engagement per se, but from the process of 'lean' manufacturing they had adopted. It was argued that 'lean' as a philosophy and a set of practices which was imposed on all units, provided a coherence to their global activities:

> Standards in our factories, whether they're in North America, Germany or China, or India or wherever, are the same. In the sense of the delivery, the safety, the quality and the way that we treat our people is the same.
>
> Commercial Director – UK

Their implementation of lean principles had a strong communication focus with daily communication briefings, lasting a minimum of 15 minutes, at the beginning of every shift, in every factory anywhere in the world, being required. Managers at GKN described a broad, common definition of employee engagement, which was designed to ensure that every employee across the company understands how their job fits into the 'bigger picture' and therefore has a 'clear line of sight' between their work and the objectives of the corporation. However, it was recognized that there are regional variations in the drivers of employee engagement. For instance, in India with poverty for some parts of the population remaining a constant feature of everyday life, GKN acknowledged that the quality of the facilities, for example the canteen and the lavatories, count as important hygiene factors in driving the engagement of the local workforce. Whilst hygiene factors might not be seen to drive engagement in the more affluent West, the HR team believed that they were drivers of engagement in India. The corporate centre therefore recognized the impact of different cultures:

> I think engagement means different things in different cultures. But engagement manifests itself around maybe some of the corporate social responsibility issues. I mean, the Indian plants do an awful lot within their communities so that, in a sense, the employees are very engaged around a sense of community, maybe more than the UK, and they take a pride in the business and get engaged in the business, not through the management style as we would see it, but through other things.
>
> Group HR Director – UK

These 'other things' referred to here included providing highly safe and clean sanitary facilities within plants. The provision of such facilities was seen as contributing to the community by providing the workforce with somewhere clean and pleasant to wash. Likewise, providing facilities where computer training can be offered into the local communities was also seen to be important. However, the centre also strived to prevent some of what they saw as negative, local cultural norms from taking root within their plants. For example, they tried to eradicate what they called 'clanism' in India, which is where local management favour employees on the basis of family ties or caste.

GKN HR function at the group level also recognized that there are factors in addition to culture which affect how employee engagement manifests itself in practice. They cite, for instance, the recent economic context impacting their European operations:

> Employee engagement in a declining market is equally as important, but I'm not sure we've got our heads around whether it's different in a declining market. I mean, because as you're doing difficult things around the world, you know, we're shutting plants, in the last 12 months we've shed several thousand people from the organization. I mean, how you maintain engagement in that kind of environment in a positive sense is one of the challenges for us.
>
> Group HR Director – UK

Employee engagement in Europe

Both AkzoNobel and GKN Corporate Centres recognized the impact of the economic context on the drivers of engagement and how employee perceptions and expectations are born out of their experiences of employment. A number of interviewees indicated that many staff in Europe felt insecure as a result of on-going reorganizations, downsizing, restructuring and rebranding, which had been brought about by merger and acquisition activity over recent years.

However, it was noted that due to employment protection legislation, particularly in the Netherlands, Dutch workers were actually comparatively well-protected, in comparison to their counterparts in India. Yet it was recognized that it was the employees in India who felt relatively secure as a result of the recent, rapid economic growth, despite weaker employment protection:

> In India, in China, you know, in Asia in general, I think they feel relatively secure, they don't have the same level of employment security as you have in Western Europe with the contracts, but that's a function of just they see continuing growth, you know, business growth and in job maintenance or creation.
>
> Corporate Centre Director – The Netherlands

Similarly, GKN mentioned the impact of trade union activity upon the type of engagement a company may intend and what the company can realize when they run their own communications alongside parallel trade union channels:

> If you have a tradition of a powerful trade union, who are the intermediary between management and the workforce, a lot of communication happens through that channel and the unions are still important in the UK. And the workforce will still have at least one eye on the views of the trade union in terms of what's happening.
>
> Group HR Director – UK

Driving employee engagement in European plants was seen as a task requiring hard work and investment by the local leadership, with communication being seen as a key mechanism. Similarly, local managers believed that they needed to invest time in this activity, particularly given the higher levels of uncertainty employees were experiencing as a result of what they saw as continuous change within the company:

> Engagement comes down to strong leadership with a vision that shows where we need to be in the future. It comes down to taking away responsibility from the unions in terms of communication and getting your shop floor masses singing the same songs and themes as senior management. It's certainly not a short journey. You have to work on it continually. You have employee involvement, you have morning briefings, afternoon briefings.
>
> UK Factory Manager

Employee engagement in India

Managers in both the manufacturing and engineering MNCs in India defined employee engagement in a similar fashion to their Western corporate centres, identifying the significance of both job and organizational engagement. They described two strands, first, for the employee to 'own' the job they have and know what they are expected to do, and second to know and identify with where the company is heading. The importance of organizational engagement was stressed:

> I think that being engaged to the organization is much bigger than being engaged to the job. The sum total of all engagements with the job is never equal to the organizational engagement.
>
> HR Manager – India

Thus, it would appear that the definitions used by managers in these companies in both the West and India were broadly similar, with keywords such as passion, commitment, motivation, being happy and, crucially, alignment with the organization's objectives and values being used. However, it was acknowledged that the drivers were very different and also depended upon the type of employee and their motivation to work.

A local GKN manager in India identified two types of employees in their factories, what they termed 'workmen', or 'stayers', and the more mobile managerial group of employees. The 'workmen' tend also to be smallholders who farm small plots of land around their houses, in order to grow food for their families. Their factory work provides additional income for other needs. They continue to farm their land and traditionally pass it on to the next generation of their families. The second group is the managerial talent pool, who are more mobile and vulnerable to being attracted away from the organization by the offer of higher levels of remuneration:

> So there is [*sic*] two cultures here. There is those satisfied with whatever they have and the other culture is 'want to do something with their life'. So those are both the cultures here.
>
> Factory Manager – India

Local managers indicated that community activities were key to driving employee engagement within the 'stayers' group. GKN in India has a Works Committee which organizes picnics, family events and also a Safety Committee. Parents of young workers are invited to visit and tour the plant. In addition, managers try to attend certain events which take place in the workmen's houses, such as house warming ceremonies, marriages, child birth or 'suffering'. For example, one explained, 'There's a person suffering from cancer – the other day we'd collected a lot of money to see what we can all do'. GKN also provides training for local children in the summer in how to use computers. The thinking behind these various activities was to bring the people closer together, through what local GKN managers call 'connectivity'.

AkzoNobel also promoted similar community based activities through what they termed the 'Employee Relationship Programme'. Their managers emphasized the importance of celebrating birthdays and setting up social clubs.

GKN in India have a motto which says Stay, Serve and Say. In practice the 'stayers' tend to clock up many years of service with the company. At the time of the research, some already had over 20 years of service. Service is seen as an emotional connection with the organization:

> It's a very emotional thing. The Indian culture thrives on emotion. The question that you ask me about the Indian context, the Indian culture. If you look back into the mythology of India it reflects on tremendous respect for the elders and a respect which is very difficult in today's world. So we come from that culture. We come from a culture where you have sacrifice as a must. You know, we are taught by our parents that this amount of money or effort, you have to sacrifice for that. You come from an Indian culture which talks about respect. So when you come here and you see that there are three social responsibility or CSR projects and you find people never think before donating.
>
> Plant Director – India

The 'Say' aspect of the motto is more problematic in this context. The local workforce were reported to have difficulty in implementing the GKN norm of speaking up and challenging upwards:

> In India people who are senior, we call them different, we add them Mr or Ji. In Indian context we put a Ji which means respect for you. Like Ellen Ji or Anushka Ji. Automatically this comes out of what we are taught, groomed up in life. But it's quite different in GKN.
>
> Plant Director – India

What was different in GKN was that the company expected the local employees to be less deferential in the way they address managers, for example not using Ji (Mr), but rather using first names.

For those employees who are potentially more mobile because they have valuable, transferrable skills, further training and access to personal development were seen to be key drivers of engagement and therefore the MNC's ability to retain them. Another motto used in GKN India which symbolizes this is 'Earn, Learn and Grow':

> And when I was telling you Earn, Learn and Grow, the learn part comes here. And this is very strong in GKN. They teach you a lot, they teach you, they put you on the track. They make you work. They develop your competency. There are development programmes identified in the PDP for the talent pool.
>
> Plant Director – India

The Tesco HSC also faced similar challenges in retaining staff, who were highly 'poachable' by other companies. These interpretations of the Indian employment culture illustrate the very different labour markets in which they are operating within their sector and their region. Tesco HSC managers defined the attitude of younger Indians towards employment as being loyal to themselves first and as such being prepared to move jobs if another employer offers them a higher salary. In order to build engagement with these employees, they reported that a large amount of time was spent in one-to-one meetings with staff, investing in creating a close 'affiliation' between the corporate brand and the employee. Tesco HSC indicated that they encouraged a culture of 'innovation and creativity' in order to appear an attractive workplace. They also reported that the growth in demand for talent in 'young India' had been slowing following the financial crisis of 2008, with talented Indian employees returning from the UK and US, because of the decrease in job opportunities there. They believed, however, that Tesco HSC was seen as a 'safe bet' as an employer in uncertain times, because of its strong brand.

Finally, like the European units, local line managers in all three MNCs were seen as critical in engaging staff and the communication carried out by these line managers was seen as vital in maintaining engagement. It was seen as the line manager's role to convert job engagement into employee engagement, in other words to ensure that the 'emotional' engagement with the organization exists alongside the job engagement:

> Basically communication goes on every morning, every section. There is in one meeting, at every section and his supervisor or second line person conducts it. So in the morning there is communication, what are the priorities, what are the problems, visitors, everything is communicated. And they also say their problems also, heat is going up, it is difficult to work there because of temperature. So these types of things, communication is there.
>
> Plant Manager – India

Tesco HSC similarly reported a large investment of time and human resources being spent on communication:

> We need to have more connection with employees on a personal level, rather than send them information through email. We have seen it works better if we have more one-to-ones, more meetings. If you are able to connect with them then this leads to increased motivation.
>
> HR Manager – India

HR managers in Tesco reported that a lot more attention was given to individualized communication in India than anywhere else in the company.

Discussion and conclusions

Overall, there was little variation in the definitions of employee engagement employed in each of the different countries. HR teams in the Corporate Centres identified the importance of both engagement with the job, or work and with the organization. Equally, managers in local operations in both Europe and India emphasized that, for them, employee engagement was about engagement with the job, coupled with engagement with the organization. However, where the findings showed variation between countries was in relation to some of the antecedents of employee engagement. The variation in these antecedents was not just seen as being due to cultural differences, but also due to the state of local/regional labour markets, the economic context, both globally and locally and the expectations of employees within different countries.

To expand on the above, cultural differences between the manufacturing and engineering units in Europe and their counterparts in India accounted for the greater emphasis given in the Indian units to community activities. This seemed to reflect the higher levels of in-group collectivism (House et al., 2004) of those local, more rural areas. Interestingly, these activities were specifically geared to the less mobile employees that were labelled as the 'stayers'. Meaningfulness, as an antecedent of engagement, was derived from the inter-meshing of the employer within the local community.

In contrast, in the same workplaces it was recognized that there was another, albeit smaller group of more mobile and more professional staff, who due to their transferrable skills, were seen to be easily poached by other employers. For this more individualistically oriented group access to *job resources and personal resources* were seen as drivers of their engagement with the employer. In the large manufacturing and engineering MNC units, local managers tried to ensure this group was engaged through offering them training and development opportunities within the company. This group of employees were viewed as having a different set of values and aspirations, mainly concerned with seeking out the best earning opportunities. This more individualistic orientation is in line with the observations of other commentators (Krishnan and Singh, 2007; Budhwar and Varma, 2011). Whereas the manufacturing and engineering MNCs tried to counteract this individualism with offering greater training and development opportunities, Tesco HSC concentrated on making the climate and culture innovative and creative and by playing on the strength of the Tesco global brand as an employer in which one could feel both security and pride. This also illustrates the regional differences within India and thus the diversity of employment experience within this vast, but unified country (Varma, 2007).

The specific economic context within the different countries also played a part in how employees perceived their level of safety and security, another driver of employee engagement. The European units reported a workforce with a feeling of uncertainty, some of whom, particularly in the UK, had seen a gradual, but persistent, decrease in workforce numbers for more than a decade. In Europe employees were less engaged, their expectations of their career and employment prospects had been based on an earlier more positive economic climate. The reality of globalization had meant that much of the growth in their employing organizations was occurring outside Europe in emerging economies such as India. Managers reported employees feeling as though they were being subjected to constant change. Whilst constant change in India was experienced in a positive way, because it was associated with growth, in Europe change was associated with retrenchment and downsizing. As one director remarked, employee engagement is much easier in times of growth when the aims of the company can be easily aligned with those of the employee – both parties can benefit from growth. However, one of the MNCs participating in the study had had to reduce its workforce by 20 per cent following the financial crisis, and in a period of such significant downsizing the drivers of employee engagement became very different. In that scenario the drivers became more about maintaining trusting relationships with the union and the workforce: 'The way we managed it, with an open and focused approach, and the constant answering of questions and not delaying in answering questions, was key to restoring relations and trust very quickly' (HR Manager – UK).

Paradoxically, although the European workforces felt they had less job security than in previous years, and therefore recorded lower levels of engagement with the employer, in fact, due to local labour laws, they experienced greater job security than their colleagues in India. This was particularly true in the Netherlands. In India employees reported feeling secure. Although they had lower levels of employment protection than their counterparts in Europe, they could see an economy around them that was growing and that made them feel positive. In addition, their standard of living was improving relative to their past. However, it must be noted that although India may be growing, poverty remains centre stage (Narayan, 2011).

The drivers of engagement that were common across the different national contexts, and across employee groups (those who were mobile and those who were 'stayers') were the importance of communication and the critical role of line managers. It was through investment of time and resources into various communication initiatives that the MNCs hoped to build an engagement between the organization and the employee. In effect they were trying to create a *meaningful* connection between the large globally spread corporate entity and the local units in India.

Taken together, what do these findings mean for MNCs considering employee engagement across their operations? First, the data show that for these kinds of organizations the meaning of employee engagement is broadly similar, regardless of location. This implies that, at least at one level, employee engagement is a universal concept. Therefore it is also implied that there is some value in exploring employee engagement on a global basis and that meaningful comparisons can be made on a cross-country basis. However, the data also show differences between countries (and in the case of India within a country) in relation to the factors which influence and contribute to levels of engagement. It seems that national context in relation to culture, institutions and economic circumstances are important determinants of the factors influencing engagement.

In the light of the importance of employee engagement in influencing organizational performance, these findings suggest that MNCs might be advised to pursue global strategies in relation to employee engagement, but there is a need to recognize that the implementation of practices intended to enhance engagement levels must take account of context and be locally integrated. In particular, what was noteworthy about the Indian context was the importance of corporate social responsibility provision within local communities to the ongoing generation of engagement with the workforce. We argue therefore that engagement is not only influenced by aspects of national culture and that MNCs need to extend their localization to the framework of institutions and the current economic conditions.

Notes

1 For example, in 2011 the UK Government launched the 'Engage for Success Campaign' with the support of senior business leaders, which was designed to increase awareness of the power and potential of employee engagement.
2 The findings presented in this chapter are drawn from a project on employee engagement in multi-national enterprises funded by the Society for Human Resource Management Foundation.

References

Bhatnagar, J. (2009), 'Talent management in India', in *The Changing Face of People Management in India*, P. Budhwar and J. Bhatnagar (eds), Routledge, Abingdon, pp. 180–206.
Bjorkman, I. and Budhwar, P. (2007), 'When in Rome. . .? Human resource management and the performance of foreign firms operating in India', *Employee Relations*, 29(6): 595–610.

Blessingwhite Intelligence (2011), *Employee Engagement Report 2011: Beyond the numbers: A practical approach for individuals, managers and executives*, Blessingwhite, NJ, USA.

Boselie, P., Paauwe, J. and Richardson, R. (2003), 'Human resource management, institutionalization and organizational performance: A comparison of hospitals, hotels and local government', *International Journal of Human Resource Management,* 14(8): 1407–29.

Brewster, C., Sparrow, P., Vernon, G. and Houldsworth, E. (2011), *International Human Resource Management*, CIPD, London.

Budhwar, P. (2012), 'Management of human resources in foreign firms operating in India: the role of HR in country-specific headquarters', *International Journal of Human Resource Management*, 23(12): 2514–31.

—— (2001), 'Human resource management in India', in *Human Resource Management in Developing Countries*, P. S. Budhwar and Y. A. Debrah (eds), Routledge, London, pp. 75–90.

—— and Bhatnagar, J. (2009), *The Changing Face of People Management in India*, Routledge, London.

—— and Sparrow, P. (2002), 'In integrative framework for understanding cross-national human resource management practices', *Human Resource Management Review*, 12(3): 377–403.

—— and Varma, A. (2011), 'Emerging HR management trends in India and the way forward', *Organization Dynamics*, 40: 317–25.

—— and Varma, A. (2007), 'HRM teaching and research in India', *Proceedings from Academy of Management Meeting*, 5 August 2007, Philadelphia, PA.

Census of India (2011), available at http://censusindia.gov.in/2011-prov-results/prov_results_paper1_india.html [accessed December 2012].

Central Intelligence Agency (2012), *The World Factbook*, available at https://www.cia.gov/library/publications/the-world-factbook/geos/in.html [accessed December 2012].

Evans, P., Pucik, V. and Bjorkman, I. (2011), *The Global Challenge: International Human Resource Management*, McGraw-Hill, New York.

Hall, P. A. and Soskice, D. (2001), *Varieties of Capitalism: The Institutional Foundations of Comparative Advantage*, Oxford University Press, Oxford.

Hofstede, G. (1980), *Culture's consequences. International differences in work-related values*, Sage, Thousand Oaks, CA.

House, R., Hanges, P., Javidan, M., Dorfman, P. and Gupta, V. (2004), *Culture, leadership and organizations: The GLOBE study of 62 societies*, Sage, Thousand Oaks, CA.

Hui, C., Lee, C. and Rousseau, D. M. (2004), 'Employment relationships in China: Do workers relate to the organization or to people?', *Organization Science*, 15(2): 232–40.

Kahn, W. A. (1990), 'Psychological conditions of personal engagement at work', *Academy of Management Journal*, 33(4): 692–724.

Khatri, N. (2011), 'A taxonomy of supervisor-subordinate exchanges across cultures', *IIMB Management Review*, 23: 71–80.

——, Ojha, A. K., Budhwar, P., Srinivasan, V. and Varma, A. (2012), 'Management research in India: Current state and future directions', *IIMB Management Review*, 24: 104–15.

Krishnan, S. and Singh, M. (2007), 'Indian intention to quit', *Proceedings from the Academy of Management Meeting*, August 8, 2007, Philadelphia, PA.

Macey, W. H. and Schneider, B. (2008), 'The meaning of employee engagement', *Industrial and Organizational Psychology*, 1(1): 3–30.

Maslach, C., Schaufeli, W. B. and Leiter, M. P. (2001), 'Job burnout', *Annual Review of Psychology*, 52: 397–422.

Narayan, S. (2011), 'Why is India losing its war on hunger', Oxfam report, 31 May.

Rathi, N. (2004), 'Human resource challenges in Indian software industry: An empirical study of employee turnover', PhD thesis.

Saks, A. M. (2006), 'Antecedents and consequences of employee engagement', *Journal of Managerial Psychology*, 21(7): 600–619.

Schaufeli, W. B., Martinez, I. M., Pinto, A. M., Salanova, M. and Bakker, A. B. (2002), 'Burnout and engagement in university students: A cross national study', *Journal of Cross-Cultural Psychology*, 33(5): 464–81.

Schuler, R. S. and Rogovsky, N. (1998), 'Understanding compensation practice variations across firms: The impact of national culture', *Journal of International Business Studies*, 29(1): 159–77.

Syed, S. (2012), *India invites ever more foreign investment* [homepage of BBC News], available at: http://www.bbc.co.uk/news/business-19632237 [accessed 18 October 2012].

The Economist (2011), *Building India Inc. A weak state has given rise to a new kind of economy. Without reform, it will hit limits*, available at http://www.economist.com/node/21533396 [accessed 18 October 2012].

Vance, R. J. (2006), *Employee Engagement and Commitment: A guide to understanding, measuring and increasing engagement in your organization*, SHRM Foundation, Alexandria, VA.

Varma, A. (2007), 'HRM Teaching and Research in India', *Proceedings from the Academy of Management Meeting*, 5 August 2007, Philadelphia, PA.

Vorhauser-Smith, S. (2012), *How to stop employee turnover in India*, available at http://www.forbes.com/sites/sylviavorhausersmith/2012/07/02/how-to-stop-employee-turnover-in-india/ [accessed 24 June 2013].

Wang, L., Bishop, J. W., Chen, Z. and Scott, K. D. (2002), 'Collectivist orientation as a predictor of affective organizational commitment: a study conducted in China', *International Journal of Organizational Analysis*, 10(3): 226–39.

Whitley, R. (1999), *Divergent Capitalisms: The Social Structuring and Change of Business Systems*, Oxford University Press, Oxford, UK.

Wong, C-S., Wong, Y-T., Hui, C. and Law, K. S. (2001), 'The significant role of Chinese employees' organizational commitment: implications for managing employees in Chinese societies', *Journal of World Business*, 36(3): 326–40.

Zhang, A. Y., Tsui, A. A., Song, L. J., Li, C. and Jia, L. (2008), 'How do I trust thee? The employee-organization relationship, supervisory support, and middle manager trust in the organization', *Human Resource Management*, 47(1): 111–32.

Part 3

Employee engagement

Critical perspectives

11 Engagement

A murmuration of objects?

Tom Keenoy

Each day, our tribe of language holds what we call the 'world' together.

(O'Donohue, 1997: 13)

Introduction

In the market-place of ideas – for that is indubitably what we are dealing with here – 'engagement' is the most recent solution proposed to address what Frederick Taylor identified as 'soldiering' (Thompson, 2003). Taylor's seminal question – How should managers motivate employees to be more productive? (Jacques, 1996) – has preoccupied management scholars ever since. In between times this core issue has morphed across countless complex discursive iterations from Human Relations to Japanization, through productivity bargaining to business process engineering and 'soft' HRM. It is also implicated in previous constructs designed to stimulate what is now being called 'employee engagement': these include attempts to improve job satisfaction, enrich tasks, promote participation, stimulate involvement, harness the promise of empowerment or self-managed teams and engineer high commitment or high performance management systems. All such initiatives have been pursued alongside an ever more complex raft of performance-related reward systems designed to improve productivity in one way or another.

Of course, advocates of engagement might object that such initiatives are different or even 'lesser' motivational mechanisms. MacLeod and Clarke in their recent report for the UK government Department for Business, Innovation and Skills (2009: 9; emphasis added) dismiss the possibility that engagement is merely the latest managerial fad (see Chapter 12) and insist it involves 'crucial differences' for 'an engaged employee experiences a blend of job satisfaction, organisational commitment, job involvement and feelings of empowerment. *It is a concept that is greater than the sum of its parts.*' Well, maybe so. However, it remains far from clear what these 'crucial differences' might amount to. For example, of the 50 different definitions of engagement they identified, the one they seem to privilege is:

> Engagement is about creating opportunities for employees to connect with their colleagues, managers and wider organisation. It is also about creating an environment where employees are motivated to want to connect with their work and really care about doing a good job ... It is a concept that places flexibility, change and continuous improvement at the heart of what it means to be an employee and an employer in a twenty-first century workplace.
>
> (MacLeod and Clarke, 2009: 8)

This is a normative rather than an analytic or operational defintion and, as such, offers an idealized and aspirational vision of what 'engagement' might accomplish in practice. The implicit strategic managerial objectives it embodies are both unexceptional and – like motherhood and apple pie – could be endorsed by managers, employees, consultants, professional bodies, governments and management scholars alike (of course, such discursive approval does not necessarily translate into pragmatic management action). Nevertheless, we could replace the term 'engagement' with 'job involvement', 'empowerment', 'high performance management' or any of the other putative solutions to the problem of soldiering and it would read in an equally coherent and plausible fashion. So, the questions posed in this chapter are: what kind of 'object' is 'engagement' and what, if anything, makes 'engagement' a distinctively different conceptual-theoretic 'object' from its predecessors? To offer some partial answers to these questions, a small number of indicative (as opposed to representative) objects are interrogated in some selective detail in order expose the 'crucial differences' which confront anyone trying to make sense of 'engagement'.

Tracking objects

Perhaps paradoxically, the majority of texts across the 'engagement narrative' commence by observing there is no agreement as to what the term encompasses. This makes any evaluation problematic. Without such a singular conception, one solution is to track the variety of concepts-in-use through the various networks which have emerged to construct, promote, enact, practice, sell and research objects called 'employee engagement'.

The idea that – both as everyday social actors and as social scientists – we 'construct' social reality by framing events, behaviours and action through language is far from novel (Astley, 1985; Berger and Luckmann, 1966; Gergen, 2000; Goffman, 1959; Fairclough, 1995; Searle, 1995; Keenoy et al., 1997) and discourse analysis is now a well established methodology across the management disciplines (Grant et al., 2004). Discourse analysts explore the discursive and social processes through which language (and other signs) are deployed to re-present and project social realities. More generally, there is concern with how particular discourses may reflect the interests of those constructing text, may exclude or marginalize possible alternative readings and with how discourse may be deployed to shape social subjectivities. The discursive analysis which follows draws significantly – but, for the most part, unobtrusively – on the insights of actor–network theory (Callon, 1986; Law, 1986; Latour, 2005; Law and Hassard, 1999) and sensemaking (Weick, 1995) in an attempt to illustrate how the presumptively novel 'engagement narrative' has come to colonize contemporary management discourse about how to motivate employees to 'go the extra mile' for themselves, their managers and their organizations. Hence, making sense of 'engagement' involves tracking this 'object' through the variety of actor-networks which – for a variety of reasons – have enrolled themselves to promote its utility, value, meaningfulness and legitimacy.

For Latour, objects can be simultaneously discursive and – because they have material social consequences – 'real'. However, knowing where to start 'tracking' our object is far from clear. 'Employee engagement' makes its presence felt across a wide range of alternative texts from a variety of interested network-actors with multiple, diverse and – sometimes – countervailing purposes. In order to avoid ascribing priority to any of the myriad defini-tions, the term 'textscape' will be used to encompass the cacophony of voices which are privileging different objects *within* the 'engagement narrative', all of which are trading off the same metaphorical construct. Analysis is further complicated because, as we shall see, these (different) objects interweave across the narrative. More specifically, a textscape refers to:

> the multiplex intertextualities which inform and underpin the meaning(s) of any given piece of discourse. Discursive construction is designed to communicate meanings (which implicates the listener or reader), but all meanings are context dependent (that is, all texts implicate other texts). [However it is] merely a linguistic device (or, perhaps, a *methodological* metaphor) which can be employed to symbolize any (or all) of the mutually implicated 'layers' of discursive interconnections and interpenetrations within and between texts.
>
> (Keenoy and Oswick, 2004: 141)

In short, it is an analytic device designed to facilitate and discipline interpretation. It permits us to identify and explore the major objects constructed by policy-makers, consultants, practitioners and academics which are circulating across the textscape and attempt to examine each in their own terms. In following these objects and attempting to plot their criss-crossing trajectories, the objective is to develop an account of how network actors interact and make sense of engagement which 'will *perform* the social in the precise sense that some of the participants in the action – through the controversial agency of the author – will be *assembled* in such a way that they can be *collected* together' (Latour, 2005: 138). Well, as ever, that is the ambition.

The policy objects

Although this is an arbitrary choice intended to articulate the overall analysis, it is useful to start with the 'policy object',[1] for – with respect to the increasing enactment of the engagement narrative in the UK – the key driver appears to be the singular boost provided by government sponsorship (see also Chapter 14). Empirically, this is embodied in the MacLeod Report (MacLeod and Clarke, 2009) which has emerged as a vital document (and social actant) circulating among all the other interested social actors – HR managers, consultants, professional associations and academics (as well as their journals and associated publishers) – all of whom can be seen as having a vested interest in the success (or failure) of the narrative as an influential or performative discourse.

Whatever else it may be, employee engagement is clearly a 'political object' which was launched in 2009 by Lord Mandelson with the suitably over-zealous claim that the Report:

> sets out for the first time the evidence that underpins what we all know intuitively, which is that only organisations that truly engage and inspire their employees produce world class levels of innovation, productivity and performance.
>
> (MacLeod and Clarke, 2009:1)

It was subsequently re-launched with an 'Engagement Taskforce' by David Cameron (2011) who, with similar rhetorical acumen, was also able to frame the engagement narrative as integral to his own political vision:

> This initiative fits well with our agenda of devolved power and authority and shows how effective companies can be when they feel empowered. I am delighted that the

Employment Engagement Taskforce has come together to develop practical ways to help all employers learn from the best, to break down barriers to engagement and to raise the profile of this whole agenda.

Such political enactment adds the cachet of political legitimacy to those promoting it. As management consultants People Insight (2012) inform us, engagement 'is now a national priority, with . . . a mission to boost UK productivity and competitiveness'. Hence, what apparently started out as an object deemed to illustrate aspects of individual motivation at work (Kahn, 1990) has been translated by those with political interests into a malleable property of 'organization' and hence ostensibly subject to (re)direction through public policy and managerial *fiat*.

The Report was produced in eight months and this 'social context of text production' (Fairclough, 1995) appears to have had a detrimental effect on the overall coherence of the text. The authors' discursive task involved collecting, digesting and summarizing a vast array of disparate data sources which included meetings with a wide variety of public, private and third sector leaders, companies across all sectors, unions and academics; over 30 round-table consultation events and some 300 online responses; trawling though numerous management consultancy surveys extolling the virtues of 'engagement' as well as 50 case studies (Clarke, 2010). This sounds like a formidable evidential base. However, with this particular assemblage of persuasive discursive artefacts, appearances prove deceptive.

While exploring the somewhat peremptory central claim of the Report:

> Despite there being some debate about the precise meaning of employee engagement there are three things we know about it: it is measurable; it can be correlated with performance; and it varies from poor to great.
>
> (MacLeod and Clarke, 2009: 10)

it is important to remember the authors are not constructing an 'academic object' and, throughout, their policy objectives take precedence over what might be considered academic niceties. As the Report unfolds, it becomes clear there are good narrative reasons to avoid a more precise framing of the object for, the more the authors consider the 'evidence', the more elusive, differentiated and intangible it becomes.

There are early hints of this intrinsic ambiguity. Despite total conviction of its practical utility to generate significant productivity gains, they tread cautiously: 'Engaged employees have a sense of personal attachment to their work and organisation' and – recognizing this is sometimes a matter of 'feel' rather than measurable data – note that business leaders told them, 'You know it when you see it' (MacLeod and Clarke, 2009: 7), a metaphor which recurs frequently in the textscape. In this respect, the plausability of the narrative depends less upon precise linguisitic useage, conceptual clarity or the systematic evaluation of robust evidence than it does upon building a smorgasbord of intuitive evidential fragments which the authors insist *must* add up to something which they have decided to call 'engagement'. And they seem unconcerned by the possible methodological weaknesses across their analyses. For example, although they point out that:

> comparisons between studies should be avoided unless care is taken to match the methodologies, particularly the variables being measured . . . there are varying definitions of engagement; some focus on one element of engagement (emotional, cognitive, behavioural); others focus on one or several but not all of the drivers. Still

other studies look at different performance outcomes (such as retention, performance measures, profit, productivity, customer service).

(MacLeod and Clarke, 2009: 35)

They then proceed to cite a series of management consultancy and academic studies without taking this *caveat* into account. In consequence, the reader cannot judge whether they are comparing like with like. However, no such methodological reservations frame their evaluation of the 50 case studies of 'exemplar organizations' (Clarke, 2010) which, for narrative purposes, carry their analysis throughout the Report. Symptomatic of what might be described as a cavalier approach to the relationship between evidence and claim is their unreflective endorsement of the face validity of the case studies. Although 'Original material for the case studies has been supplied by the organisations themselves' (MacLeod and Clarke, 2009: 34), at no point does this cause them to question the evidential probity of these self-reported 'successes'.

While the cases include much of interest, all too often – and understandably – they read like self-serving press-releases from the organization in question which extol the undoubted virtues of the HR departments' initiatives to improve employee relations. The authors seem oblivious to the possibility that those deputed to write responses to the consultation might construct the best possible case on behalf of their organization (and themselves). Unsurprisingly, having been called upon to (re)present their organization, they enacted what Goffman (1959) calls a 'front-stage' performance. It is unclear whether these 'cases' were selectively edited prior to inclusion, and it seems unlikely any were followed up to verify the claims. Two not untypical cases should suffice to underline the potential fragility of such an approach. In a 200-word 'case-study' from KPMG, the informant reports the company successfully implemented a programme of voluntary short-term working. As the Head of Engagement commented:

> We were open with colleagues about the need to introduce additional flexibility in our staffing arrangements . . . *It is a clear indicator that staff at KPMG feel a shared ownership for the organisation's fortunes,* and I am very sure that we would not have achieved such a positive response *without the high level of engagement between staff and management.*

(MacLeod and Clarke, 2009: 27; emphases added)

While this may be an accurate account, the company's Head of Engagement seems unlikely to be the most impartial source of such information. Clearly, there are a variety of other less-flattering explanations as to why staff might agree to such an arrangement. A similar caution applies to the second example which relates to events at JCB. Following the financial crisis in 2008, JCB negotiated a shorter working week with the union. Employees endorsed an agreement which meant that – in exchange for a 34-hour working week – the company could avoid declaring 332 redundancies. The case concludes with: 'This is *widely regarded in JCB as a successful employee engagement exercise* during the most difficult trading environment that the company has ever seen' (MacLeod and Clarke, 2009: 26; emphasis added).

While this managerial interpretation is not implausible, it is equally possible the outcome reflects the benefits of having a unionized workforce which – when faced with the harsh reality of market-relations – chose to demonstrate they are clearly 'engaged' with their fellow workers.

Predictably, the case studies are immensely varied in both their situational contexts and the kind of initiatives being adopted. These include the adoption of engagement surveys, the introduction of continuous improvement, involvement schemes and self-managed teams, reforms to collective bargaining relationships, examples of sickness and absenteeism reduction, improvements in 'well-being', suggestion schemes, promoting staff-advocacy and an employee-sensitive merger strategy as well as almost ubiquitous examples of 'improving communication'. And they range in size from a small charity caring for the homeless and an employee-owned school uniform supplier, through SMEs, household name retailers, banks and engineering companies to global players including Microsoft and Google. Such decontextualized variation begs the question: what does the term 'employee engagement' *not* cover?

The wider analytic point here concerns the range and diversity of practice the authors embrace when using the term. It was noted above that there are good discursive reasons for MacLeod and Clarke to avoid any precise specification of the object being tracked here, for their examples 'suggest that when it comes to engagement, *it is not a case of inventing something new; good practice is out there*, transforming organisations and transforming lives' (MacLeod and Clarke, 2009: 24; emphasis added). This suggests there might be a deeper underlying more general construct which informs what they clearly sense unifies their examples. Insofar as it is possible to arrive at any meaningful generalization about the case studies, it is that all show clear traces of what is usually called 'employee-centred management practice'. This is a notion which, refreshingly, goes all the way back to McGregor's (1960) highly influential Theory Y,[2] the idealized management style which assumes employees are creative beings who can be trusted to exercise self-control, accept responsibility, contribute with ingenuity to goal-setting and problem solving and respond best when they are listened to and treated with dignity and respect. As an approach, it embraces self-control and self-direction.

In stark contrast, his Theory X insisted that directive imposed control is the only answer. In effect, what MacLeod and Clarke seem to be doing is treating engagement as a metaphor encompassing every form of 'Theory Y practice' they come across. Such a view is reinforced by the critical importance they attach to the development of 'soft skills' among managers (MacLeod and Clarke (2009: 82) and the frequency with which they are critical of 'command-and-control' management. (McGregor himself also directly associated this metaphor with Theory X.) More precisely, in terms of the discursive construction of their object, MacLeod and Clarke deploy engagement as an 'empty' or 'floating signifier', thus permitting a process of continual conceptual elision in which the construct means whatever the reader or speaker chooses it to mean in the context in which it is used. This reading seems to be the only possible way to make narrative sense of the disparate array of 'exemplary' benefits which allegedly flow from 'engagement' practices. Nor should this conclusion be surprising, for this rather more commonplace panacea for the problems of 'soldiering' – employee-centred management – is also pre-figured early in the Report when they point out that, 'The way employee engagement operates *can take many forms . . .* and *the best models are those which have been custom-developed for the institution*' (MacLeod and Clarke, 2009: 4; emphases added).

In passing, it should be noted that the choice of McGregor is neither fanciful nor arbitrary, for his construct embodies an archetypal idealization of 'good management', discursive traces of which can be found historically across a wide range of supposedly 'novel' management objects. As was noted about textscapes in general:

> In terms of temporality, we contend that an instance of discourse is informed by a retrospective context, a realtime context, and a projective context. In short,

the past, the present, and future are simultaneously embedded within a discursive event.

(Keenoy and Oswick, 2004: 138)

Of course – despite citing numerous legitimizing academic semiotics – the MacLeod Report was not written with an academic audience in mind.[3] Its purpose was to shape and drive public policy and to embolden and inspire positive managerial action in difficult times. As such, its 'discursive value' lies precisely in this intrinsic ambiguity and all-embracing character, for it permits managers and others to embrace it as a 'discursive driver' of action without ever having to be over-concerned about what it might mean. Thus, it becomes an all-purpose managerial object which can be deployed to accomplish *something*. It should also be self-evident that, discursively, the policy narrative had to *appear* to be new and novel; academic coherence and credibility are optional embellishments. In that respect, MacLeod and Clarke have constructed, if not created, a highly successful object.[4]

However, as all this suggests, what they have certainly not done is construct, evidence and illustrate that engagement is a distinctively different conceptual-theoretic object from those which preceded it. Fortunately, such academic nit-picking is of marginal concern to the second set of actors who have enrolled themselves into the network promoting the discourse of engagement: the management consultants who have indeed enacted it as 'a concept that is greater than the sum of its parts' (MacLeod and Clarke, 2009: 9).

The consultants' objects

For the consultancy industry, 'engagement' is a newish trope underpinning their present products. In contrast to the ambiguous multi-faceted aspirational policy object, the consultants' object presents itself to the reader as a seemingly far more coherent and self-confident entity. Engagement is portrayed with a much narrower range of identit(ies), all of which can be captured and measured through metrics of considerable semiotic persuasiveness. The latter are then deployed to clearly demonstrate its capacity to transform a wide range of attitudinal, behavioural and organizational features which are systematically evidenced though their reflection in indices of improved productivity, performance and a variety of enhanced bottom-line values. 'With proven links to productivity, customer engagement, quality, retention, safety, and profit, Gallup's unique employee engagement approach blends strategic analysis with practical steps and advice to change how leaders view their work, their employees, and their customers' (Gallup, 2012a). Unsurprisingly, it emerges as a formidable and desirable object with direct links to a cornucopia of positive change. Unlike the policy object, consultancies steer managers toward management practices which usually involve installing appropriate 'drivers' to ensure significant improvements in engagement. There is also a sense that 'engagement' is something which can be 'done to' or 'extracted from' employees through 'leadership'. Hence, for Mercer (2012) engagement is 'about the ability of leaders to inspire and align their people around the way forward at the desired pace, involving a planned communication effort that is integrated with all the other leadership and change activities'.

The source of this composite image – a variety of management consultancies' on-line web pages[5] – might be seen as problematic. Such 'front-stage' texts are essentially designed to advertise the companies' long successful experience in advising organizations while simultaneously marketing their products. But to dismiss such constructions as commercial hyperbole would be to critically underestimate the central role consultants have played in constructing, promoting and driving the engagement narrative from the outset by, as Callon (1986) puts it, 'mobilising allies'. For example, prior to his core role in constructing the policy object, David MacLeod co-authored *The Extra Mile: How to Engage Your People to Win* (MacLeod and Brady, 2007). According to the publisher's blurb, this book 'is the result of four years of research into engagement by a joint team from Cass Business School and Towers Perrin [and] drew on the results of various studies and surveys which together totalled 33 million respondents'. That eye-watering number refracts the massive data-banks built up over years now held by the major consultancies. Those surveys are heavily cited in the general literature and provide a critical evidential stream in both the MacLeod Report and the subsequent follow-up document which, listing the sources used, tell us their 'evidence comes from academic research, and from *research using data compiled by research houses such as Towers Watson, Kenexa, Hay, Aon-Hewitt and Gallup*' – a remark which carries the discursive implication that academic and consultancy 'research' procedures and findings may be considered of equivalent legitimacy and validity (Rayton et al., 2012: ii; emphasis added). Hence, arguably, the intertextual presence and influence of the consultants' 'objects' might be seen as setting the parameters of the discursive agenda for all the other social actors who have enrolled themselves in constructing 'engagement'. In short, the consultants' role appears to be fundamental and, in this respect they may well qualify as 'policy entrepreneurs' – social actors who 'from outside the formal positions of government, introduce, translate, and help implement new ideas into public practice' (Roberts and King, 1991: 147).

Predictably, definitions vary – not least because each consultancy needs to construct a distinctive unique sales proposition (USP) to position themselves in a highly competitive market. Reading across the websites, there seems little fundamental difference between their constructions, and all share an emphasis on the core measurable and provable direct relationship between engagement, performance, productivity and bottom-line values. This commercial contextual priority places a premium on constructing seemingly distinctive semiotic images which project a novel conception of and approach to 'engagement'. With the discursive default set on hyperbole, this provides a rich, if occasionally confusing set of possibilities.

Since it is a mediating text between the consultants' objects and the policy object, it is useful to start with MacLeod and Brady's (2007: 11) observation that, 'In seeking to harness this elusive quality, organisations have an advantage: in general people actually *want* to be engaged.' So, what is this 'elusive quality'?

> The simplest definition is this: it is the employee's willingness to put discretionary effort into their work in the form of time, brainpower and energy above and beyond what is considered adequate [and the] purpose of promoting engagement is to increase performance, efficiency and company resilience. [However] Mere contentment, in fact, may be the enemy of engagement. [Hence] Consequences – both good and bad – should be built into the organization to encourage and reinforce discretionary effort.
>
> (MacLeod and Brady 2007: 11–13)

While not overtly declaring that employees' 'discretionary effort' should become subject to managerial *fiat*, this formulation implies that the 'extra mile' should be a 'normal' and legitimate managerial expectation (which comes at no extra cost). A more visible object has been constructed in a book written by two senior managers at Towers-Perrin: Gebauer and Lowman (2009). They offer a richer narrative of their object than is found on the web pages which combines data from three sources: the Towers Perrin Global Workforce Survey – an online survey of 90,000 randomly selected full-time employees from mid- to large size companies across 18 countries which covers all age-groups and job-types; the 'world's largest employee normative database updated annually from over 2 million employees across 40 countries'; and 'real life', a metaphor referring to a 'year of interviewing' employees at all levels. For them:

> an engaged employee *understands* what to do to help her company succeed, she *feels* emotionally connected to the organization and its leaders, and she is willing to put that knowledge and emotion in *action* to improve performance, her own and the organisation's.

Although this embodies what might be regarded as the idealized 'good' employee, what informs this thoughtful and organizationally focused definition is the assumption that authentic engagement involves a combination of 'head, heart and hands' which, they suggest, clearly differentiates engagement from alternative tropes such as company loyalty, job-engagement or professional commitment – none of which presupposes that employees will necessarily be *fully* engaged. Hence, it projects itself as a novel conceptual-theoretic object and certainly depicts an 'elusive quality' about a highly sensitive psycho-social individual 'state-of-mind'. However, it reads more like a rare situated phenomenon to be observed, for example, among those driven single-minded entrepreneurs building their own business from scratch rather than something which could be statistically derived from a decontextualized random sample of contracted employees working in mid- to large size companies completing an online engagement survey. In other words, while it is a plausible object, it is also one which seems most unlikely to be captured through the methods deployed to trap it. However – illustrating the intertextual connections across the network – their object is echoed (and elaborated upon) in a subsequent academic construction:

> We [conceptualize engagement] as the investment of an individual's complete self into a role . . . In engagement, organisation members harness their full selves in active, complete work role performances by driving personal energy into physical, cognitive and emotional labours. Engaged individuals are described as being psychologically present, fully *there*, attentive, feeling, connected, integrated, and focussed in their role performances. They are open to themselves and others, connected to work, and focussed in their role performance.

> (Rich et al., 2010: 617, 619)

In contrast, Kenexa's (2012a: 1), aptly named 'White Paper', defines engagement as 'the extent to which employees are motivated to contribute to organizational success. It involves how willing an employee is to apply discretionary effort to accomplishing tasks important to the achievement of organizational goals.' It is measured by responses to four scale items:

- I am proud to tell people I work for my organization.
- Overall, I am extremely satisfied with my organization as a place to work.
- I would recommend this place to others as a good place to work.
- I rarely think about looking for a new job with another organization.

Substantively, these have little or nothing to do with respondents' work-tasks and, intuitively, appear to be using 'I like where I work' as a proxy for employee engagement.

Consultants also need to be able to demonstrate the discursive plausibility of their objects, a task partly accomplished through semiotic graphics with highly visible labels which, perhaps fortuitously, portray a worryingly large number of employees with lower and, occasionally, pathological levels of engagement. For example, Aon-Hewitt (2010) offer a 'Global Engage-O-Meter' depicting four categories of engagement – 'destructive' (30 per cent), 'serious' (15 per cent), 'indifferent' (20 per cent) and 'high performance' (35 per cent). Towers-Perrin (2007) display their 'Engagement Gap', which separates the 'disengaged' (8 per cent) and 'disenchanted' (30 per cent) from the 'enrolled' (41 per cent) and 'engaged' (21 per cent). However, the most vivid artefact is a box-graphic in the Gallup Business Journal™ (2012) which analytically differentiates 'Three Types of Employees'. First, 29 per cent are 'Engaged employees [who] work with passion and feel a profound connection to their company. They drive innovation and move the organization forward'; second, some 56 per cent are depicted as 'Not-Engaged employees [who] are essentially "checked out." They are sleepwalking through their workday, putting time – but not energy or passion – into their work'; and third, we encounter 15 per cent described as 'Actively Disengaged employees [who] aren't just unhappy at work; they're busy acting out their unhappiness. Every day, these workers undermine what their engaged co-workers accomplish.' Employees, it would seem, are no longer 'our most valuable assets'.

As these examples indicate, the vital discursive semiotics which both enact and empower consultants' objects are the statistical artefacts which emerge from surveys. These 'actants' – which are deployed to motivate social action – are the intertextual threads routinely cited to build the engagement narrative by other actors enrolled in constructing the textscape. The surface semiotic plausibility of these metrics remains largely unquestioned (but see Crush, 2009). Hence, it is possible for Rayton et al. (2012: ii) to categorically declare:

> The UK has an employee engagement deficit. Survey after survey indicates that only around one third of UK workers say they are engaged – a figure which leaves the UK ranked ninth for engagement levels amongst the world's twelve largest economies.

The database appears powerful. Kenexa (2012b) 'have more experience conducting engagement surveys than anyone – 850 million employee responses in our three year rolling database'; Gallup (2012b) 'maintains the world's most comprehensive historical and comparative employee engagement databases [which] contains data collected in 67 languages from more than 17 million respondents in 175 countries worldwide' (updated annually); while Aon-Hewitt's (2010) review is based on 'Our global employee engagement research from 2008 to 2010 [and] represents 6.7 million employees working in over 2,900 organizations', a sample which expanded to 9.7 million employees across 3,100 organizations by 2012 (Aon Hewitt, 2012).

The question is: what accounts for the allegedly troubling persistent finding 'that only around one third of UK workers say they are engaged'? Among the statistical signifiers on display, by far the most visible are the overall mega-sample sizes and a bewildering array of percentages deployed to imply causation between engagement levels and attitudes, performance, productivity, well-being and a variety of bottom-line values. Such surveys clearly 'measure' something: the trend data appear to refract marginal changes in the level of 'felt' employee economic (in)security and/or job satisfaction, while the more specific causal claims remain very difficult to evaluate.

The problem lies in the absence of sufficient methodological detail. In consequence, discursively, the consultants' narratives are necessarily sustained through the sheer semiotic machismo of sample size and surface legitimacy endowed by the 'global' scope of the data. Context, culture and representativeness are not discussed in sufficient detail and there is not a margin of error in sight. Nor – from the web pages visited – is there any helpful elaboration of the distributions of respondent answers. As is well known, the interpretation of such distributions is critically dependent on where one 'cuts' the data in order to fix the parameters of the descriptive categories devised to analyse the findings. While scrupulous statistical probity insists such categories ought to mirror the original equidistant scale categories, it is not unusual for analysts (and not only consultants) to group or collapse scale category responses to create more visible and comprehensible images of the object under scrutiny.

Unfortunately, we do not know how how consultancies 'cut' their distributions and this makes a more considered evaluation impossible. However, there is a more mundane technical property of statistical distributions which is salient in this context: no matter what length of scale is used and irrespective of changes (upward or downward) in the level of 'measured engagement' over time, there will *always* be 30 per cent of respondents' who *could* be classified as displaying either high or low levels of engagement if the distribution is 'cut' into groups of equal frequency. Hence, there is just a possibility that the 'engagement deficit' is no more than an entirely predictable and 'normal' statistical property of survey data rather than the harbinger of economic decline in GB plc.

Despite occasional resort to tilting at managerialist windmills in the foregoing (Delbridge and Keenoy, 2010), this is certainly not to imply that consultants' objects do not merit very serious consideration. Both as social actants in their own right – managers may utilize, if not defer to, such objects to inform their decision-making about employees – and as fundamental discursive drivers of the wider engagement narrative, they are very successful social constructions. Moreover, despite the market-oriented hyperbole, what emerges between the lines of the semiotics which inform the consultants' objects is a generic emphasis on six managerial practices listed in the conclusions of the much-cited IES summary review of engagement: good quality line management, two-way communication, effective internal co-operation, a focus on development, commitment to employee well-being and clear, accessible HR policies and practices. As the IES authors note, 'These clearly resemble the common drivers [of engagement] found in the literature' (Robertson-Smith, and Markwick, 2009: 53). As this also suggests, consultants have probably not discovered a 'silver bullet' to improve worker productivity or increase earnings per share, but are merely restating the historic practices which engender McGregor's iconic Theory Y management style.

The practitioners' objects

'Practitioners' refer to those social actors who take on the task of enacting the object: they are discursive mediators or – more graphically – the discursive midwives recruited, either voluntarily or of necessity, to bring the object to life. In effect, they translate and transform what we might call the 'raw discourse' from policy makers, consultants and academics into 'practical objects' which are then deployed to socially engineer employee attitudes, feelings, behaviours and – if all this 'works' – positive organizational outcomes. Unsurprisingly, because they act within the situated constraints of their own particular organizations and individual circumstances, what emerges invariably refracts those constraints.

A pivotal practitioner is the Chartered Institute of Personnel and Development (CIPD) which is best regarded as a 'qualifying association' (Millerson, 1964). Human Resource Management is conventionally portrayed as a profession and its professional body, the CIPD – with over 135,000 members across 120 countries – proclaims it is 'setting the global standards for best practice in HR' (CIPD, 2012c), However, critically – with respect to engagement – it remains unable to control the identity and facticity of 'best practice'. For, despite enacting institutional controls over the semiotic emblems of professionalism, the CIPD qualification does not ensure exclusive jurisdiction over HR practice (see also Friedson, 2001). Unfortunately, 'anyone' can do it. Hence, the CIPD is limited to a reactive role in mediating the trajectory of salient objects fashioned for it by others. This deeply discomfiting position finds reflection in how the CIPD has translated engagement.

It offers an engagement web page (CIPD, 2012a) designed to service an exemplary range of informational and professional needs. These include policy documents, factsheets, toolkits, podcasts, organized events and books reporting commissioned research. Among these texts, the most visible is a succinct *Factsheet* which crafts the 'CIPD object' to ensure the CIPD retains a distinctive voice within the engagement textscape. Initially (CIPD, 2012a) employee engagement is loosely framed as a phenomenon which:

> *can be seen* as a combination of commitment to the organisation and its values and a willingness to help out colleagues (organisational citizenship). It goes beyond job satisfaction and is not simply motivation. *Engagement is something the employee has to offer: it cannot be 'required' as part of the employment contract* [emphasis added].

While this construction mimics the dominant imagery of the policy and consultants' objects, it casts doubt upon the novelty of 'engagement' and overtly distances the CIPD from any possible suggestion that employee discretion can be 'demanded' from employees. This focus is underlined by an explicit insistence (CIPD, 2012b) that engagement is, first and foremost, something which *employers* have to work for:

> When employers deliver on their commitments *(when by their actions they fulfil employees' expectations)* they reinforce employees' sense of fairness and trust . . . and generate a positive psychological contract between employer and employee [emphasis added].

They agree engaged employees 'will help promote the brand and protect the employer from the risks associated with poor service levels or product quality' and that the 'first step is to measure employee attitudes'. However, in describing the merits of such surveys there is no free extra mile on offer and there is a not unsubtle shift in the narrative ordering of priorities, for:

> in both private and public sectors . . . The results typically show what employees feel about their work on a range of dimensions including, for example, *pay and benefits, communications, learning and development, line management and work-life balance* [emphasis added].

In addition, there is 'no definitive all-purpose list of engagement "drivers"' although their own research found that the three main drivers are: 'having opportunities to feed your views upwards; feeling well-informed about what is happening in the organisation'; and 'believing that your manager is committed to your organisation'. This list is underpinned by calling on the IES study (Robertson-Smith and Markwick, 2009) which offers a similar set of generic

Theory Y type managerial practices. And the *Factsheet* concludes with a quite singular assertion which clearly differentiates the CIPD object:

> Engagement is *not about driving employees to work harder but about providing the conditions under which they will work more effectively* – it is about *releasing* employees' discretionary behaviour. This is more likely to result from a healthy work life balance *than from working long hours* [emphasis added].

Although the expressed 'CIPD Viewpoint' broadly endorses the engagement narrative, it is not regarded as a novel object. Indeed, the CIPD appears distinctly underwhelmed, for their own narrative is informed by an almost hard-nosed realism about what can realistically be expected from employees, a stance which clearly distances them from the enthusiasm with which engagement has been embraced by other network-actors. And there also seem to be some deeper historical intertexts informing this aspect of the textscape.

It is not so long since the CIPD had to address a previous challenge to its institutional claim to define those 'best practices', for, in the mid-1980s, the discourse of HRM presented a quite singular threat. Discursively, HRM not only confronted pluralist-oriented personnel management with a unitarist managerial conception of HR as a potentially integrative strategic business role but also, inadvertently, it generated an identity crisis for what was then the 'Institute of Personnel Management' (Fombrum et al., 1984; Guest, 1987; Legge, 1995/ 2005). This crisis was not overcome without suitable syllabus changes to its professional qualification, a strategic merger with the Institute of Training and Development in 1994 and the prestigious award of 'Chartered' status in 2003 (CIPD, 2012d). In this respect, it is notable that, apart from an initial cursory reference to that 'extra mile', there is not a single reference in the CIPD *Factsheet* to any of those management consultancy surveys and 'research houses' which feature in the MacLeod Report and its supportive evidence[6] (see also, CIPD, 2010 and CIPD, 2011). In consequence, the CIPD has constructed an astutely crafted, conservative and quietly political object designed to preserve their autonomy as the institutional guardian of McGregoresque-style people-oriented HR practice.

However, if recent commentaries which seriously question the future for such a traditional approach to HR practice prove accurate (Organizational Dynamics, 2011; Management-Revue, 2009; Bach and Edwards, 2013), then there is a fine and potentially perilous line between standing for historic values and practices, and failing to effectively embrace some uncomfortable changes. As Albert et al. (2009: 4,14) pointedly remind us – echoing Legge (1978) – not only does HR continue to suffer from 'a lack of self-confidence, undervaluation by both practitioners and users, and a confused idea of what its own professional mission should be', but:

> many organisations are operating in a cultural lag from the traditional psychological contract . . . Organisations now employ a multitude of models (part-time, job shares, remote working, contract, shared services, outsourcing etc.) for organising their workforce but, largely, retain the artefacts of a traditional contract (e.g. career paths, benefits etc.) which they cannot (realistically) deliver.

For HR managers, the frontline midwives, engagement confronts them as an ambiguous though, since they are accustomed to the assembly-line of HR 'buzzwords', not necessarily such a potentially troublesome object. This is richly detailed in a qualitative study by Luisis-Lynd and Myers (2010) which is tucked away among the CIPD web pages. Through interviews with 12 senior HR professionals they identify and explore an aptly named object: 'engagement-in-the-wild'. They found a diverse range of situated concepts-in-use being deployed to encompass, enact and measure engagement-in-practice; and these meanings

> are largely free of any constraints which academics or, indeed, practitioners might wish to impose [and] include compound, nebulous, or vague definitions, faith in causes and consequences which themselves may overlap with these definitions, and acceptance of the resulting ambiguity.
>
> (ibid.: 1)

Only one organization had a formal definition of engagement, but only one respondent thought it a passing fad. This might seem curious, but a remark from one respondent hints at why this might be so:

> I'm sure that, *like every other buzzword*, we'll stop saying 'engagement' and we'll probably call it something else. But it won't matter really, *because the underlying concept is not new. So, the concept of engagement mattering has always been there, will always be there, it might well be called something else.*
>
> (ibid.: 15; emphasis added)

Once again, the ghost of McGregor's Theory Y appears to be lurking within the discursive undergrowth of the engagement textscape.

Indicative support for Luisis-Lynd and Myers' (2010) analysis comes from a Kings College 2011 survey based on 350 responses from senior HR professionals across a broad cross-section of sectors and organizational sizes (Clinton and Wollard, 2012). The authors note that '*the idea of engagement has become firmly embedded in HR strategy*' and conclude that maintaining 'employee engagement remains the major challenge identified for 2012' (ibid.: 13; emphasis added). Foremost among the coping strategies devised by HR managers to 'manage' the engagement narrative appear to be 'recycling and repackaging traditional ideas', for:

> despite a range of varying definitions, most survey respondents conceptualise and utilise employee engagement through a more traditional lens. *Over 75 per cent of those that measure engagement do so using measures of job satisfaction, organisational commitment and identification with values.*
>
> (ibid.: 15; emphasis added)

And – confirming Luisis-Lynd and Myers' (2010) analysis – it is also observed that 'Surprisingly, significantly fewer organizations (around 33 per cent) use engagement measures that include additional or discretionary effort, or organizational citizenship (working for the benefit of others or the organisation as a whole).' These HR managers are 're-using old concepts [which] may even contradict how an organisation defines it' with the possible consequence that there may well be 'a difference between how it is conceptualized and how it is actually measured', for 'most are not necessarily talking about the same idea'. In a remark that may disturb *aficionados*, the authors also note that 'Additionally many organisations may be measuring something different to what they believe is being measured' (ibid.: 15).

While not even the ghost of McGregor makes an appearance in these survey findings, it is difficult to resist the broader observation that, for HR practitioners, engagement has not generally been embraced with any enthusiasm. The constraints under which they must display their professionalism leaves them little choice but to acknowledge and incorporate this 'buzzword' within their discursive armoury and, through their daily practice, construct methods to enact it. However, what appears to emerge is a pragmatic and pale refraction of MacLeod's ambitions, the consultants' hyperbole or the exquisite academic idealization offered by Rich et al. (2010).

The academic objects

The choice of Frederick Taylor as the godfather of engagement was not entirely arbitrary, for his experience is instructive. He is perhaps the first significant management scientist whose object was written down, twisted, expropriated and – in his case – used against him in the famed congressional hearings (Thompson, 2003). Ever since, as with the Kahn (1990) initiated construction of engagement, potentially useful academic objects have endured a similar fate through the discursive translations of those with managerial objectives. However, a not dissimilar process of intertextual elaboration, conceptual blending, theoretical fine-tuning and progressive transformation can also be seen to characterize scholarly endeavour to 'develop' this new field. While usually construed as the process of 'normal science', it is important to note that academics also have not insignificant material interests in the market-place of ideas. While the construction of novel ideas is a touchstone for policy and consultancy network actors, in these increasingly performative times, they are of equal significance for academics. Despite the insulation of those metaphorical ivory towers, academic actors enrolled in the engagement narrative may be seen as responding to institutional pressures to secure research funding, construct publishable objects with ostensibly novel semiotic imagery as well as launch innovative teaching programmes to generate income.

Fortuitously, the major academic objects which populate the engagement textscape are portrayed in detail elsewhere in this volume and will not be (re)presented here. There are two other reasons for deferring consideration of these objects until this point. First, it seems that, as a containable conceptual-theoretic and empirical object, academics have lost any privileged voice in controlling the identity and direction of the social actant, 'engagement'. This is not necessarily an unwelcome development, and might well be regarded as a measure of the success of the academic object in colonizing the daily life of management discourse. While this may lead to putative improvements in managerial practice, simultaneously, it generates additional academic research agendas and research funding. But, secondly, and perhaps paradoxically, as the academic objects become ever more fine-grained, it might also result in the academic voice becoming increasingly marginalized (as occurred with much of the research in HRM; see Armstrong, 2000; Editor's Forum, 2007). While reference to academic semiotics will likely remain important for legitimatory purposes, practical applications and social enactment of the object itself is in the hands of other actors.

However, there are two emblematic academic objects which merit discursive consideration because they refract what might be called the core and periphery of the academic objects in circulation. The core object is Macey and Schneider's (2008) 'The meaning of employee engagement', a widely cited article which offers a seemingly highly respected 'framework for understanding the elements of employee engagement' while simultaneously addressing the discursive agendas of policy-makers, consultants, practitioners and academics. Contextually, it is notable that both authors are spokespersons for a Californian management consultancy, the Valtera Corporation (Macey is the founder and CEO; while Schneider is also listed as a University of Maryland professor). Valtera (2012) describes itself as a 'leading authority on workforce performance' and advises on:

> true engagement [which] means your employees mirror and actively promote your organization's goals and ethics. They go out of their way to do their jobs. They feel energized on the job. They help their fellow employees.

The analysis echoes this corporate narrative and, from the first line of the abstract onwards, the authors are unequivocal about their managerialist agenda:

> Our goal is to present a conceptual framework that will help both researchers and practitioners recognize the variety of meanings the engagement construct subsumes and the research traditions that give rise to or support those meanings. We believe that this is important in itself as it creates a working model for how the research literature can influence practice and vice versa.
>
> (Macey and Schneider, 2008:4)

To this end, we are informed that 'we choose to focus on *only those aspects of engagement that have positive valence*', a stance which they believe 'is crucial to developing conceptual precision in that *it maintains a clear intentional focus on benefits that inure to the organization*' [and] '*we simply choose to arbitrarily exclude . . . models of behavior that focus on withdrawal, maladaptive behavior, or other disengagement phenomena*' (ibid.: 4; emphasis added). And thus, having sanitized their object of desire by intimating that non-compliant behaviours are likely pathological, they proceed to offer a discursively disinfected analysis of the complex and conceptually nuanced psychological conceptions of engagement: state engagement, behavioural engagement and trait engagement. This is accomplished through a series of primarily normative expectations dressed up as 14 semiotically persuasive 'propositions'. For example, they eschew the 'folk definition of employee engagement (e.g. "going the extra mile")' in preference of a seemingly more scientific object: 'Proposition 8: Engagement behavior includes actions that, given a specific frame of reference, go beyond what is typical, usual, ordinary, and/or ordinarily expected' (ibid.: 16).

Unsurprisingly, their overall conclusion is a normative aspiration: 'having engaged employees may be a key to competitive advantage. This will be especially true if we can show how the engagement construct produces effects at levels of analysis of concern to management' (ibid.: 25).

For our purposes, this article illustrates not only the practical managerial ambition embedded in the textscape, but also the potentially distortive impact of framing analysis through the medium of 'positive' psychology. It should be stressed that the authors have been crystal clear about their intentions and their elegant inter-text would grace the pages of any management consultancy website. However – and this underlines the point that text cannot be understood outside the context in which it is deployed – it was published between the covers of *Industrial and Organizational Psychology*. Although it is by no means the only such text written by consultants,[7] it is precisely this social location which permits it to project itself as a putatively impartial 'academic article' as it circulates throughout the actor-network.

In total contrast, the peripheral object is *Alienation from work: Marxist ideologies and twenty-first-century practice* (Shantz, Alfes and Truss, 2012), which – because of the seemingly discordant framing – is one of the most thought-provoking articles in the textscape of engagement. While all three authors are involved in building the mainstream academic object, this text specifically explores what has been called the 'dark side of engagement' which is concerned with issues such as dis-engagement, burnout and workaholism (Bakker et al., 2011; Maslach and Leiter, 1997). In this questionnaire-based study the analysis is framed as a response to proponents of 'Critical HRM' and takes Marx's concept of alienation as the starting point. The authors astutely distance themselves from Marxians who are concerned with the 'structural conditions in capitalist society [which] create alienation' and frame their own approach to alienation as 'an individual, malleable social-psychological' artefact which is defined as 'a dissociate state of the individual in relation to the product or process of work' (ibid.: 4,6). This permits them to creatively explore in some detail three 'precursors' of alienation (the absence of employee voice, person–job fit and meaningfulness at work) and two consequences of alienating work (emotional exhaustion and low levels of well-being) in their analyses of engagement practices with the potential to ameliorate alienating work contexts.

While Marxian purists might kerfuffle at such usage, Shantz et al. are by no means the first to re-imagine alienation as a socio-psychological object. Its discursive significance within the textscape of engagement is threefold. First, it enlists (and incorporates) a construct – alienation – which has been portrayed as the 'opposite of engagement' (ibid.: 16) as a network-object. Second, it translates this historic *political* characteristic of a collective (i.e. the working class) into a mutable individual psycho-social 'state' subject to change through managerial intervention. Third, although this object (re)connects engagement to a much wider range of critical sociological and institutional academic literatures, it also offers up what some in 'Critical HRM' might see as a fruitful discursive point of entry to critique the whole engagement project for, in contrast to Macy and Schneider (2008) who exclude 'disengagement phenomena', Shantz et al. (2012) embrace a more plausible but also a more fragile object.

Conclusion: alternative objects?

This chapter has attempted to demonstrate that 'engagement' can be usefully understood as a conceptual 'object' that can be tracked through the social constructions of social actors enrolled in a network to enact their preferred objects through text, research, social practices and marketing. Inevitably and – in sociological terms – 'naturally', these objects manifest identities which refract these actors' competing interests and objectives. And, despite their variable ontology, these objects have material consequences which take the form of policy outputs, management consultancy products, professional HR practices, academic publications and, of course, both direct and indirect social and economic impacts on the work lives of employees who, as ever, exercise some constrained choices in how they interact with the object. With such conflicting conceptions, it is simply not possible to fix the identity of 'engagement' in any satisfactory fashion. As noted elsewhere, identities are projected 'through the circuitry of the structural context' and are 'more accurately seen as co-constructed or dialogical entities which are "fabricated" through discourse, "staged" through performance and "fictionalized" through text' (Ybema et al., 2009: 305). This is less daunting than it sounds, for it is also the case that all those enrolled in the network propagating the object develop more or less hazy inter-subjective understandings of what others take the object to mean. Hence it is possible for me, having joined the network, to offer (yet another) trustfully plausible account of what it might 'really' mean (Weick, 1995).

Although it finds its origins in the positive psychology of Kahn (1990), the analysis offered here suggests this object has, in effect, taken on a life of its own (or, more precisely, a series of parallel lives). This underlines the point that the nature of an object depends not upon any properties intrinsic to the object itself, but reflects the narrative (and privileged) expectations of observers who are, in effect, *creating* the identity in question (Keenoy, 1999; Weick, 1999). In other words, our observations refract how we frame our 'seeing' and, hence, social actors may construct qualitatively different identities for what is ostensibly the same object. Making sense of such mutable objects requires privileging some readings over others. Since none can escape the discursive framings we deploy to construct 'reality', whatever the formal academic criteria deployed, in the final analysis they will invariably refract the ethical touchstones which shape the observers' perceptual frame. Mine should be fairly self-evident through the tone and direction of the narrative developed above.

One possible way into evaluating the engagement textscape is to ask whether it represents continuity, change or transformation with respect to our discursive understandings of how best to manage employment relations. Concerning continuity, as with the construct of HRM, engagement emerges as a multi-faceted holographic facticity (Keenoy, 1999). Insofar as it has a discernible lineage, it has been argued there are powerful generic echos of McGregor's Theory Y informing the various objects: far from being a 'novel' construct, employee engagement may be seen as a metaphorical reincarnation of employee-centred management practice. The construct can also be aligned with debates about the so-called 'hard-soft' strategems which informed analyses of the projected social practices of HRM (Guest, 1987; Legge, 1995/2005; Truss et al., 1997; Keenoy, 1997). That debate can be seen as having reimagined and reconfigured McGregor's Theory Y to meet the very considerable pressures on managers to accomodate the changes consequent on the 1980s de-regulation of markets and the rise of neo-liberal economic policies. Managers had to devise HR strategies to meet both employee expectations (i.e. discursively 'soft' practices) and the shareholders' short-termist expectations (i.e. the discursively 'hard' practices). However, the parallel if less visible concern in the engagement textscape with burnout and workaholism also resonates with contemporary concerns about attempts by management to 'govern the soul' of employees (Rose, 1999; Costea et al., 2008). In this latter respect, the engagement textscape may refract a quietly desperate attempt to enrol employees into an 'inspiring' and optimistic narrative during a period of unprecedented economic restraint for, while 'we are all in it together', the only reward on offer to secure those essential 'extra miles' is an individualistic psycho-social experience of 'engagement'. (For semiotic glimpses of this phenomenon see some of the tweets on the Engage for Success, 2012 web page or the more histrionic contributions on Scoop.it. 2012 – a site which collates 'popular' advice on how to enhance employee engagement).

With respect to change, the one potentially significant conceptual-theoretic development is the novel emphasis on the analytic heuristic of 'positive psychology' which frames many of the academic objects (Kahn, 1990; Schaufeli and Bakker, 2004; CIPD, 2010). A psycho-logistic perspective came to dominate the now-stalled HRM-performance project (Guest, 2011) and HRM more generally (Keenoy, 2009), a process which also facilitated the (discursive) managerialist shift from pluralist to unitarist employee relations policies and practices. However, the academic engagement narrative seems to anticipate a micro-focus on the employee–work relationship and an even greater priority being accorded to the 'individual' as both the source of and the solution to the problems of work motivation. Such a development will likely position the engagement academic research agenda as marginal to broader institutional employment issues (e.g. fairness, the living wage, full-time contracts, pay-levels, equality, legal protection, the role of unions) which tend to frame the agendas of those interested in the socio-economic regulation of the employment relationship. If the latter becomes redefined as an almost exclusively personal and psycho-social relationship, engagement may come to be regarded merely as a transient managerial and ideological distraction for, as yet, we have not seen the emergence of the institutional mechanisms which drove the discourse of HRM to prominence in the late 1980s (e.g. re-naming of university departments, professorships, mainstream courses on engagement and dedicated academic journals).

Finally, if one is persuaded by the promise of the policy and consultancy objects, then socio-economic transformation with unheralded improvements in a wide range of performance indicators are just over the horizon. This hyperbole of 'transformation' has become an unreflective discursive commonplace ever since the introduction of the (*sic*) 'excellence' discourse by Peters and Waterman (1982), who fundamentally reconfigured language use across the discourses of management science. As ever, context is critical and, with the possible exception of the practitioners, network actors have generally downplayed the insidiously destructive impact of the present highly dispiriting economic climate which – at the level of employee experience in Europe and North America – seems to have no tangible end in sight. For the immediate future, those consultancy surveys of global engagement trends all suggest a downward drift reflecting progressive dissatisfaction with work-rewards. In the UK context, a workforce of some 29 million is characterized by 20 per cent who do not earn a 'living wage' (KPMG, 2012); 30 per cent in part-time work (ONS 2012); an expansion of temporary work and underemployment, an increasing use of zero-hours contracts (Unison, 2012); proposals to lengthen public sector working hours (Syal, 2012); progressive reductions in the levels of benefit protection for low-paid employees; and a situation in which even the middle classes can no longer sustain private childcare (Resolution Foundation, 2012). Alongside recession and falling living standards, these are hardly promising trends from which to anticipate a transformation in employee engagement inspired by putatively 'mediocre managers' (People Management, 2012).

The far more interesting and troubling question here concerns possible alternative 'transformations'. There are growing signs of social instability and potential resistance in advanced and formerly prosperous societies across continental Europe and some observers (Vidal, forthcoming) predict an ever-increasing disaffection associated with post-Fordist socio-economic trends in capitalist societies. Echoing the bleak UK trends noted above, Vidal argues that the relative institutional employment security and decent wages which characterized the Fordist period are now being progressively (and necessarily) undermined. Despite technological advances and a reduction in low autonomy work this is, seemingly paradoxically, combined with a persistent expansion in the proportion of low wage work and an ever-increasing deterioration in the distribution of incomes and wealth. Shantz et al. (2012: 17) concluded that 'Marx's ideas on the factors that give rise to the alienation of labour from the production process have been shown to be as relevant today as they were then [1844].' While their concern was to reductively reconfigure estranged labour in terms of the psycho-social disengagement narrative, what Vidal's analysis suggests is that we may still have much to learn from the insights of Marxian political economy. In what was both a political and a policy object, Marx's celebrated *Communist Manifesto* (2008: para 18) graphically declared:

> The bourgeoisie cannot exist without constantly revolutionising the instruments of production, and thereby the relations of production, and with them the whole relations of society . . . Constant revolutionising of production, uninterrupted disturbance of all social conditions, everlasting uncertainty and agitation distinguish the bourgeois epoch from all earlier ones. All fixed, fast-frozen relations, with their train of ancient and

venerable prejudices and opinions, are swept away, all new-formed ones become antiquated before they can ossify. All that is solid melts into air, all that is holy is profaned, and man is at last compelled to face with sober senses his real conditions of life, and his relations with his kind.

Despite its archaic rhetorical elegance, the analytic prescience of these observations resonates deeply with our contemporary crisis. And, while Marx's optimism of a worker-led societal transformation has not and may not bear the fruit he imagined, far less appealing oppressive regimes remain possible in the wake of a deepening capitalist crisis. Such a conclusion may seem pessimistic (and, personally, I hope it is) but, nonetheless, it does carry far greater plausibility than the projected transformation of capitalist labour market-relations through employee engagement initiatives.

Acknowledgements

I am indebted to Martin Edwards, Di Kelly, Aoife McDermott, Johanna Macneil, Joe O'Mahoney, Piers Myers, Cliff Oswick, Victoria Wass and Stuart Wollard, who all commented constructively on earlier drafts.

Notes

1   The term does not originate with MacLeod and Clarke (2009) – a seminal honour usually accorded to Kahn (1990). Management consultants were conducting engagement surveys for some years before 2009. However, in the UK literature, the MacLeod Report is a singular reference point and appears to have galvanized others in the actor-network which is building the 'engagement' narrative.
2   The thinking behind Theory Y was informed by Maslow's iconic hierarchy of needs, one of the intellectual sources of 'positive psychology'. Notably, Carson (2005: 459) argues that Theory Y is a precursor of 'self-directed work teams, self-management, job enrichment, and empowerment, to name a few. Each of these concepts takes a bow to McGregor's concept of giving employees more responsibility and watching them flourish'.
3   A subsequent document provides a more detailed and robust summary account of 'The Evidence' to support the policy object. However, it was 'written with an audience of chief executives and chief financial officers, as well as investors, shareholders, company analysts in mind and will also be available to all those managers and leaders who are still semi convinced that this topic needs prioritising' (Rayton et al., 2012: i), a remark which not only marginalizes academics but also, to a mildly paranoid reader, might read like a list of potential management consultancy clients. (However, see also Callon, 1986 on the importance of 'mobilising allies' across networks.)
4   Following endorsement from the coalition government in 2011, MacLeod and Clarke have been able to institutionalize the 'engagement movement' through the 'Engage for Success' (2012) website. This is an online resource centre which posts information about new work, developments, cases, meetings and – inevitably – also runs a Twitter account.
5   Although what HR consultancies say and offer is broadly similar, it is far from easy to identify what might constitute a 'representative' sample of consultancies. This section is based on management consultants' websites; those selected are included because their work is much cited in the textscape or they offer interesting, alternative and useful illustrations of how the 'consultancy object' has been discursively constructed, defined and measured.
6   Although, the last time the web page was consulted – November 2012 – the CIPD was co-sponsoring a conference on engagement with Hay Group Insight.
7   For example, in Albrecht's (2010) Handbook, of 65 contributors, 17 are from management consultancies. While this illustrates the progressive colonization of academic objects by other network actors, it also alerts us to the possibility that it is no longer possible to sustain a meaningful distinction between 'academic' and 'non-academic' engagement objects.

References

Albrecht, S. L. (ed.) (2010) *Handbook of employee engagement perspectives, issues, research and practice*, Cheltenham: Edward Elgar Publishing.

Albert, A., Sullivan J. and Wong, W. (2009) *Quality people management for quality outcomes: The future of HR review of evidence on people management*, London: available at The Work Foundation www.theworkfoundation.com/assets/. . ./qualitypeoplemanagement [accessed October 2012].

Aon Hewitt (2010) http://www.aon.com/. . ./Trends_Global_Employee_Engagement_Final.pdf [accessed October 2012].

—— (2012), Trends in Global Employee Engagement, available at http://www.aon.com/attachments/thought-leadership/Trends_Global_Employee_Engagement_Final.pdf [accessed October 2012].

Armstrong, M. (2000) The name has changed but has the game remained the same?, *Employee Relations*, 22, 6:576–89.

Astley, W. G. (1985) Administrative science as socially constructed truth, *Administrative Science Quarterly*, 30, 4:497–513.

Bach, S. and Edwards, M. (eds) (2013) *Managing human resources: Human resource management in transition*, London: Wiley & Sons.

Bakker, A. B., Albrecht, S. L. and Leiter, M. P. (2011) Work engagement: Further reflections on the state of play, *European Journal of Work and Organizational Psychology*, 20(1): 74–88.

Berger, P. L. and Luckmann, T. (1966) *The social construction of reality: a treatise in the sociology of knowledge*, London: Penguin.

Callon, M. (1986) Some elements of a sociology of translation. Domesticating the scallops and fishermen of St Brieuc Bays, in Law, J. (ed.) *Power, action, belief: A new sociology of knowledge?* London: Routledge and Kegan Paul.

Cameron, D. (2011) 'Prime Minister launches engagement task force', available at http://www.govtoday.co.uk/?option=com_content&view=article&id=6808:task-force-to-improve-levels-of-employee-engagement-&catid=111:business [accessed October 2012].

Carson, C. M. (2005) A historical view of Douglas McGregor's Theory Y, *Management Decision*, 43(3): 450–60.

CIPD (2010) Creating an Engaged Workforce, available at http://www.cipd.co.uk/NR/rdonlyres/DD66E557-DB90-4F07-8198-87C3876F3371/0/Creating_engaged_workforce.pdf [accessed July 2012].

—— (2011) Management competencies for enhancing employee engagement, available at http://www.cipd.co.uk/hr-resources/research/management-competencies-for-engagement.aspx [accessed October 2012].

—— (2012a) Engagement, available at http://www.cipd.co.uk/hr-topics/employee-engagement.aspx [accessed October 2012].

—— (2012b) Employee Engagement *Factsheet*, available at www.cipd.co.uk/hr-resources/factsheets/employee-engagement.aspx [accessed October 2012].

—— (2012c) CIPD Global website, available at http://www.cipd.co.uk/global/ [accessed October 2012].

—— (2012d) History of HR and the CIPD (Revised October 2012) *Factsheet*, available at http://www.cipd.co.uk/hr-resources/factsheets/history-hr-cipd.aspx [accessed November 2012].

Clarke, N. (2010) Presentation to Scottish CIPD, available at http://www.cipd.co.uk/branch/scottishpartnership/_events/Nita+Clarke+presentation.htm [October 2012].

Clinton, M. and Woollard, S. (2012) The state of HR: facing continuing uncertainty, available at http://www.kcl.ac.uk/sspp/departments/management/learningboard/index.aspx [November 2012].

Costea, B., Crump, N. and Amiridis, K. (2008) Managerialism, the therapeutic habitus and the self in contemporary organizing, *Human Relations*, 61(5): 661–85.

Crush, P. (2009) Engagement Surveys: Gallup and Best Companies face criticism, HR Magazine, available at file:///C:/Documents%20and%20Settings/User/Desktop/A/Engagement/Consultants/Joh%27s%20Page%20-%20original%20engagement-surveys-gallup-best-companies-criticism.htm [accessed October 2012].

Delbridge, R. and Keenoy, T. (2010) Beyond managerialism? *International Journal of Human Resource Management*, 21(6): 801–19.

Editors' Forum, (2007) Editors' Forum on the research-practice gap in HRM, *Academy of Management Journal*, 50(5): 985–1054.

Engage for Success (2012) Engage for Success website, available at http://www.engageforsuccess.org/ [accessed November 2012].

Fairclough, N. (1995) *Critical discourse analysis: the critical study of language*, London: Longman.

Fombrun, C. J., Tichy, N. and Devanna, M. A. (1984) *Strategic human resource management*, New York: Wiley.

Friedson, E. (2001) *Professionalism, the third logic: On the practice of knowledge*, Chicago, IL: University of Chicago Press.

Gallup (2012a) Gallup employee engagement, available at http://www.gallup.com/strategicconsulting/employeeengagement.aspx [accessed October 2012].

—— (2012b) Employee engagement: What's your engagement ratio? Brochure downloaded from Gallup (2012a) [accessed October 2012].

Gallup Business Journal™ (2012) Gallup study: Engaged employees inspire company innovation, 12 October 2006, available at file:///C:/Documents%20and%20Settings/User/Desktop/A/Engagement/Consultants/Gallup%202006%20-%203%20kinds%20of%20eye.htm [accessed October 2012].

Gebauer, J. and Lowman, D. (2009) *Closing the engagement gap*, London and NY: Portfolio, Penguin (Kindle edition).

Gergen, K. J. (2000) *An invitation to social constructionism*, London: Sage.

Goffman, E. (1959) *The presentation of self in everyday life*, New York: Doubleday Anchor.

Grant, D., Hardy, C., Oswick, C. and Putnam, L. (eds) (2004) *Handbook of organizational discourse*, London: Sage.

Guest, D. E. (1987) Human resource management and industrial relations, *Journal of Management Studies*, 24(5): 503–21.

—— (2011) Human resource management and performance: still searching for some answers, *Human Resource Management Journal*, 21(1): 3–13.

Jacques, R. (1996) *Manufacturing the employee: management knowledge from the 19th to 21st centuries*, London: Sage Publications.

Keenoy, T. (1997) Review article: HRMism and the languages of re-presentation, *Journal of Management Studies*, 34(5): 825–41.

—— (1999) HRM as hologram: A polemic, *Journal of Management Studies*, 36(1): 1–23.

—— (2009) Human Resource Management, in Alvesson, M., Bridgman, T. and Willmott, H (eds), *The Oxford handbook of critical management studies*, Oxford: Oxford University Press.

—— and Oswick, C. (2004) 'Organising Textscapes', *Organization Studies*, 25(1): 145–53.

Kenexa (2012a) Engagement Trends Over Time (White Paper), available at http://khpi.com/R-D-Library/White-Papers?page=3 [accessed October 2012].

——(2012b) Kenexa website, available at http://www.kenexa.com/Solutions/EmployeeSurveys?gclid=CPHBm8XD7bMCFSnJtAodbE8A_g [accessed October 2012].

KPMG (2012) Living wage research for KPMG, available at http://www.kpmg.com/uk/en/pages/default.aspx [accessed October 2012].

Latour, B. (2005) *Reassembling the social: An introduction to actor-network-theory*, Oxford: Oxford University Press.

Law, J. (ed.) (1986) *Power, action and belief: A new sociology of knowledge?* London: Routledge & Keegan Paul.

Legge, K. (1978). *Power, innovation and problem-solving in personnel management*, London: McGraw-Hill.

—— (1995/2005). *Human resource management: Rhetorics and realities*, 10th anniversary edn. Basingstoke: Palgrave Macmillan.

Luisis-Lynd, L and Myers, P. (2010) How, why and when are organisations today 'engaging with engagement'?, available at www.cipd.co.uk/NR/rdonlyres/. . .563E. . ./LuisisLyndandMyers.pdf [accessed October 2012].

Macey, W. H. and Schneider, B. (2008) The meaning of employee engagement. *Industrial and Organisational Psychology*, 1(1): 3–30.

MacLeod, D. and Brady, C. (2007) *The extra mile: How to engage your people to win*, Harlow: Financial Times/ Prentice Hall.

—— and Clarke, N. (2009) *Engaging for Success: Enhancing Performance through Employee Engagement*, Office of Public Sector Information.

Management Revue (2009) *Special Issue*, The end of personnel? Managing human resources in turbulent environments, A. Reichel and W. Mayrhofer (eds), *Management Revue*, 20(1): 000–000.

Maslach, C., and Leiter, M. P. (1997), *The truth about burnout: How organizations cause personal stress and what to do about it*, San Francisco, CA: Jossey-Bass.

Marx, K. and Engels, F. (2008) *The Communist manifesto*, London: Pluto Press.

Mercer (2012) Employee engagement, available at http://www.mercer.com/services/Employee-Engagement [accessed October 2012].

Millerson, G. (1964) *The qualifying associations: a study in professionalization*, London: Routledge & Kegan Paul.

McGregor, D. (1960) *The human side of enterprise*, NY: McGraw-Hill.

ONS (2012) Labour Market Statistics, October figures, available at http://www.ons.gov.uk/ons/rel/lms/labour-market-statistics/October-2012/statistical-bulletin.html [accessed November 2012].

O'Donohue, J. (1997) *Anam Cara*, London: Bantam Books.

Organizational Dynamics (2011) *Special Issue*, The Future of Human Resource Management, edited by W. Cascio and J. Boudreau, *Organizational Dynamics*, 40(4).

Peters, T. J. and Waterman, R. R. (1982) *In search of excellence: Lessons from America's best-run companies*, NY: Harper & Row.

People Insight (2012) People Insight employee engagement, available at http://www.peopleinsight.co.uk/employeeengagement.html [accessed October 2012].

People Management (2012) Mediocre managers risk undermining engagement, CIPD warns, 14th December 2012, available at http://www.peoplemanagement.co.uk/pm/articles/2012/12/mediocre-managers-risk-undermining-engagement-cipd-warns.htm [accessed December 2012].

Rayton, B., Dodge T. and D'Analese, G. (2012) Employee engagement – the evidence, available at http://www.engageforsuccess.org/ [accessed November 2012].

Resolution Foundation (2012) Counting the Costs of Childcare, available at http://www.resolutionfoundation.org/publications/counting-costs-childcare/ [accessed October 2012].

Roberts, N. C. and King, P. J. (1991) Policy Entrepreneurs: Their Activity Structure and Function in the Policy Process, *Journal of Public Administration Research and Theory*, 1(2): 147–75.

Robertson-Smith, G. and Markwick, C. (2009) Employee engagement: A review of current thinking, *Institute for Employment Studies*, Brighton: University of Sussex.

Rose, N. (1999) *Governing the soul: the shaping of the private self*, London: Free Association Books, 2nd edn.

Scoop.it (2012) Employee engagement enhancement, available at http://www.scoop.it/t/employee-engagement-enhancement [accessed November 2012].

Searle, J. (1995) *The construction of social reality*, London: Allen Lane, The Penguin Press.

Shantz, A. Alfes, K. and Truss, C. (2012) Alienation from work: Marxist ideologies and twenty-first-century practice, *The International Journal of Human Resource Management*, 1–22, iFirst, available at http://dx.doi.org/10.1080/09585192.2012.667431 [accessed October 2012].

Schaufeli, W. B. and Bakker, A. B. (2004) Job demands, job resources, and their relationship with burnout and engagement: a multi-sample study, *Journal of Organisational Behaviour*, 25(3): 293–315.

Syal, R. (2012) Leaked documents reveal plan to lengthen public sector working hours, *The Guardian*, 10th October 2012, available at http://www.guardian.co.uk/politics/2012/October/10/leaked-documents-public-sector-hours?INTCMP=SRCH [accessed October 2012].

Thompson, K. (ed.) (2003) *Early sociology of management & organizations Volume 1: Scientific management*, London: Routledge.

Towers-Perrin (2007) *The Towers Perrin 2007–2008 Global Workforce Study: Insights to Drive Growth*, available at http://www.peoplepartners.com/white_papers/The_Towers_Perrin.pdf [accessed October 2012].

Towers Watson (2012) *2012 Global Workforce Study: UK Findings*, available at http://www.towerswatson.com/united-kingdom/research/7556 [accessed October 2012].

Truss, C., Gratton, L., Hope-Hailey, V., McGovern, P. and Stiles, P. (1997) Soft and hard models of human resource management: a reappraisal, *Journal of Management Studies*, 34(1): 53–73.

UNISON (2012) Zero Hours Contracts, available at http://www.unison.org.uk/file/Zero%20 Hours%20Factsheet.pdf [accessed December 2012].

Valtera (2012) Valtera website, available at http://www.valtera.com/ [accessed November 2012].

Vidal, M. (forthcoming) Low-autonomy work and bad jobs in postfordist capitalism, *Human Relations*.

Weick, K. E. (1995) *Sensemaking in Organizations*, Thousand Oaks, CA: Sage Publications.

—— (1999) Theory Construction as Disciplined Reflexivity, *Academy of Management Review*, 24(4): 797–806.

Ybema, S., Keenoy, T., Oswick, C., Beverungen, A., Ellis, N. and Sabelis, S. (2009) Articulating Identities, *Human Relations*, 62(3): 299–22.

12 Employee engagement

Fashionable fad or long-term fixture?

David E. Guest

As employee engagement enjoys its days in the sun, lauded by national policy-makers, management consultants and top managers as a path to pursue to improve organizational performance, advocates might reflect on the lessons from the history of management fads and fashions. Like employee engagement, T-groups, quality circles, business process reengineering and *In Search of Excellence* all had their period of glory, only to fade into the background as enthusiasm waned or more attractive alternatives appeared on the horizon. The aim of this chapter is to consider whether employee engagement will follow the path of the faded stars or become more firmly established at the heart of continuing good management practice. The chapter starts by describing the characteristics of management fads and fashions before going on, in the light of these, to assess the specific case of employee engagement. The conclusions will veer towards pessimism about its long-term prospects.

The nature of management fads and fashions

Abrahamson, one of the academics most closely associated with the study of management fashions, describes a management fashion as 'a relatively transitory collective belief, disseminated by management fashion setters, that a management technique leads to rational management progress' (1996: 257). An overlapping definition, but this time of management fads, is offered by Gibson and Tesone who suggest that they are 'widely accepted, innovative interventions into the organization's practices designed to improve some aspect of performance. Fads either evolve into new management practices or are abandoned as failures' (2001: 122–3). In an article specifically considering whether employee engagement is a management fad, Wefald and Downey (2009) distinguish fads, fashions and folderol, drawing on a distinction offered much earlier by Dun33nette (1966). They view fads as short-term ideas that soon disappear and folderol as useless ideas, sometimes based on repackaging of old ideas, that crop up from time to time. In contrast, they view fashions more positively as approaches that become established as normal behaviour.

These definitions reveal an absence of a clear consensus about what we mean by management fashion. However, there is the implication in each of the definitions that there may be superficial innovations or ideas that are commonly described as passing fads and there are fashions that may be transitory, as Abrahamson suggests, or can become an established part of management practice, as the other two definitions imply. Despite the more superficial connotation of a fad and the indications of some interchangeability of terms, we will use the term 'management fashion' in this chapter. We will work with the definition used by Abrahamson and will adopt his criteria. The only qualification is that for the purposes of this chapter we will slightly amend his definition from 'a relatively transitory belief' to 'a potentially transitory belief' to reflect the fact that it is too soon to judge the long-term status of employee engagement.

Abrahamson's careful definition contains a number of key elements, each of which can be considered in its own right. First, management fashions are relatively transitory, implying some kind of life cycle. Second, there is a collective belief, suggesting that the fashion is widely adopted within a management population. Third, the role of 'management fashion setters' is highlighted, indicating that their role deserves particular attention. Fourth, specific management techniques are presented as a core feature of management fashions. Finally, there is an emphasis in each case on a specific fashion as a rational path to organizational progress. Each of these elements will be explored in more detail.

A characteristic of many fads and fashions is that they are likely to be transitory. A number of writers have considered the life-cycle of management fashions. Abrahamson, for example, explored this by reviewing the spread of publications about quality circles, revealing a rise, peak and decline. Gibson and Tesone use the approach adopted by Ettorre (1997) to study the life cycle of five specific management fashions, namely management by objectives, sensitivity training, quality circles, total quality management and self-managed teams. Ettorre identified five stages described as discovery, wild acceptance, digestion, disillusionment and hard core. The last two phases may need to be somewhat redefined since this life cycle implies that all management fashions end in failure. Yet an argument presented in Japan for the apparent decline of interest in total quality management was that it had become so deeply embedded in organizations and was so taken-for-granted that any organization without it was unlikely to survive. As Gibson and Tesone note, in the USA management by objectives may not be viewed as a path to organizational salvation but it retains a place in the established practice of many organizations, perhaps within the performance appraisal process. We may therefore need to acknowledge, in line with Gibson and Tesone, that fashions may end up as established practices. We need to consider the likelihood that this will happen in the case of employee engagement.

The second element in Abrahamson's definition emphasizes the collective belief among managers that a particular fashion should be adopted. In other words, it attains mass appeal, reflected in the attention it receives in the media, at conferences and among management consultants. As a management fashion takes off, and particularly if certain trend-setting organizations are seen to be associated with it, then the chances that managers in many organizations will seek to adopt the fashion is increased, in line with the standard tenets of mimetic isomorphism (DiMaggio and Powell, 1983). With respect to employee engagement, it will therefore be important to consider how far organizations and leading managers are eager to be associated with the approach.

A major influence on managers and their organizations will be the role of the promoters of the management fashion, a feature of Abrahamson's third criterion, as discussed further in Chapter 11. Management fashion setters are particularly likely to be management consultants. In promoting a particular fashion, they will often espouse an evidence-based approach, reflected either in some form of quantitative data collected by the consultants or in case studies of organizations where the new approach has been successfully applied. Academics, particularly Business School academics, can have a role to play. Examples from the past include McGregor and Herzberg while more recent examples include Kaplan with the balanced score card and Porter with his approach to strategy. However, the main proponents of management fashion have been business consultants who have an interest in marketing ideas that are perceived as innovative and relevant and associated with their organization. At the same time, they can also create a demand by articulating an opportunity or highlighting an underlying concern and presenting it in a language that appeals to managers. McKinsey have been particularly successful in this and the *In Search of Excellence* phenomenon of the 1980s (Peters and Waterman, 1982) is one of their outstanding examples, even though both the authors had more or less parted company with McKinsey by the time the book was published. A more recent example is their marketing of *The War for Talent* (Michaels, Handfield-Jones and Axelrod, 2001) that has effectively tapped management anxieties about whether their organization is able to attract and retain top management talent.

Abrahamson argues that management fashions do not appear spontaneously but are deliberately constructed or created by fashion setters to market to fashion followers. As already noted, these trend setters can include consultants, management gurus, business schools and occasionally 'hero' managers. To be successful, they must sense market readiness and then create a demand. One mechanism for this is finding the appropriate rhetoric to arouse management interest. This can take the form of case study-based anecdotes about organizations that have benefitted from applying the promoted fashion. And in the same way that important people wearing a new clothing fashion are likely to promote it, so a successful organization adopting a new management fashion can do the same – and provide a telling case study. A key feature is then the dissemination of the new fashion. Here the mass media, management conferences and popular books and articles can be used. In the past the *Harvard Business Review* has proved a particularly influential means of communicating new management fashions.

The fourth element in Abrahamson's definition of management fashions is the emphasis on rational techniques. As he argues, management fashion is in some respects more demanding than aesthetic fashions which, he suggests, have to be beautiful and modern whereas management fashion also has to appear rational and progressive. In other words, a core part of the successful selling of management fashion is to present it as having a strong underlying rationale. It may sometimes be dressed up as a theory but more often as a solution to a problem, reflected in a specific technique or practice that managers need to introduce in their organization, preferably with the help of a consultant. In other words, most successful management fashions give managers something concrete to do. Occasionally, the techniques or action can be left rather vague. *In Search of Excellence* recommended eight broad areas for action but taken together these amounted to a major programme of organizational cultural change. The concept of 'the learning organization' (Senge, 1990) also contained only rather diffuse recommendations for action, despite its plausibility and attractive rhetoric, and this may have helped to hasten its decline as an area for concrete rational action to improve organizational performance.

Finally, and we have already alluded to this, management fashions attract attention because they highlight the potential for rational progress. In this respect they are a basis for management optimism. By taking appropriate action, there is every chance of a better future. To many managers, particularly in difficult times or when there are high levels of uncertainty, this can be particularly appealing. Therefore, on this criterion, the challenge for employee engagement is to demonstrate that it offers a more attractive future.

The analysis of management fashion has become a significant topic of academic research in its own right and has resulted in many books of varying quality and numerous articles. If we applied Ettorre's life cycle to this research, we might discover that it has waxed and waned and for some years has been in decline. One reason for this is a general decline in new management fashions. Arguably, they had their heyday in the last decades of the twentieth century. Maybe consultants and business school academics have run out of ideas. Maybe the market is less receptive and has grown more sceptical. However, since 2000, the main claims to a traditional management fashion probably include talent management and employer branding. And, of course, employee engagement.

We will consider whether employee engagement fits the criteria set out by Abrahamson for a management fashion. A later section will also evaluate its chances of graduating to an established practice. Before this, however, it is necessary to define what we mean by engagement.

What is engagement?

Engagement is a positive term. Most people would agree that on the whole it is better to be engaged than disengaged in what one is doing, including what one does at work. However, the term also lacks precision. For the purposes of this chapter, I will draw a distinction between what I will term 'academic' and 'consultancy' definitions. There is inevitably a degree of overlap, but the distinction goes beyond terminology to reflect differences in precision, theorization, level of analysis and empirical support, and is therefore important.

As discussed earlier in this volume, academic approaches to engagement are usually traced to the work of Kahn and to an article published in 1990 (Kahn, 1990). He has subsequently argued (Kahn, 2010) that a stimulus to his interest was a dissatisfaction with extant theories of motivation and the need for a more nuanced approach that allowed for variation in motivation such that it could be treated as a transitory state. He defined engagement as 'the simultaneous employment and expression of a person's 'preferred self' in task behaviours that promote connections to work and to others, personal presence (physical, cognitive, and emotional) and active, full performance' (1990: 700). It is relevant to motivation in the sense that it is concerned with the allocation of personal resources to work activities and as such is primarily concerned with work behaviour.

Schaufeli, Bakker and Salanova (2006) offered a more attitudinally focused variant on Kahn's definition, suggesting that work engagement is a 'positive, fulfilling work-related state of mind that is characterized by vigour, dedication and absorption' (2006: 702), as described in Chapter 1. Furthermore, they suggested that it is a relatively stable psychological state. The Dutch group also developed a measure, the Utrecht Work Engagement Scale, including a short nine-item version, that has become probably the most widely used measure in academic research on engagement. Rich, Lepine and Crawford (2010) have criticized this measure because, in their view, it conflates certain antecedents with the state of engagement. They developed their own measure in an attempt to stay true to Kahn's original more behavioural definition. Their research demonstrated an association between scores on their scale and some behavioural indicators but more work is needed to evaluate their measure, particularly their attempt to measure emotional energy. Both academic approaches imply that engagement is a state that can be affected by a range of external factors, including short-term work experiences and personal mood, and as such is potentially transitory (see the research of Sonnentag, Dormann and Demerouti, 2010). However, both argue that it need not be short-lived.

Macey and Schneider (2008), in a comprehensive review of the available literature, have explored the meaning of engagement and attempted to provide an integrative framework. Essentially, they distinguish between trait, state and behavioural engagement. Trait engagement reflects an individual disposition to be more or less engaged and provides a necessary reminder that not everyone will wish to be enthusiastically engaged, even when the circumstances might appear to merit it. State engagement reflects the feeling of being engaged, is characterized by energy and absorption and is reflected in familiar attitudes such as commitment and involvement. Behavioural engagement is defined as extra-role behaviour and extends to forms of proactive activity such as job crafting (Bakker, 2010). These may be viewed either as manifestations of engagement, in line with Kahn's perspective or as outcomes of engagement, in line with Schaufeli's more attitudinal perspective. However we know, for example, that there are a range of factors that influence organizational citizenship or extra role behaviour (Podsakoff, Mackenzie, Paine and Bachrach, 2000), so there is a question about how closely it can be linked distinctively to engagement. Harrison, Newman and Roth (2006) have presented a counter-argument, suggesting that there is so much concept redundancy in the more attitudinal measure of engagement that an alternative integrated concept of behavioural engagement, reflected in performance, attendance and citizenship behaviour, is more useful. However, there has been much less research on Kahn's concept of behavioural engagement and therefore its utility in this context remains open to question.

The charge of concept redundancy needs to be seriously addressed and has been the focus of some of the major reviews of attitudinal engagement (Christian, Garza and Slaughter, 2011; Cole, Walter, Bedeian and O'Boyle, 2011). One of the challenges for the long-term establishment of the concept of employee engagement, therefore, as discussed in Chapter 1, is demonstrating its distinctiveness as a construct. There appears to be some overlap with related constructs such as involvement and commitment. Indeed both are cited by Macey and Schneider, along with satisfaction and empowerment, as reflections of the state of engagement. The meta-analyses cited above broadly support the view that when compared with these variables, engagement in work is a distinct construct. The relationship with burnout is more controversial. In an early paper, Schaufeli seemed to support the view that burnout and engagement were opposite ends of a continuum (Maslach, Schaufeli and Leiter, 2001) but more recently he and colleagues have argued that they are conceptually and empirically distinct (Schaufeli, Taris and van Rhenen, 2008). However Cole et al. (2011) suggest that on the basis of the empirical evidence emerging from their meta-analysis, they are best viewed as two sides of the same coin.

Newman, Joseph and Hulin (2010) provide a slightly different perspective. First, they argue for the presence of what they term an 'A-Factor' that explains much of the common variance between job satisfaction, affective organizational commitment, job involvement and employee engagement. Second, they suggest that this set of associations and common variances is just as strong as that between the three components of dedication, vigour and absorption in the Utrecht measure of employee engagement. They accept that more research needs to be done to establish the level of overlap. They also note that their higher-order attitudinal construct is associated with a range of outcomes and is therefore potentially useful. At the same time, they adopt the approach more often found in the US literature of focusing on behaviour and argue for a further higher order construct that captures various aspects of performance ranging from citizenship behaviour to (low) absence.

Drawing this analysis together, there appears to be some consensus around the characteristics of work engagement, although there is a degree of uncertainty about the importance of trait factors. There is an established measure, although it is not without its critics. And there is some indication that high levels of engagement, as reflected in the measures, are associated with a range of positive outcomes (see, for example, Rich, Lepine and Crawford, 2010; Salanova, Agut and Peiro, 2005; Christian et al., 2011).

The origins of the alternative consultancy approach to employee engagement that has attracted the attention of many organizations, is more difficult to identify. It can probably be associated, to a significant extent, with the longstanding survey work of the Gallup organization, as discussed in Chapter 11. Over a period of time, and aided by focus groups and careful statistical analysis, their extensive workplace audit measure, which covered many aspects of job satisfaction, was whittled down to what became known as the Gallup 12. This included a global measure of job satisfaction and a range of potential antecedents of job satisfaction. As Harter, Schmidt and Hayes (2002) define it, employee engagement in this context 'refers to the individual's involvement and satisfaction with as well as enthusiasm for work' (2002: 269). They go on to explain that the 12 items 'explain a great deal of the variance in what is defined as "overall job satisfaction" . . . we refer to them as measures of employee engagement to differentiate these actionable work-group-level facets from the more general theoretical construct of "job satisfaction"'. This is a revealing statement in so far as it first defines employee engagement but then goes on to say that they are operationalizing it quite differently as the antecedents of job satisfaction. This operational definition has been a cause of much confusion and criticism.

One implication of the Gallup approach, as outlined by Harter, Schmidt and Hayes, is that the measure of engagement predicts job satisfaction. This is not the same as aligning it to motivation or performance. The extensive literature on the relationship between job satisfaction and performance (for a review see Judge, Thoresen, Bono and Patton, 2001) confirms an association but no clear causal relationship. Furthermore, Schneider, Hanges, Smith and Salvaggio (2003), reporting on longitudinal data from company attitude surveys, show that there is just as much evidence to support the view that financial performance affects satisfaction as the more common assumption that satisfaction affects firm performance. Harter, Schmidt and Hayes (2002), on the basis of a unit level analysis, reported a positive association between their measure of engagement and a range of performance indicators but the data are cross-sectional and, therefore, particularly in view of the findings of Schneider et al., it would be inappropriate to infer causality.

As discussed in Chapter 15 of this volume, Gallup is only one of a number of consultants who have developed measures of employee engagement. For example, Towers Watson has also developed a widely used measure. A key distinguishing feature of this second general approach to employee engagement is that it is focused at the unit or organizational level of analysis. Therefore whereas the academic approach of Kahn, Schaufeli and colleagues focuses on work engagement at the individual level, the consultancy version addresses the work group, the unit or the organizational level and is more concerned with organizational engagement. What is unclear is whether by using this term Gallup created an interest in employee engagement or adapted the title of their measure to capture an already growing interest among organizations in the idea of engagement.

The UK is one of a number of countries where there has been a particular interest in employee engagement not only at the organizational but also at government level (see Chapter 14 of this volume). The government sponsored a review of the potential of employee engagement. The resulting report 'Engaging for Success' (Macleod and Clarke, 2009) stated that the review had been provided with over 50 different definitions of employee engagement by interested parties, confirming a lack of clarity about the concept. In the end, the definition the report settled on was 'a workplace approach designed to ensure that employees are committed to their organization's goals and values, motivated to contribute to organizational success, and are able at the same time to enhance their own sense of well-being' (Macleod and Clarke, 2009: 9). This definition sets the goals of employee engagement and provides criteria by which to determine whether employees express or display engagement. It differs from many other approaches in highlighting employee well-being alongside more typical organizationally-oriented outcomes as a goal of engagement. However it does not outline 'the approach' that needs to be adopted to promote engagement.

The advocacy of employee engagement has been supported by successive governments and 'Engaging for Success' has been followed up by a series of initiatives to promote employee engagement throughout industry and the public sector. The case is backed by various survey figures suggesting that at least 30 per cent of the working population is not engaged while only about 30 per cent are highly engaged. A mass of case study evidence from organizations which appears to show that there is an association between more organizational engagement, or, at least, higher scores on consultancy measures of employee engagement and a range of performance outcomes, makes the argument appealing to managers. However, in many of these cases, the definition and measurement of employee engagement is left unclear, as is the evidence of any causal link. Nevertheless, this does not appear to stand in the way of enthusiastic advocacy of the general case for organizational employee engagement.

The challenging and seemingly unanswerable question is, why did industry and government become interested in employee engagement? A range of surveys over recent years have revealed that levels of employee engagement are one of the main concerns of organizations. For example, an annual survey of over 300 organizations conducted by the King's College London Human Resource Management Learning Board in conjunction with the law firm Speechly Bircham has consistently revealed that managers place employee engagement at the top of the list of major issues facing HR functions (Clinton and Woollard, 2012).

Is engagement a management fad?

In assessing whether employee engagement is a management fad or fashion, or instead is likely to become firmly established in the long term, it will be useful to distinguish between what I have termed the academic and consultancy approaches. These can be considered against the criteria for a management fashion set out by Abrahamson.

The first criterion mentioned by Abrahamson is that management fashion is transitory. However this must be set alongside the argument of Gibson and Tesone (2002) that fashions can disappear because they move out of fashion or because they become established as more or less standard management practice. In his own research, Abrahamson traces the rise and fall of management fashion, notably for quality circles. What is less clear is how to define 'transitory'. In academic circles, research fashions can last for well over a decade, reflecting the time required to undertake research, get it published and then wait for the criticism and adaptation of ideas. Industry may take decades to pick up on the ideas. A good example from the last century is the work of Herzberg whose two-factor or motivator-hygiene theory (Herzberg, 1966) generated a mass of research over a period of ten to fifteen years and then disappeared from the academic community. But his two-factor theory and its advocacy of job enrichment lived on for a much longer time in the management consciousness, no doubt aided by some academic management departments and textbooks where his ideas are still presented.

The academic interest in employee engagement has been traced back to Kahn's paper in 1990 and this interest shows no signs of abating. For reasons that are outlined more fully below, there is a case for claiming that this has become an established area of academic interest and research rather than a passing fad. One factor that may affect its longevity is whether it can demonstrate discriminant validity. As noted above, some authors have suggested that it overlaps strongly with concepts such as commitment and involvement, although the meta-analyses seem to confirm that it is distinct. There is a separate debate about the Utrecht measure and whether the version of employee engagement associated with it can be clearly distinguished from burnout which was the focus of the earlier research by the Utrecht team. Based on their meta-analysis, Cole et al. (2011) conclude that it is not sufficiently distinct. However these potentially controversial issues can also provide a continued stimulus to research on employee engagement. On this basis, it can be argued that the academic form of work or job engagement appears to have achieved a respectable degree of longevity and cannot reasonably be described as a passing fad or fashion.

The longevity of the consultancy version of engagement is more difficult to assess. Its genesis can be traced to around the turn of the century and the 2002 article by Harter and colleagues, so it has experienced about a ten-year period of growth. If it is driven by consultants, it can be expected to thrive as long as it provides a basis for competitive advantage and consultancy fees. When this changes, and more particularly if something comes along to take its place as the latest focus for improving employee performance, then it may experience a swift decline. Similarly, like many topics that interest governments, the interest may be transitory. In both cases, marketing depends on novelty or convincingly demonstrated positive impact. When employee engagement begins to look tired, or if we reach a point where people in organizations feel they have taken it as far as it can go, then it will fade. It is probably too early to judge whether it is a passing fashion but for reasons outlined below, there are grounds for suspecting that this might be the case. One straw in the wind, noted in the 2012 King's College survey, was the first sign of a decline in initiatives to promote employee engagement (Clinton and Woollard, 2012).

The second criterion for a management fashion is that there is a collective belief that the topic is important and deserves widespread attention. The academic version appears to reflect this. It is increasingly common to see research articles on engagement. It is also becoming the focus of reviews and meta-analyses, implying a critical mass of studies. Furthermore, it is becoming a popular topic for books, as the present book attests. Several other books have been published or are in the pipeline and it is becoming a chapter topic in many human resource textbooks (see for example Peccei in Bach and Edwards, 2013). All this implies acceptance of employee engagement in the academic community as a topic worth studying. For it to survive in the longer term, it will need to be backed by a stronger evidence base addressing antecedents and consequences. To date there is remarkably little longitudinal research exploring these issues. Without it, a strong critical backlash, already beginning in the various meta-analysis-based reviews, is likely to follow.

The consultancy version of employee engagement also appears to meet this second criterion. As noted above, it is viewed as a top concern among a wide range of human resource managers. The UK Engaging for Success movement has managed to gain the commitment of an impressive range of top business leaders as well as supporting case study evidence from a lot of organizations. Interest and, by implication, belief that there is something worthwhile about employee engagement appears to be widespread. Abrahamson refers to 'adoption' rather than mere interest in a management fashion. This poses something of a problem for employee engagement since it is not clear what adoption means in practice. One criterion that appears to be popular is the use of opinion surveys to measure levels of engagement. In the King's College survey in 2012, 50 per cent of organizations reported using an in-house employee survey to gauge engagement while 42 per cent used external third parties to conduct surveys. When it came to action to improve engagement the main activities cited were 'more effective leadership and management of staff', 'developing better staff relations with line managers', 'improved learning and development opportunities' and 'greater employee participation in decision-making'. However, levels of activity in each of these areas except the last one had decreased over the previous year. Nevertheless, on this criterion, the consultancy version of employee engagement can reasonably be described as a management fashion.

A third criterion for a management fashion is that there should be fashion setters. These are the champions of the movement who, at least for a time, can attract a large audience of management enthusiasts to hear them advocate the new fashion. In the academic field, such champions are notably absent. There are no 'management gurus' writing best-selling books for an eager management audience. The most prolific output is to be found in academic articles, often written by Dutch authors such as Schaufeli and Bakker. In this respect, therefore, it appears that the academic focus reflects a serious academic endeavour rather than a movement marketed on the management or even the business school circuit. In this respect it differs from a number of other management fashions that have been promoted by academics to a predominantly management audience.

The consultancy approach to employee engagement is also unusually lacking in champions. As Macey and Schneider (2008) note, engagement has been heavily marketed by consultancy firms in the USA and the same holds true for the UK. For example, it has been strongly promoted by the Gallup organization and other consultancy organizations such as Towers Watson. In the UK, as noted above, there has been endorsement by government ministers and notably initially by Peter Mandelson, then Secretary of State for Employment, when the Engaging for Success report was initiated and published. The figureheads for the government-sponsored movement to promote employee engagement have been David MacLeod and Nita Clarke who co-authored the Engaging for Success report. However, there is a limited life for the kind of activity they have been involved in. They have launched a range of activities, a set of conferences and workshops, a so-called 'guru' group, a web page and Twitter page and a series of case studies. All these are marketing the idea of employee engagement and the need for engagement. Beyond this, it is not clear what they will do. The risk is that without the oxygen of publicity provided by their energy, and after organizations have had two or three employee engagement surveys and nothing much has changed, the enthusiasm will wane. With respect to the importance of fashion setters, therefore, employee engagement does not fit the Abrahamson concept of a management fashion. The absence of such figures may affect the sustainability of the concept as a focus for management interest.

Abrahamson's fourth criterion for a management fashion is that it advocates specific management techniques. In other words, it tells management what it should do. Employee engagement is most unusual in this respect in that it is relatively silent on action. It is presented as a good thing that everyone should want but there is rather little about how they should get it. The distinctive feature of both academic and consultancy perspectives is the provision of tools to assess levels of engagement in the form of attitude surveys. For the academics, the tool is something like the Utrecht Work Engagement Scale. For the consultants it is the Gallup 12 or the equivalent offered by other consultancies. Action is therefore conducting a survey. As noted above, the King's College survey confirmed that the use of surveys is widespread but also identified the kinds of action that some organizations undertake to promote engagement. None of these actions, such as more effective leadership and more learning and development opportunities, is in any way uniquely linked to employee engagement and all would fit equally well with steps to enhance organizational commitment or employee involvement. It may well be helpful if interest in engagement stimulates organizations to take more action in these areas. But this does not represent a distinctive management technique. On this basis, therefore, both perspectives on employee engagement do not appear to meet this criterion for a management fashion. This may not matter for the academic perspective but it could be a potentially fatal shortcoming for the consultancy version of employee engagement.

The final criterion outlined by Abrahamson for a management fashion is that it can be presented as a rational path to more successful organizational outcomes. This implies the presence of convincing evidence that promoting employee engagement leads to positive outcomes. Given the espoused support for an evidence-based approach to aid management decisions (Rousseau and Barends, 2011) there is usually a strong attempt to provide convincing evidence. The quality of such evidence may vary according to whether the focus is on the academic or the consultancy approach to engagement.

For the academic approach, the rational case will typically be reflected in convincing and consistent evidence of an association between engagement and specified outcomes. To be fully convincing, this should be particularly reflected in longitudinal studies with appropriate controls. This is not the place for a full review but much of the relevant research is summarized in a meta-analysis by Christian, Garza and Slaughter (2011) of 90 studies. They found a strong association between engagement and both task and contextual performance. They also found that engagement explained added variance after including measures of satisfaction, commitment and involvement, confirming that it explains performance above and beyond these potentially overlapping constructs. However, we need to be somewhat cautious in concluding that this analysis offers clear rational support to engagement. Only a small proportion of the studies measured performance and a majority used self-rated performance. Furthermore, most were cross-sectional, raising questions about causality. On this basis, we might argue that the results are encouraging but not yet convincing.

The consultancy literature operates, at least in part, on a somewhat similar basis by showing an association at the organizational level between overall higher levels of employee engagement and organizational performance (see, for example, Harter et al., 2002). The Engaging for Success movement has produced a report titled 'Nailing the Evidence' (Rayton, Dodge and D'Analeze, 2012) which reviews a body of evidence that purports to explore the causal relationship between employee engagement and a wide range of performance outcomes. The report is designed to convince managers as well as sceptics in the academic community. Unfortunately, it does not offer any definition of employee engagement and much of the academic research cited in the report addresses commitment, job satisfaction and other widely researched variables. It therefore risks reinforcing the academic scepticism about the utility and discriminant validity of the consultancy version of employee engagement. Furthermore, many of the studies are conducted at the individual level and while they address relevant outcomes such as citizenship behaviour and labour turnover, these are more proximal measures than the kind of financial benefits at the organizational level that are often claimed for employee engagement.

The more analytic sources of evidence are usually set alongside case studies of organizations that have successfully applied something that they label employee engagement. The problem with many of these cases is that there is a considerable variety and often a lack of clarity about what they have done to enhance engagement and there is little information about other changes that have been occurring that might have affected any outcomes. Nevertheless, the telling of compelling stories forms an important part of the process of convincing managers that ideas such as employee engagement are worth taking seriously. On this criterion of presenting a rational case, we can therefore argue that employee engagement is following a path to the promise of progress that has been well trodden by other management fashions. In summary, despite these attempts to present an evidence-based case, the quality of the evidence for the academic approach focusing on work engagement remains less than wholly convincing while the consultancy approach with its focus on organizational engagement is deeply unconvincing.

Discussion and conclusion

We have used Abrahamson's criteria for a management fashion to assess the current state of employee engagement. One initial conclusion is that while the concept of management fashion would seem to be particularly appropriate as a framework within which to consider employee engagement, it also has some limitations. For example, there is a clear negative connotation about management fads, but this also extends to the idea of a management fashion. Yet, as Gibson and Tesone (2001) and Wefald and Downey (2008) suggest, a fashion may be short term or may be a first necessary step on the road to becoming an established and effective management practice. A second potential problem is that Abrahamson has helpfully identified five criteria, but it is unclear whether all are equally important or all are essential. Therefore, some innovations may be swiftly adopted without the fanfare and marketing associated with fashions. Others may be so weak that they struggle to meet only a couple of the criteria. Still others may be particularly strong on one or two criteria but have nothing to offer on others. In other words, the Abrahamson list provides some useful criteria and a framework within which to explore the question of whether employee engagement is likely to be a long-term or short-term management fashion, but leaves considerable scope for judgement. Perhaps the important underlying question is whether employee engagement has legs – is it here to stay? To answer this question, we need to review and weigh the dimensions provided by Abrahamson.

One of the attractions of engagement is that it is clearly a good thing. Managers are attracted to the concept because they like the idea of having engaged employees and dislike the prospect of having disengaged employees. As Wefald and Downey note, they are also likely to associate engagement with positive behaviours and therefore positive organizational outcomes. While there is the beginning of a debate about the 'dark' side of engagement, reflected, for example, in the kind of proactive behaviour that results in 'stealing' the attractive elements of the jobs of others and leaving them to undertake the more routine activities (Bakker, 2010), this has yet to be seriously explored. It is therefore an easy starting point to get most people to agree that employee engagement should be a goal of organizations, in other words, to establish a collective belief that organizations should promote employee engagement. However, beyond intuitive attraction and the belief that it is a good thing, the interest among managers in engagement may be shaped by two further less obvious factors.

The first of these is an underlying anxiety that levels of engagement are low and that this may have damaging consequences. This reflects the marketing by consultants and there seems to be a commonly cited figure in the UK indicating that only 30 per cent of the workforce is highly engaged. This can be linked to another management fashion, the war for talent. In some cases, the anxiety is associated with the fear that employees have been somewhat harshly treated during the prolonged economic downturn. At the very least, they have had to lower expectations about rewards and promotions and have sometimes had to work more intensively to pick up the work of others who have left and not been replaced. The fear is that if and when the economy improves and employment opportunities pick up, many employees will want to move on. There will be an exodus of talent. There is good evidence that employees demonstrating low commitment are more likely to leave (Mayer et al., 2001). Insofar as engagement is often described in terms of commitment, the risk of low engagement is a loss of talented staff. Increasing the levels of engagement offers a means of retention. Engagement then becomes a kind of insurance policy.

The second underlying factor concerns the view that engagement is a good thing. It is a short step to argue that employees ought to be engaged. In other words, engagement is part of their citizenship behaviour. This raises the moral question of how engagement is used and where the responsibility for engagement lies. Part of the argument is that engagement – or organizational commitment and involvement – is too low and ought to be higher. The question can then be asked – who is responsible for ensuring high engagement? At one extreme, there may be the promise of something for nothing; get higher engagement and organizational performance goes up. An approach closer to exchange theory suggests that if employees are well treated they will choose to be engaged. Indeed, invoking the norm of reciprocity (Gouldner, 1960), they may feel obliged to be engaged. However the debate rather underplays what management must do to earn engagement from employees. In all the debates, there is certainly no hint, for example, that in return for the apparently greater contribution associated with higher engagement, employees should receive higher pay.

The topic of employee engagement is replete with case studies of organizations that claim to have used employee engagement successfully to help to achieve organizational goals. In some cases, one of these goals is the smooth management of workforce reductions. This raises ethical questions about how far employees can be expected to participate in activities that save costs for the organization at the expense of jobs. In general, the unions have been supportive of the principles of employee engagement. The key element that might justify this is the nature of the 'voice' that appears to form a key underpinning of engagement activity. If, as in the case of many redundancy programmes, it is merely consultative, then the term 'engagement' may be inappropriate. Archie Norman has been held up as a paragon of management enthusiasm for engagement, largely on the basis of his success in turning round Asda. As he proudly records, one of his early activities was to de-recognize the union. With the oppositional voice reduced, a management agenda for engagement becomes more straightforward but based on the quieting of a traditional collective employee perspective. The interrelationship between voice and engagement is discussed further in Chapter 13 of this volume.

A potentially critical challenge for organizational engagement is that it lacks practices, even though practices are viewed by Abrahamson as lying at the core of a management fashion. Indeed it can be argued that this is the key factor likely to limit engagement's longevity as a management fashion. It is not clear what you 'do' with engagement. The Engaging for Success report identified four 'enablers' of engagement. These are a strong strategic narrative about the organization, managers who are able to engage their staff, employee voice and organizational integrity. However, these are couched at such a level of generality and are such obviously 'good' things to do, rather like engagement, that they do not provide a clear basis for action. They are not practices. The practice that has been marketed in association with engagement is the use of attitude surveys. These purport to provide a measure of the level of engagement and whether it has changed. What the survey can less easily do is point to the practices that will enhance engagement, although most surveys will give some clues. However, in this consultancy approach to engagement, there are no specific practices that all managers can utilize. As noted earlier, once organizations have repeated the surveys, they may tire of the process and abandon them. They may continue to espouse engagement as a desirable state but not as a useful means of improving outcomes.

A further anomaly of engagement as a management fashion is that it lacks fashion leaders. There are few individuals actively promoting it in the UK, with the exception of the authors of Engaging for Success. They have been highly successful in gaining the endorsement of top level industrialists, trade union leaders and government representatives. But beyond this, there is an absence of champions. Instead the promotion is largely left to the consultants. The same cannot be said of the academic perspective which has been strongly supported in both Europe and the US by a specific group of researchers. More particularly in Europe, there is a distinct group associated with the use of the Utrecht scale who have been prolific in publishing papers on work engagement.

The counter to the argument that managers will tire of engagement surveys when they are unable to leverage them to improve performance would be a rational case, based on sound evidence, that policies and practices to enhance engagement bring rewards. In this respect, the advocates of the consultancy version of engagement may have missed a trick by not paying more attention to work engagement of the sort that has attracted the attention of academics. They have focused much more on identifying antecedents of engagement. For example, one meta-analysis (Crawford et al., 2010) finds that there is a strong association between work engagement and job variety, work-environment fit, task significance and opportunities for development. By implication, if these features of work are promoted, then the outcome will be enhanced engagement. Other studies suggest that this in turn will be associated with a range of positive proximal outcomes. We know less about how this affects overall organizational performance, but it would seem to be a potentially fruitful avenue to explore. However, employers seem typically more interested in organizational engagement with its much weaker analytic framework and poorer evidence base.

Given the failure to develop a coherent set of practices to enhance organizational engagement, there must be a significant risk that it will lose its attraction among managers. In the UK at present, there is what is increasingly termed an 'engage for success movement', led by the authors of the Engaging for Success report. If they were to cease to champion it and to maintain a sense of progress within the movement, then the energy will drop. It is likely that while academic engagement will continue to act as a focus of research for some considerable time, the status of the consultancy approach has yet to become firmly established as part of management practice. The risk must be that it will soon join the pantheon of laudable aspirations with which we can all agree, including happiness, quality, growth and sustainability; goals that most of us would like to pursue, concepts that some people think we can measure, but goals that remain ultimately elusive in many if not most cases.

References

Abrahamson, E. (1991). 'Management fads and fashions: The diffusion and rejection of innovations'. *Academy of Management Review*, 16: 586–612.

—— (1996). 'Management fashion'. *Academy of Management Review*, 21: 254–85.

Bakker, A. (2010). 'Engagement and "job crafting": Engaged employees create their own great place to work'. In S. Albrecht (ed.). *The handbook of employee engagement: Perspectives, issues, research and practice.* Cheltenham: Edward Elgar. pp. 229–44.

Christian, M., Garza, A. and Slaughter, J. (2011). 'Work engagement: A quantitative review and test of its relations with task and contextual performance'. *Personnel Psychology*, 64: 89–136.

Clinton, M. and Woollard, S. (2012). *Facing continuing uncertainty: The state of HR.* London: King's College, London and Speechly Bircham.

Cole, M., Walter, F., Bedeian, A. and O'Boyle, E. (2011). 'Job burnout and employee engagement: A meta-analytic examination of concept proliferation'. *Journal of Management*, 20: 1–32.

DiMaggio, P. and Powell, W. (1983). 'The iron cage revisited: Institutional isomorphism and collective rationality in organizational fields'. *American Sociological Review*, 48: 147–60.

Dunnette, M. (1966). 'Fads, fashions, and folderol in psychology'. *American Psychologist*, 21: 343–52.

Ettore, B. (1997). 'What's the next business buzzword?' *Management Review*, 86 (8), 33–5.

Gibson, J. and Tesone, D. (2001). 'Management fads: Emergence, evolution, and implications for managers'. *Academy of Management Executive*, 15: 122–33.

Gouldner, A. (1960). 'The norm of reciprocity: A preliminary statement'. *American Sociological Review*, 25, 161–78.

Harrison, D., Newman, D. and Roth, P. (2006). 'How important are job attitudes? Meta-analytic comparisons of integrative behavioural outcomes and time sequences'. *Academy of Management Journal*, 49: 305–25.

Harter, J., Schmidt, F. and Hayes, T. (2002). 'Business-unit-level relationship between employee satisfaction, employee engagement, and business outcomes: A meta-analysis'. *Journal of Applied Psychology*, 87: 268–79.

Herzberg, F. (1966). *Work and the nature of man*. New York: Thomas Y. Crowell Co.

Judge, T., Thoresen, C., Bono, J. and Patton, G. (2001). 'The job satisfaction–job performance relationship: A qualitative and quantitative review'. *Psychological Bulletin*, 127: 376–407.

Kahn, W. (1990). 'Psychological conditions of personal engagement and disengagement at work'. *Academy of Management Journal*, 33: 692–704.

—— (2010). 'The essence of engagement: lessons from the field'. In S. Albrecht (ed.). *The handbook of employee engagement: Perspectives, issues, research and practice*. Cheltenham: Edward Elgar. pp. 20–30.

Macey, W. and Schneider, B. (2008). 'The meaning of engagement'. *Industrial and Organizational Psychology*, 1: 3–30.

MacLeod, D and Clarke, N. (2009). *Engaging for success: Enhancing performance through employee engagement*. London: BIS.

Maslach, C., Schaufeli, W. and Leiter, M. (2001). 'Job burnout'. *Annual Review of Psychology*, 52: 397–422.

Meyer, J., Stanley, D., Herscovitch, L. and Topolnytsky, L. (2001). 'Affective, continuance and normative commitment to the organization: A meta-analysis of antecedents, correlates and consequences'. *Journal of Vocational Behavior*, 61: 20–52.

Michaels, E., Handfield-Jones, H. and Axelrod, B. (2001). *The war for talent*. Boston, MA: Harvard Business School Press.

Newman, D., Joseph, D. and Hulin, C. (2010). 'Job attitudes and employee engagement: considering the attitude "A-factor"'. In S. Albrecht (ed.). *The handbook of employee engagement: Perspectives, issues, research and practice*. Cheltenham: Edward Elgar. pp. 43–61.

Peccei, R. (2013). 'Employee engagement at work: An evidence-based review'. In S. Bach and M. Edwards (eds). *Managing human resources*, 5th edn. Chichester: Wiley. pp. 336–63.

Peters, T. and Waterman, R. (1982). *In search of excellence*. New York: Harper and Row.

Podsakoff, P., Mackenzie, S., Paine, J. and Bachrach, D. (2000). 'Organizational citizenship behaviours: A critical review of the theoretical and empirical literature and suggestions for future research'. *Journal of Management*, 26: 513–63.

Rayton, B., Dodge, T. and D'Analeze, G. (2012). *The evidence: Employee engagement task force 'Nailing the Evidence' Workgroup*. Report.

Rich, B., Lepine, J. and Crawford, E. (2010). 'Job engagement: Antecedents and effects on job performance'. *Academy of Management Journal*, 53: 617–35.

Rousseau, D. and Barends, E. (2011). 'Becoming an evidence-based practitioner'. *Human Resource Management Journal*, 21: 221–35.

Salanova, M., Agut, S. and Peiro, J-M. (2005). 'Linking organizational resources and work engagement to employee performance and customer loyalty: The mediation of service climate'. *Journal of Applied Psychology*, 90: 1217–27.

Schaufeli, W., Bakker, A. and Salanova, M. (2006). 'The measurement of work engagement with a short questionnaire: A cross-national study'. *Educational and Psychological Measurement*, 66: 701–16.

Schaufeli, W., Taris, T. and van Rhenen, W. (2008). 'Workaholism, burnout and engagement: Three of a kind or three different kinds of employee well-being?' *Applied Psychology: An International Review*, 57: 173–203.

Schneider, B., Hanges, P., Smith, B. and Salvaggio, A. (2003). 'Which comes first: Employee attitudes or organizational financial and market performance?' *Journal of Applied Psychology*, 88: 836–51.

Senge, P. (1990). *The fifth discipline*. New York: Doubleday.

Sonnentag, S., Dormann, C. and Demerouti, E. (2010). 'Not all days are created equal: The concept of state work engagement'. In A. Bakker and M. Leiter (eds). *Work engagement: A handbook of essential theory and research*. New York: Psychology Press. pp. 25–38.

Wefald, A. and Downey, R. (2009). 'Job engagement in organizations: fad, fashion or folderol?' *Journal of Organizational Behavior*, 30: 141–5.

13 Employee voice and engagement

John Purcell

Introduction

The four pillars necessary to support employee engagement identified by MacLeod and Clarke (2009) in their comprehensive report include 'employee voice' alongside leadership, engaging managers and integrity. 'Voice' has received the least interest in the three years since the report was launched compared to the significant attention paid to leadership, integrity and managerial behaviour, as reflected in the chapters of this book. The opportunity for employees to have a voice in management decision taking is fundamental in influencing attitudes and behaviour toward the organization that employs them, and in building cooperation with managers and fellow workers.

Part of the reason for this neglect is that employee voice can be challenging for managers and questions their prerogatives for unilateral decision making. As MacLeod and Clarke (2009: 75) put it, voice becomes a building block for engagement when 'employees' views are sought out, they are listened to and see that their opinions count and make a difference. They speak out and challenge when appropriate. A strong sense of listening and of responsiveness permeates the organisation.' Recent evidence from the 2011 Workplace Employment Relations Study (WERS) underlines the connection with engagement. Eighty five per cent of the 21,000 employees surveyed 'who were satisfied with their involvement in decision-making felt proud to work for their organization, compared to 35 per cent who were dissatisfied' (van Wanrooy et al., 2013: 19).

The question this chapter seeks to answer is why there is an assumed causal relationship between voice and engagement. If such a link can be identified, it becomes easier to assert the policy and practice implications.

The promise of employee engagement is that it puts the employee centre stage, but what then follows has to be a careful analysis of the factors that lead employees to be engaged. It is all too easy to jump to conclusions. Following the publication of the MacLeod report (2009), according to Arkin (2011), it appeared that most action focused on the use of 'suggestion schemes, recognition rewards and getting employees to buy into corporate values'. The attempt to get employees to buy into corporate values is especially worrying, since employee engagement is relegated to brand management and 'employees are viewed in a passive role (with) engagement seen as something that be driven by the organization, rather than something that is largely under the control of employees' (Francis and Reddington, 2012: 272). There is little recognition that employee voice is a two-way process where employees have an opportunity to give their views, ask questions and engage in dialogue with managers, including senior managers. Voice is not merely a passive response to managerial blandishments.

For Farndale et al.,

> the root of employee voice lies in influence being shared among individuals who are hierarchically unequal. In essence, voice relates to employees' ability to influence the outcome of organizational decisions by having the opportunity to advance their ideas and have them considered.
>
> (2011: 114)

Voice must therefore be an alternative to managerial unilateralism and can be seen as challenging.

The chapter first considers what engagement really means since there are many definitions and approaches to the subject. It shows how there are strong links and overlaps with earlier studies on organizational commitment. This allows a consideration of the antecedents of engagement looking at fairness, justice and trust. It is necessary to ask, in the third section of the chapter, how engagement has fared in the recession. The fourth section looks at how engagement can be improved through enhancing employee voice, especially in the work of employee representatives interacting with senior managers on strategic and policy issues. The conclusion asks whether government action is required to bolster employee voice via better regulations.

What is engagement?

We need to try to get to a definition of employee engagement, since otherwise we find ourselves in a Tower of Babel conversation where no-one is listening to anyone else. As has been highlighted elsewhere in this volume, it is not easy to find an acceptable definition and some authors refer to the whole field as an 'industry' (Welbourne, 2011), for want of ever finding an accepted definition, or a 'folk theory', another term used to avoid a definition (Macey and Schneider, 2008). One way to do this is to profile the 'engaged employee'. Here is one example, originally developed by Kahn (1990), taken from Rich, Lepine and Crawford (2010: 619, emphasis in the original):

> In engagement, organization members harness their full selves in active, complete work role performances by driving personal energy into physical, cognitive and emotional labours. Engaged individuals are described as being psychologically present, fully *there*, attentive, feeling, connected, integrated, and focussed in their role performances. They are open to themselves and others, connected to work, and focussed in their role performance.

And that is not all. It is not just role performance that matters. As well as having 'feelings of persistence, vigour, energy, absorption, enthusiasm, alertness, and pride' (Macey and Schneider, 2008: 12), the engaged employee will 'demonstrate initiative, proactively seeking opportunities to contribute, and going beyond what is . . . typically required' (ibid.: 15). And just to emphasize the need to be totally focused, Saks (2006: 602) showed that there is clear evidence that 'participation in outside activities [is] a negative predictor [of engagement]'.

Not surprisingly, we find reference to 'depletion theories' (Macey and Schneider, 2008: 13) or the 'dark side' of engagement where employees who try to enact all of their roles are 'experiencing burnout, health problems and disengagement' (Welbourne, 2011: 97). Welbourne identifies five core roles which the engaged employee is expected to contribute to: as a job holder, an innovator, a team member, a person with a career and as an organizational member (ibid.: 91). These are all areas where employees are expected to exercise their discretionary behaviour (Caza, 2012: 153–6). This leads Welbourne (2011: 94) to ask,

> can leaders expect employees to do more of the non-core job roles and still keep doing more of the core job role? . . . And are today's organizations asking employees to be super people who go above and beyond in everything?

Not surprisingly, there are fears that 'engagement can drive work intensification, with employers coming to *expect* employees to "go the extra mile" as a matter of course [with] overtime becoming normalized [and probably unpaid]' (Rees et al., 2013 emphasis in the original).

Under the definition of engagement as exceptional work attitudes, feelings and behaviour – which must mean it is always a minority activity – 'average task performance does not typically define engagement, nor does coming to work on time or doing what the boss expects' (Macey and Schneider, 2008). But as Newman and Harrison (2008: 35) point out in a refreshing paper titled 'Been there, bottled that', good attendance, doing one's job well and being a good citizen 'is precisely what it means to be engaged'. Using a car-driving metaphor, they suggest that to be engaged is to be 'in gear', and, of course, when the engine is not in gear it is 'idling', running slowly and is disconnected.

What evidence of the extent of engagement we have gives some support to this more sensible approach. In an employee survey in the companies belonging to the engagement consortium at Kingston Business School, led by Katie Truss, 43 per cent were nearly always strongly engaged while a third were rarely engaged and never strongly so – the so-called 'flat-liners'. Ten per cent were reliable and consistent while 14 per cent became engaged in episodes when undertaking a particular task (Truss and Soane, 2010). In the Civil Service, the overall level of engagement was 56 per cent in 2010 (Bach and Kessler, 2012: 137). It would seem generally the case that around a third of employees are not engaged, or disengaged, with the remainder showing some attributes of engagement. This will vary according to the job performed. Managers and professional workers are expected to have higher levels of engagement than those in jobs which emphasize routine efficiency, where there are low levels of involvement and little opportunity for discretionary behaviour, often found among front-line service workers in fast food outlets, supermarkets and high-volume call centres (Boxall, Ang and Bartram, 2011: 1527).

Psychologists tend to focus on 'state' engagement, meaning the psychological feelings and emotions of doing the job in terms of involvement, commitment, attachment and mood (Macey and Schneider 2008: 5), but this is not much more than the familiar territory of 'overall job attitude' (Newman and Harrison, 2008: 35). Behavioural engagement is, arguably, of more interest than work-related attitudes (ibid.: 34) since this is where engagement is most obviously related to outcomes. These can be seen in job performance, adaptability, lower levels of sickness absence, less labour turnover as well as broader behaviours coming under the general heading of organizational citizenship behaviour (OCB) or pro-social behaviour and voluntary cooperation. Good examples would be taking part in problem-solving groups, helping new starters and even becoming an employee representative.

A more useful distinction than state and behavioural engagement relates to the objects of engagement: engaged with what and whom? While it is possible to generate quite a long list covering the job, co-workers, customers, the immediate line manager and senior management, it is more helpful to delineate between job engagement and organizational engagement, in a sense between the immediate and the more remote. Measures used to rate job engagement are remarkably similar to those used to assess job satisfaction, job involvement and job challenge. Newman and Harrison (ibid.) describe this as old wine in new bottles.

This does not diminish the validity of job engagement, indeed it adds to it, since these aspects of jobs have been studied exhaustively over half a century or more. It is no surprise to find that, according to Saks (2006: 603), 'job engagement is associated with a sustainable workload, feelings of choice and control, appropriate recognition and reward, a supportive work community, fairness and justice, and meaningful and valued work'. The obvious policy implications, according to Saks, are 'training for line managers and job design interventions' to build in autonomy, challenge and variety. This is correct but it is not enough. There is nothing here promoting voice. Indeed, none of the definitions cited here makes any reference to voice, voice systems or voice outcomes.

The value of organizational engagement is that it recognizes the firm as a social entity, a source of identification beyond the job. This is where the notion of organizational commitment is more helpful than engagement since it is of long standing and has been extensively studied. For a person to show high levels of organizational commitment requires 'a strong belief in and acceptance of an organization's goals and values, a willingness to exert considerable effort on behalf of the organization, and a strong desire to maintain membership in the organization' (Mowday, Steers and Porter, 1979: 226). In particular, the distinction between three forms of commitment is valuable (Meyer and Allen, 1991). Affective commitment concerns the feelings of affection or belonging that a person has towards the organization and the line manager and is positively associated with organization citizenship behaviour. Normative commitment relates to employees, like nurses, who often feel they should be, and are, focused on their job for its social value. Continuance commitment is not really commitment at all in these senses, but refers to people trapped in their organizations since the cost of leaving is too high. They are more likely than others to be disengaged.

Alongside organizational commitment is the idea of the psychological contract: an individual's beliefs about the terms of their relationship with the organization that employs them (Rousseau, 1995). Employees reciprocate the kind of treatment they receive from management as the employment relationship unfolds. This is where perceived organizational support (POS) comes in as part of social exchange theory (Eisenberger et al., 1986). Saks (2006: 613) reports that perceived organizational support was the only significant predictor of both job and organizational engagement, while organizational engagement was a much stronger predictor of all of the outcomes than job engagement. A basic tenet of social exchange theory is that 'relationships evolve over time into trusting, loyal and mutual commitments as long as the parties abide by certain "rules of exchange" and engagement is a two way relationship between the employer and employee' (Saks, 2006: 603). It is not a short-term fix and, as the psychological contract asserts (Rousseau, 1995), it is most often found where people have more open-ended, relational contracts. One logic of this is that people on short-term contracts such as agency staff, and those in closely defined and controlled routine work, are likely to have transactional contracts and less inclined to become engaged.

The antecedents of engagement

Since perceived organizational support, according to Saks (2006), is the only significant predictor of both types of engagement, it becomes much easier to hunt for their antecedents. It is here that we can begin the search for the contribution of voice in generating employee engagement. There is widespread agreement that fairness, justice and perceptions of trust are crucial causal influences both at the level of the job, thus drawing attention to the role of the line manager, and at the organizational level where the spotlight falls on top management.

'Fairness', unlike employee engagement, is a widely recognized and often-used term in everyday working life relating to beliefs of how people should treat each other in social and economic exchanges. Castellano (no date) summarizes the consequences of feelings of fairness:

> When employees feel that they are being treated fairly, they reciprocate through the performance of citizenship behaviours . . . To be fair, procedures should be applied consistently; be free from bias; ensure accurate information is collected; a mechanism exists to correct mistakes; conforms to standards of ethics and morality; and ensure that opinions of groups affected are taken into account . . . Fairness of procedures that determine the amount and distribution of organizational resources are particularly important . . . as well as favourable treatment from supervisors.
>
> (pp. 10–13)

We can recognize this as a statement of good employment relations practice which includes avenues for voice to ensure that opinions of groups affected are taken into account. What is particularly important about voice and fairness is the well-established observation that people will still rate a procedure as fair 'if they had a voice, even if they knew that what they said had little or no influence on the decisions made . . . voice has a value beyond its ability to shape decision-making processes and outcomes' (Tyler and Blader, 2003: 351), a conclusion supported by Farndale et al. (2011) in their research.

The problem with fairness, like engagement, is that it can be a bit too vague. The idea of justice in organizations (Folger and Cropanzano, 1998) has more bite since we are able to distinguish four types of justice: distributive, procedural, interactional and informational. Distributive justice is the perceived fairness of the outcome of a decision, like the distribution of performance related pay. Procedural justice concerns the way in which the decision came to be taken, the information collected, the openness of the process and the extent to which people's views were taken into account. This could be work allocation among team members or the management of redundancy, to give but two examples. Increasingly procedural justice is linked to interactional justice, the interpersonal quality of the interaction between the employee and the immediate manager, or higher level manager, and with fellow team members. Thus, 'procedural justice judgements play a major role in shaping people's reactions to their personal experience . . . in particular about being treated with respect' (Tyler and Blader, 2003: 350).

Increasingly, procedural justice research focuses on pro-social outcomes such as how to build trust, encourage responsibility and obligation, generate intrinsic motivation and creativity and stimulate voluntary cooperation (ibid.: 351). A distinction can be made between the formal quality of the decision-making process, the informal decision making, the formal quality of treatment and the informal treatment. 'People focus heavily on issues of procedural justice of their group because they find procedural justice information to be the most useful identity-related information they have about their groups' (ibid.: 356). 'Group' means both the work team and the wider organization. To be able to identify with something or someone is part of belonging and closely related to affective commitment. Thus it is argued that procedural justice, intertwined with interactional justice, provides identity security (ibid.: 358), a rather obscure term for a good job, in a good work environment run by a good organization. The importance of this is that it can provide a realistic meaning to perceived organizational support. In some quarters perceived organizational support is seen as the employer providing good pay, secure jobs and career opportunities – the classic staple diet of the HR department. Procedural justice points the finger at processes of management, the behaviour of line managers and of senior management, the way they treat people with respect, the transparency of their decision-making processes and their openness to employee views and voice.

The final type of organizational justice is informational. Fuchs and Edwards (2012: 41–2) suggest that 'informational justice perceptions are shaped through accounts and explanations provided by organizational authorities about reasons as to why certain procedures were chosen and why certain outcomes were distributed in a certain way'. This is central to the generation of trust. Informational justice can be especially important in positively influencing employees' attitudes and behaviour in change initiatives (ibid.: 42). It flows through to procedural and interactional justice since 'accounts and explanations' are often provided by middle and lower level managers who will also be involved in taking action at the local level, for example in a corporate restructuring exercise. It is here that the link with voice is clearest. The accounts and explanations of senior managers to change initiatives is strongly linked to perceptions of justice in the way decisions are taken and transmitted and the opportunity employees have to make suggestions, ask for more information and explore the consequences. This may be direct with senior managers in workforce meetings or via employee representatives and, in addition, be transmitted by line managers in team briefing sessions and problem-solving groups.

It is trust which links the four forms of justice, especially where there are more open-ended, or relational, expectations. In an occupational analysis of factors associated with high levels of organizational commitment the Bath University team, using 2004 Workplace Employment Relations Survey data, found that 'trust in management' was the dominant factor for each of the eight major occupations studied (Purcell et al., 2009: 102). No other factor had the same explanatory power. Trust, like engagement, is a risk. It requires hope for the future and expectations of others, especially leaders. In particular Hope-Hailey, Searle and Dietz (2012) conclude from their study of trust that leaders have to have the ability to do the right or best thing; are guided by some principles of benevolence or well-meaning, especially in treating people with respect; have integrity and honesty; and are predicable. Searle et al. (2011: 1072) summarize the evidence on the link between information sharing and trust:

> Information sharing, or open communication, was found to play a pivotal role in building trust between employees and management ... the frequency and openness of communication enhances trust in the system. In line with this, the meta-analysis of Cohen-Carash and Spector (2001) shows that interactional fairness, which includes open communication between managers and employees, positively affects trust in the organization.

This is where we should be worried. It has been suggested by Arkin (2011) that there is 'a growing trust deficit between people at the bottom and the top of organizations', what Saks (2006: 600) calls an 'engagement gap'. The evidence from the UK Civil Service engagement survey in 2010 is not very encouraging. Only just over a third (36 per cent) agreed that 'overall I have confidence in the decisions made by my organization's senior managers' and an even smaller proportion, 27 per cent, felt that 'change is managed well in my organization'. As we have already noted, having a voice, even if the decision is not changed, is strongly linked to perceptions of procedural justice, but in the Civil Service only

32 per cent agreed that 'I have an opportunity to contribute my views before decisions are made that affect me' (Bach and Kessler 2012: 138). This negativity is reflected in the 2011 CIPD Employee Outlook Survey. The survey reports net scores: the proportion of people agreeing with a statement minus those disagreeing. The minus scores, where a majority of respondents disagreed with a statement, were found in relation to questions about trust in directors/senior managers (–4), and having confidence in these top people (–4). There were positives concerning treating employees with respect (+6) and having a clear vision of where the organization is going (+12). But the most negative score came in answer to the statement, 'Senior managers/directors consult employees about important decisions'. Here the net score was –29, by far and away the lowest score in the survey.

Research by Farndale et al. (2011: 123) showed how important trust in senior managers was. Organizational commitment was directly related to perceptions of voice, but was also mediated through line managers and senior managers. While the mediation effect line via managers was relatively weak, the mediation effect of trust in senior managers 'is stronger than the direct relationship . . . almost substituting it'. They conclude that 'employees who believe they have an opportunity to voice their opinions regarding proposed changes to a higher level in the organization and believe that they can influence the decision making, show higher commitment to the organization'. They are much more likely, therefore, to be engaged.

There is one final dimension to engagement which is often neglected. The psychology experts in this field suggest that 'one potential avenue (for research) is whether engagement manifests itself as a property of work groups or teams . . . facilitating the development of a common purpose and cohesiveness?' (Rich, Lepine and Crawford, 2010). Of course it does! You can find references in the literature to 'collective efficacy: people's shared beliefs in their collective power to produce desired results'. This is 'not simply the sum of efficacy beliefs of individual members but as an emergent group-led activity' (Francis and Reddington, 2012: 273). This is collective engagement where people are recognized as social animals with group dynamics and identities. This is why we find reference to 'work climate' or 'organizational culture'. As Chris Rees and colleagues put it, 'trust in senior managers and strong employee-line manager relationships thus constitute key components of the "organizational climate" required for engagement to flourish' (Rees et al., 2013).

Engagement in the recession

There is, as yet, no clear impression of what has happened to employee engagement in the recession. It was reported in 2006 that engagement levels in the USA were on the decline and 'there is a deepening disengagement among employees today' (Saks, 2006: 600), but this was before the financial collapse in 2008. There is some evidence from Ireland, where the recession was, and remains, profound. Bill Roche and his colleagues published a study in 2011 based, in the main, on surveys and focus groups with HR professionals. The results are not very encouraging. 'Specific programmes for engagement', they report, 'were not much in evidence . . . and it had sometimes been necessary to park employee engagement initiatives' (Roche et al., 2011). In terms of management action 'the dominant pattern involved, in the main, one way (top-down) communication, more intensive work regimes, a new concern to manage under-performance and discipline and the suspension of profit sharing or performance bonuses' (ibid.: 121–2), none of which will do much to boost engagement. In terms of best practice identified by the Irish HR managers, by far the most prominent was 'the importance of intensive communications with staff and unions regarding the commercial pressures confronted by firms and the responses deemed appropriate' (ibid.: 119). This would fit with informational justice and it did seem to be a new approach, but it did not appear to include employee voice in a two-way dialogue.

One example of voice in the recession, from a study of consultation (Hall and Purcell, 2012) is an American-owned multi-national which decided to cut staffing levels at its Welsh plant by two-thirds and move work to lower-cost countries. It had a 'hybrid' staff council where unions represented the manual workers and non-union staff representatives spoke for the administrative and professional staff. The council was closely involved in the redundancy and restructuring plan to a remarkable extent over a long period, including direct communication with the workforce in teams or small groups. An employee survey had been conducted before the troubles and was repeated afterwards with those staff that remained on site. The results were startling: 'How good are management here at seeking employees' views?' The proportion giving positive responses went up from 41 to 79 per cent. 'How good are managers here at keeping their promises?' This rose from 37 to 77 per cent. 'How fair are managers?' Positive responses increased from 50 to 76 per cent. Organizational commitment increased from 70 to 90 per cent. One respondent wrote in the survey form:

> The past 14 months has been a huge challenge to the company and its employees. Levels of consultation and communication reached unprecedented levels following the announced closure of two-thirds of manufacturing operations. Workplace consultation has delivered an amazing result considering the scale of job cuts. Levels of quality, productivity, safety and attendance all exceeded the average run-rate for the previous two years.
>
> (Hall and Purcell, 2012: 142)

In this case it was voice via collective consultation procedures – often ignored by some proponents of the engagement agenda – that made a major contribution to boosting levels of employee engagement, even in adverse economic circumstances.

Direct voice systems conducted by front-line managers in team briefing, problem solving groups and informal dialogue are widely used (van Wanroory et al., 2013: 18) and are more highly valued by employees than representative voice systems (Purcell and Geogiades, 2007). They often provide the basis for building employee engagement and commitment (Farndale et al., 2011).

Research at Selfridges in Manchester in 2001 and 2003 (Purcell et al., 2009: 31–6, 67–75) provided evidence of the link with organizational commitment. The employees were interviewed twice about their views on management and the organization. Looking at the results of the first-year survey, senior managers took the view that the results showed the front line managers were not providing staff with enough support and attention, for example they did not meet the employee standards in the company value statement 'I know my opinion and contribution is welcomed'. The employees did not appear to believe that they had much voice and were not listened to. The action that followed included substantial training, some weeding out of poor performing front line managers, and the introduction of a development-based appraisal scheme based around conversations between the line manager and each member of staff.

In the second-year survey, organizational commitment had increased substantially as had people's perceptions of job influence, and their views on management conduct, especially in 'responding to suggestions from employees'. There is nothing particularly remarkable in these case studies. The key in each was the imagination and foresight of some senior managers, and in one case a union leader, to see what was possible and to drive it though in a way that established better voice systems and built on fairness, justice and trust as well as contributing to performance improvements, as it did in both cases. While trade union leaders generally play little part in the national campaign to promote employee engagement, at the local level involvement in partnerships with employers and via consultative committees provides the basis for working on means to enhance engagement by promoting employee voice.

Can levels of engagement be improved?

At the heart of employee engagement are employees' feelings, beliefs and attitudes concerning their job, their co-workers, the customers, their manager, and concerning the organization as a whole and especially the senior management team. We know that if employees believe that the organization and its management, at the local and top levels, provide support to them as a person, a person with feelings and beliefs about fairness and wanting some development, they are likely to respond with cooperative behaviours of benefit to the firm. The key players are line managers, especially front-line managers and the top management. While there are limits to how many employees are likely to be engaged, or 'in gear', given the prevalence of bad jobs, and reluctance by some to devote much energy to their job, the overall level of engagement or commitment could grow. Employee engagement is best seen as an outcome of managerial activity to build perceptions of trust, fairness and organizational justice, especially procedural and interactional or interpersonal justice. These are the antecedents of engagement and are closely related to the employees' perceptions that they have an effective voice, their opinions are sought and they are listened to and their views treated with respect.

The question remains on how trust, fairness and justice are built. Each are essentially processes establishing the quality of the interactions between management and employees. MacLeod and Clarke recognized this and homed in on leadership, engaging managers, employee voice and integrity (2009: 74–116). More emphasis needs to be given to employee voice, without detracting from the other three pillars of engagement. Voice is a multifaceted activity which is most obviously connected to the generation of trust, fairness, and procedural and informational justice. These days, virtually all of the emphasis on employee voice is focussed on direct communication and involvement through team briefing, workforce meetings, problem solving groups and, to a much lesser extent, via employee surveys. Employees get most information from their line manager and well-run briefing group meetings allow for questions, discussion and some dialogue. The good line manager will, in any case, spend time talking informally with their staff, for example in task allocation, problem solving and work issues, especially in coping with change. In order for a sense of procedural justice to flourish employees need to understand the rationale for decisions and why certain actions were necessary, as well as judging how fair they were. Explaining, sharing and justifying takes place through dialogue, or voice.

The advent of social media may change the way employers communicate with staff and open up new opportunities for employees to link with each other and express their views to senior management. As Smith and Harwood (2011: 3) recognize, the full potential for using social media to improve employee voice practices has yet to be realized. They suggest that 'social media tools allow rapid sharing of data across organizational hierarchies and this opening up of organizational data flow is perhaps one of the most fundamental impacts upon organizations'. In particular, they suggest two areas likely to be influenced by social media: the potential for managers to share information and consult employees, and for employees to gain a stronger collective voice. The latter may stem from employees being able to respond rapidly to items discussed in consultative committees, and representatives may equally be able to gain closer relationships with their constituents. Although not identified by Smith and Harwood, it is also possible that consultative committees could become eclipsed by social network forms of direct communication.

Top level voice through employee representatives

There are limits, however, to how far direct communication and involvement can meet the requirement for informational justice. Top managers are out of the loop, and while they may use a wide array of communication methods, including social media, these are in the main top-down forms of communication. They do not give employees a voice. Collective consultation, a form of top level voice between senior managers and employee representatives, is curiously out of fashion, if it ever was in fashion, except during the Second World War. So too, is partnership with trade unions, after a flurry of enthusiasm some ten years ago. In both, the distinctive characteristic is senior managers briefing employee representatives on major plans and strategies, exploring the need for the decision and, especially, working through the consequences and how best to ensure a fair and just implementation.

This is where informational justice can be achieved. Collective consultation crucially requires senior managers to bring big issues to the consultative committee or staff council. Many are reluctant to do so, which goes some way in explaining why trust in senior managers is so low, as revealed by the CIPD survey, noted earlier. Two other key activities are building an effective group of staff representatives able to forge a common purpose, and linking the staff council to the direct communication and involvement practices at shop floor level so that they do not become isolated. When embedded voice practices on the shop floor, led by front-line managers, co-exist with top level consultative committees, run by senior managers, the effect on employee engagement and commitment is greater than each by themselves (Purcell and Georgiades, 2007). There is reasonably compelling evidence that the use of multiple voice channels has the strongest effect in building organizational commitment, and engagement (Purcell and Hall, 2012).

A good definition of voice through consultation, drawn from wider European experience, is 'a right to be informed of planned measures in advance and to have an opportunity to express an opinion prior to implementation' (Budd and Zagelmeyer, 2010: 492). This requires the establishment of a consultative committee where representatives of employees, drawn from recognized trade unions or directly elected by employees, or both, meet with senior managers to discuss planned business and HR changes as well as issues raised by employees. Trade unions have always shown some ambivalence since they prefer collective bargaining and fear that some employers would use consultative committees as substitutes for unions. There are plenty of examples of employers doing just that. Employers, for their part, have often favoured forms of employee involvement, but object to legal enforcement of consultative committees especially where these appear to limit their prerogatives.

The probability of having a consultative body grows with the size of the organization. Only around a quarter of workplaces with 200 or more employees did *not* have a consultative committee either on site or at a higher level. What is particularly interesting is that two-thirds of these consultative committees were non-union and only 11 per cent organized exclusively by the recognized union. Around one in five (22 per cent) had a mixture of union and non-union representatives working alongside each other. These are generally called 'hybrids'

(Hall et al., 2010). The use of hybrid consultative committees is particularly noteworthy. In workplaces where there is a union representative, hybrids now constitute around half of all consultative committees, showing how union and non-union representatives can work together.

Not all consultative committees are the same. While it is common for work organization, future plans and employment issues to be discussed, the crucial difference is how management tables items for discussion, if at all. There is clear evidence that where managers look to the committee to consider policy options, they will judge the committee to be influential. In contrast, where managers have already taken a decision before discussing it at the consultative committee, the scope for influence is considerably less (Kersley et al., 2006).

This was confirmed by Hall et al. (2010) in their longitudinal research in 25 organizations. Two main types of consultative committees were evident. The 'active consulters' were organizations where management took a pro-active approach to consultation and put proposed business decisions, like restructuring, on the agenda. Often this needed special meetings to be called and for information to be given in confidence prior to a public announcement. For there to be a meaningful discussion the employee representatives had to be organized as a coherent body. This was recognized by management which often took steps to encourage training and allow representatives to meet by themselves to work through how to respond to the proposals. In contrast, in other companies management saw the role of the consultative committee to be a communication body. The 'communicators' rarely placed business decisions on the agenda, and where this did happen, it was usually after the event. Most of the topics discussed were raised by employee representatives but these tended to be housekeeping matters, sometimes lapsing into 'tea and toilets' issues. It was rare for there to be an effective body of employee representatives since all they had to do was to attend the meetings a few times a year. While both the 'active consulters' and the 'communicators' used direct communication and involvement methods with the workforce, in the latter's case this tended to 'crowd-out' the consultative committee since it had little opportunity to contribute anything distinctive.

Management is always the dominant partner in consultation since it is they who are setting the key parameters to the agenda. The 'communicators' saw consultation as a means of communication between senior managers and employees. The emphasis was on the creation of harmonious relationships, integration and building engagement. The active consulters had much the same aims but saw these being achieved through employee representatives becoming involved in the management of change and the achievement of consensus, especially over the implementation of decisions.

In 2008 the Information and Consultation of Employees Regulations (ICE for short) came fully into force in the UK for undertakings with 50 or more employees. The intriguing question was whether this would give a substantial boost to the formation of consultative committees and encourage top level employee voice, as it was designed to do. The EU sees the provision of information and the practice of consultation as a 'fundamental right' in the same way as there is a fundamental right not to suffer from discrimination in employment. The way the regulations are drawn up in the UK gives considerable freedom to choose the form and frequency of consultation. The need to take steps to set up a consultative body is only 'triggered' when 10 per cent or more of the employees ask for one. What evidence we have suggests that very few employees have organized themselves to exercise this right (Hall et al., 2012).

There is nothing to stop an employer from setting up a consultative committee without an employee request. There is technical advantage in doing so, from the employer's perspective, as the committee can be established as a so-called 'pre-existing agreement' (PEA), provided a majority of employees in a ballot have backed it or all employee representatives have endorsed it. The advantage of a PEA from an employer's perspective is that the procedures and topics of consultation are not pre-determined and can be designed to suit the organization. Unlike where a committee results from an employee request under the regulations, a PEA does not provide employee representatives with the right to complain to the Central Arbitration Committee (CAC), nor any right to time off or training. Some companies have responded to the regulations by setting up a consultative committee but many have not, and the 'do nothing' option is clearly available in the absence of a request from employees. The 2011 WERS first findings (van Wanrooy et al., 2013) show that there has been no growth in the number of consultative committees since the Regulations came into force. This raises questions on how effective the Regulations are and whether they should be strengthened to promote employee voice.

Conclusion

Employee engagement is worth pursuing, not as an end in itself, but as a means of improving working lives and company performance. The evidence of positive business outcomes is as strong as you can get it, even if it is never conclusive. And employee engagement is a classic win-win initiative since it is associated, when done properly, with better employee well being as well as wealth creation. It puts employees at the heart of the enterprise since it is they who judge their managers for their fairness, trust and acting with justice and who, in return, work better in their job, cooperate in innovation and change, and support the organization which employs them.

For this to be achieved, there have to be effective voice systems in place both at the level of the shop floor and close to the boardroom. If senior managers really want their employees to be engaged they will have to be committed to multiple channels of employee voice which give people a real chance of influencing policy and business decisions. All the considerable evidence from across Europe shows that employers need to be stimulated by legislation to take action to set up top level voice systems such as consultative committees or works councils. Looking across a wide range of countries in their comprehensive study of participation Heller et al. (1998:14) conclude that 'indeed laws and other legally binding rules provide a major explanation for differences in the extent of actual participation across countries'. This is because 'the law legitimises participation . . . and gives employees clout to insist that participation takes place' (ibid.: 214).

The ICE Regulations in the UK are weak and do not give the same level of rights to employee representatives as found in European Works Councils or in collective redundancy consultation. The Secretary of State, Vince Cable, admitted as much when he told the House of Commons that 'this potentially powerful mechanism for employees has been underutilized to date'.[1] If the government is serious in wishing to promote employee engagement it could stimulate employee voice by strengthening the regulations. Hall and Purcell (2012: 172–8) suggest how this could best be done.

Note

1 See http://www.publications.parliament.uk/pa/cm201212/cmhansrd/cm120123/debtext/120123-0
001.htm#12012313000594.

References

Arkin, A. (2011) 'In engagement working?' *People Management*, 1 November 2011.

Bach, S. and Kessler, I. (2012) *The modernisation of the public services and employee relations*. Basingstoke: Palgrave Macmillan.

Boxall, P. and Purcell, J. (2011) *Strategy and human resource management*, 3rd edn. Basingstoke: Palgrave Macmillan.

——, Ang, S. and Bartram, T. (2011) 'Analysing the "Black Box" of HRM: Uncovering HR goals, mediators and outcomes in a standardized service environment'. *Journal of Management Studies* 48(7): 1504–32.

Budd, J. and Zagelmeyer, S. (2010) 'Public policy and employee participation' in A. Wilkinson, P. Golan, M. Marchington and D. Lewin (eds) *The Oxford handbook of participation in organizations*. Oxford: Oxford University Press, pp. 476–503.

Castellano, W. (no date) *A new framework of employee engagement*. Centre for Human Resource Strategy, Rutgers, the State University of New Jersey.

Caza, A. (2012) 'Typology of eight domains of discretion in organizations'. *Journal of Management Studies* 49(1) 144–77.

CIPD (2011) *Employee outlook 2011*. London: CIPD.

Cohen-Carash, Y. and Spector, P. (2011) 'The role of justice in organizations: A meta-analysis'. *Organizational Behaviour and Human Decision Processes* 86: 278–321.

DTI (2007) 'Workplace representatives: A review of their facilities and facility time'. Consultative Document, January. London: Department of Trade and Industry.

Eisenberger, R., Huntington, R., Hutchinson, S. and Sowa, D. (1986) 'Perceived organizational support'. *Journal of Applied Psychology* 79: 617–26.

Farndale, E., Van Ruiten, J., Kelliher, C. and Hope-Hailey, V. (2011) 'The influence of perceived employee voice on organizational commitment: an exchange perspective'. *Human Resource Management* 50(1): 113–29.

Folger, R. and Cropanzano, R. (1998) *Organizational justice and human resource management*. Thousand Oaks, CA: Sage.

Francis, H. and Reddington, M. (2012) 'Employer branding and organizational effectivness' in H. Francis, L. Holbeche and M Reddington (eds) *People and organizational development: A new agenda for organizational effectiveness*. London: CIPD, pp. 260–85.

Fuchs, S. and Edwards, M. (2012) 'Predicting pro-change behaviour: the role of perceived organizational justice and organizational identification'. *Human Resource Management Journal* 22(1): 39–59.

Hall, M., Hutchinson, S., Purcell, J., Terry, M. and Parker, J. (2010) *Information and consultation under the ICE regulations: Evidence from longitudinal case studies*. Employment Relations Research Series No 117 London: Department of Business, Innovation and Skills, at http://www.bis.gov.uk/assets/biscore/employment-matters/docs/i/10-1380-information-consultation-ice-regulations.

—— and Purcell, J. (2012) *Consultation at work: Regulation and practice*. Oxford: Oxford University Press.

Heller, F., Pusic, E., Strauss, G. and Wilpert, B. (1998) *Organization participation: Myth and reality*. Oxford: Oxford University Press.

Hope-Hailey, V., Searle, R. and Dietz, G. (2012) 'Organizational effectiveness: How trust helps' *People Management* 30–5.

Kahn, W. (1990) 'Psychological conditions of personal engagement and disengagement at work'. *Academy of Management Journal*, 33: 692–724.

Kersley B., Alpin, C., Forth, J., Bryson, A., Bewley, H., Dix, G. and Oxenbridge, S. (2006) *Inside the workplace: Findings from the 2004 Workplace Employment Relations Survey*. London: Routledge.

Macey, W. and Schneider, B. (2008) 'The meaning of employee engagement'. *Industrial and Organizational Psychology* 1: 3–30.

MacLeod, D. and Clarke, N. (2009) *Engaging for success: Enhancing performance through employee engagement*. A report to Government. London: Department for Business, Innovation and Skills.

Marginson, P. and Meardi, G. (2010) 'Multinational companies: transforming national industrial relations' in T. Colling and M. Terry (eds) *Industrial relations: Theory and practice*, 3rd edn. Chichester: Wiley pp. 207–31.

Meyer, J. P. and Allen, N. J. (1991). 'A three-component conceptualization of organizational commitment: Some methodological considerations'. *Human Resource Management Review*, 1: 61–98.

Mowday, R., Steers, R. and Porter, L. (1979) 'The measurement of organizational commitment'. *Journal of Vocational Behaviour*, 14(2): 224–47.

Newman, D. and Harrison, D. (2008) 'Been there, bottled that: Are state and behavioural work engagement new and useful construct "wines"'. *Industrial and Organizational Psychology* 1: 31–6.

Purcell, J. and Geogiades, K. (2007) 'Why should employees bother with worker voice?' in R. Freeman, P. Boxall and P. Hayes (eds) *What workers say: Employee voice in the Anglo-American workplace*. Ithaca, NY: ILR press, 181–97.

——, Kinnie, N., Swart, J., Rayton, B. and Hutchinson, S. (2009) *People Management and Performance*. London: Routledge.

—— and Hall, M. (2012) *Voice and participation in the modern workplace: Challenges and prospects*. Acas Future of Workplace Relations discussion paper series, London: Acas.

Rees, C., Alfes, K. and Gatenby, M. (2013) 'Employee voice and engagement: connections and consequences'. *International Journal of Human Resource Management* 24(14): 2780–98.

Rich, B., Lepine, J. and Crawford, E. (2010) 'Job engagement: antecedents and effects on job performance', *Academy of Management Journal* 53(2): 617–35.

Roche, W., Teague, P., Coughlan, A. and Fahy, M. (2011) *Human resources in the recession: Managing and representing people at work in Ireland*. Dublin: The Stationery Office.

Rousseau, D. (1995) *Psychological contracts in organizations*. Thousand Oaks, CA: Sage.

Saks, A. (2006) 'Antecedents and consequences of engagement'. *Journal of Managerial Psychology*, 21(7): 600–19.

Searle, R., Den Hartog, D., Weibel, A., Gillespie, N., Six, F., Hatzakis, T. and Skinner, D. (2011) 'Trust in the employer: the role of high-involvement work practices and procedural justice in European organizations'. *International Journal of Human Resource Management* 22(5): 1069–92.

Smith, S. and Harwood, P. (2011) *Social media and its impact on employers and trade unions*. Employment Relations Comment, London: Acas.

Truss, K. and Soane, E. (2010) 'Engaging the "pole vaulters" on your staff'. *Harvard Business Review* March, p. 24.

Tyler, T. and Blader, S. (2003) 'The group engagement model: procedural justice, social identity, and cooperative behaviour'. *Personality and Social Psychology Review* 7(4): 349–61.

van Wanrooy, B., Bewley, H., Bryson, A., Freeth, S., Stokes, L. and Wood, S. (2013) *The 2011 workplace employment relations study first findings*. London: Department for Business, Innovation and Skills.

Welbourne, T. (2011) 'Engaged in what? So what? A role-based perspective for the future of employee engagement' in A. Wilkinson and K. Townsend (eds) *The future of employment relations: New paradigms, new developments*. Basingstoke: Palgrave Macmillan.

Part 4

Employee engagement in practice

14 Relevance of employee engagement across cultures from the perspective of HR professional associations

Amanda Shantz, Jordan Schoenberg and Christopher Chan

Introduction

Most research on work engagement has been conducted in either North America or Western Europe. This is not surprising given that the two mainstay theoretical models were developed by William Kahn (1990) in the United States (see Chapter 4) and William Schaufeli and Arnold Bakker (2006) (see Chapters 1 and 7, respectively) from Europe. There is little research that examines whether engagement is considered a relevant construct in other parts of the world (cf. Bakker et al., 2011; Shimazu et al., 2008; Wajid et al., 2011).

Examining the extent to which work engagement is relevant in different national contexts is important for at least two reasons. First, contextualization is a necessary, albeit often ignored step in the development of theory (Rousseau and Fried, 2001), whereby 'context' is broadly defined as a set of factors surrounding a phenomenon that exerts some direct or indirect influence on it (Whetten, 2009). Context-effects such as national culture are central to understanding organizational phenomena and hence cross-cultural analysis is increasingly becoming a distinctive feature of organizational scholarship (Rousseau and Fried, 2001; Whetten, 2009). Second, understanding whether engagement has found relevance in different national contexts provides practical knowledge for human resource professionals who work in multi-national organizations, as discussed in Chapter 10 of this volume. In multi-national organizations, employees bring to the workplace diverse cultural backgrounds and varied skill sets derived from an eclectic array of personal histories. It is therefore difficult for employers to achieve high levels of engagement with a standardized approach to the treatment of a workforce. Human resource professionals thus stand to benefit from progress in the cross-cultural understanding of engagement.

The purpose of this chapter is to examine the extent to which engagement has entered the lexicon of human resource management professionals in different national and cultural contexts. To do so, we examined the websites of personnel management associations – institutions that are responsible for propagating standards of best practice in the management of human resources. Like previous research that has analyzed websites as the basis of understanding cultural differences (e.g. Cho and Cheon, 2005; Taylor, 2006; Tong and Robertson, 2008; Zhang, Sakaguchi, and Kennedy, 2007), personnel management websites were content analyzed for reference to employee engagement in order to determine the extent of its relevance.

We analyzed the data by contrasting the countries under study by their respective levels of human, social, and cultural capital (Parboteeah, Cullen, and Lim, 2004). Human capital captures a country's level of material wealth, mean educational level, and economic stability. Social capital refers to the extent to which a country's members are socially integrated, and is associated with Hofstede's (2001) cultural dimension of individualism/collectivism, that is, the extent to which a culture emphasizes individuality versus interdependence. Cultural capital indicates cultural characteristics that may predispose a country to embrace engagement and is operationalized in the present study by a country's religiosity, and Hofstede's (2001) measures of power distance and uncertainty avoidance. Power distance refers to the extent to which members of a culture expect and accept that power is distributed unequally, and uncertainty avoidance is concerned with the level of acceptance for uncertainty and ambiguity within a society. Although these three forms of capital are often examined at the individual level, we adopt Parboteeah et al.'s (2004) approach and examine human, social, and cultural capital at the national level.

This chapter is organized as follows. First, we explain the role of the personnel management association and discuss its value in conveying information regarding the relevance of employee engagement and issues in human resource management. Second, we present our methodology, followed by the findings. Third, we conclude and make suggestions for the future of cross-cultural research in employee engagement.

The personnel management association

The role of a professional association is to 'enable the formation and reproduction of shared meanings and understandings' (Farndale and Brewster, 2005: 36). As such, a professional association strives to establish a distinct body of knowledge and to derive a set of core competencies to which members of a profession adhere. The human resource management function has been shown to qualify as a profession by Farndale and Brewster (2005) who found that:

> The picture emerging of HRM professionalism across the globe is one of a field in which there is an active sense of community identity; where guidelines and training on specialist activities and codes of ethics are readily available, and where there is a common body of knowledge from which the field is drawing.
>
> (p. 46)

Education and training provisions within the human resource management function are numerous and wide-ranging; examined courses are offered as part of certification programs. There is ample evidence to suggest that personal management associations are disseminating a common body of knowledge from which the human resource management profession is drawing.

It is the job of the personnel management association to have its proverbial 'finger' on the 'pulse' of the private, public, and third sectors. Its prospect for sustainability as an organization is dependent on its ability to produce relevant research that is of concern to human resource managers. The personnel management association thus focuses its energies on relevant issues in human resource management that promote effectiveness and sustainability in the workplace. As such, the national personnel management association offers a unique perspective into the relevance of engagement and its meaning across cultures.

Personnel management associations are found across the globe. In our search, we found at least 120 in countries from all major continents (see Table 14.1). They varied as to their purpose, membership numbers, and depth of services provided to members. The purpose of the present study was to examine whether there were systematic differences in the extent to which 'engagement' featured on the websites. We do so by leveraging Parboteeah et al.'s (2004) framework for examining cross-national differences. They suggested that nations can

Table 14.1 Personnel management associations

Organization name	Acronym	Location	Number of members	Website
Human Resources Professional Association	HRPA	Canada	19000	http://www.hrpa.ca/Pages/Default.aspx
National Human Resources Association	NHRA	USA		http://www.humanresources.org/website/c/
College and University Professional Association for Human Resources	CUPAHR	USA	*1800	http://www.cupahr.org/
Professionals in Human Resources Association	PIHRA	USA	3500	http://www.pihra.org/
National Association of African Americans in Human Resources	NAAAHR	USA	1100	http://www.naaahr.org/Home.html
American Council on International Personnel	ACIP	USA	*200	http://www.acip.com/
Canadian Society for Training and Development	CSTD	Canada	12500	http://www.cstd.ca/
Asociacion Mexicana en Direccion De Recursos Humanos	AMEDIRH	Mexico	7000	http://www.amedirh.com.mx/
South Africa Board for People Practices	SABPP	South Africa		http://www.sabpp.co.za/
Human Resource Council of South Africa	HRCOSA	South Africa		http://www.workinfo.com/free/downloads/hrcosa.htm
Foundation for Human Resources Development	FHRD	Malta		http://www.fhrd.org/
Chartered Institute for Personnel and Development	CIPD	UK	135000	http://www.cipd.co.uk/
Albanian Human Resource Society	AHRS	Albania		http://www.albaniahr.org/index.php
China Human Resource and Training Association	CHRATA	China	*350	http://chrata.jobschina.org/
National Human Resources Development Network	NHRDN	India	12500	http://www.nationalhrd.org/
Pakistani Society of Human Resource Management	PSHRM	Pakistan		http://pshrm.webs.com/
Singapore Human Rights Institute	SHRI	Singapore	3000	http://www.shri.org.sg/
Council of Hong Kong Professional Associations	COPA	China		http://www.copa.hk/
Japan Human Resource Society	JHRS	Japan		http://www.jhrs.org/
People Management Association of the Philippines	PMAP	Philippines	*1800	http://www.pmap.org.ph/
Bangladesh Institute of Human Resource Management	BIHRM	Bangladesh		http://www.bihrm.org/bihrm/
Arabian Society for Human Resource Management	ASHRM	Saudi Arabia		http://www.ashrm.com/visitor.php
Institute of Personnel Management Sri Lanka	IPMSL	Sri Lanka		http://www.ipmlk.org/
Australian Human Resources Institute	AHRI	Australia	20000	http://www.ahri.com.au/
Hong Kong Institute of Human Resource Management	HKIHRM	China	4600	http://www.hkihrm.org/ihrm_eng/index.asp
Society for Human Resource Management	SHRM	Global	250000	http://www.shrm.org/
International Association for Human Resource Information Management	IHRIM	Global	2000	http://www.ihrim.org/

(continued)

Table 14.1 Personnel management associations *(continued)*

Organization name	Acronym	Location	Number of members	Website
International Public Management Association for Human Resources	IPMAHR	Global	1000+	http://www.ipma-hr.org/
World Federation of People Management Associations	WFPMA	Global	450000	http://www.wfpma.com/
Asia Pacific Federation of Human Resource Management	APFHRM	Global	**15	http://www.apfhrm.com/index.php
European Association for People Management	EAPM	Global	**31	http://www.eapm.org/
African Federation of Human Resource Management Associations	AFHRMA	Global	**16	http://www.wfpma.com/members/region/afhrma
International Federation of Training & Development Organizations	IFTDO	Global	500000	http://www.iftdo.net/default.asp
Organization of Human Resource Development	OHRD	Afghanistan		http://www.ohrd-net.org/
Human Resource Professionals of Antigua and Barbuda	HRPAB	Antigua and Barbuda		http://www.facebook.com/pages/Human-Resource-Professionals-of-Antigua-and-Barbuda/185175518169971?v=info
Human Resources Club Armenia	HR Club Armenia	Armenia		http://hrclub.am/
Bahamas Human Resources Development Association	BHRDA	Bahamas		http://bhrda.shrm.org/
Bangladesh Society for Human Resources Management	BSHRMBD	Bangladesh		http://www.bshrmbd.org/
Human Resources Management Association of Barbados	HRMAB	Barbados		http://hrmab.org.bb/
Institute of Human Resources Management of Botswana	IHRM Botswana	Botswana	245	http://www.ihrmbotswana.com/
Bulgarian Human Resources Management and Development Association	BHRMDA	Bulgaria		http://www.bhrmda.bg/
Cyprus Human Resource Management Association	CyHRMA	Cyprus		http://www.cyhrma.org/
Austrian Center for Productivity and Efficiency	OPWZ	Austria	400	http://www.opwz.com/
Personnel Managers Club Belgium	PM Club	Belgium		http://www.pmclub.be/
People Management Forum	PMF	Czech Republic	*300	http://www.peoplemanagementforum.cz/
Association of Human Resource Managers in Denmark	PID	Denmark	940	http://www.pid.dk/
Association of Personnel Development in Estonia	PARE	Estonia	300	http://www.pare.ee/eng
Finnish Association for Human Resource Management	HENRY	Finland	2800	http://www.henryorg.fi/page?pageId=1
Association Nationale des Directeurs des Ressources Humaines	ANDRH	France	5000	http://www.andrh.fr/
German Association for Personnel Management	DGFP	Germany	2000	http://www.dgfp.de/
Greek Personnel Management Association	GPMA	Greece	650	http://www.gpma.gr/
Hungarian Association for Human Resources Management	OHE	Hungary	*279	http://www.ohe.hu/

Name	Abbreviation	Country	Members	URL
Associazione Italiana Direzione Personale	AIDP	Italy	3000	http://www.aidp.it/
Latvian Association of Personnel Management	LAPM	Latvia	269	http://www.lpva.lv/
Macedonian Human Resources Association	MHRA	Macedonia	100	http://www.mhra.mk/
Nederlandse Vereniging voor Personeelsmanagement & Organisatieontwikkeling	NVP	Netherlands	5000	http://www.nvp-plaza.nl/site/nl/
Human Resources Norge	HR Norge	Norway	2850	http://www.hrmorge.no/
Polish Human Resources Management Association	PHRMA	Poland	2000	http://www.pszk.pl/
Portuguese Association of Human Resource Managers	APG	Portugal	1500	http://www.apg.pt/
Human Resources Club Romania	HR Club Romania	Romania	350	http://www.hr-club.ro/ro/
National Personnel Managers Union	NPMU	Russia	5000	http://www.kadrovik.ru/
Organization Association of HR Professionals	HR-Asocijacija	Serbia	120	http://www.hr-asocijacija.org.rs/
Slovak Association for Human Resources Management	ZRRLZ	Slovakia	108	http://www.zrrlz.sk
Slovenian Human Resource Association	SHRA	Slovenia	1000	http://www.skz.si
Asociacion Espanola De Direccion y Desarrollo De Personas	AEDIPE	Spain	4000	http://www.aedipe.es/
Swedish Association of Human Resources Management	HR Sveriges HR Forening	Sweden	5600	http://www.sverigeshrforening.se/
Human Resources Swiss	HR Swiss	Switzerland	4000	http://www.hr-swiss.ch/
Türkiye Personel Yönetimi Derneği	PERYON	Turkey	3000	http://www.peryon.org.tr
National Institute for Personnel Management	NIPM	India	11000	http://nipm.in/
Indonesian Society for People Management	PMSM	Indonesia		http://www.hrcentro.com/vendor_sdm/pmsm_indonesia
Malaysian Institute of Human Resource Management	MIHRM	Malaysia	4000	http://www.mihrm.com/
Human Resources Institute of New Zealand	HRINZ	New Zealand	2000	http://www.hrinz.org.nz/
Chinese Human Resources Management Association	CHRMA	Taiwan		http://www.chrma.net/
Personnel Management Association of Thailand	PMAT	Thailand		http://www.pmat.or.th/
Society of Human Resource Management & Productivity	SHRM&P	Cambodia		http://www.shrmp.com.kh/home/
Society for Human Resource Management Ethiopia	SHRME	Ethiopia		
Rwandan Human Resources Management Association	RHRMA	Rwanda		
Institute of Human Resource Management Kenya	IHRM Kenya	Kenya		http://www.ihrm.or.ke/alpha/
Institute of Personnel Management Namibia	IPM Namibia	Namibia		http://www.ipmnamibia.org/
Chartered Institute of Personnel Management of Nigeria	CIPM Nigeria	Nigeria		http://www.cipmnigeria.org/
Human Resource Managers' Association of Uganda	HRMAU	Uganda		http://www.hrmau.org
Zambia Institute of Human Resource Management	ZIHRM	Zambia		http://zihrm.org/
Japan Society for Human Resource Management	JSHRM	Japan		http://www.jshrm.org/

(continued)

Table 14.1 Personnel management associations (continued)

Organization name	Acronym	Location	Number of members	Website
Institute of People Management South Africa	IPM South Africa	South Africa		http://www.ipm.co.za/
Institute of People Management Swaziland	IPM Swaziland	Swaziland		
Institute of People Management Zimbabwe	IPMZ	Zimbabwe	6592	http://www.ipmz.org.zw/
Human Resources Association of Tanzania	HRAT	Tanzania		
Asociacion De Recursos Humanos De la Argentina	ADRHA	Argentina	9138	http://www.adrha.org.ar/
Circulo Ejecutivos Recursos Humanos	CERH	Chile	150	http://www.cerhchile.cl/
Asociacion Paraguaya De Recursos Humanos	APARH	Paraguay	168	http://www.aparh.org.py/
Asociacion Peruana De Recursos Humanos	APERHU	Peru	265	http://www.aperhu.com/
Asociacion Venezolana De Gestion Humana	AVGH	Venezuela	350	http://www.anri.org.ve/
Asociacion De Gestion Humana	ACRIP	Columbia	735	http://www.acripnacional.org/
Asociacion De Gestion Humana Del Ecuador	ADGHE	Ecuador	580	http://www.adghe.com/
Asociacion Bolviana De Gestion Humana	ASOBOGH	Bolivia	100	http://www.asobogh.com.bo/
Asociacion Nacional De Profesionales De Recursos Humanos De Panama	ANREH	Panama	290	http://www.arhpanama.org/html/
Asociacion Costarricense De Gestores De Recursos Humanos	ACGRH	Costa Rica	355	http://www.acgrh.net/
Asociacion De Ejecutivos De Recursos Humanos De Nicaragua	AERHNIC	Nicaragua	250	http://www.aerhnic.org/
Asociacion De Gerentes De Recursos Humanos	AGRH	Guatemala	187	http://www.agrhgt.org
Canadian Council of Human Resources Associations	CCHRA	Canada		http://www.cchra.ca/en/
Federacion Interamericana De Asociaciones de Gestion Humanas	FIDAGH	Global	**15	http://www.fidagh.org/
North American Human Resource Management Association	NAHRMA	Global	*9	http://www.nahrma.org/
Egyptian Human Resource Management Association	EHRMA	Egypt	230	http://www.ehrma.net/
Fiji Human Resources Institute	FHRI	Fiji		http://fhri.org.fj/
Ghana Employers Association	GEA	Ghana		http://www.ghanaemployers.com/geanew/index.php
Papua New Guinea Human Resources Institute	PNGHRI	Papua New Guinea	500	http://www.pnghri.org.pg
Israeli Society for Human Resources Management	ISHRM	Israel		http://www.ishrm.org.il/
Human Resources Management Association of Jamaica	HRMAJ	Jamaica	300	http://www.hrmaj.org/

Organization	Abbreviation	Country	Number	URL
Jordanian Human Resources Management Association	JHRMA	Jordan		http://jhr-ma.com/inside.php?src=cons&consId=1
Korea Management Association	KMA	South Korea		http://www.kma.or.kr/
Personalo Valdymo Profesionalu Asociacija	PVPA	Lithuania		http://www.pvpa.lt/?language=EN
Malta Employers Association	MEA	Malta		http://www.maltaemployers.com/Default.aspx?tabid=1149
Mongolian Human Resources Institute	MHRI	Mongolia	500	http://www.mhri.mn/index.php?module=menu&cmd=content&id=1670&menu_id=426
Moroccan Association of HR Professionals	AGEF	Morocco		
Oman Human Resources Association	OHRA	Oman		
National Human Resources Development Council	NHRDC	Seychelles		http://www.nhrdc.sc/
Human Resources Management Association of Trinidad & Tobago	HRMATT	Trinidad and Tobago	700	http://www.hrmatt.com/1content/en/index.aspx
Asociacion Dominicana De Administradores De la Gestion Humana	ADOARH	Dominican Republic		http://www.adoarh.com.do/
Asociacion De Profesionales Uruguayos en Gestion Humana	ADPUGH	Uruguay		http://www.adpu.org/
Brazilian Association of Human Resources	ABRH	Brasil	6336	http://www.abrhnacional.org.br/

be examined in relation to their human, social, and cultural capitals. Before presenting exploratory hypotheses along with the results regarding whether employee engagement relevance is a function of a nation's human, social, and cultural capital, we turn to the methodology employed in this study.

Methodology

The websites of 11 national personnel management associations were chosen for content analysis so as to be inclusive of varying levels of human, social, and cultural capital. We ensured our sample was diverse in terms of geographic representation; our sample includes national personnel management associations from North America, Europe, Africa, and Asia (see Table 14.2). Our estimates for human capital were informed by macroeconomic data provided by the World Bank (see Table 14.3). Estimates on the social and cultural capital spectra were derived from Hofstede's country-specific measures of individualism, power distance, and uncertainty avoidance (http://geert-hofstede.com/countries.html).

Although Hofstede's work on culture is the most widely cited cultural typography (Bond, 2002), his observations and analyses have not escaped criticism. Criticisms tend to be leveled at five issues: (1) surveys are not suitable for measuring cultural differences; (2) nations are

Table 14.2 National personnel management associations under study

AHRI	Australian Human Resources Institute	Australia
ANDRH	Association Nationale des Directeurs des Ressources Humaines	France
CIPD	Chartered Institute of Personnel and Development	UK
DGFP	Deutsche Gesellschaft für Personalführung	Germany
HKIHRM	Hong Kong Institute of Human Resource Management	Hong Kong (China)
HR Sveriges	Centrum för Personal and Utveckling	Sweden
HRPA	Human Resources Professionals Association	Canada
IPM South Africa	Institute of Personnel Management – South Africa	South Africa
JHRS	The Japan HR Society	Japan
PMPAP	People Management Association of the Philippines	Philippines
SHRM	Society for Human Resource Management	USA

Table 14.3 Human capital levels by country

Country	GDP per capita (PPP)	GDP rank	Education index	Education rank	Weighted mean rank	Human capital ranking
Australia	39721	5	.993	1	3.6	4
USA	48112	2	.978	3	2.35	1
UK	35657	7	.957	6	6.65	7
Canada	40370	4	.991	2	3.3	2
France	35246	8	.968	5	6.95	8
Germany	39491	6	.954	7	6.35	6
Sweden	41467	3	.974	4	3.35	3
South Africa	10960	10	Not ranked	11	10.35	11
Hong Kong	50551	1	.879	10	4.15	5
Japan	34314	9	.949	8	8.65	9
Philippines	4119	11	.888	9	10.3	10

Sources: World Bank (2011), UN Development Index

not the best units for studying culture; (3) Hofstede's original study used data from the subsidiaries of one company, namely, IBM, and is therefore unable to account for differences across national cultures; (4) the original IBM data that was used as the basis of Hofstede's work is old, and therefore obsolete; (5) there are insufficient cultural dimensions in the classic four or five typology (e.g. McSweeney, 2002).

Hofstede (2002) countered these arguments in stating that: (1) surveys should not be the sole manner to collect data; (2) nations are usually the only units of analysis available for comparison, and hence are better than nothing; (3) there have been a number of additional studies that confirm the cultural dimensions, conducted by other scholars and at different time periods; (4) only data that remained stable across two subsequent surveys were used in the analyses of the IBM data and third-party replications demonstrate validity; (5) additional dimensions have already been defined, and if others argue that more dimensions are necessary to more fully understand culture, Hofstede (2002) stated that 'candidates are welcome to apply' (p. 1356). Although not all of Hofstede's work stands up to scrutiny, the majority of his findings have been replicated and hence the dimensions are useful for guiding multi-national practitioners in understanding cultural differences (see also Chapter 9).

We used the program NVivo© to perform the content analysis. Each website was searched for reference to the word 'engagement'. Once such a reference was identified, the web page on which engagement appeared was captured and imported into NVivo©. An iterative data collection process in NVivo© was used to aggregate the following personnel management association-specific measures:

- Absolute frequency of references to engagement
- Absolute frequency of pages referencing engagement
- Relative frequency of references to engagement

'Absolute frequency of references to engagement' conveys an overall assessment of relevance; 'absolute frequency of pages referencing engagement' is a more specific assessment of relevance, as a performance management association with X 'number of pages' conveys a higher level of relevance than a personnel management association with (X-1) 'number of pages'; 'relative frequency of references to engagement' is the ratio of the number of time 'engagement' is mentioned on the website, divided by the total number of words on the website.

Finally, we used NVivo© to produce graphical representations of our findings. For each national personnel management association website, we used NVivo© to generate a 'tag cloud' and a 'tree map'. A 'tag cloud' is a graphical representation of frequency of word reference, where words that are mentioned more frequently are shown in larger font, and words that are mentioned less frequently are shown in smaller font. A 'tree map' is also graphical representation of frequency of word reference, where words that are mentioned more frequently generate 'boxes' with larger areas and words that are mentioned less frequently generate 'boxes' with smaller areas. The frequencies with which 'engagement' is mentioned on each of the websites under study are found in Table 14.4.

Human capital

Human capital refers to 'the knowledge, skills, competencies and attributes embodied in individuals that facilitate the creation of personal, social and economic well-being'

Table 14.4 Frequency of mentions of engagement on websites

Country	Absolute mentions	Ranking	Absolute pages	Ranking	Relative mentions
Australia	14	5	6	4	.34%
France	6	8	5	7	0%
UK	106	1	10	2	1.65%
Germany	1	10	1	10	0%
Hong Kong	20	3	8	3	.52%
Sweden	13	7	6	4	0%
Canada	N/A	N/A	N/A	N/A	N/A
South Africa	13	6	6	4	.25%
Japan	15	4	3	8	0%
Philippines	3	9	2	9	0%
USA	102	2	15	1	.67%

(OECD, 2001: 18). Countries with high levels of human capital have high levels of material wealth, education, and they are economically stable.

Table 14.4 shows that the personnel management associations in the UK and the USA included the most absolute mentions to engagement, and the most absolute web pages that featured engagement. With a GDP of $15.09T, the United States generates the most economic wealth in the world. With a GDP of $2.43T, the United Kingdom is ranked seventh globally in terms of gross economic wealth. With such high levels of material wealth, it is no surprise that both countries are ranked among the most well-educated in the world, with the United States ranking fourth and the United Kingdom ranking seventh according to a recent ranking published by the Wall Street Journal (Sauter and Hess, 2012). Both the United States and the United Kingdom have highly developed, diverse economies that operate within relatively stable economic conditions. Despite natural fluctuations in unemployment rates (to which all countries are systematically exposed), the labor markets in the United States and the United Kingdom are historically stable due to sound infrastructure and high levels of education.

Such economic conditions may give rise to well-established human resource management functions, and ultimately to engagement construct relevance. In countries with high levels of economic wealth, the government, along with private and public sector firms, subsidize research in personnel management and invest time and money into the human resource management function. This, among other reasons, may induce growth in professional associations related to these fields. In fact, the largest national personnel management association in terms of membership is Society for Human Resource Management (SHRM) in the United States, with over 180,000 private and institutional members. In the United Kingdom, the Chartered Institute of Personnel and Development (CIPD) has over 120,000 members. The CIPD owes its status as the second-largest personnel management association in terms of membership to the British government and its role in including personnel management in policy discussion. The 1960s saw an 'increasing desire for the institute to become more influential in government policy and to make a greater contribution to national debates' in personnel management (Farndale and Brewster, 2005: 37). The institute ultimately gained chartered status – or official government recognition of practical competence – in 2000.

With sustained levels of membership and concurrent revenue streams, these national personnel management associations have the capacity to focus on a wide array of issues in human resource management, one of which is employee engagement. On the website of SHRM, engagement was referenced 102 times on a total of 15 pages. On the website of CIPD, engagement was referenced 106 times on a total of 10 pages. References to engagement appeared in a variety of contexts, including in press releases, journal publications, advertisements for consulting services, and within 'issues' or 'research' web pages. On the website of CIPD, the word engagement accounted for 1.65 per cent of all words on web pages – further evidence of the UK's commitment to engagement as not only relevant in absolute terms, but also comparatively relevant.

Although countries with lower levels of human capital referenced engagement, it appeared less frequently. On the website of PMAP (the Philippines), engagement was referenced, but only three times and on only two web pages. With a GDP of $.22T and a significantly lower quality-of-life index value than in the United States or United Kingdom (6.403 versus 7.615 and 6.917, respectively), the Philippines and its human resources management function are less concerned with the engagement of the Filipino workforce, and more invested in issues such as wage management and labor regulation (Bitonio Jr., 2008). The same can be said for South Africa and its Institute of People Management (IPM). In a country whose economy is in its infancy, HR practitioners are primarily concerned with other concepts such as leadership. Here, establishing a versatile labor market imbued with basic tenets of morality (e.g. care, honesty, gratitude, fairness, humility, trust, and respect) appears to take precedence over instituting initiatives to generate high levels of employee engagement (Lambourne, 2010).

Lower levels of engagement relevance in countries with lower levels of human capital may be attributed to the lack of comparative importance of engagement within the context of economic instability and a less-developed labor market. According to the International Labor Organization, the labor market in the Philippines has failed to meet expectations, as the labor force grows at a faster rate than the economy is able to create jobs. Out of a total workforce of 56.8 million, 10.1 million are underemployed and only 17.7 million are working within a formal employment relationship (Bitonio Jr., 2008). More fundamental issues within the Filipino labor market may take precedence over the engagement construct; it would seem more important for the human resources management function in the Philippines to address a systematic lack of supply in the labor market than to ensure that those currently working are engaged (World Bank, 2010). While relevant, engagement within the context of economic instability is not at the forefront of the human resource management function.

Social capital

Social capital refers to 'the sum of the actual and potential resources embedded within, available through and derived from the network of relationships possessed by an individual or social unit' (Nahapiet and Ghoshal, 1998: 243). Beilmann and Realo (2012), Durkheim (1969), and Realo and Allik (2009) have found that social capital tends to be higher in more individualistic than collectivistic countries. Herein, we refer to a country's level of social capital by its corresponding level of individualism. Table 14.5 orders the nations under study in terms of their levels of individualism.

Individualism refers to the degree of interdependence a society maintains among its members. It is a direct measure of the extent to which members of a given society define themselves in terms of 'I' or 'we'. In highly individualistic societies (e.g. Australia, UK, US), individuals are interested in achieving their personal goals and that of their immediate family members. In highly collectivist societies (e.g. Hong Kong, Japan,

Table 14.5 Country level measure of individualism

Country	Individualism
Australia	High
UK	High
Canada	High
USA	High
France	Medium
Germany	Medium
Sweden	Medium
South Africa	Medium
Hong Kong	Low
Japan	Low
Philippines	Low

Philippines), individuals consider themselves 'group' members, exchanging collective concern for loyalty (Hofstede, 2001).

There is a clear association between high levels of individualism and higher frequency of reference to engagement. The most individualistic cultures (in order) are the United States, Australia and the UK (ranked 1, 5, and 2 respectively in absolute mentions of engagement). The least individualistic cultures (in order) are Hong Kong, the Philippines, and Japan (ranked 3, 9, and 4 respectively in absolute mentions of engagement). Despite the lack of a clear linear relationship between Hofstede's measure of individualism and absolute reference to engagement, countries that are more individualistic tend to reference engagement more often than countries that are collectivist in nature.

Interestingly, within industrial relations discourse the terms individualism and collectivism are often treated as interchangeable with unitarist and pluralist approaches, respectively (Storey and Bacon, 2006). That work engagement is embraced to a greater extent in individualistic countries is congruent with the assertion that work engagement has been approached from a unitarist standpoint. Like many other human resource management concepts and theories, there is an implicit assumption in the engagement literature that it is possible and desirable to align the interests of employers with employees (e.g. Pfeffer, 1998; Ulrich and Broadbank, 2005). Recently, scholars have questioned the unitarist underpinning of work engagement, suggesting that employers and employees have a plurality of interests that do not necessarily coincide (e.g. Jenkins and Delbridge, 2013; see Chapters 11, 12, and 13 of this book).

Cultural capital

Cultural capital refers to non-financial resources that foster non-economic phenomena. In the context of engagement, cultural capital refers to levels of cultural dimensions that indicate the propensity of a country's human resource management function to value engagement. The cultural dimensions that were chosen in the present study to indicate cultural capital include religiosity, and Hofstede's measures of power distance and uncertainty avoidance.

Religiosity signifies the importance of religion. Table 14.6 presents the responses to a question posed by Gallup: 'Is religion important in your daily life?' The total proportion of 'yes' answers is used to measure national religiosity. According to the survey results, the most religious country among those studied is the Philippines, and the least religious country is Sweden. The United States is relatively religious with 65 per cent of survey respondents

Table 14.6 Country level measure of religiosity

Country	Gallup measure of religiosity
Philippines	High
South Africa	High
USA	Medium-High
Canada	Medium
Germany	Medium
Australia	Medium
France	Low
UK	Low
Hong Kong	Low
Japan	Low
Sweden	Low

claiming that religion is an important part of their everyday lives. Only 27 per cent of survey respondents in the United Kingdom answered similarly.

We did not find a systematic relationship between religiosity and frequency of reference to engagement. With similar levels of engagement construct relevance, the United States and the United Kingdom exhibit vastly different levels of religiosity (65 per cent and 27 per cent, respectively). Moreover, countries with similarly low levels of engagement construct relevance also exhibit vastly different levels of religiosity; see France at 30 per cent, Philippines at 96 per cent). Our findings are, however, consistent with the tendency of the poorest countries to express higher levels of religiosity than those countries with high levels of economic wealth. According to Gallup, the most religious countries surveyed are relatively poor, with a GDP per capita measure of < $5000. Some theories posit that religion plays a more functional role in poorer countries, where religion is necessary to cope with the daily rigors of poverty (Crabtree, 2010). For the poorest, most religious countries (e.g. South Africa, Philippines), reference to engagement is comparatively low. Yet it is likely that this pattern is not due to religiosity, but to the more fundamental condition of poverty and consequent low level of social capital. The pattern of results may also be explained by the nature of religions, whereby some are more communitarian than others.

Hofstede's measure of power distance expresses the attitude of a culture toward inequality. It is defined as the extent to which less powerful members of an organization expect and accept unequal distribution of power (Hofstede, 2001). We therefore might expect a country with a low measure of power distance to have a keen interest in employee engagement – employees in such a country are frequently dissatisfied, demand justification for unequal distribution of power and strive to equalize it (Hofstede, 2001). Table 14.7 presents the order of power distance in the countries under study. In the United States, organizations tend to be 'flatter' whereby managers exert less control over employees; in hierarchical structures managers tend to rely on their employees for their expertise. Employees in countries characterized by high power distance tend to expect centralization, and desire leaders who provide direction (Hofstede, 2001).

We find that high levels of engagement construct relevance are positively associated with low levels of power distance. In cultures where power inequality is considered unacceptable, we find high levels of reference to *engagement* within their national personnel management associations (e.g. UK, US versus Philippines, Hong Kong, and France). This finding can be attributed to the perceived infallibility of supervisors in cultures with high levels of power distance. Brockner et al. (2002) argued that in cultures with high levels of power distance,

Table 14.7 Country level measure of power distance

Country	Power distance
Philippines	High
France	Medium-High
Hong Kong	Medium-High
Japan	Medium
South Africa	Medium
Canada	Low
UK	Low
Germany	Low
Sweden	Low
USA	Low
Australia	Very Low

the decisions of high-ranking supervisors are granted immediate legitimacy by employees, whereas the decisions of lower-ranking employees are automatically discounted. Carl et al. (2004) noted that the power of those in high-ranking positions is unquestionable in countries with high levels of power distance; employees in such countries are obliged to be respectful of their superiors' status and concurrent authority. Employees do not analyze the decisions of their supervisors in such cultures; in fact, the supervisor–employee relationship can almost be characterized as one of dependence of the latter on the former, both for direction and guidance.

The perceived infallibility of supervisors in countries with high levels of power distance may devalue the importance of an engaged workforce, thereby explaining the disparity between reference to engagement in the United Kingdom and the United States versus the Philippines, Hong Kong, and France. If employees accept the authority of their supervisors, then the extent to which they are engaged is of peripheral concern. These employees are obliged to follow the direction of their supervisors; their productivity is more dependent on their ability to follow direction as opposed to the extent to which they invest their personal selves in their work-roles. On the contrary, employees in the United States and United Kingdom are depended upon for input and are predisposed to question the decisions of their supervisors. In countries with low levels of power distance, productivity is not so much a function of an employee's ability to follow direction, but rather of an employee's creativity and ability to generate novel ideas. In these countries, engagement construct relevance is high, as engaged employees have been shown to be more creative, and ultimately more productive.

Engagement construct relevance is similarly influenced by Hofstede's uncertainty avoidance dimension, which measures the degree to which a society is uncomfortable with uncertainty and ambiguity (Hofstede, 2001). Countries with high levels of uncertainty avoidance maintain rigid codes of belief and tend to feel uncomfortable when confronted with unorthodox behavior and new ideas. Countries with low levels of uncertainty avoidance embrace uncertainty and feel comfortable generating and implementing new ideas (Hofstede, 2001). Table 14.8 presents the rank order of the countries under study in relation to uncertainty avoidance.

Despite the lack of a clear linear relationship between uncertainty avoidance and reference to engagement, it seems that relatively low levels of uncertainty avoidance are necessary to observe high levels of engagement construct relevance. Low levels of uncertainty avoidance are associated with an 'acceptance of new ideas, innovative products and a willingness to try

Table 14.8 Country level measure of uncertainty avoidance

Country	Uncertainty avoidance
Japan	High
France	High
Germany	Medium-High
Australia	Medium
South Africa	Medium
Canada	Medium
USA	Medium
Philippines	Medium
UK	Low
Hong Kong	Low
Sweden	Low

Table 14.9 Consolidation of tables 14.5–14.8

Country	Individualism	Power distance	Uncertainty avoidance	Religiosity
Japan	Low	Medium	High	Low
France	Medium	Medium-High	High	Low
Germany	Medium	Low	Medium-High	Medium
Australia	High	Very Low	Medium	Medium
South Africa	Medium	Medium	Medium	High
Canada	High	Low	Medium	Medium
USA	High	Low	Medium	Medium-High
Philippines	Low	High	Medium	High
UK	High	Low	Low	Low
Hong Kong	Low	Medium-High	Low	Low
Sweden	Medium	Low	Low	Low

something new or different' (Hofstede, 2001). Because a primary benefit of an engaged workforce is enhanced creative ability (Bakker and Xanthpolouou, 2013), it would seem that for engagement to be relevant within a country's human resource management function, the country must embrace uncertainty. Our findings are consistent with this notion, as the four personnel management association websites with the most absolute references to *engagement* are low on the uncertainty continuum.

Discussion

Total frequency of references to engagement on the websites of national personnel management associations is a crude indicator of engagement construct relevance. Regardless, our findings attest to the cross-cultural relevance of engagement, and suggest that its relevance and ultimately its meaning vary across cultural dimensions.

Cross-cultural theory was not a focus of organizational behaviour research until the 1980s, when the introduction of cultural typographies accelerated the contemporary examination of cross-cultural differences in work-related behavior (e.g., Hofstede, 1990; House et al., 2004; Trompennaars, 1993). These categorizations are used to both understand differences in work-related behavior across cultures, and also to question the hegemony of theoretical models developed in the West. A growing body of cross-cultural research in human resource management confirms that work-related employee attitudes and behavior vary across cultures. We believe that employee engagement is no exception.

Further cross-cultural research in employee engagement is needed if we are to fully realize its value to the human resource management function. Our analysis suggests that engagement is a relevant construct in the West, however it is of less importance in other national contexts. Future research should focus on establishing a theoretical framework that helps explain divergence in the way engagement is understood across cultures. In today's increasingly multicultural and globalizing workplace, it is imperative for executives, especially HR executives, to be cognizant of how to elicit a productive work environment through effective employee engagement. Furthermore, an appreciation of how the various cultural forces may affect engagement could lead to a better understanding of the dynamics between employees, managers, and leaders in the organization. Given that various cross-cultural researchers have questioned the universalities of various management practices (Budhwar and Debrah, 2009; Chiang and Birtch, 2007; Tung and Verbeke, 2010), any HR policies and practices to engage workers need to be carefully implemented. These uncertainties point to the need for executives to be culturally aware and sensitive. Thus, it is necessary for them to participate in cross-cultural and sensitivity training.

Understanding the interaction of discrete cultural factors and the contextual meaning of employee engagement will ultimately allow human resources professionals to customize the employer–employee relationship, which has been shown to increase organizational efficiency. For example, in Australia, workplace initiatives such as effective change management, employee involvement, learning and development, role clarity, and teamwork have been shown to increase employee engagement (Parkes and Langford, 2008). In a UK study by Alfes, Shantz, Truss and Soane (2013), positive working conditions, experiences of HRM practices, perceived organizational support, and quality of interactions with line managers were essential to promoting employee engagement. Studies done in North America have found that employees are likely to be engaged when they find their workplace climate to be positive and when they can derive meaning from their work (Fairlie, 2011; Kernaghan, 2011). Gillet, Huart, Colombat and Fouquereau (2012) have found that self-motivation (or the desire to participate in activities for the sole purpose of seeking pleasure) acts through perceived organizational support (including support from trainers) to encourage engagement among the French police. In Germany and Sweden, research has found that it is necessary to provide social support in organizations and autonomy in order to increase engagement (Taipale, Selander, Anttila and Nätti, 2011; Vincent-Höper, Muser, and Janneck, 2012). Providing job relevant resources to challenging job demands (De Braine and Roodt, 2011) and organizational support to promote work–family balance (Mostert and Rathbone, 2007) were found to encourage greater employee engagement in South Africa. Fong and Ng (2012) have argued that Hong Kong employees are more engaged when holistic care is provided to help them to reduce their stress level and burnout. While organizations should pay attention to group harmony and employee support when it comes to Japanese employees (Inoue et al., 2010), others have cautioned the over-reliance of survey data in Japan given the tendency to moderate their responses (Mastrangelo, 2013; also see Chapter 9 in this book).

Meanwhile, in the Philippines, strategies for engaging employees could include the use of performance management systems and provision of competitive employee benefits (Resurreccion, 2012). While employee engagement appears to be enacted via the organization's work climate, cultural forces may determine the priorities that employers should emphasize in order to engage workers in various cultural configurations. Future research should determine whether the abovementioned findings are culturally bound, or generalize to other national contexts.

In the 2010 study of electronics giant Best Buy, Smith and Cantrell found that individual customization within the context of a diverse workforce increased engagement levels and ultimately, financial efficiency. Because each employee had 'different abilities, work styles and preferences, as well as different motivations for working', managers at Best Buy realized that there could be no single way of treating all employees that would yield similarly high levels of employee engagement (Smith and Cantrell, 2010: 2). As such, they fostered an individualized approach whereby employees were permitted to define their own best practices according to their varying strengths and skill sets. Smith and Cantrell found that this individualized approach 'doubled the rate of increase in employee engagement', with each .10 increase in engagement (on a scale of 5.0) resulting in an estimated +$100,000 profit per store, per annum. In sum, defining engagement cross culturally will allow human resource professionals at multi-national organizations to more effectively customize their approach to the employer–employee relationship, thereby increasing levels of employee engagement and ultimately, economic efficiency. The results of Smith and Cantrell (2010) attest to the benefit human resource professionals stand to gain from progress in the study of cross-cultural employee engagement.

Whetten (2009) advocates for the inclusion of context-sensitive organizational theory in context-sensitive organizational research. An established cross-contextual theory in engagement would generate innovative insight into organizational phenomena in different contexts, ultimately enhancing the overall comprehensiveness and efficacy of theory in engagement. Ultimately, we echo the sentiments of Steers and Sanchez-Runde (2002: 214) by calling for a 'significant increase in rigorous, comprehensive and theory-based studies' that further our understanding of engagement across cultures.

Further progress in the study of engagement can be achieved by inclusion of both emic and etic research approaches. In an operational context, *emic* refers to the 'presence of an actual or potential interactive context' between a researcher and an informant who inhabits a particular cultural context (Harris, 1976). *Etic*, on the other hand, refers to the 'non-essential status' of the researcher–informant interaction (Harris, 1976). Emic approaches yield data concerning meanings unique to particular cultures, whereas etic approaches yield data concerning cross-cultural generalizability. Brett et al. (1997) argued that cultural differentiation in organizational phenomena may be so great as to require the use of multiple research concepts to address the same research question. As the prevalence of the engagement construct has been shown to vary across cultures, the use of both emic and etic concepts would be appropriate here. Evidence suggests that there is a dearth of comparative research making use of this multi-conceptual approach. Rousseau and Fried (2001, 22) point out that 'comparative research in either etic or emic form is still relatively infrequent in organizational research, particularly in studies focused on the experiences of workers rather than firms'.

In conclusion, the findings herein have discrete, practical implications for management scholars and human resource management practitioners. We have shown the relevance of the employee engagement construct, and believe that its inclusion in the GLOBE project, which is a large-scale international research study focusing on societal and organizational culture, would help to foster a maximally productive and efficient workforce – a workforce that is ultimately, engaged.

References

Alfes, K., Shantz, A. D., Truss, C., and Soane, E. C. 2013. The link between perceived human resource management practices, engagement and employee behavior: A moderated mediation model. *International Journal of Human Resource Management*, 24(2), 330–51.

Bakker, A. B., Shimazu, A., Demerouti, E., Shimada, K., and Kawakami, N. 2011. Crossover of work engagement among Japanese couples: Perspective taking by both partners. *Journal of Occupational Health Psychology*, 16(1), 112–25.

—— and Xanthpolouou D. (2013). Creativity and charisma among female leaders: The role of resources and work engagement. *International Journal of Human Resource Management*.

Beilman, M. and Realo, A. 2012. Individualism – collectivism and social capital at the individual level. *Trames*, 16(3), 205–17.

Bitonio Jr., B. E. R. 2008. *Labour market governance in the Philippines: Issues and institutions* [pdf], available at http://www.ilo.org/wcmsp5/groups/public/---asia/---ro-bangkok/---ilo-manila/documents/publication/wcms_123202.pdf [accessed 28 January 2013].

Bond, M. H. 2002. Reclaiming the individual from Hofstede's ecological analysis – A 20-year odyssey: Comment on Oyserman et al. *Psychological Bulletin*, 128(1), 73–7.

Brett, J., Tinsley, C., Janssens, M., Barsness, Z., and Lytle, A. L. 1997. New approaches to the study of culture in industrial/organizational psychology. *New Perspectives on International Industrial/ Organizational Psychology*, 75–129.

——, Tinsley, C. H., Janssens, M., Barsness, Z. I., and Lytle, A. L. 1997. *New approaches to the study of culture in industrial/organizational psychology*. In P. C. Earley and M. Erez (eds), New perspectives on international industrial/organizational psychology. San Francisco, CA: New Lexington Press, pp. 75–129.

Brockner, J., Ackerman, G., Greenberg, J., Gelfand, M. J., Francesco, A. M., Chen, Z. X., Leung, K., Bierbrauer, G., Gomez, C., Kirkman, B. L., and Shapiro, D. 2001. Cultural and procedural justice: The influence of power distance on reactions to voice. *Journal of Experimental Social Psychology*, 37(4), 300–15.

Budhwar, P. and Debrah, Y. A. 2009. Future research on human resource management systems in Asia. *Asia Pacific Journal of Management*, 26, 197–218.

Carl, D., Gupta, V., and Javidan, M. 2004. Power distance in cross-cultural leadership, in R. J. House, P. J. Hanges, M. Javidan, P. W. Dorfman, and V. Gupta (eds) *Culture, leadership, and organizations: The global leadership and organizational effectiveness (GLOBE) study of 62 societies*. Thousand Oaks: Sage Publications, pp. 513–63.

Chiang, F. F. T. and Birtch, T. 2007. The tranquility of management practices: Examining cross-national differences in reward preferences. *Human Relations*, 60(9), 1293–330.

Cho, C. H. and Cheon, H. J. 2005. Interactivity on Japanese versus American corporate websites. *Journal of International Consumer Marketing*, 17(4), 41–63.

Crabtree, S. 2010. Religiosity highest in world's poorest nations. *Gallup World*, [online] 31 August 2010, available at http://www.gallup.com/poll/142727/religiosity-highest-world-poorest-nations.aspx [accessed 28 January 2013].

De Braine, R. and Roodt, G. 2011. The job demands–resources model as predictor of work identity and work engagement: A comparative analysis. *SA Journal of Industrial Psychology*, 37(2), 1–11.

Durkheim, E. 1969. *The division of labor in society*. New York: The Free Press.

Fairlie, P. 2011. Meaningful work, employee engagement, and other key employee outcomes: Implications for human resource development. *Advances in Developing Human Resources*, 13(4), 508–25.

Farndale, E. and Brewster, C. 2005. In search of legitimacy: Personnel management associations worldwide. *Human Resource Management Journal*, 15(3), 33–48.

Fong, T. C. T. and Ng, S. M. 2012. Measuring engagement at work: Validation of the Chinese version of the Utrecht work engagement scale. *International Journal of Behavioral Medicine*, 19(3), 391–7.

Gillet, N., Huart, I., Colombat, P., and Fouquereau, E. 2012. Perceived organizational support, motivation and engagement among police officers. *Professional Psychology: Research and Practice*, no pagination specified.

Harris, M. 1976. History and significance of the emic/etic distinction. *Annual Review of Anthropology*, 5, 329–50.

Hofstede, G. 2002. Dimensions do not exist: A reply to Brendan McSweeny. *Human Relations*, 55(11), 1355–61.

—— 2001. Culture's consequences: Comparing values, behaviors, institutions and organizations across nations (2nd edn). Thousand Oaks, CA: Sage.

—— 1990. *Cultures and organizations: Software of the mind.* New York: McGraw-Hill.

House, R. J., Hanges, P. J., Javidan, M., Dorfman, P. W., and Gupta, V. 2004. *Culture, leadership, and organizations: The GLOBE study of 62 societies.* Thousand Oaks, CA: Sage Publications.

Inoue, A., Kawakami, N., Ishizaki, M., Shimazu, A., Tsuchiya, M., Tabata, M., Akiyama, M., Kitazume, A., and Kuroda, M. 2010. Organizational justice, psychological distress and work engagement in Japanese workers. *International Archives of Occupational and Environmental Health*, 83(1), 29–38.

Kahn, W. A. 1990. Psychological conditions of personal engagement and disengagement at work. *Academy of Management Journal*, 33(4), 692–724.

Kernaghan, K. 2011. Getting engaged: Public-service merit and motivation revisited. *Canadian Public Administration*, 54(1), 1–21.

Jenkins, S. and Delbridge, R. in press. Context matters: Examining 'Soft' and 'Hard' approaches to employee engagement in two workplaces. *International Journal of Human Resource Management.*

Lambourne, W. 2010. *Leadership: Living the care and growth values* [pdf], available at http://www.schuitema.co.za/articles/Living%20the%20Care%20and%20Growth%20Values.pdf [accessed 28 January 2013].

Mastrangelo, P. M. 2013. Will employee engagement be hijacked or reengineered? In J. Vogelsang, M. Townsend, M. Minahan, D. Jamieson, J. Vogel, A. Viets, C. Royal, and L. Valek (eds). 2012. *Handbook for strategic HR: Best practices in organizational development from the OD network.* New York: American Management Association, pp. 368–74.

McSweeney, B. 2002. Hofstede's model of national cultural differences and their consequences: A triumph of faith – a failure of analysis. *Human Relations*, 55, 89–118.

Mostert, K. and Rathbone, A. D. 2007. Work characteristics, work–home interaction and engagement of employees. *Management Dynamics*, 16(2), 36–52.

Nahapiet, J. and Ghoshal, S. 1998. Social capital, intellectual capital, and the organizational advantage. *Academy of Management Review*, 23(2), 242–66.

OECD 2001. *The well-being of nations: The role of human and social capital.* OECD Publications, Paris.

Parboteeah, K. P., Cullen, J. B., and Lim, L. 2004. Formal volunteering: A cross-national test. *Journal of World Business*, 39, 431–41.

Parkes, L. P. and Langford, P. H. 2008. Work–life balance or work–life alignment? A test of the importance of work–life balance for employee engagement and intention to stay in organizations. *Journal of Management & Organization*, 14, 267–84.

Pfeffer, J. 1998. *The human equation: Building profits by putting people first.* Boston, MA: Harvard Business School Press.

Realo, A. and Allik, J. 2009. On the relationship between social capital and individualism–collectivism. *Social and Personality Psychology Compass*, 3(6), 871–86.

Resurreccion, P. F. 2012. Performance management and compensation as drivers of organization competitiveness: The Philippine perspective. *International Journal of Business and Social Science*, 3(21), 20–30.

Rousseau, D. M. and Fried, Y. 2001. Location, location, location: Contextualizing organizational research. *Journal of Organizational Behavior*, 22, 1–13.

Schaufeli, W. B. and Bakker, A. B. 2006. The measurement of work engagement with a short questionnaire, a cross-national study. *Educational & Psychological Measurement*, 66(4), 701–16.

Shantz, A., Alfes, A., Truss, C., and Soane, E. 2013. The role of employee engagement in the relationship between job design and task performance, citizenship and deviant behaviours. *The International Journal of Human Resource Management.*

Shimazu, A., Schaufeli, W. B., Kosugi, S., Suzuki, A., Nashiwa, H., Kato, A., Sakamoto, M., Irimajiri, H., Amano, S., Hirohata, K., and Goto, R. 2008. Work engagement in Japan: Validation of the Japanese version of the Utrecht work engagement scale. *Applied Psychology: An International Review*, 57(3), 510–23.

Smith, D. and Cantrell, S. 2010. A workforce of one. *Accenture Outlook* [pdf], available at http://www.accenture.com/us-en/outlook/Pages/outlook-journal-2010-workforce-of-one.aspx [accessed 28 January 2013].

Steers, R. M. and Sanchez-Runde, C. J. 2002. Culture, motivation, and work behavior. In M. J. Gannon and K. L. Newman (eds), *The Blackwell Handbook of Cross-Cultural Management*, Oxford: Blackwell, pp. 190–216.

Storey, J. and Bacon, N. 1993. Individualism and collectivism: Into the 1990s. *International Journal of Human Resource Management*, 4(3), 665–84.

Taipale, S., Selander, K., Anttila, T., and Natti, J. 2011. The role of job demands, autonomy, and social support. *International Journal of Sociology and Social Policy*, 31(7/8), 486–504.

Taylor, J. 2006. Statutory bodies and performance reporting: Hong Kong and Singapore experience. *Public Organization Review*, 6(3), 289–304.

Tong, A. M. C. and Robertson, K. 2008. Political and cultural representation in Malaysian websites. *International Journal of Design*, Special Issue, 2(2), 67–79.

Trompenaars, F. 1993. Riding the waves of culture: Understanding cultural diversity in business. New York: McGraw-Hill.

Tung, R. L. and Verbeke, A. 2010. Beyond Hofstede and GLOBE: Improving the quality of cross cultural research. *Journal of International Business Studies*, 41(8), 1259–74.

Ulrich, D. and Broadbank, W. 2005. *The HR value proposition*. Boston, MA: Harvard Business School Press.

United Nations Development Programme 2008. *Human development report 2007/08: Fighting climate change, human solidarity in a divided world*, available at http://hdr.undp.org/en/reports/global/hdr2007-8/ [accessed 27 February 2013].

Vincent-Hoper, S., Muser, C., and Janneck, M. 2012. Transformational leadership, work engagement and occupational success. *Career Development International*, 17(7), 663–82.

Wajid, R. A., Zaidi, N. R., Zaidi, M. T. and Zaidi, F. B. 2011. Relationship between demographic characteristics and work engagement among public sector university teachers of Lahore. *Interdisciplinary Journal of Contemporary Research in Business*, 3(6), 110–22.

Whetten, D. A. 2009. An examination of the interface between context and theory applied to the study of Chinese organizations. *Management and Organization Review*, 5(1), 29–55.

World Bank 2010. *Philippines skills report: Skills for the labor market in the Philippines*. Report No. 50096-PH.

—— 2011. *World databank: World development indicators – GDP (PPP) Per Capita*, available at http://databank.worldbank.org/ddp/home.do?Step=12&id=4&CNO=2 [accessed 27 February 2013].

Zhang, X., Sakaguchi, T., and Kennedy, M. 2007. A cross-cultural analysis of privacy notices of the global 2000. *Journal of Information Privacy & Security*, 3(2), 18–36.

15 Measuring and understanding employee engagement

Luke Fletcher and Dilys Robinson

Introduction

Employee engagement has generated interest among a range of stakeholder groups including academics (e.g. Kahn, 1990; May et al., 2004; Schaufeli et al., 2002), HR practitioners (e.g. Harter et al., 2002), consultancies (e.g. Masson et al., 2008), and government policy-makers (e.g. MacLeod and Clarke 2009). As this interest in employee engagement has rapidly increased over the last decade (as highlighted by Wilmar Schaufeli in Chapter 1 of this volume), so has the desire to measure, evaluate, and benchmark levels of engagement within and between organizations.

Measurement is powerful, because 'what gets measured gets attention' (Eccles, 1991: 131). Performance dashboards, of which the 'balanced scorecard' (Kaplan, Norton, 1992) is a well-known example, attempt to ensure that all the major factors contributing to an organization's success are being measured – related to operations, customers, finance and employees. A performance indicator that represents the extent to which employees are engaged can constitute a useful headline measure for the 'employee' section of the dashboard or scorecard. However, there has been a lack of a unifying definition or framework (MacLeod, Clarke, 2009; Truss, Mankin and Kelliher, 2012) and so there exists a wide range of 'employee engagement' indicators.

Therefore, this chapter aims to (a) provide a review of the main ways in which employee engagement has been measured; (b) give insight into issues that may occur when designing and implementing such measures; and (c) consider implications in regards to presenting and interpreting engagement scores. Whilst covering academic material, this chapter is designed with the practitioner in mind. Two short case studies illustrating how employee engagement can be measured and evaluated in practice are discussed at the end of this chapter.

Overview and review of employee engagement measures

As discussed in the first chapter of this volume, a useful organizing framework when examining the wide range of literature on employee engagement is that of Shuck's (2011) systematic review. He identified four main approaches to defining engagement, which can also be utilized when exploring measures of engagement: (a) The Burnout-Antithesis Approach; (b) The Needs-Satisfying Approach; (c) The Satisfaction-Engagement Approach; and (d) The Multidimensional Approach. As each of the approaches and the seminal contributions to each are discussed in various chapters in this volume, particularly Chapter 1, the focus here is in relation to the operationalization and measurement of engagement.

Note that all measures detailed in this chapter can be found via the corresponding full reference given in the bibliography at the end of the chapter.

Measures from the burnout-antithesis approach

Measures developed from the Burnout-Antithesis Approach draw directly from the established literature on burnout – a negative psychological syndrome that comprises emotional exhaustion, cynicism and reduced professional self-efficacy (Maslach, Schaufeli and Leiter, 2001). Engagement was initially theorized as being the polar opposite construct of burnout and was measured by reverse scoring burnout questionnaire scales (Maslach and Goldberg, 1998). However, as research progressed, some scholars argued that the antithesis of burnout could not simply be examined in this way – engagement was in fact a distinct (positive psychological) construct that should be defined and measured separately. The main contribution from this approach has been from Schaufeli and Bakker's (2003) work engagement construct (Utrecht Work Engagement Scale – UWES) and from Shirom's (2004) Vigor construct (Shirom-Melamed Vigor Measure – SMVM).

The UWES (Schaufeli and Bakker, 2003) is currently the most widely used and validated measure. It has been used with 60,000+ individuals across the world (Schaufeli and Bakker, 2010). It comes in the form of a 17-item questionnaire scale and a shortened 9-item version. Respondents are asked to rate the frequency (on a seven-point scale from 'never' to 'always/every day') with which they have experienced a number of feelings/thoughts over the last year, and are categorized as feelings of Vigor (e.g. *'At my work, I feel that I am bursting with energy'*), Dedication (e.g. *'I am enthusiastic about my job'*), and Absorption (e.g. *'I am immersed in my work'*). It has been used in a variety of contexts and has been found to predict both individual-level performance-related and wellbeing-related outcomes (Halbesleben, 2010).

The SMVM (Shirom, 2004) examines 'vigor': a specific 'positive affective response to one's ongoing interactions with significant elements in one's job and work environment' (p. 12). Although vigor is a core dimension of the UWES, the SMVM explores its content more broadly and argues that it is distinct from Schaufeli et al.'s (2002) construct of work engagement. Shirom (2004) developed and tested a three-factor vigor construct that included physical strength (e.g. *'I have experienced a feeling of vitality'*), emotional energy (e.g. *'I feel I am capable of investing emotionally in co-workers and customers'*), and cognitive liveliness (e.g. *'I feel mentally alert'*). Respondents are asked to rate the frequency (on a seven-point scale from 'almost never' to 'almost always') with which they had experienced each of those feelings over the previous 30 workdays. The resulting 14-item questionnaire was initially validated using a sample of 87 employees in two hi-tech companies in Israel. The SMVM has since been mainly used in health research (mostly in Israel) and has been found to predict various health and obesity indicators (e.g. Shirom et al., 2012).

The measures from the burnout-antithesis approach seem to focus on activated forms of energy, which are highlighted by the kinds of adjectives used, e.g. bursting, vitality, inspiring, resilient, alertness. Both the UWES and the SMVM adopt a frequency response format, i.e. 'how often do you feel this way?' This is most likely because both are linked with burnout, which is typically measured via instruments utilizing frequency formats. This frequency approach reflects the way in which outcomes of burnout, such as mental health conditions, are assessed based on occurrences of a feeling/behaviour within a given timescale. It would, therefore, make logical sense to measure an antecedent, such as burnout, in a similar way. However, when compared with other engagement measures this frequency format is in direct contrast with all the other approaches which use an 'extent of agreement' format, i.e. the strength of feeling. This difference is highlighted later in this chapter.

Measures from the needs-satisfying approach

Measures developed from the needs-satisfying approach draw directly from the theoretical propositions and empirical findings of Kahn's (1990, 1992) work on 'psychological engagement'. With regard to what constitutes engagement, Kahn (1990) states that the construct captures the physical, cognitive and emotional aspects of one's preferred self that are simultaneously employed and expressed when performing one's job role. From his qualitative research, examples of such aspects are given, for example an architect 'flying around the office', focused on creating aesthetic yet functional designs, and being empathetic to others' feelings. Three measures of engagement have been developed (and published) using this operationalization as an explicit foundation: May, Gilson and Harter's (2004) psychological engagement measure; Rich, LePine and Crawford's (2010) job engagement measure; and Soane, Truss, Alfes, Shantz, Rees and Gatenby's (2012) Intellectual Social Affective (ISA) engagement measure.

May et al.'s (2004) psychological engagement measure was the first to operationalize Kahn's (1990) three-factor conceptualization of engagement. It is a 13-item questionnaire scale, validated via a sample of 213 employees from a large insurance firm in the US. Respondents indicate the extent (on a five-point scale) with which they agree or disagree with each statement, categorized as emotional engagement (e.g. *'My feelings are affected by how well I perform my job'*), cognitive engagement (e.g. *'Time passes quickly when I perform my job'*), and physical engagement (e.g. *'I exert a lot of energy performing my job'*). This measure has been used in other academic research, such as Olivier and Rothmann (2007) and Chen, Zhang and Vogel (2011). Both of these studies focused on the psychological antecedents to engagement based on Kahn's (1990) theory, with Chen et al. (2011) examining one outcome (knowledge sharing) as well. Taken together with May et al.'s (2004) study, they all found that meaningfulness exhibited the strongest relationship with engagement, followed by availability, with safety demonstrating the weakest (see Chapter 3 for detail). However, when focused on the relationship with outcomes, this scale may not be as useful. When compared with the UWES this measure performed less well in terms of convergent and predictive validity, even though it may be more aligned with broader definitions of engagement (Viljevac, Cooper-Thomas and Saks, 2012).

Rich et al.'s (2010) job engagement measure aimed to map onto Kahn's (1990) conceptualization. Therefore, they drew upon various existing scales to develop their measure of engagement, such as Brown and Leigh's (1996) work intensity measure, as well as Russell and Barrett's (1999) measure of core affect. Through modifying statements from these sources as well as filling out the content domain with additional statements developed by themselves, their measure of engagement corresponds well with Kahn's (1990) three-factor conceptualization. The final 18-item questionnaire scale was validated via a sample of 245 US firefighters. Respondents state the extent (on a five-point scale) to which they agree or disagree with each statement in relation to their own thoughts/feelings about their job, categorized under the headings of emotional engagement (e.g. *'I am proud of my job'*), cognitive engagement (e.g. *'At work, I pay a lot of attention to my job'*) and physical engagement (e.g. *'I try my hardest to perform well on my job'*). A recent research study by Alfes, Shantz, Truss and Soane (2013) used a shortened version of this scale (adopting a seven-point rather than five-point scale) within the UK context. Both studies found engagement, measured using this scale, predicted behavioural outcomes that are important to the organization, e.g. organizational citizenship behaviours, task performance and intention to quit. Rich et al. (2010) specifically found that engagement had strong explanatory power in predicting such outcomes, even after the effects of job involvement, job satisfaction and intrinsic motivation were accounted for in analyses. Moreover, Alfes et al.'s (2013) study highlighted that engagement should not be examined in isolation; one must also consider how the broader social climate (such as perceptions of organizational and line manager support) may moderate the engagement–outcome relationship.

Soane et al.'s (2012) ISA engagement measure builds upon Kahn's (1990) theorizing whilst also considering recent reviews and discussions in the engagement domain (such as Shuck, 2011; Bakker, Albrecht and Leiter, 2011; Parker and Griffin, 2011). From an initial set of 21 items, a final 9-item questionnaire scale (representing the most parsimonious item set) was validated via a sample of 683 employees from a retail organization in the UK. This validation process also found that the ISA measure explained additional variance above the UWES in predicting in-role performance, organizational citizenship behaviours and turnover intentions. This analysis indicates that the ISA measure could be more useful than the UWES in relation to predicting individual-level behavioural outcomes. Earlier versions of this scale have been used in CIPD commissioned projects (Alfes et al., 2009). Respondents are asked to state the extent (on a seven-point scale) to which they agree or disagree with each statement with regard to their own thoughts/feelings about their job, categorized as intellectual engagement (e.g. *'I focus hard on my work'*), social engagement (e.g. *'I share the same work values as my colleagues'*), and affective engagement (e.g. *'I feel positive about my job'*).

These measures within the needs-satisfaction approach suggest that engagement has an activated emotional dimension (i.e. positive feelings about one's work/job that go beyond being satisfied and happy), as well as a heightened cognitive dimension (i.e. feeling intellectually stimulated by one's work/job). The third dimension has been viewed by May et al. (2004) and by Rich et al. (2010) as the enablement of physical energies, typically in the form of exerting energy/effort and trying hard. In contrast to the other measures, Soane et al. (2012) make a distinction between state and behaviour, and so do not include this physical energy dimension (as it may refer more to behaviour rather than to a psychological state). Instead, they revisited Kahn's (1990) findings and identified a key, yet previously neglected, component of engagement: the perceived social connectedness between the individual and their co-workers, which includes sharing the same work-related attitudes, goals and values. It may be of interest to those exploring engagement from this approach to examine this feature in more depth.

Measures from the satisfaction-engagement approach

Given its popularity within the management consultancy and HR practitioner domains, a variety of measures have been developed from the satisfaction-engagement approach. The main purpose of these measures is to provide managers with a tool that can be used to improve areas of work and organizational life (Harter, Schmidt and Hayes, 2002). Therefore this approach focuses on specificity of managerial action and workplace interventions (e.g. Macleod and Clarke, 2009); and so employee engagement measures, from this approach, typically examine the individual's connection with the wider work and organizational environment rather than with the specific job/organizational role or work activities.

The extent to which the content of these indicators is in the public domain varies and, even when in the public domain, the method of analysis is normally not disclosed. To illustrate the content that is often found, the following measures where content is in the public domain will be examined: the Gallup Workplace Audit (i.e. 'Gallup Q12') (Harter, Schmidt and Hayes, 2002); the Institute for Employment Studies (IES) (Robinson, Perryman and Hayday, 2004); the UK's annual NHS staff survey and the UK civil service 'People Survey' (Department of Health, 2012b; Civil Service, 2011); and an academic instrument by James, McKechnie and Swanberg (2011).

As discussed elsewhere in this volume, the Gallup Q12 is probably the most internationally recognized and adopted measure from this approach. The Gallup Organization's 12-item measure is designed to capture 'the individual's involvement and satisfaction with as well as enthusiasm for work' (Harter, Schmidt and Hayes, 2002: 269) whereby respondents are asked to rate (on a five-point scale) the extent to which they disagree or agree with each statement. Although it has been used extensively in many organizations around the world and has been shown to predict various business-unit performance indicators (Harter, Schmidt and Hayes, 2002), there have been many criticisms levelled at the measure (Schaufeli and Bakker, 2010; Briner, 2012; Macey and Schneider, 2008). Specifically, rather than measuring 'engagement', the Gallup Q12 may instead be assessing the extent to which a range of positive and motivational working conditions are present (Little and Little, 2006) (e.g. clear expectations – *'Do I know what is expected of me at work?'*, supportive supervisor/co-workers – *'Does my supervisor, or someone at work, seem to care about me as a person?'*, and personal development – *'This last year, have I had opportunities at work to learn and grow?'*).

The IES defines engagement as: 'A positive attitude held by the employee towards the organization and its values' (Robinson, Perryman and Hayday, 2004). From this definition, a 12-item employee engagement measure was designed to cover the following: (a) pride in the organization (e.g. *'I speak highly of this organization to my friends'*); (b) belief that the organization provides good products/services and enables the employee to perform well (e.g. *'I would be happy to recommend this organization's products/services to my friends and family'*); (c) a willingness to behave altruistically and go beyond what is required (e.g. *'I try to help others in this organization whenever I can'*); and (d) an understanding of the 'bigger picture' (e.g. *'I find that my values and the organization's are very similar'*). Respondents rate the extent to which they agree or disagree with each statement (on a five-point scale). This measure was initially validated with over 10,000 employees across a large number of organizations, many of which were in the public sector (Robinson, Hooker and Hayday, 2007). Its usage is primarily as a diagnostic tool alongside measures of key 'drivers' such as feeling valued and involved, job satisfaction and good quality management.

The annual NHS (Department of Health, 2012b) and civil service (Civil Service, 2011) staff surveys use engagement measures that have been developed for use within the context of the NHS (provider trusts in England) and the civil service (government departments in the UK) respectively. The NHS uses a 9-item 'employee engagement' measure, which includes elements of engagement with the job (e.g. *'I am enthusiastic about my job'*) although it is primarily concerned with organizational purpose, positive advocacy and confidence in the service provided (e.g. *'I would recommend my organization as a place to work'*). The civil service's engagement indicator has five statements focusing on organizational pride, identity, advocacy and attachment (e.g. *'I feel a strong personal attachment to my department'*). In both these surveys, respondents rate the extent to which they agree or disagree with each statement (on a five-point scale). Both the NHS and the civil service use these indicators as part of a wider employee engagement strategy that includes benchmarking and setting action plans for business units/departments within their organizations as well as developing organization-wide capabilities that can foster engagement, such as managerial skills or HR initiatives.

James et al. (2011) devised and tested an eight-item 'employee engagement' questionnaire scale with a sample of 6,047 employees from a large US retail company. This captured the emotional (e.g. *'I really care about the future of this organization'*); cognitive (e.g. *'It would take me a lot to get me to leave this organization'*); and behavioural (e.g. *'I am always willing to give extra effort to help this organization succeed'*) connection with the company. Respondents rate the extent to which they agree or disagree with each statement (on a five-point scale). This study focused on job-related antecedents rather than outcomes of engagement, and found that supervisory support and recognition, work scheduling autonomy/satisfaction and job clarity were important predictors of engagement.

All measures from this approach focus on the connection the individual has with the organization, rather than with the job or work activities. This connection mainly constitutes an attachment to, and an alignment with, the organization and its values. This reflects the well-established attitudinal construct of 'affective commitment' (Meyer and Allen, 1991), which 'refers to the employee's emotional attachment to, identification with, and involvement in the organization' (p. 67). In many engagement measures from this approach, one or two items ask about the individual's intention to stay with (or leave) the organization, which has been found to be an important outcome of affective commitment (Meyer et al., 2002).

Another fundamental area that is examined by measures from the satisfaction-engagement approach concerns the desire to perform voluntary behaviours on behalf of the organization, such as helping co-workers, putting in extra effort or advocating the organization to friends. Again, these parallel other widely researched and well-established constructs of (a) 'discretionary effort' (Dubinskya and Skinner, 2002) which signifies the degree to which an individual 'willingly' gives extra effort, time, or energy to help the organization succeed or to help reach its objectives; and (b) 'organizational citizenship' (Podsakoff et al., 2000) which refers to a collection of behaviours that are acted out voluntarily, are not part of one's job description and are intended to benefit either specific individuals or the wider organization. These include helping behaviour (e.g. assisting co-workers with work-related problems), sportsmanship (e.g. sacrificing personal interests for the good of the work group/organization), and organizational loyalty (e.g. advocating working for the organization or using their goods/services).

Although each of the 'employee engagement' indicators from the satisfaction-engagement approach displays high reliability and has been tested in a variety of sectors and settings over time, it is important to remain critical of what is really being measured. With this mixture of constructs many have argued that this form of 'engagement' may just be an overall 'employee attitude' factor rather than a new construct called 'employee engagement' (see arguments by Newman et al., 2010). Furthermore, many academics consider that some features described above, such as value alignment, may be antecedents and others, such as discretionary effort, may be outcomes of the 'experience' of engagement (e.g. Rich, Lepine and Crawford, 2010; Saks, 2008; Alfes et al., 2013). The boundaries between antecedents, engagement and outcomes need to be more rigorously defined. This will help identify specific ways in which engagement operates and functions; and how these processes may be influenced by unique business and individual circumstances. Being clear about boundaries will enable a more sophisticated and nuanced understanding of how to tailor engagement strategy to suit a particular context.

Measures from the multidimensional approach

The multidimensional approach is one of the most recent developments in the employee engagement field, and stems from Saks's (2006) research. This approach is very similar to that of the needs-satisfaction approach (i.e. Kahn, 1990) as it focuses on role performance; however, it is distinct in the fact that it differentiates between the foci of the job and of the organization (as highlighted in Chapter 1). Therefore employee engagement can be measured via two related, yet distinct constructs – job engagement and organizational engagement (see also Chapters 10 and 13).

Saks (2006) devised two six-item questionnaire scales: one measuring job engagement (e.g. *'This job is all consuming, I am totally into it'* and *'I really throw myself into my job')*; the other measuring organizational engagement (e.g. *'One of the most exciting things for me is getting involved with things happening in this organization'* and *'Being a member of this organization makes me come alive')*. Taken together, this overall employee engagement measure was designed to capture the individual's 'psychological presence in their job and organization' (p. 608) and focused on activated psychological responses such as feeling alive, exhilarated and consumed. Respondents indicate the extent (on a five-point scale) with which they agree or disagree with each statement.

Saks's (2006) multidimensional engagement scale was validated with a sample of 102 employees from a range of jobs and organizations, mainly in Canada. The results of the study also suggested that although job and organizational engagement may have some common antecedents (e.g. perceived organizational support); they may also have some different antecedents (e.g. job characteristics were more strongly related to job engagement whereas procedural justice was more strongly related to organizational engagement). This indicates that job and organizational engagement may be related, yet distinct constructs. Moreover, both job and organizational engagement were found to correlate positively with the outcomes of job satisfaction, organizational commitment, intention to quit and organizational citizenship behaviours. These findings indicate that a multidimensional approach is of value and could be useful in the future development of employee engagement theory and practice. This idea is discussed further in Chapter 10.

Common measurement issues

There are three major issues to consider when measuring any phenomenon via self-reported questionnaire scales: (a) validity, (b) reliability, (c) response formats and biases. The aim here is to give the essence of these issues and how they relate to measuring engagement; in Chapter 9, the relevance of these issues from a cross-cultural perspective is explored.

Validity

Validity is firstly concerned with whether the measure fully captures the construct of interest. This is known as 'content validity', whereby all items should reflect the overall definition, and should adequately cover all aspects of that construct. Problems with content validity arise when the measure includes antecedents such as 'My job challenges me'; outcomes of engagement such as 'I help out my colleagues when they have a problem'; or refer to other confounding phenomena such as 'I often work more than my contracted hours'. These aspects may well be related to engagement, yet may not be part of the experience of engagement itself.

Moreover, validity is concerned with how the construct is statistically correlated to theoretically related constructs. This is known as 'convergent validity'. In addition, the construct should be statistically related to important outcomes in the 'real-world', either at the same time-period (concurrent validity) or an outcome in the future (predictive validity). For example, engagement scores today should predict job performance tomorrow.

Lastly, the measure should be statistically distinct from other similar, yet different constructs (discriminant validity). For example, engagement is part of a wider domain of positive psychological constructs, such as job satisfaction. However, it theoretically differs from these and so measures of engagement should be substantially different, statistically, from these other measures (this also assumes that measures of other constructs are also valid and reliable). The most important 'difference' is in terms of antecedents and outcomes. For example, if job satisfaction and job engagement have the same antecedent's and both predict, to similar degrees, the same outcomes, then there is a major problem with differentiating the two constructs.

This final aspect has been the most debated in regard to engagement. Some have argued that there is significant crossover between engagement and other well-established constructs, and have provided evidence to support this view (Newman, Joseph and Hulin, 2010; Wefald and Downey, 2009; Cole, Bedeian and O'Boyle, 2012). Thus, the suggestion is that engagement may, in its current form, be a 'redundant' concept. On the other hand, many others disagree and find evidence that engagement is a novel and valuable concept (Rich, Lepine and Crawford, 2010; Warr and Inceoglu, 2012; Hallberg and Schaufeli, 2006). This type of debate is common and is healthy when a construct, like engagement, is still relatively new to scientific scrutiny. However, a time will soon come when some form of agreement needs to be reached on how engagement 'adds value' to theory and practice.

Reliability

Reliability is concerned with the measure being stable and consistent. When designing self-report questionnaire scales, one must be aware of at least two types of reliability: (a) test-retest reliability and (b) internal consistency reliability.

Test-retest reliability means that if a person were to complete the survey again, under similar conditions, they would have a similar score. If the two scores are dramatically different then the scale may not be deemed reliable. This is typically used when the construct being measured is itself deemed to be temporally stable, such as personality traits. However, as engagement has been found to fluctuate across days and across weeks (Sonnentag, Dormann and Demerouti, 2010), this type of reliability may not enable a suitable judgement of an engagement measure's stability and consistency. This is because engagement is, theoretically and empirically, a psychological state and so an individual's level of engagement changes in accordance to alterations in their situation or environment. Because some aspects may be fairly stable over time (such as belief in the organization's values or work-role fit), this leads to the individual experiencing a 'typical' or 'standard' level of engagement. However, as many other aspects may change regularly, such as work tasks, workloads and social support, the individual's level of engagement will dip above and below their 'standard' level within the course of the workday and workweek (Sonnentag et al., 2010).

Internal consistency reliability refers to the extent to which items within a scale 'hang together' such that if a respondent strongly agrees to one positively worded statement within the scale, the respondent should agree or strongly agree with most other positively worded statements in the scale. Internal consistency is measured via Cronbach's alpha (for more details see Rust and Golombok, 2009; Field, 2009). As a rule of thumb, for the measure to be deemed of acceptable reliability Cronbach's alpha values should be above .70 (range from .00 to 1.00).

Most measures of engagement from the academic community have good levels of internal consistency as well as demonstrating construct and convergent validity due to the rigorous statistical testing undertaken in scholarly scientific research. However, some measures produced by consultancies may not undergo such thorough testing, and so it is recommended to ask the publisher/consultancy to ensure that the scale is both reliable and valid (see Rust and Golombok, 2009). Many should be able to provide these and will be able to show, with confidence, that their measure is indeed psychometrically acceptable. Furthermore, practitioners can take the initiative to conduct either concurrent or predictive validation studies in order to demonstrate that the measure of engagement that they use is linked to key performance outcomes, such as sales or performance appraisal scores. This would also help build a good evidence base and business case for future engagement projects.

Response formats

Table 15.1 summarizes the three most common response formats used in engagement measures. Some use the typical five-point agree-disagree Likert scale whereas others use a seven-point variant of this. At first glance, this may appear a trivial difference, yet studies have shown, albeit not in engagement measurement, that seven-point Likert scales may be more suitable than five-point counterparts: they have been found to be more sensitive at capturing the respondent's 'true' evaluation of a statement whilst maintaining statistical robustness (Finstad, 2010). In other words, it allows the respondent to give a judgement that better reflects their actual subjective feeling. When answering questionnaires, respondents are asked to categorize abstract thoughts and feelings that they might not regularly reflect on in everyday life. Therefore it is important to allow the respondent enough choice that enables them to identify a category that best matches their evaluation, but not too much choice as to make categories less meaningful and less distinct. A seven-point Likert scale seems to strike a good balance between choice and structure. Other measures (such as UWES) use a seven-point never-always frequency scale that may also include timeframe references, such as a few times a year, month, week or day.

Table 15.1 Comparison of different response scales

	Usual instruction	*Response categories*
5-point Likert extent scale	Please rate the following statements according to how much you agree or disagree with each	Strongly Agree, Agree, Neutral, Disagree, Strongly Disagree
7-point Likert extent scale	Please rate the following statements according to how much you agree or disagree with each	Strongly Agree, Agree, Slightly Agree, Neutral, Slightly Disagree, Disagree, Strongly Disagree
7-point frequency scale	Please read each statement and decide if you ever feel this way about your job. If you have never had this feeling, cross the '0' (zero) in the space after the statement. If you have had this feeling, indicate how often you feel it by crossing the number (from 1 to 6) that best describes how frequently you feel that way.	Never, Almost never (a few times a year), Rarely (once a month or less), Sometimes (a few times a month), Often (once a week), Very often (a few times a week), Always (every day)

Although these different response formats adopt a 'Likert scale' approach, they may not be readily comparable with each other, especially when one is concerned with strength of feeling (i.e. agree/disagree) and the other is concerned with frequency of feeling (i.e. never/always). Despite this, there may be opportunities to explore the intersection of strength and frequency of engagement, and examine whether this has any impact on how engagement is understood. Strength of feeling refers to the intensity of the experience, whereas frequency of feeling reflects the temporal nature of the experience. This becomes important when examining the phenomenon within its wider context, when considering short-term versus long-term implications, and when comparing with other similar phenomena.

For instance, if an experience is high in intensity, yet low in frequency, it might have a sharp, short-term effect on an outcome, for example the introduction of new equipment may cause disruption whilst employees get to know how to use it; whereas if an experience is low in intensity, yet high in frequency, it may have a gradual, long-term effect on an outcome, for example repeated failure on the part of a manager to acknowledge employees' successes could lead over time to growing frustration and upset. In relation to engagement, Alfes et al. (2009) utilized both extent and frequency response formats for the same engagement measure and so were able to explore each separately as well as together. They found that the percentage of the sample that could be categorized as 'highly engaged' (i.e. scoring > 4.50 out of 5.00) varied accordingly: 8 per cent of respondents reported that they were engaged to a 'great extent', 18 per cent reported that they were engaged 'very frequently' at work, and 5 per cent of the sample were engaged to a 'great extent' and that this occurred 'very frequently' – i.e. extent and frequency plotted together). This indicates that although individuals felt engaged frequently (i.e. daily or weekly) they did not always feel this as a highly intense experience.

Another consideration is 'acquiescence bias', which is a tendency for individuals to agree or disagree with all items regardless of their content. To reduce the likelihood of this occurring, most psychometric guides (such as Rust and Golombok, 2009) agree that both positively and negatively worded items should be used. However, this has not been applied in relation to many engagement measures, except May et al. (2004). This may partly be due to the influence of the positive psychology movement on the employee engagement field (see Chapter 2 of this volume), which has advocated for a specific focus on 'the positive features that make life worth living' (Seligman and Csikszentmihalyi, 2000: 5). The question for the future is what to include as 'negative' items.

As the focus of the measure is to capture engagement, i.e. a positive phenomenon, and not to capture negative phenomenon that may be qualitatively different, such as burnout (Maslach et al., 2001), it makes deciding suitable 'negative' items difficult. Moreover, one must balance this with the consideration regarding the absence of 'engagement' and how statements should reflect this, yet not cross boundaries with those 'negative' constructs. This highlights the importance of having a precise definition and operationalization of the construct and being clear on how, theoretically and empirically, it is different from other phenomena. There are other forms of response biases, particularly in regards to culture, which are highlighted in Chapter 9 of this volume.

Presentation and interpretation considerations for practitioners

The manner in which engagement indicators are calculated and presented varies considerably, which can cause confusion. This section addresses three areas: the ways in which the indicator is calculated and presented; the categorization of individuals or groups depending on their level of engagement; and the use of benchmarking.

Calculation and presentation

An engagement indicator is, typically, a collection of statements, grouped into a single measure. The first way of presenting the results is to simply add up the percentage of those who express a positive view by selecting either the 'agree' or 'strongly agree' options. This means that the statements are usually positively expressed, as any negatively expressed statements would have to be reverse-scored. The latter option is usually avoided by survey providers, as it can be confusing for respondents to understand, and sometimes the organization itself is reluctant to include any negative statements.

The benefit of the simple 'percentage agreeing or strongly agreeing' presentation is that it is easy to understand and use within an organizational context, where, for example, a headline organizational score of '80 per cent of our employees are engaged, compared with a target of 75 per cent' might be presented on a performance dashboard or scorecard. However, an apparently positive result can be misleading without a further examination of the distribution of responses, to assess:

• the percentage in the 'agree' and 'strongly agree' categories (the 80 per cent could be broken down, for example, as 40 per cent in each of these categories, as a more positive 60 per cent 'strongly agree' and 20 per cent 'agree', or conversely as a less positive 20 per cent 'strongly agree' and 60 per cent 'agree').

• the percentage in the neutral, 'disagree' and 'strongly disagree' categories (the 20 per cent who have not expressed positive views might all be in the neutral midpoint category of 'neither agree nor disagree', or might all be expressing strong disagreement, which could indicate a serious problem for the organization that is congratulating itself for exceeding its overall target of 75 per cent and now finds that one-fifth of its employees are clearly disengaged).

The practical difficulty of using percentage distributions is that they are not easy to explain to managers, who tend to prefer a single target to aim for. This has led to the use of 'net' scores, where the percentage expressing disagreement/strong disagreement is subtracted from the percentage expressing agreement/strong agreement. Although this refinement yields a single figure, it can lead to those opting for the neutral mid-point to be ignored. This could mean that the organization fails to realize that a significant number of its employees do not have a view one way or another about a particular issue – which could in turn indicate either indifference to, or a lack of knowledge of, the issue.

The second method is to express the indicator as an overall figure between 1 and 5, using a mean average. This requires the allocation of 'scores' to each response category, so that 'strongly disagree' is allocated 1, 'disagree' 2, 'neither agree nor disagree' 3, 'agree' 4 and 'strongly agree' 5. Again, the scoring for negatively expressed statements has to be reversed so that 1 becomes 5, 2 becomes 4, and so forth. This process will typically lead to an indicator that is expressed as a number such as 3.67 or 3.95 (in simple terms, the higher the better). This might be expressed on a performance scorecard as 'our engagement score is 3.92 compared to a target of 3.80, and a big increase on last year's score of 3.75'. The calculation of an overall 'score' has the benefit of yielding a number that can be used easily for comparisons (year-on-year, or between different groups of employees), but it has disadvantages too.

• The allocation of 1 to 5 for each response category assumes that the distance between each category is equal – whereas in reality an individual employee might feel only a small difference in view between the neutral midpoint and the 'disagree' categories, but a huge gulf between 'disagree' and 'strongly disagree'.

- A mean score can mask differences that might appear on an examination of the full distribution of responses. To use an extreme example, a mean of exactly 3 could indicate that every employee has opted for the neutral midpoint, but it could also mean that 50 per cent 'strongly agree' and 50 per cent 'strongly disagree'.

In terms of examining the distribution of scores from this approach, the variance and standard deviation can be calculated. These examine the average variability across the dataset: if large in relation to the mean, then it indicates a wide spread of scores (i.e. data points are not closely clustered around the mean); if small in relation to the mean, then it indicates a narrow spread of scores (i.e. data points are closely clustered around the mean). Therefore, the second disadvantage of 'masking differences' is reduced as one can examine how close the range of scores are from the mean score. For instance, two organizations have the same mean score of 4.0 (out of 5.0), yet Organization A has a standard deviation of 0.1 and Organization B has a standard deviation of 0.5. This indicates that although both have high average levels of engagement, Organization A has a tighter spread of scores and thus has a more stable level of engagement (across workforce) than Organization B.

Employee profiling

It is tempting to start categorizing the workforce into groups such as 'highly engaged', 'unengaged' or 'disengaged'. Although there can be a rationale behind such categorization – for example, based on the percentage distribution of scores – in practice it would appear that such categorization is often done in a fairly arbitrary way, based on convenient cut-off points. For example, anyone scoring below the midpoint of 3 might be labelled 'disengaged', those scoring between 3 and 3.24 'unengaged', 3.25 to 3.99 'engaged' and 4 and above 'highly engaged'. While these descriptions represent a convenient shorthand, it then becomes tempting to assign characteristics to people in these groups, and to assume they behave in similar ways. This can lead to further assumptions about the best ways of tackling 'low' engagement scores and the likely benefits of different interventions. Someone returning an 'unengaged' score might simply be too new to the job to be certain about his or her views; a naturally cautious personality not given to extreme responses; or an employee who is satisfied but not necessarily engaged. Similarly, 'highly engaged' individuals may invest so much into their jobs and the organization that they are vulnerable to sudden changes of view if they perceive that the organization has let them down in some way (Masson et al., 2008).

Blinded by benchmarking?

Several survey houses and research organizations that have developed their own engagement measures offer their customers external benchmarking, using their large databases of survey data collected from many different clients. This enables organizations to compare their engagement indicator results with those of other, similar organizations – 'similar' having several possible meanings, such as size, location, sector, product/service range and workforce composition. For example, consultancies typically analyse trends within as well as differences between large organizations within particular industries or sectors, such as retail or finance. This information can then be purchased and is often used as a marketing/bargaining tool by consultancies. It is, of course, essential to compare like with like in terms of the engagement indicator used and the method of calculating and presenting the results. Used thoughtfully – for example by a group of HR professionals from comparable organizations using the same survey product, who come together to share their results, note similarities and differences, and describe the impact of interventions – they can bring real benefits. However, careful consideration needs to be given to weigh up the potential advantages against the disadvantages before embarking on what can be quite a costly and time-consuming exercise.

- Having to use an 'off-the-shelf' engagement indicator may not be suited to an organization with its own terminology and circumstances. Some companies use both their own in-house engagement measures (for internal comparisons) and a standard measure (for external benchmarking) (Robinson, Perryman and Hayday, 2004).
- Benchmarking can induce a false sense of security. A chief executive who is informed, for example, that his or her company is 'in the upper quartile' in terms of the engagement score, could lead to a decision not to progress with detailed survey analysis. This could in turn mask serious engagement issues in certain areas of the organization.

Another alternative is internal benchmarking, which may provide more specific detail on how engagement is experienced across the organization. Depending on the size of the organization and number of respondents, a considerable number of internal comparisons are possible. Examples include: by gender, ethnicity and age group; by location, region and country; by length of service group, staff type, grade or level; by type of employment contract; by working pattern; by managerial or operational roles. If the same engagement measure has been used over several years, analysis of trends over time also become possible, which enables the organization to track changes in engagement levels, both overall and by employee group.

In addition, the engagement measure can be compared to other indicators of performance used within the organization to gain a more rounded picture. The possibilities vary depending on the nature of the organization and its business, and the way that data are collected and analysed, but could include: absence rates, employee turnover rates, productivity, customer satisfaction, quality measures such as error or scrap rates, and out-turn measures such as sales.

How is employee engagement measured and evaluated in practice?

Case study: Employee engagement at Mace

Mace is an international consultancy and construction company that operates in 65+ countries, has a workforce of 3,700 from a range of occupational groups, and has a turnover of over £1 billion. Between 2007 and 2009 Mace participated in phase one of the Kingston Engagement Consortium Project. This project aimed to measure and understand 'psychological' engagement, as well as its main drivers and outcomes, within each of the participating organizations. This small case study is detailed within a more comprehensive report commissioned by the CIPD (Alfes et al., 2009). A total of 180 employees from Mace completed a range of questionnaires and a subset was interviewed.

Employee engagement was defined as *'being positively present during the performance of work by willingly contributing intellectual effort, experiencing positive emotions and meaningful connections to others'* (Alfes et al., 2009: 6), and was measured using an earlier version of Soane et al.'s (2012) ISA scale. Mace employees were asked to rate each statement twice. once according to the extent to which they felt that particular way (on a five-point scale – strongly agree, agree, neutral, disagree and strongly disagree) and again according to the frequency by which they felt that particular way (i.e. on a five point scale – never, a few times a year, once a month, once a week and daily). Both extent (i.e. how much) and frequency (i.e. how often) of engagement were examined so that engagement could be viewed from 'various angles'. Furthermore, aspects of the work, managerial and organizational environment were also assessed along with key outcomes such as appraisal and job performance ratings.

The results indicate that the majority of Mace employees were highly or very highly engaged (> 4.0 out of 5.0) with their jobs, both in terms of extent (i.e. 78 per cent high/10 per cent very high) and frequency (i.e. 60 per cent high/28 per cent very high). Furthermore, only 1 per cent to 2 per cent were weakly engaged (< 2.0 out of 5.0) in terms of extent or frequency. Although the majority felt a strong sense of engagement, they felt this around once a week rather than every day. Therefore, Mace could increase engagement by focusing on the tasks and interactions that employees participate in on a day-to-day basis. This was combined with the interviews to give a richer understanding. From this integrated analysis, Alfes et al. (2009) identified organizational and managerial practices that were positively contributing to as well as those that were hindering or preventing their employees' engagement.

The benefits of measuring and understanding engagement in this way are highlighted by Alexandra Michael, Employee Engagement Manager at Mace:

> It has given employees a voice and has provided figures to support our business case for engagement activity. More importantly, it has helped us to understand the complexity of employee engagement. For example, some of our people are highly engaged despite having experienced less than adequate line management – why is that? Others are highly engaged with their projects but less so with the company itself – should we see this as a problem? Having an understanding of these complexities and anomalies has been most helpful in shaping our engagement strategy.

Case study: Employee engagement in the NHS

Every NHS provider trust in England conducts an annual staff survey using a survey contractor from an approved list and a standard questionnaire (with potential for adding questions to explore further topics and/or specific issues). The core questionnaire covers personal development; job satisfaction; management; the organization; and health, wellbeing and safety. The nine-statement engagement indicator uses statements taken from different sections of the questionnaire.

NHS organizations can choose whether to survey a random sample of staff, or carry out a census survey of all staff. Regardless of the option chosen, data from the completed questionnaires of a random sample of between 600 and 850, depending on the size of the organization, are transferred to the NHS Staff Survey Co-ordination Centre.

The approved survey house produces a report for each NHS organization with which it is contracted. In addition, the NHS Staff Survey Co-ordination Centre produces a standard report for every participating NHS organization. These standard reports, which are in the public domain, enable trusts to benchmark their results, particularly against those of similar organizations (for example acute trusts, mental health trusts, ambulance trusts).

Within the standard report, the engagement indicator is presented as the headline result. Possible scores range from 1 to 5, with higher scores indicating greater engagement. To use an example from the 2011 report for Salford Royal NHS Foundation Trust, the score for the Trust in 2011 was 3.86 compared with 3.88 in 2010, and a national average for acute Trusts in 2011 of 3.62. This score places the Trust in the highest (best) 20 per cent when compared with Trusts of a similar type (Department of Health, 2012a).

The engagement indicator is broken down into three sub-dimensions called 'key findings' (KFs). KF31 is described as the 'percentage of staff able to contribute towards improvements at work' and consists of three statements: e.g. *'I am able to make improvements happen in my area of work'*. KF34 is described as 'staff recommendation of the trust as a place to work or receive treatment' and consists of three statements: e.g. *'If a friend or relative needed treatment I would be happy with the standard of care provided by this organization'* (this advocacy statement is gaining in prominence within the NHS as it can be linked to the overall development of a 'Friends and Family' indicator within the patient satisfaction survey). Finally, KF35 is labelled 'staff motivation at work' and consists of three statements: e.g. *'I look forward to going to work'*.

This case study illustrates how engagement is measured and presented within one sector. It suggests that, for the NHS at least, some aspects of engagement are sector-related (for example, the advocacy statement in the paragraph above is specifically related to healthcare treatment) while others (such as the motivation example above) could be applied to any organizational context. It also illustrates that engagement is multi-faceted, in this case having three sub-dimensions.

Conclusion

This chapter has given an overview of the current ways in which employee engagement is measured. It has been acknowledged that there are differing approaches to defining and measuring engagement, and so Shuck's (2011) systemic review was used as an organizing framework. Although caution is required when deciding, designing, presenting and interpreting engagement questionnaire scales, they do hold significant value. A measure that represents the extent to which employees are engaged can be a major contributor towards understanding overall organizational performance, providing it is properly understood and used consistently.

References

Alfes, K., Shantz, A., Truss, C. and Soane, E. (2013) 'The link between perceived human resource management practices, engagement and employee behavior: A moderated mediation model', *The International Journal of Human Resource Management*, 24(2): 330–51.

——, Truss, C., Soane, E., Rees, C. and Gatenby, M. (2009) *Creating an engaging organisation: Findings from the Kingston Employee Engagement Consortium Project*, London: CIPD.

Bakker, A. B., Albrecht, S. L. and Leiter, M. P. (2011) 'Key questions regarding work engagement', *European Journal of Work and Organizational Psychology*, 20(1): 4–28.

Briner, R. (2012) 'Just how bad an idea is employee engagement?', *ESRC Seminar Series: Employee engagement, Organisational Performance and Individual Wellbeing – Exploring the evidence, developing theory*.

Brown, S. P. and Leigh, T. W. (1996) 'A new look at psychological climate and its relationship to job involvement, effort, and performance', *Journal of Applied Psychology*, 81(4): 358–68.

Chen, Z., Zhang, X. and Vogel, D. (2011) 'Exploring the underlying process between conflict and knowledge sharing: A work-engagement perspective', *Journal of Applied Social Psychology*, 41(5): 1005–33.

Civil Service (2011) *People Survey 2011*. Available at http://resources.civilservice.gov.uk/wp-content/uploads/2011/11/CSPS-2011-question-set.pdf [accessed 05/02/2012].

Cole, M. S., Bedeian, A. G. and O'Boyle, E. H. (2012) 'Job burnout and employee engagement: A meta-analytic examination of construct proliferation', *Journal of Management*, 38(5): 1550–81.

Department of Health (2012a) *2011 National Staff Survey: Results from Salford Royal NHS Foundation Trust*. Available at http://nhsstaffsurveys.com/cms/uploads/Individual%20Trust%20reports%202011/NHS_staff_survey_2011_RM3_full.pdf. [accessed 05/02/2012].

Department of Health (2012b) *National NHS Staff Survey 2012*. Available at http://nhsstaffsurveys.com/cms/uploads/Questionnaires/Staff%20Survey%202012%20-%20Core%20Questionnaire_final.pdf. [accessed 05/02/2012].

Dubinskya, A. and Skinner, S. (2002) 'Going the extra mile: Antecedents of salespeople's discretionary effort', *Industrial Marketing Management*, 31: 589–98.

Eccles, R. G. (1991) 'The Performance Measurement Manifesto', *Harvard Business Review*, 69(1): 131–7.

Field, A. (2009) *Discovering statistics using SPSS*, 3rd edn, London: Sage Publications.

Finstad, K. (2010) 'Response interpolation and scale sensitivity: Evidence against 5-point scales', *Journal of Usability Studies*, 5(3): 104–10.

Halbesleben, J. R. B. (2010) 'A meta-analysis of work engagement: Relationships with burnout, demands, resources, and consequences' in A. B. Bakker (ed.) *Work engagement: A handbook of essential theory and research*. New York: Psychology Press, pp. 102–17.

Hallberg, U. E. and Schaufeli, W. B. (2006) 'Same same but different? Can work engagement be discriminated from job involvement and organizational commitment?', *European Psychologist*, 11(2): 119–27.

Harter, J. K., Schmidt, F. L. and Hayes, T. L. (2002) 'Business-unit-level relationship between employee satisfaction, employee engagement, and business outcomes: A meta-analysis', *Journal of Applied Psychology*, 87(2): 268–79.

James, J., McKechnie, S. and Swanberg, J. (2011) 'Predicting employee engagement in an age-diverse retail workforce', *Journal of Organizational Behavior*, 32: 173–96.

Kahn, W. A. (1990) 'Psychological conditions of personal engagement and disengagement at work', *Academy of Management Journal*, 33(4): 692–724.

—— (1992) 'To be fully there: Psychological presence at work', *Human Relations*, 45(4): 321–49.

Kaplan, R. S. and Norton, D. P. (1992) 'The Balanced Scorecard – Measures that drive performance', *Harvard Business Review*, 70(1): 71–9.

Little, B. and Little, P. (2006) 'Employee Engagement: Conceptual Issues', *Journal of Organizational Culture, Communications and Conflict*, 10(1): 111–20.

Macey, W. H. and Schneider, B. (2008) 'The meaning of employee engagement', *Industrial and Organizational Psychology: Perspectives on Science and Practice*, 1(1): 3–30.

MacLeod, D. and Clarke, N. (2009) *Engaging for success: Enhancing performance through employee engagement*, London: Department of Business, Innovation and Skills.

Maslach, C. and Goldberg, J. (1998) 'Prevention of burnout: New perspectives', *Applied & Preventive Psychology*, 7(1): 63–74.

——, Schaufeli, W. B. and Leiter, M. P. (2001) 'Job burnout', *Annual Review of Psychology*, 52(1): 397–422.

Masson, R. C., Royal, M. A., Agnew, T. G. and Fine, S. (2008) 'Leveraging employee engagement: The practical implications', *Industrial and Organizational Psychology: Perspectives on Science and Practice*, 1(1): 56–9.

May, D. R., Gilson, R. L. and Harter, L. M. (2004) 'The psychological conditions of meaningfulness, safety and availability and the engagement of the human spirit at work', *Journal of Occupational and Organizational Psychology*, 77(1): 11–37.

Meyer, J. P. and Allen, N. J. (1991) 'A three-component conceptualization of organizational commitment', *Human Resource Management Review*, 1(1): 61–89.

——, Stanley, D. J., Herscovitch, L. and Topolnytsky, L. (2002) 'Affective, continuance, and normative commitment to the organization: A meta-analysis of antecedents, correlates, and consequences', *Journal of Vocational Behavior*, 61: 20–52.

Newman, D. A., Joseph, D. L. and Hulin, C. L. (2010) 'Job attitudes and employee engagement: Considering the attitude "A-factor"' in S. L. Albrecht (ed.) *The handbook of employee engagement: Perspectives, issues, research and practice*, Cheltenham, UK: Edward Elgar, pp. 43–61.

Olivier, A. and Rothmann, S. (2007) 'Antecedents of work engagement in a multinational oil company', *SA Journal of Industrial Psychology*, 33(3): 49–56.

Parker, S. K. and Griffin, M. A. (2011) 'Understanding active psychological states: Embedding engagement in a wider nomological net and closer attention to performance', *European Journal of Work and Organizational Psychology*, 20(1): 60–7.

Podsakoff, P., MacKenzie, S., Paine, J. and Bacharach, D. (2000) 'Organizational citizenship behaviors: A critical review of the theoretical and empirical literature and suggestions for further research', *Journal of Management*, 26: 513–63.

Rich, B. L., Lepine, J. A. and Crawford, E. R. (2010) 'Job engagement: Antecedents and effects on job performance', *Academy of Management Journal*, 53(3): 617–35.

Robinson, D., Hooker, H. and Hayday, S. (2007) *Engagement: The Continuing Story*, Brighton, UK: Institute for Employment Studies.

——, Perryman, S. and Hayday, S. (2004) *The drivers of employee engagement*, Brighton, UK: Institute for Employment Studies.

Russell, J. A. and Barrett, L. F. (1999) 'Core affect, prototypical emotional episodes, and other things called emotion: Dissecting the elephant', *Journal of Personality and Social Psychology*, 76(5): 805–19.

Rust, J. and Golombok, S. (2009) *Modern psychometrics: The science of psychological assessment*, 3rd edn, London: Routledge.

Saks, A. M. (2006) 'Antecedents and consequences of employee engagement', *Journal of Managerial Psychology*, 21(7): 600–619.

—— (2008) 'The meaning and bleeding of employee engagement: How muddy is the water?', *Industrial and Organizational Psychology: Perspectives on Science and Practice*, 1(1): 40–3.

Schaufeli, W. B. and Bakker, A. B. (2003) *UWES: Utrecht work engagement scale preliminary manual*, Department of Psychology, Utrecht University, The Netherlands.

—— and Bakker, A. B. (2010) 'Defining and measuring work engagement: Bringing clarity to the concept' in A. B. Bakker (ed.) *Work engagement: A handbook of essential theory and research*, New York: Psychology Press, pp. 10–24.

——, Salanova, M., González-Romá, V. and Bakker, A. B. (2002) 'The measurement of engagement and burnout: A two sample confirmatory factor analytic approach', *Journal of Happiness Studies*, 3(1): 71–92.

Seligman, M. E. P. and Csikszentmihalyi, M. (2000) 'Positive psychology: An introduction', *American Psychologist*, 55(1): 5–14.

Shirom, A. (2004) 'Feeling vigorous at work? The construct of vigor and the study of positive affect in organizations' in D. Ganster and P.L. Perrewe (eds) *Research in Organizational Stress and Well-being Vol. 3*, Greenwich, CT: JAI Press, pp. 135–65.

——, Melamed, S., Berliner, S. and Shapira, I. (2012) 'The effects of vigour on measures of obesity across time', *British Journal of Health Psychology*, 17(1): 129–43.

Shuck, B. (2011) 'Four emerging perspectives of employee engagement: An integrative literature review', *Human Resource Development Review*, 10(3): 304–28.

Soane, E., Truss, C., Alfes, K., Shantz, A., Rees, C. and Gatenby, M. (2012) 'Development and application of a new measure of employee engagement: The ISA Engagement Scale', *Human Resource Development International*, 15(5): 529–47.

Sonnentag, S., Dormann, C. and Demerouti, E. (2010) 'Not all days are created equal: The concept of state work engagement' in A. B. Bakker (ed.) *Work engagement: A handbook of essential theory and research*, New York: Psychology Press, pp. 25–38.

Truss, C., Mankin, D. and Kelliher, C. (2012) 'Chapter 12: Employee Engagement' in C. Truss, D. Mankin and C. Kelliher (eds) *Strategic human resource management*, 1st edn, Oxford: Oxford University Press, pp. 219–33.

Viljevac, A., Cooper-Thomas, H. D. and Saks, A. M. (2012) 'An investigation into the validity of two measures of work engagement', *The International Journal of Human Resource Management*, 23(17): 3692–709.

Warr, P. and Inceoglu, I. (2012) 'Job engagement, job satisfaction, and contrasting associations with person–job fit', *Journal of Occupational Health Psychology*, 17(2): 129–38.

Wefald, A. J. and Downey, R. G. (2009) 'Construct dimensionality of engagement and its relation with satisfaction', *Journal of Psychology*, 143(1): 91–111.

16 Case studies in employee engagement

Kerstin Alfes and Selma Suna Yeltekin Leloglu

Introduction

In the previous chapters of this book, leading scholars have provided theoretical insights into the nature of the concept of engagement, its antecedents and its consequences. The purpose of this chapter is to illustrate how engagement can be enacted in a business context. Four practitioners were asked to share their experiences of the development and implementation of engagement initiatives in their respective organizations. The organizations differ with regard to their size, the industry or sector they are operating in and the challenges they are currently facing. However, what they have in common is a genuine interest for engaging their workforce. The four case studies provide insights from the experiences of practitioners actively involved in promoting engagement. They should not be interpreted as 'best practices' that are readily transferable to other organizations. Rather, they provide valuable ideas that might be adapted by other organizations to inform their actions and processes.

Department for Work and Pensions

Joyce Henderson

The Department for Work and Pensions (DWP) is one of the largest Whitehall government departments – with around 100,000 employees. It has a large operational arm of around 90,000 people and a set of corporate functions which supports this and develops policy. Its role, in addition to processing and paying unemployment and other benefits and pensions, is to deliver the coalition priorities on welfare reform. This involves introducing Universal Credit, implementing a Work Programme, reforming pensions and supporting disabled people into work where possible. DWP operates through network (telephony) as well as face-to-face customer services. DWP has undergone significant transformation in the last few years, through streamlining, re-structuring and embracing digitalization. Universal Credit and pensions will primarily be delivered online in the future.

DWP has run a People Survey since 2002. The surveys have always been championed by HR which also provides the resource for co-ordinating the survey process internally. Post survey action planning is devolved to the business, however, and is not project managed from the centre.

DWP has a somewhat unconventional engagement strategy. Engagement is seen as an enabler of the transformation that is now underway. There has been a move away from a focus on improving scores ('transactional engagement') to a broader concern to improve the organizational experience ('transformational engagement') and thereby improve engagement outcomes. Within this approach, engagement in DWP is viewed as an outcome of progress on creating the conditions for engagement. The survey and engagement results continue to help identify the organization's strengths and weaknesses and where effort needs to be applied for engagement to be strengthened. This feeds into the development of the business strategy. This is an insight-led approach as opposed to a target-driven approach.

In its early stages, the survey (now called People Survey) was seen as a staff satisfaction survey and contained a set of topics highlighting important organizational themes. Although engagement was not a familiar concept at this stage, an early proxy was in use, as people were asked to choose five items from a list of those aspects of working life most important to them.

From 2004/2005, a self-made Engagement Index was constructed. This early approach to engagement comprised a set of questions considered to be important to measure, including leadership, job satisfaction and change. These were not derived from a statistical model of engagement and therefore had limited value in predicting business outcomes. There was, however, growing awareness of the need to demonstrate causality within the structure of the results, as opposed to some 'useful looking' information.

From 2006, a key driver analysis was used within the survey. This helped to explore the drivers or influencers of engagement and identify actionable areas of improvement. This provided a more coherent 'story' of the results and helped shift the focus from the numbers to the narrative. The driver analysis helped identify, through statistical modeling, what factors were influencing (i.e. most correlated with) the engagement outcomes DWP had identified (a subset of survey questions, the Engagement Index). The key drivers were mapped on a quadrant diagram which compared driver impact with driver performance. This showed, for example, that the organization had drivers which were influential and high performing (such as people's relationship with their work); high performing but low impact (such as inclusion and fair treatment); and high impact and low performing (such as leadership and the management of change), an area where it was felt that DWP needed to improve.

In subsequent years, the addition of engagement segmentation reports further deepened the insight available from the engagement surveys. Distinct groupings of employees were identified in terms of how they answered the engagement questions, from very positive to very negative. Each group or segment had a distinct attitudinal and demographic profile in terms of how other questions in the survey were answered. DWP was able to see that the segments varied, in some cases quite dramatically, in terms of how employees felt about DWP, the type of job they did and even geographical location.

The results of the survey were increasingly being used to drive corporate action: for example, feedback that staff felt they were not being listened to influenced a number of interventions such as a Back to the Floor programme for senior managers, a Senior Civil Servant Leadership Framework to develop engagement skills of senior leaders, a Bright Ideas portal and a Making a Difference programme to develop and engage frontline leaders.

The Back to the Floor programme aimed to bridge the gap between senior managers and operational teams. Senior leaders spent up to a week with a frontline team, learning the ropes of a delivery role (coached by a staff member) and absorbing the issues and challenges within the office. DWP's Permanent Secretary did this several times and blogged on the intranet about his learning curve and his experiences. The objectives of the programme included developing a more positive view of senior managers and identifying where improvements could be made in the processes. In practice, the programme had mixed results, with visits sometimes being viewed as 'royal visits' and outcomes having variable impact.

A new programme, 'Twinning' has replaced this since 2011. This took heed of feedback from Back to the Floor that the value of the programme could be enhanced by building more enduring relationships as opposed to one-off experiences. The programme has been re-designed to engender more fruitful partnerships (of at least a year's duration), and build confidence and trust between every operational site and a twinned senior leader. The aim is to connect operational staff with the DWP vision and story, provide senior leaders with insight into operational life, place operational service delivery at the heart of DWP's purpose and ultimately drive up engagement.

The Making a Difference Programme was an ambitious approach to re-energizing and reconnecting staff with DWP. Successive surveys had shown that many employees were neutral about or disengaged with DWP. The programme aimed to motivate first-line leaders, and through them, the teams they managed. A number of large-scale events (touching nearly 10,000 leaders) were held throughout the UK to initiate the programme. Attendees were challenged to consider their management style and the impact this had on the people they were leading. A range of inputs and media were used on these events including an interactive theatre workshop and inspirational inputs from senior leaders. Participants identified personal challenges and took these away to work on, coached by senior colleagues either one-to-one or via action learning sets. An intranet site was developed containing support materials. The programme had some impact on engagement levels generally as well as the credibility of line managers (a strength which had already been identified and now improved further).

Despite some good progress year on year, some areas of organizational experience have proved consistently challenging, including level of pride in DWP, an increasing disconnect between staff and senior managers and management of change. The announcement of a major efficiency review across government (requiring reductions in DWP of 30,000 by March 2008) undoubtedly impacted people's level of engagement with DWP, how valued people felt and perceived commitment to customer service.

From October 2009, DWP's survey became part of the Civil Service People Survey (CSPS) covering nearly half a million civil servants. This allowed the Civil Service to exploit economies of scale, standardize the measurement of engagement and support efforts to raise engagement. It also acknowledged the changing context of austerity in which government departments were now operating, expressed in the following way by Sir Gus O'Donnell, former Cabinet Secretary and head of the Home Civil Service.

> The Civil Service faces unprecedented challenges tackling complex policy issues every day. In order to meet these challenges we must harness the talents of all our staff to the full. Our employee engagement programme enables us to do this by understanding and improving civil servants' experience of work, helping to ensure that they have access to the opportunities they need to achieve success in their roles. This, in turn, supports our drive to deliver improved public services and better outcomes for citizens.

A number of employee engagement pathfinder surveys in 2007 and 2008 helped to validate the content of the new questionnaire including the Engagement Index and drivers of engagement for civil servants. It was recognized that the public sector context differed from private sector sufficiently to require careful attention to survey design to ensure validity of the tool and credibility for civil servant respondents. DWP has benefited considerably from this collective effort in terms of efficiency in delivering such a large survey (for over 100,000 people), sharing tools and best practice and having access to a range of benchmark data.

Adopting the Civil Service People Survey 'Say Stay Strive' engagement model also allowed DWP to articulate for the first time what it meant by engagement.

Ongoing change in the wake of the economic downturn since 2008 has provided the backdrop for DWP's continuing engagement journey. There have been significant impacts on civil servants, resulting from the Spending Review in 2010 and subsequent changes to civil servants' terms and conditions. Maintaining engagement has proved challenging in this climate. The DWP Investor in People report in 2010 expressed this as follows:

> Simplistically the organization is moving from a highly efficient paternalistic culture. This provided at least the promise of stability, progression and recognition. The culture was/is outstanding at managing processes to deliver often very challenging targets. Now however the organization is striving to move towards a culture that encourages creativity, releases energy and finds increasingly effective ways of achieving all kinds of outcomes. This requires a whole new set of management and operational skills.
>
> (Investor in People Report, 2010)

There has been no let-up in the pace of change since then. DWP is leading an ambitious programme of welfare reform in the lead up to the introduction of Universal Credit in 2013. In 2011 it undertook significant re-structuring as well as experiencing ongoing reduction in staff numbers.

There are a number of key people challenges emerging from the current context. These highlight senior leadership, DWP's future and the management of change. This is reflected in the engagement drivers in the People Survey: Leadership and the management of change is the key driver of engagement for DWP and across government, and one of the biggest challenges. This includes elements such as leadership vision, leadership credibility and the ability to drive major change affecting every level of the organization. Scores have remained persistently low over a number of years.

Despite this, DWP has some enduring strengths; most of staff enjoy their work, feel a sense of accomplishment and remain committed to delivering a quality customer service. Given the choice, most staff (over 80 per cent) would like to continue working for DWP. Work is the second ranked driver of engagement and is high performing.

Line management is a key enabler of engagement and this is also a particular strength in DWP (the third ranked driver of engagement). Despite the challenging context, line manager skills have continued to improve over several years, notably in giving recognition, openness to ideas and motivating people to be effective in their job.

The insight gained from DWP's recent engagement surveys has underlined an urgent need to address the loss of identification and pride in DWP, the disconnect between frontline staff and leaders and the need to develop a more innovative and collaborative culture to deliver the challenging agenda ahead. It has also been recognized that a data driven approach is not the answer to developing an engaged workforce, important as it is to monitor progress.

Since 2011, the business has progressed at pace to restructure, aligning the business arms of DWP into one entity, 'One DWP', developing a new culture that responds to future business needs initially through a set of cultural principles, encouraging innovation through a Bright Ideas portal and introducing the 'DWP Story'. The Story is the start of a process to engage, inspire and re-align DWP employees with the future vision and direction of DWP. This recognizes the importance of creating strong relationships at every level.

Amongst the cultural challenges is putting first what works for the claimant, customer and Operations (or 'inverting the triangle'). This is a challenge for colleagues in the corporate centre, whose responsibilities (e.g. for policy, HR practices, IT) must include what they can do to improve the service claimants and customers receive; but it's also a challenge for each part of Operations, to make sure their responsibilities (for job-broking, benefit processing, telephony) combine effectively to provide an excellent service.

These initiatives represent a new chapter in the way DWP engages with its people. One DWP is a new way of thinking and working – it's about doing things that consider the whole of DWP rather than just the part that individuals work in. Dialogue is at the heart of the approach. The DWP Story is a simple ongoing narrative that sets out for everyone DWP's purpose and agenda and the energy and ideas required to deliver that. The ambition is high, to create an 'extraordinary' department. There has been an avoidance of cascading information or designing processes around it to maintain the integrity of person-to-person contact. 'Our Road Ahead' is a complementary document that sets out the priorities over the next five years, the ways of working required and stories of how people are making this a reality.

Since the middle of 2012, DWP's senior leaders have delivered the Story to their people through visits to teams and have participated in events all over the UK. This is the start of a cascade process through the management layers. Managers and HR business partners will play an ongoing role in supporting this. DWP wants its employees to be engaged in the DWP Story and have carefully designed the approach to increase engagement. An intranet site has been developed to provide basic background and share people's own DWP stories about what they are doing locally to change the culture and create a more unified, coherent and collaborative organization. It will not happen overnight but a promising start has been made.

In some ways these are radical and counter-cultural approaches for what has traditionally been a very process-oriented and bureaucratic organization, more comfortable with hitting targets than engaging in conversations. It has taken some bravery to embark on this new way of doing things.

Is it working? The results of DWP's most recent survey suggest that it is. Not only have scores increased across the board, suggesting a shift in hearts and minds, but, significantly, improvements have occurred in the most challenging areas, senior leadership, change and engagement with DWP. Some of these improvements are still on a low base but suggest that a corner has been turned after years of discouraging results. There are early signs that the DWP Story is having an impact, even on some of the most disengaged staff. It appears that we are definitely embarked on the road ahead with renewed confidence.

Marks and Spencer

Gillian D'Analeze

Company background

Marks and Spencer (M&S) are one of the UK's leading retailers, with over 21 million people visiting their stores each week. M&S offer high quality clothing and home products, as well as quality foods, responsibly sourced from around 2,000 suppliers globally. M&S employ over 78,000 people in the UK and abroad, and have over 700 stores, plus an expanding international business.

M&S are the number one provider of womenswear and lingerie in the UK, and have a rapidly growing market share in menswear, kidswear and home, due in part to its growing online business. Overall, M&S's clothing and homeware sales account for 49 per cent of the business, with the other 51 per cent being foods.

M&S is known for their 'green' credentials as a result of a five-year social and eco plan, Plan A, which amongst other things has driven the company to become the UK's first retailer to become carbon neutral and send no waste to landfill, achieving this in 2012.

Engagement background

When Simon Marks founded Marks and Spencer 127 years ago, he based his 'people policies' on the fundamental belief that a happier workforce is a more productive workforce. M&S believes that it is the talent and commitment of their people that will drive the business forward and deliver better service. This is a belief that M&S continues to carry in 2012, with employee engagement being one of the main business priorities.

M&S has always had a strong reputation of being a good employer. Part of the employee value proposition when employees joined M&S was that they would be 'looked after' and that M&S was a 'good company to work for'. However, M&S had previously never measured this or the value that this added to the overall profit of the business. M&S have been discussing employee engagement for a number of years, with conversations starting to take place across the business about how to engage their people to maximize business performance and how to define and embed behaviours and attitudes that are fit for the future. M&S identified the need to sustainably engage their people within the organization and take proactive steps to do this.

M&S knew that their employee engagement levels were high and increasing year on year despite the challenging external environment. However, the company was conscious that they were moving into an era where the focus on cost was more important than ever, and as such there was an increasing need to differentiate the company from their competitors. It was felt that in order for the company to implement new customer initiatives and increase productivity and discretionary effort, a highly engaged workforce was paramount.

Engagement strategy

In recognition of the importance of employee engagement to commercial performance and the need for a more sophisticated approach, in 2010 M&S set up an Employee Engagement Centre of Expertise within the HR function, tasked with the development of the engagement strategy. Prior to this, the company's engagement survey had been managed by the Learning and Development team, with the engagement agenda driven more locally by HR Business Partners. Following this, in 2011 Marc Bolland, CEO and Tanith Dodge, HR Director joined a government taskforce, Engage for Success, which was established to take forward the work of the 2009 MacLeod Report into employee engagement in the UK, commissioned by the Department for Business, Innovation and Skills (BIS). By this point, the company had undertaken extensive internal and external research and both this and the MacLeod Report helped shape their employee engagement strategy. M&S wanted the strategy to drive continued and enhanced engagement globally supporting a more open, honest and adult business culture. The strategy took a more sophisticated approach, reinforcing engagement in all aspects of the employee life cycle and forward business planning. It focused on embedding engagement into the company's daily practices in order to ensure engagement was a lived experience for employees, rather than just an area of focus at the time of the regular engagement survey.

In order for M&S to communicate the strategy to staff, they first needed to define what was meant by engagement in M&S in simple terms:

> Great engagement makes sure employees are committed to the goals of the business and motivated to contribute to them. Engaged employees have a sense of pride and a personal attachment to their work and organization; they are motivated and able to give their best to help the organization succeed.

To support this, M&S developed a framework focusing on the following areas:

- **Maximizing business initiatives**
  To maximize the value of our business plan and business initiatives it is really important our teams are fully engaged in what the business plans are, how things are changing and what they will be expected to do differently as a result of any change. We need to join up business initiatives and make sense of them for our people in a way that engages them, gives them clarity and confidence and drives sustained value.
- **Employer brand**
  Communicating a clearly defined employee brand enables us to attract and retain talent, particularly in new international markets. It enables us to make decisions about our people with more authority and best positions us to build on and leverage the great things about our employer brand to drive business and brand loyalty.
- **Employee voice**
  Encouraging our employees to participate in our business by asking for ideas, opinions and views. Provide new opportunities and new channels to encourage more regular and open dialogue across the business. Our employees are part of the solution; they know better than anyone else what is going on and often have the answers.
- **Developing engaging line managers**
  We want our managers to focus their teams and offer them scope, we want them to treat people as individuals and to coach and stretch their teams. We will provide our managers with resources and current information to support them in engaging and getting the best out of their people.
- **Inclusion and wellbeing**
  Manage and maintain our leading market position in employability, inclusion and wellbeing.

Measurement process and correlations

M&S has conducted an in-house employee satisfaction survey, Your Say, since 2000. In 2006 M&S sourced an external provider and started to report an engagement score. The data gathered allowed M&S to identify emerging themes and benchmark against their competitors. It further allowed M&S to identify correlations between engagement and business outcomes, predominantly sales, absence and service, and further the potential positive movement of each of these that an increase in employee engagement would bring. This had a significant impact on the attitude of managers towards engagement in terms of its value.

Prior to 2011, the response to the yearly Your Say survey was mostly a transactional action planning process; however, in 2011 M&S moved away from this and introduced management teams making commitments in liaison with their people, initiating a more transformational approach towards engagement. This 'ditching of the action plans' was symbolic, and represented a shift in focus for the business and a mindset change for many line managers who had traditionally approached engagement merely as a task to be completed.

Introducing a 'Your Manager' score into the survey, and refining the questions asked, have provided the data required to support managers make positive changes. This is of great importance as research indicates that direct line managers make the most significant impact on how engaged an employee feels. To drive this, the survey provides all managers with over five direct reports a Personal Manager's report, which gives very direct feedback on what their teams think of their management approach. Managers are encouraged to use the reports in addition with open dialogue with their teams to develop their leadership style.

Although the M&S Your Say survey had been measuring employee engagement for a number of years with great success, in 2012 M&S made further enhancements to their engagement survey. First, M&S introduced quarterly pulse surveys to keep a regular temperature check. Second, the company completed a more in-depth study in order to confirm that a performance advantage existed where staff were highly engaged, and, where possible, to estimate the value it had delivered. This longitudinal study (four years of data) found that long-term employee engagement trends directly link to long-term sales performance, as stores with an improving engagement trend over four years significantly outperformed stores where engagement levels were declining (compared to respective sales targets).

This survey showed that stores with improving engagement had, on average, delivered significantly more sales to the business every year than stores with declining engagement. In addition, it showed that the third most engaged stores had significantly higher 'Mystery Shop' scores and lower absenteeism than the lowest third.

While these correlations clearly demonstrated the business case for employee engagement, embedding engagement into the M&S culture has not been without challenges. M&S continues to work hard to ensure that employee engagement moves into the transformational space, is meaningful for employees and managers and helps drive a sustainable change in leadership behaviour.

Challenges

Getting people to understand the positive impact that employee engagement could have was paramount. The engagement team needed to prove the commercial 'hook' to drive their commercial colleagues into positive action and answer the critical question – 'What would having engaged employees give the business in terms of business benefits?' As the above data were not available at time the company started to focus on engagement, the HR department carried out external and internal research which demonstrated that the commercial argument was compelling.

In addition M&S have been working hard to ensure people understand that employee engagement is not simply 'an additional job', nor is it a job that can be ticked off a list. It is about the way in which the company does business, embedded into the culture and the day-to-day routine. To this end M&S had to work hard not to compartmentalize engagement and make it an additional task to do with. Although managers were used to audits and checklists, they needed to be encouraged to think differently about engagement. While these are challenges that M&S continues to face, the language of engagement has started to be used in the business, and managers and teams are now asking for more information on the 'how', such as: 'What are the tools I need to engage my team? How can I make my managers more engaged and engaging?'

Initiatives

During 2012, M&S has launched a number of engagement initiatives in order to drive change, supporting the shift to a more transformational way of working and responding to the requests for support with regard to 'how' engagement could be embedded in the culture:

- **Engagement magazine – Engagement delivers . . . do you?**
  First, M&S introduced an internal magazine focusing on employee engagement. The magazine was produced in order to help develop engaging line managers, pulling together stories from colleagues, sharing what they had done and what had worked for them. This allowed managers to consider ideas that they could adapt and get them to think differently about engagement. It contained ideas that were simple, highlighting that small things could make a big difference. It also reinforced the idea that engagement was not a quick fix, it was a way of doing business. An example of what was contained within the magazine was a 'Take a look in the mirror' article, encouraging manager self-reflection.
- **Engagement hub**
  The engagement hub was created and made available on the company intranet in response to feedback from line managers who wanted a place to share best practice, get ideas and learn more about engaging their teams. The hub was launched in line with engagement becoming a business KPI, supporting managers with specific challenges, developing their teams or providing inspiration. One of the features of the hub is the 'foundations of employee engagement' section which includes information on: involving, recognizing, sharing, growing, inspiring and knowing your team. M&S believes that getting these foundations right are the first steps in building an engaged team. Within the engagement hub housed on the intranet, managers can access simple, effective ideas shared by their colleagues and further can share their best practice with others.
- **Line manager guide**
  This guide emphasizes the important role played by the line manager in the business; leading, engaging and motivating their teams. The guide contains practical tools and support available for both existing and new managers. The guide covers a range of usual employee lifecycle topics, such as development and opportunities, reward and recognition, managing performance and involvement and communication, but seeks to position them in terms of the positive impact they have in driving how much a person is committed to the business and how important they are.
- **People Plan A**
  There are a number of initiatives within People Plan A, the company's corporate social responsibility strategy: employability, charity fundraising, employee volunteering, diversity and wellbeing. The wellbeing package provides employee support around financial stability, physical, mental health and a wellbeing website. This site is updated with videos, podcasts, fact sheets, tools and information to provide a well-being face/platform for both line managers and employees. The site introduces a social element, encouraging group activities through corporate challenges and team opportunities in recognition of the importance of the 'team' in driving engagement.
- **Business KPI**
  Years of developing the business case for employee engagement has led to people understanding its importance. As a result, this has now influenced the business Key

Performance Indicators (KPIs), with engagement now being included in the people KPI alongside rates of absence. This was driven by the commercial arm of the business as opposed to being an HR initiative, and recognizes the large role engagement plays in the achievement of the other commercial measures. This has a number of consequences, including impact on potential bonus and pay review, and further reporting to the board.

- **Full integration**

  A measure of success so far is that the business now understands the need to consider engagement as part of future strategy, with the employee engagement team now considered stakeholders in all new business initiatives. They are sought out for their advice, and focus on ensuring a strong connection between work streams around the theme of engagement, in order to inspire and enthuse colleagues about the future direction of the business. M&S has a measure on this in their Your Say Survey which has increased in recent years.

- **International strategy**

  In line with international growth plans, M&S is currently developing an engagement strategy for the international business, implementing territory-specific plans that recognize that one size does not fit all. This is being built on the work M&S has completed in the UK business.

Learning

There are a number of key considerations when driving employee engagement in an organization. First, the need to understand the business benefit and how to communicate that message: making it a simple and compelling argument, backed up where possible by tangible evidence (either internal or external). Second, it is important that employee engagement becomes a way of doing business as opposed to it being an accessory or a one-off. It is a way of working that needs to be embedded into the culture of the company, and as such needs buy in and ownership from the top and a strong commitment to measure and act on the results.

The Co-operative Group Pharmacy[1]

Liz Bramley

The Co-operative Group structure and diverse business portfolio (with core interests in food, banking, pharmacy, funerals and legal services) makes it a unique UK high street retailer. In addition, there are non-customer facing businesses such as farming and property. Historically, the businesses had operated independently with little customer crossover. Over the last seven years, this family of businesses has progressively moved closer together under The Co-operative brand. In 2009, the Group acquired Somerfield and its banking arm merged with Britannia Building Society. In 2010, it undertook the biggest retail re-branding and integration programme in UK corporate history.

The Group's objective has been to align all colleagues, working in diverse businesses, to a common core set of shared values, to improve the consistency of employee experience and to instill strong positive feelings in colleagues about working for The Co-operative, regardless of which businesses the colleagues work in.

Improving the level of engagement is always a long-term people and business strategy. However, it is not simply a matter of ticking boxes and recording numbers on scales. It is about understanding what drives colleague engagement and also understanding how engagement affects business performance across a whole range of different trading circumstances. Once understood, the task is to translate understanding into actions and positive change across all businesses.

The Co-operative Group has been actively measuring and managing levels of colleague engagement since 2004. The Group uses a measure which focuses on the expected outcomes from an engaged colleague, which was informed by William Kahn's 1990 research. The Group was also interested in the research which appeared to demonstrate a positive relationship between employee engagement and business performance. Also, as an ethical employer, the Group was interested in some of the early research which suggested that higher levels of engagement were also beneficial to employees' wellbeing and happiness. The Group's strategy provides a measurement framework alongside a statistical analysis of the different engagement drivers for colleagues working within different Group businesses and functions. Managers and leaders at every organizational level are encouraged to take direct responsibility for engagement.

The Group Director of Human Resources was keen to employ what in 2004 was a very forward-thinking approach to human capital management. There were a number of driving forces behind the Pharmacy focus on employee engagement. Firstly, the Group employee engagement team had been able to clearly demonstrate that key KPI's either improved or worsened year on year at branch/store level, depending on how employee engagement levels moved year-on-year; building a compelling business case for change. Secondly, the Group Board monitored business performance through a balanced scorecard, which included a measure of employee engagement. The Board was keen to encourage improvements in employee engagement as part of its overall governance responsibilities. Employee engagement also formed a small part of the senior manager bonus incentive scheme and so there was a small financial incentive attached to building engagement. This focus was aimed at signaling that how business performance was achieved, was of interest to the Board, rather than just the performance itself.

Unfortunately, employee engagement is not something that can be delivered by internal communication or HR professionals in isolation. The Co-operative has discovered that engagement is only significantly improved when operational line managers and leaders, internal communications, marketing, IT and HR professionals all work together to consider the impact of their own work on colleagues' employee engagement levels. The Group understands that support functions have a role to play, particularly in building rational engagement.

The Group measures employee engagement annually in the autumn. It also conducts 'temperature checks' once or twice a year across a sample of colleagues. The frequency of interim measures may be reduced or increased within different businesses according to their individual requirements. The vast majority of the Group's 100,000 colleagues anonymously complete a paper survey called 'Talkback', with staff that have access to a computer completing an identical online version. The survey is comparatively long, with around 80 questions (including a suite of demographics) but the Group believes that not only does this allow it to ask about a wide range of aspects of the employee experience, it also believes that a longer survey is in line with its stated aims of becoming an exemplary employer and also reflects its concern for the quality of the colleague experience. The Group works with an external partner to ensure that colleagues can be comfortable that the survey really is anonymous and they are able to freely express their views.

Leaders and line managers take responsibility for colleague engagement and the role of the Group employee engagement team is to ensure that communications and action plans are created at every level of the organization and to challenge managers to build an ongoing dialogue with their teams so that engagement becomes a daily concern rather than an annual 'event'.

Manager support packs provide useful ideas on how to raise employee engagement and deal with specific priorities. In early 2011 around 6,500 results and action planning packs were distributed to managers across the Group, to enable plans to be discussed and implemented within teams that will continue to change people's working lives for the better.

Using insight from Talkback, leaders of the different Group businesses integrate engagement considerations into their business and people strategies. At the Group centre, engagement insight is similarly fed into supporting function strategies, e.g. within HR; the development of a Group-wide recognition scheme, an award winning online leadership development portal and the introduction of total rewards statements, to name but a few.

In 2007, The Co-operative Group undertook a significant merger with United Co-operatives. In particular the Group's Food, Pharmacy and Funeral businesses separately went through a significant programme of operational integration. Over the following few years and supported by the Group's employee engagement strategy and best practice measurement framework, engagement in the majority of the Group businesses and functions continued to steadily improve. However, engagement levels within the Pharmacy business remained relatively unchanged and the Group's Management Executive acknowledged that they had some challenges in raising levels of engagement.

For a number of years, overall colleague engagement levels within the Pharmacy business had remained stubbornly stable but behind the Group average, whilst other businesses and functions were experiencing steady improvements over time. Pharmacy HR recognized the influence Pharmacy managers had on levels of engagement, and also acknowledged that although their managers were highly skilled pharmacists, they may not have undergone any focused people management training. This was compounded by the difficulty in sourcing qualified Pharmacists to provide cover whilst other managers were in training. Additionally, employee voice and recognition were also identified as key drivers of engagement that needed to be worked on.

The Pharmacy HR and leadership team looked at the drivers or aspects of employment which were most important to Pharmacy colleagues and identified a high-level plan to address and improve both the visibility and effectiveness of key drivers. The majority of drivers which required improvement generally involved more straightforward or rational aspects of the employment experience. The Pharmacy business, and the Group in general, was fortunate in that emotional connection to The Co-operative brand and the organization was very strong, due to authentic adherence to co-operative values and principles that have been in place since 1844.

The Pharmacy team set the following objectives in order to improve employee engagement levels:

1   Improve the overall capability of managers to engage and lead their teams.
2   Improve understanding of the Pharmacy strategy and how people contribute towards achieving strategic objectives through their day-to-day work.
3   Improve understanding about the wider Pharmacy business, the role it plays within the Group and the communities where it trades and the challenges and opportunities it faces.
4   Improve regular communications to branch colleagues.

5   Improve the opportunity for branch colleagues to provide feedback and suggest ideas that will contribute to business success.
6   Improve opportunities to be recognized for going the extra mile.

In order to achieve its specific engagement objectives, the Pharmacy business implemented a number of key business programmes.

1   First, the Pharmacy Executive committed to identifying training that would be suitable for pharmacy managers; highly skilled health professionals were taught to think logically, and have a meticulous eye for detail, but were less prepared when it came to management and colleague engagement. A specialist programme for tailored management training was designed and implemented for all Pharmacy managers.
2   The Pharmacy leadership team also supplemented its bi-annual programme of strategy and performance road shows with a strategic plan publication which clearly communicated the Pharmacy vision and mission. The published plan also articulated the six strategic goals, plans to achieve the goals and details of how success would be measured.
3   Pharmacy developed its own colleague publication. The 'Together' magazine was for, and about, pharmacy colleagues, and was a direct response to verbatim comments within the Talkback survey results. The Co-operative Pharmacy was itself the amalgamation of a number of merged pharmacy businesses, so 'Together' helped colleagues to feel part of a larger cohesive business, channeling their enthusiasm in a consistent direction. The 'Together' magazine has now been replaced by the Group's US magazine; however, US still heavily features Pharmacy specific content, whilst also enabling Pharmacy colleagues to understand more about the wider family of businesses.
4   The communications and HR teams also collaborated to create 'PIP'. PIP stands for People in Pharmacy and was quickly established as a character brand that signaled a particular communication or initiative as being focused on engagement and a response to what Pharmacy colleagues had said via Talkback. Using technology, the weekly communication cascade to Pharmacy branch managers and employees was significantly improved.
5   Pharmacy colleagues have been encouraged to have a voice and be creative in their approach to improving the business. 'What's the big idea?' is the challenge that 'PIP' offers to Pharmacy colleagues. Everyone has the opportunity to submit a suggestion, and everyone gets a response which Pharmacy understands from the colleague survey, is important for engagement. As a 'thank you' for entering, everyone receives a small token prize. Depending upon the quality and impact of the idea, bronze, silver or gold 'PIP' badges are awarded. The initiative has provided valuable insights from the people who know our customers best – our colleagues.
6   The Pharmacy team understood that the 'PIP' scheme recognition need not be expensive, and they stressed the importance of it encouraging effective manager communication. Recognition should make people feel valued, be visible, be immediate, be cumulative, and should associate the desired behavior with the reward. The 'PIP' scheme met all of those criteria but in addition the business also holds an annual 'PIP' awards night, providing the opportunity to recognize and reward outstanding performance.

Since the Pharmacy leadership team has implemented the above and other colleague engagement initiatives, levels of engagement have markedly improved. In the space of twelve months, engagement scores increased by five percentage points and engagement levels now appear to be moving much more in line with the Group as a whole.

The most significant improvements in perceptions across more than 5,500 respondents were: how involved and prepared people felt when change was planned, how strongly people felt a sense of connection to The Co-operative and how willing people were to advocate the Group as a place to work to their family and friends. On average, scores for these questions improved by nine percentage points.

The business has also been able to demonstrate a predictive relationship at branch level between engagement levels in one year and performance across a number of KPI's in the following year. Overall, the Pharmacy business is performing better and responding well to the challenging trading conditions it faces.

The key lessons that The Co-operative Group has understood and the Pharmacy business has put into practice in relation to building employee engagement are:

1   To be successful in significantly improving engagement from a stubbornly stable baseline, it requires a holistic approach which tackles the main drivers of engagement simultaneously.
2   In order to be successful, change needs to take place at every level. Team level action plans are an important aspect of helping people feel involved, but often the greatest opportunity for positive change arises in those aspects of the work experience which are not controllable at team level, but can only be changed by the Leadership.
3   The process of building engagement does not have to be expensive, but it does need to be a coordinated effort by operational line management, senior and middle leadership, human resources and internal communications. It is also important that other functions such as Finance and IT have an awareness of how they may be affecting employee engagement, either through change projects or day-to-day operations.
4   Manager awareness of the scale of the impact they have on employee engagement is extremely important.
5   It is also important to identify hygiene factors which do not contribute to higher engagement, but do hinder efforts to build engagement.
6   It is helpful to signal this holistic approach by the use of a brand, emblem or character which helps tie all of the action elements together and provides regular visible reinforcement of the change.

KIA Motors (UK) Ltd

Gary Tomlinson

Kia overview

Kia Motors (UK) Ltd is part of HMG, the Hyundai Motors Group, which consists of both the Hyundai and Kia automakers and various ancillary companies within the group. This case study is focused on the Kia organization within the UK, which is a wholly owned subsidiary of the Kia Motors Corporation based in Seoul, South Korea.

The engagement strategy outlined in this case study is being further developed and implemented as part of a global project team comprising HR representatives from across

Europe, USA, Russia and South Korea; led by the Head of HR for the UK and Ireland, Gary Tomlinson.

The UK's strategy for employee engagement has been supported by the Kia HR team, Joanna Moor HR Manager, and HR Advisors Kevin Oxlade and Amanda White.

Background

It is often said that for real change to happen individuals, whether people or companies, have to reach a point of crisis. At Kia, this point was reached in 2006 when employee engagement was at an all-time low, financial and commercial results were falling, employee turnover was at 31 per cent and the cultural malaise in the organization through lack of leadership and strategy was tangible.

At the start of 2007 a new executive team was appointed with a new CEO and President and a new British Managing Director, both of whom were receptive to ideas on how to improve the organization.

Since 2007 employee engagement has gone from being an initial idea, to a plan; and now it is firmly part of the culture and strategic agenda of the organization.

Making the business case

The business case for employee engagement is widely accepted within the Kia organization, based on the still painful memories of experiencing low levels of engagement but more positively the enhanced levels of performance achieved from having increasingly higher levels of employee engagement.

In 2007 study results demonstrating the ROI (Return on Investment) of high employee engagement were presented to the Board. For Kia the one that made the biggest impression was a study conducted by Russell Investments (formally Frank Russell) on the commercial impact on achieving a Top 100 status in the US Fortune 100 employers list (Bastock and Shaw, 2005).

The study was significant for a number of reasons – it was conducted by an organization whose core competence was around financial analysis, it crossed over a broad range of industries and across a number of social-economic factors, the Dot.Com crash, and tragically 9/11. Yet, across all of these variables, the most significant factor, appeared to be the Top 100 organizations' commitment to their people and their higher levels of employee engagement.

Although no single study has provided the 'silver bullet' and unquestionable 'proof' of the link between employee engagement and business performance, overall evidence supports the claim that employee engagement has an impact on business results, which enabled Kia to make a business case for a stronger focus on engagement.

Kia engagement model

The Kia engagement model evolved over a number of years in large part from reviewing various engagement models developed by third party consultancies, and from their experience of what worked within their organization.

In describing their engagement model, Kia utilized the metaphor of the 'ladder of engagement' consisting of a series of steps which have to be fully addressed before the next step can be taken (Figure 16.1).

Ladder of Engagement

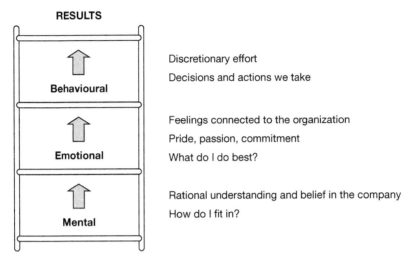

Figure 16.1 Kia's ladder of engagement

Employee engagements has three key steps:

1   *Mental/Rational*
    The first stage is the internalization or perception of individuals' understanding of the purpose of the organization and how they fit into that wider picture. This includes not only an understanding of how they are formally positioned in the organizational hierarchy, but extends to the beliefs individuals form about their contribution, the value that is placed upon them and their position in the wider organization.
2   *Emotional*
    The second stage is the emotional level, which encompasses the pride, passion and commitment individuals have for their organization.
       The emotional aspect is very important for Kia as it underlines the level of effort and commitment employees are willing to make in their jobs and collectively for their organizations. The Corporate Leadership Council (2004) found that the emotional impact on engagement was four times more powerful than the mental/rational aspect, demonstrating how much individuals are affected by their emotions.
       In Kia's experience emotional engagement was achieved by ensuring employees were able to do what they did best by having jobs that played to their strengths. For Kia this came down to effective recruitment and ongoing review of the capabilities of all their employees to ensure they were being affectively utilized.
3   *Behavioural*
    Finally, when the mental/rational and emotional aspects of employee engagement come together, employees' engagement becomes visible through their behaviour. The term widely used to describe the behavioural component of engagement is 'discretionary effort'. Managers often refer to this term as working overtime, however Kia uses it in a wider context in that it includes individuals utilizing their resourcefulness and creativity, and the level of concern they have in seeking to support their organization.

Key drivers of engagement

At Kia the engagement strategy was developed around certain key drivers of employee engagement.

SENIOR LEADERSHIP

The first driver refers to ensuring that all Board members understand and demonstrate the appropriate leadership qualities. This includes ensuring that the organization has a clear vision and strategy for organizational direction, demonstrating commitment to living the company values and showing genuine concern for the wellbeing of their team members.

ENGAGING MANAGERS

Kia acknowledges that the role of the manager is a challenging one; so investment was made to provide appropriate leadership training to ensure the managers feel fully engaged. The leadership training focused on building the coaching capability of the Kia management team utilizing the *GROW* model (Whitmore, 2009);[2] with the aim to build a pool of managers who facilitate learning through raising employees' awareness and encouraging employees to become more responsible through empowerment.

Kia also focused on building managers' awareness of their behaviour by utilizing a 360 degree tool. This tool was introduced for development purposes only and there was no link with appraisal or pay review. It was at the individual employee's discretion whether they wanted to share feedback with their line manager, however most employees choose to do so.

The aim of the leadership development programme was to build managers' capabilities by providing a toolkit of management techniques to support them in taking on bigger roles and responsibilities in the future, as career development is seen as a key factor of building engagement within Kia.

INTERNAL COMMUNICATIONS AND CORE VALUES

At Kia the internal communications model views all strategic messages as evolving through a series of transitions via four stages. This can best be explained with the example of embedding their core values:

(i) Awareness – first employees become aware of the core values and what they are and their importance to the organization.
(ii) Understanding – then they build understanding and comprehension of the values.
(iii) Involvement – then they become more actively involved and emotionally connected with the values through appreciating how they relate to them.
(iv) Committed – finally they become committed both mentally and emotionally and through this demonstrate their engagement and advocacy on the values through their behaviour.

Over the last 12 months the agenda has been on embedding the core values which for the Hyundai-Kia Motors Group are – Customer, Challenge, Collaboration, People and Globality. During 2012 Kia has run various internal workshops, which culminated in a Core Values Day, an off-site team building event centred on embedding the core values.

The Core Values Day involved all employees attending a one-day event at the Kia Oval cricket ground. The event began with presentations from Kia's President and Managing

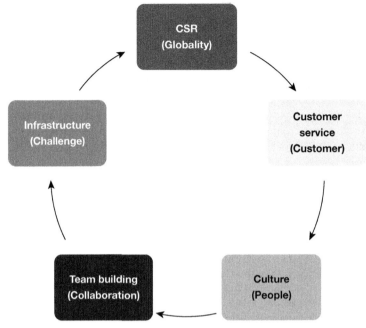

Figure 16.2 Kia's five engagement workshops

Director to give an update on business strategy and company performance. Employees were then split into five rotating workshops focused on key challenges with regard to each core value (Figure 16.2).

For example, the Value of People focused on how Kia could further enhance the culture; the value of Collaboration was centred on ways to encourage and facilitate team building; the value of Challenge was about the organization's ambitious growth strategy and ways to ensure the infrastructure was in place to support these plans.

Each workshop had a series of questions for employees to focus upon. In order to encourage momentum and guidance a facilitator was utilized from an external training consultancy.

The HR team was then tasked to put together an action plan based on ideas the employees had generated and these were shared with employees at the next employee briefing. The key initiatives introduced were:

* Corporate Social Responsibility Day – allowing employees to have one CSR holiday day to attend nominated charities.
* Customer Services – a complete review of the levels of service provided to Kia dealers and introduction of improved IT systems to further enhance the experience provided to Kia customers.
* Induction – development of a one-day training programme for employees to better understand Kia dealers and the opportunity for all staff to spend time in the 'field' at one of the dealers to build their knowledge of the Kia automotive dealers.

In addition, Kia has set a significant focus on improving the internal communications mechanisms including:

- Kia Vision (the corporate intranet) as an enabling tool to promote internal communication
- cross-functional project groups to breakdown departmental silos
- regular town hall meetings from the CEO with employee awards for outstanding contributions.

In more recent times Kia has placed a higher priority on Corporate Social Responsibility initiatives to communicate what is important to the organization and to facilitate better internal communications through cross functional working on charitable projects. Effective communications is a cornerstone of engagement as it helps employees build a clear picture of the organization and their place within it.

Measuring employee engagement

At Kia, employee engagement is measured against two employee surveys; Sunday Times Best Companies Survey and the Global HMG employee survey called CVES (Core Values Engagement Survey) which is run in partnership with Towers Watson. The surveys provide the means to measure engagement through benchmarking internally and externally, to assess engagement and identify areas for further development.

Kia's objectives for employee engagement have become more developed and progressive each year; for 2012 their Key Performance Indicators were to:

1 Achieve re-accreditation for the Investors In People[3]
  This was achieved in the summer of 2012 with the recognition within the report that *'Kia demonstrates a strong commitment to its people'*[4]
2 Increase Kia's employee engagement index by 5 per cent
  The Core Value Engagement Survey provides an overall index to measure employee engagement. In 2010 the score was 80 per cent, in 2011 this increased to 88 per cent, an overall increase of 8 per cent. Against the Towers Watson blue chip companies benchmark Kia's engagement levels were 5 per cent higher. This was reflected across all three dimensions of the Kia engagement model with the following achieved against the external benchmark: mental engagement 90 per cent (5 per cent above), emotional engagement 83 per cent (7 per cent above) and behavioural engagement 92 per cent (5 per cent above).[5] The target for 2012 is an engagement index of 90 per cent, however it is acknowledged that the current result is very positive.
3 Reduce employee turnover by 2 per cent in 2012
  Since the all-time high of 31 per cent Kia has experienced a consistent year-on-year falling of its employee turnover to 3 per cent in October 2012 (Figure 16.3).
4 Increase hire rate of internal employees for new management roles by 10 per cent
  Investment in leadership development has paid dividends with the percentage of jobs filled by internals increasing from 38 per cent over a two-year period between 2008 to 2010 to 53 per cent from 2010–12.
5 Increase the Core Value Index by 3 per cent
  The Core Value Index is the tool that Kia utilizes to assess how effectively their values have been embedded into the organization. In 2010 Kia achieved a Core Values Index of 72 per cent, in 2011 this increased to 76 per cent. This result was higher than all other benchmarks, namely 6 per cent above the internal and 5 per cent above the external benchmark.

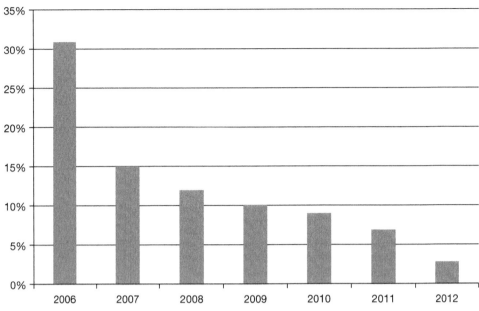

Figure 16.3 Employee turnover at Kia

Commercial results

Kia has experienced simultaneous rising of sales results and rising levels of employee engagement, suggesting a correlation between both factors.

In a difficult market environment over the last four years, Kia has seen its overall sales more than double from 31,000 in 2008 to forecasted sales in 2012 to over 65,000 sales.

Key lessons

During the last six years a number of lessons have been learnt.

1   *Support from the top*
    The most important success factor, which sometimes is overlooked by HR professionals, is ensuring genuine and real commitment from the ultimate decision maker in the organization – the President and CEO.

    At Kia the public commitment from the CEO to improving employee engagement was the fundamental catalyst of change within the organization, for two reasons. First, it contributed to gaining senior management buy-in and second, it ensured that employees knew that engagement was a business imperative and not simply another HR initiative.

    Kia's HR team were thankful to have a CEO who simply 'got it' when it came to the business case for employee engagement. Although there was some initial resistance especially from the CFO on understanding the business case, clear evidence of the benefits and the leverage of the adverse impact being experienced from high employee turnover, led to full support from the top management team.

    Organizations therefore need to provide a clear narrative of why engagement matters.

2   *Engagement as a process, not an event*

David MacLeod and Nita Clarke's report 'Engaging for Success' differentiated between two schools of engagement. First, transactional engagement, where engagement is an event related to the annual employee survey followed up with a few actions to show some commitment and second, transformational engagement, where engagement is a way of life and part of the overall business approach (MacLeod and Clarke, 2009). Over the last few years Kia has evolved from an organization that looked at engagement from a transactional perspective towards an organization where engagement is a way of life.

3   *Action over analysis*

Employee surveys play a critical role in understanding levels of engagement and developing a strategy on how to improve engagement levels. However, there is a danger of over analysis since the surveys have become increasingly sophisticated and with the use of online databases demographics and trends can be analysed forever more.

For Kia the lesson is one where actions really speak louder than words. It is critical that after careful analysis there is real action, which is followed through to ensure engagement remains a strategic focus. As the report 'Engaging for Success' colourfully quotes 'no one ever got a pig fat by weighing it'; in other words you cannot improve engagement simply by analysing survey results.

Conclusion

Kia is proud of the progression that has been made in terms of employee engagement and is very much seen as a centre of excellence within the wider global company. However, given the challenge and complexity that engagement presents, the Kia HR team are not complacent and continue to seek ways of evolving their approach and raising the bar for employee engagement.

Final thoughts

The case studies in this chapter have provided valuable insights into the engagement journeys of different organizations. Several conclusions can be drawn with regards to implementing engagement in a business context:

- No 'one size fits all' approach: The four case study organizations operate in different business contexts and have chosen different approaches to foster engagement within their workforce. Implementing the same initiatives or tools might not produce the same effect in other organizations, as the organizational culture and the working environment are likely to differ. Practitioners should therefore be inspired by the engagement initiatives presented in this chapter, but at the same time, ensure that the initiatives they implement are tailored to fit the goals and objectives of their organizations. What works well in one organization might not work at all in another organization.
- Involvement of different organizational groups: Developing and implementing engagement initiatives cannot be done by the HR department in isolation. The case studies in this chapter have provided ample evidence that engagement initiatives are much more successful if other organizational groups such as line managers, marketing and IT departments are involved and if the engagement movement has the full support of the top management. To ensure that the key decision makers support

engagement initiatives, practitioners need to be able to demonstrate a business case for engagement and show to what extent an engaged workforce can impact the organization's bottom line.

- Embedding engagement in the organizational culture: Organizations can focus on measuring engagement through staff surveys, or focus on embedding engagement into their culture and working environment. The case studies in this chapter illustrate that engagement is much more powerful when it becomes part of the way that the organization lives and operates. Measuring engagement levels of the workforce should therefore be considered only as a first step towards a more fundamental change in the attitudes and behaviors of employees, line and senior managers.

In this chapter, four practitioners have shared their experiences and provided insights into the lessons they learned when their organizations began implementing engagement initiatives. These examples might serve as inspiration for other organizations to start on or progress their own journey of engagement to reap the benefits of an engaged workforce.

Notes

1 We would like to acknowledge the Co-operative Pharmacy Leadership Team for their contribution to this case study.
2 The GROW coaching model stands for Goals, Reality, Options and Will, twin objectives of building the individuals' awareness and self-responsibility.
3 The Investors in People award is a recognized benchmark of becoming an employer of choice in the UK, and is evidence of organizations committed to engaging their people.
4 Investors in People Report 2012 on Kia UK's performance against the IIP standard.
5 The external benchmarking group includes a wide range of companies including: Canon, Diageo, Mercedes-Benz, Nestle, Toyota and Siemens.

References

Bastock, A. and Shaw, K. (2005) *Employee engagement. How to build a high performance workforce.* London: Melcrum Publishing Limited.

Corporate Leadership Council (2004) *Driving performance & retention through employee engagement.* London: The Corporate Executive Board Company (UK) Ltd.

MacLeod, D. and Clarke, N. (2009) *Engaging for success. Enhancing performance through employee engagement.* London: Office of Public Sector Information.

Whitmore, J. (2009) *Coaching for Performance.* 4th edn, Boston, MA: Nicholas Brealey Publishing Inc.

Index